Familiar Futures

Stanford Studies in Middle Eastern and Islamic Societies and Cultures

Familiar Futures

Time, Selfhood, and Sovereignty in Iraq

Sara Pursley

Stanford University Press

Stanford, California

STANFORD UNIVERSITY PRESS
Stanford, California

Printed in the United States of America on acid-free, archival-quality paper

Library of Congress Cataloging-in-Publication Data

Pursley, Sara, author.
Familiar futures : time, selfhood, and sovereignty in Iraq / Sara Pursley.
Stanford studies in Middle Eastern and Islamic societies and cultures.
Stanford, California : Stanford University Press, 2019. | Stanford studies in
    Middle Eastern and Islamic societies and cultures | Includes bibliographical
    references and index.
LCCN 2018019452| ISBN 9780804793179 (cloth : alk. paper) | ISBN 9781503607484
    (pbk. : alk. paper) | ISBN 9781503607491 (electronic)
LCSH: Economic development projects—Social aspects—Iraq. |
    Economic development—Iraq—History—20th century. | Iraq—
    History—Hashemite Kingdom, 1921-1958. | Iraq—Social conditions—
    20th century. | Iraq—Economic policy. | Iraq—Social policy.
LCC HC415.4.Z9 P87 2018 | DDC 338.9567—dc23
LC record available at https://lccn.loc.gov/2018019452

Typeset by Kevin Barrett Kane in 11/13.5 Garamond
Cover design by Rob Ehle
Cover image: Kadhim Haidar, "Ten Fatigued Horses Converse with Nothing,"
1965, from *The Martyr's Epic*, a series of paintings about the 1963 Ba'th coup
told through the story of the Battle of Karbala. Image courtesy of Barjeel Art
Foundation, Sharjah.

In loving memory of my dad, Ken Pursley

Contents

Acknowledgments

Support for the research and writing of this book was provided by a Cotsen Postdoctoral Fellowship from the Society of Fellows in the Liberal Arts at Princeton University; the American Academic Research Institute in Iraq; and the Center for the Humanities, the Ralph Bunche Institute for International Studies, and the History Program at the CUNY Graduate Center. I also thank the staff at the American University of Beirut Library, the British Library, the SOAS Library, the Wellcome Library, the Middle East Center Library at St. Antony's College, the UNESCO Archives, the Hoover Institute, the New York Public Library, the New York University Library, and the Princeton University Library.

At Stanford University Press, Kate Wahl has assiduously followed the progress of this book for a number of years now and fully lives up to her reputation in the field as an engaged, reliable, and sharp editor. I could not have hoped for two better anonymous readers of the manuscript, and I am grateful for their extremely astute and helpful comments as well as for their encouragement. Elspeth MacHattie was a superb copyeditor. I thank Gigi Mark and Leah Pennywark for their skilled and good-natured shepherding of the book through the editorial and production stages.

As the book was nearing completion and I was looking for a cover image, Sinan Antoon introduced me to the work of the Iraqi artist Kadhim Haidar, in particular his 1965 series of paintings on the 1963 Ba'th coup told through the story of the martyrdom of Husayn. I thank Sinan for the suggestion and the Barjeel Art Foundation for permission to use one of those paintings, "Ten Fatigued Horses Converse with Nothing." I am also grateful to Hassan Nadhem for connecting me with the Iraqi photographer Atheer Mohammed, who took beautiful photos of Jawad Salim's *Monument to Freedom* for the book's Epilogue.

The ideas of this book took root quite a few years ago at the Graduate Center of the City University of New York. Beth Baron read their earliest incarnations more times than she probably cares to remember and was a model of personal and intellectual generosity; I now count her among my friends. Samira Haj challenged me at every turn and helped me finally understand why I had chosen to study Middle East history in the first place. I continue to turn to her for reliably critical readings of my work. Talal Asad got me thinking about time, upending my original plan and sending me down the path that led to this book. Dagmar Herzog was simply a gift, an inspiring scholar and unexpected mentor who calmly pointed the way forward at moments of crisis, real and imagined. Ervand Abrahamian and Orit Bashkin (visiting from Chicago) provided fresh readings that helped me get out of the trees and see a bit of the forest. Last but certainly not least, I am immensely grateful to Joan Scott for her interest, support, and no-nonsense encouragement. Among many other acts of generosity, she read every chapter of both an early and a late version and helped push me over the finish line.

Also at the Graduate Center, stimulating conversations and helpful comments on early versions of the chapters were provided by Mitra Monir Abbaspour, Raja Abillama, Ozan Aksoy, Anthony Alessandrini, Andrew Alger, Arman Azimi, Zachary Berman, Mohamad Ezzeldine, Aleksandra Majstorac-Kobiljski, Sara Pekow, Jeremy Randall, Mitra Rastegar, Kutlughan Soyubol, Melis Sulos, and Seçil Yilmaz. Anny Bakalian was always supportive and made the Middle East and Middle Eastern American Center a welcoming interdisciplinary environment. Jeffrey Culang was a wonderful editorial partner during our time at the *International Journal of Middle East Studies*, and has provided helpful comments on everything from cover letters to book chapters. For their continuing friendship and insightful critiques of my work, I am especially grateful to Spencer Bastedo and Nada Moumtaz.

The Princeton Society of Fellows was an idyllic atmosphere for the near-final stages of research and writing. For their kindness and helpful feedback, I thank in particular Tineke D'Haeseleer, Molly Greene, Jonathan Gribetz, Andrew Hamilton, Thomas Hare, Mary Harper, Kevan Harris, Eric Huntington, Amaney Jamal, Stefan Kamola, Satyel Larson, Kate Liszka, David Minto, M'hamed Oualdi, Cyrus Schayegh, Daniel Sheffield, Mira Siegelberg, Susan Stewart, Max Weiss, and Muhammad Qasim Zaman.

I doubt I could have landed at a more congenial workplace than the Middle Eastern and Islamic Studies department at New York University. Zachary Lockman read most of the book in its final stages and helped me with a troublesome chapter. Ismail Alatas and Asli Igsiz provided incisive comments on the introduction that shaped its final revision. Arang Keshavarzian has been a generous unofficial mentor and a steadying presence. I love being colleagues with my favorite Arabic professor from more than a decade ago, the marvelous Ahmed Ferhadi. Marion Katz has been a very supportive chair. Ellis Garey and Gabriel Young provided invaluable last-minute research assistance. In the history department, Monica Kim has become a great friend and a pretty good writing pal to boot.

Other comrades have been acquired along the way. I am a great admirer of the work of Omnia El Shakry and Stefania Pandolfo and hope to continue the discussions we've started. Begüm Adalet and Andrew Bush both read the introduction near the end and gave excellent feedback. Kenneth Cuno and Ellen Fleischmann provided unsolicited encouragement very early in the process, for which I am grateful. In Beirut, welcome respite from the archives was provided by Samer Frangie, Khaled Al Hilli, Hazem Jamjoum, Maya Mikdashi, Nada Moumtaz, and Jeremy Randall. The late Faleh Abdul Jabar of the Iraq Institute for Strategic Studies took time to give me research advice and share his memories of the Iraqi communist movement. In London, Mubejel Baban and Bushra Perto provided me with valuable materials and insights on the League for the Defense of Women's Rights as well as their memories of Iraq in the 1940s and '50s. Alzahraa K. Ahmed was a sharp end-stage proofreader.

An ongoing conversation with Rob Miotke for most of my adult life has shaped nearly every thought I have; it is entirely apt that he came up with the title of the book, *Familiar Futures*. Jennie Portnof made a great partner in crime in this journey and I thank her for all of it. Michele Kelley helped me through some especially difficult times and is a model of how to live ethically. Steve Cosson is an inspiration and an excellent friend. This book took a while to finish and would have taken even longer without the encouragement of Nora Breen; I am grateful for that and much else. For their companionship, support, and wit, I also thank Elisabeth Abeson, Faris Al Ahmad, Jeanne Bergman, Patrick Boucher, Zahid Chaudhary, Ed Cohen, Tom de Kay, Nancy Dunbar, David Eng, Carla Freccero, Christopher Hogan, Pamela Jackson, David Kazanjian, Anna Kramarsky, Alaa Majeed, John Orcutt, Lysander Puccio, Karla Rosenberg, Mary Lou Rasmussen, Anandaroop Roy, Josie Saldaña-Portillo, Catherine Sameh, Erin Small, Eric Taylor, Elyse Wolland, Hasan Zaidi, and Catherine Zimmer.

My parents supported me every step of the way, and my brothers, Ben and Sean, inspire me with their honesty and integrity. Sean and I continue to grow together in the most unexpected ways. I wrote much of this book at our family cabin in the mountains of Idaho, using a small generator to charge my laptop. Ben hauled in books for me by snowmobile in the winter months, when the road is impassable, and dropped off elk meat in the fall. My mom, in her seventies, hiked in alone on snowshoes for quiet evenings of reading by the fire. The cabin itself is a gift from my dad, who read every word of an early version of this book and texted me delightful comments along the way. The book is dedicated to him. I wish he could have seen what it became.

Note on Transliteration and Translation

This book follows the transliteration system of the *International Journal of Middle East Studies* except that diacritical marks have been omitted. All translations are mine unless otherwise noted.

Familiar Futures

Iraqi Futures and the Age of Development

AT 6:30 AM ON JULY 14, 1958, Baghdad radio went silent for a few minutes. A new voice then came over the airwaves.

Noble People of Iraq: Trusting in God and with the assistance of the loyal sons of the people and the national armed forces, we have undertaken to liberate the beloved homeland from the corrupt crew that imperialism installed. . . . Brothers: The army is of you and for you and has carried out what you desired. . . . Citizens: While admiring your fervent patriotic spirit . . . we call upon you to remain calm and maintain order and unity . . . in the interest of the homeland.[1]

Within a few hours of this proclamation that the Iraqi Hashimite monarchy and its British life-support system had been overthrown, the streets of Baghdad were filled with jubilant supporters. The "Free Officers" of the Iraqi military who had executed the coup and installed themselves at the head of the newly declared Republic of Iraq were not communists, but the Iraqi Communist Party (ICP) and its many sympathizers were their most visible base of support. They were joined by members of the three other opposition parties that had come together in 1957 to form the United National Front and whose leaders had been apprised of the impending coup—the liberal National Democratic Party (NDP) and the two Arab nationalist parties, the Ba'th Party and the Independence Party—as well as by throngs of unaffiliated Baghdadis celebrating the monarchy's demise.

Many factors enabled a military coup in Baghdad in 1958 to be widely experienced as a popular revolution and then, in some ways, to become one. Among them was the fact that the July revolution was a future that had already been imagined by many Iraqis, or a *future past*, to borrow Reinhart Koselleck's phrase.[2] By fulfilling certain expectations (abolition of monarchy, an end to British political control, reform of agriculture), it could be experienced as an absolute temporal rupture, the end of one time and the beginning of another. On July 27, Iraq's new prime minister, 'Abd al-Karim Qasim, introduced the temporary constitution of the thirteen-day-old republic by proclaiming: "When the revolution came, uprooting tyranny and corruption, a new age began, and it inevitably cut the ties to that painful past."[3] The term *al-'ahd al-ba'id*—often translated into English as "the old regime" but more directly translatable as "the bygone era" or "the time gone by"—immediately became a common appellation for the monarchical period, already felt as belonging to the distant past.

On January 1, 1959, the communist popular front women's organization, the League for the Defense of Women's Rights, led a march through the streets of Baghdad. The women were protesting not Qasim's government but rather the monarchical regime of "the time gone by," agents of which they deemed responsible for an attempted counterrevolutionary coup in December. Their demand was for the "immediate execution of the traitors and plotters. . . . We, the women of Baghdad, will keep the fire burning in our hearts until we see the traitors' bodies hanging from the gallows."[4] Coverage of the march in the following days conveyed its violent demands, which were consistent with those of the ICP and the other communist-affiliated organizations.

But within a few weeks a new narrative had emerged. In late January, the *Illustrated London News* published a letter to the editor from the Iraqi Ministry of Development, boasting of the march as evidence of the modernity the July revolution had introduced to Iraq: "the women of Baghdad, some 50,000 including students, doctors, teachers, housewives, etc. took part in the first female demonstration in the country in support of the present government."[5] That this statement was issued by the Ministry of Development in particular points to the new regime's engagement with a global idiom of development that indexed a nation's modernity by the status of its women: their presence in public, their social and domestic work ("students, doctors, teachers, housewives, etc."), and their simultaneously apolitical or at least nonoppositional stance ("in support of the present government"). Within six months, the narrative of the march as a momentous "first," marking the dramatic entry of Iraqi women into the public sphere, had almost completely eclipsed the memory of its declared purpose and vengeful language. A July 1959 article in the communist press breathlessly recalled: "It was the first demonstration of its kind in the history of the whole Arab people. It was greater than words can express. The streets were silent. . . . Never before had the Iraqi people witnessed such an event."[6]

The taming of the women's march in official memory signaled the regime's efforts to domesticate the revolutionary movements that had initially ensured the success of the coup but then posed a threat to the new political order. Perhaps more striking is that the communist press participated in a similar rewriting of the event. The ICP had recognized Qasim's government as the legitimate agent of the bourgeois or capitalist phase of the two-stage revolution leading to socialism, and in the summer of 1959 it retreated from its demand for a share in government. In both official and ICP narratives, the communist women's public action was transformed into a reassuring harbinger of an already familiar future at which Iraq was now arriving. Simultaneously, the women as private individuals were domesticated through reference to their reproductive, future-oriented work, within both the familial and the social domains, thereby transforming them from "political" to "sociological" agents, as Denise Riley has written of similar discourses elsewhere. "Both this 'social' and 'women' lean forward, as concepts, into a future which is believed to sustain them. . . . If 'women' can be credited with having a tense, then it is a future tense."[7]

Familiar Futures

The 1959 Baghdad women's march and later retellings of it point to several different, overlapping, and often paradoxical registers I have in mind for this book's title, *Familiar Futures*. In one register, Iraqi futures were familiar because they were already somebody else's past or present. Thus, revolutionaries of all stripes celebrated the felicitous occurrence of the coup on Bastille Day, and asserted that diverse initiatives of the post-revolutionary state, from the People's Court to the land reform law, were repetitions of 18th-century French originals. It was this temporal imaginary that made the women's march legible as the "first demonstration of its kind in the history of the whole Arab people." Modernity here appears as transformative, a radical break with the past, even while its trajectory is always already known. This register thus contains its own paradox: it was the very familiarity of the Iraqi revolution as a future past that allowed it to be experienced as the beginning of a new time.

There were significant differences between the political parties that supported the coup, especially in 1958 and 1959 over the question of whether Iraq should unite with Syria and Egypt in the newly created United Arab Republic. The most serious conflict, often erupting as a bloody street war, was between the communists and the Ba'thists. But the parties also shared certain understandings of what was required of the new regime to legitimate the coup as the long-awaited revolution. Most of all, they called on the state to create a sovereign and stable political space in which capitalist economic development could unfold. In doing so, they stressed the need to combat "lethargy" or "stagnation" in the economy as a whole and/or in the bodies of the country's laborers. The recurring word used for this condition was *jumud*, literally "a frozen state."[8] At the same time, many called for the "suspension"—*tajmid*, from the same root as *jumud*, literally "freezing"—of various kinds of political mobilization in the present. Thus, key NDP leaders called for the *tajmid* of all political party activity, including their own, while communists sometimes worked to suspend urban and rural labor unrest in the interest of the ICP's primary "slogan" during the revolutionary era, "defending the republic."[9] In other words, the overcoming of economic stagnation or *jumud* was widely seen as depending on the enforcement of political stagnation or *tajmid*. In the second register of the book's title, then, Iraq's futures were familiar because they were to be managed repetitions of its present, at least for certain subjects (such as workers and peasants) and/or in certain domains (such as the political).

This book is about the role of conceptions and practices of sexual difference in stabilizing the tensions between these two orientations of modern historical time toward the future, that is, between modernity as a transformative promise and as a repetition of the same. For example, in the revolutionary era (1958–63), women's work in the public domain of the social and the private domain of the family often appeared as critical to both parts of the process described above, that is, to the conquering of *jumud* and the enforcement of *tajmid*. What Riley describes as the "future tense" of "women" rests on that category's association with biological reproduction and child-raising on the one hand and with modernizing pedagogical and social reform projects on the other. A third, and analytically central, register of the book's title thus relates to the recurring prominence of ideas about family life and sexual difference to the future-oriented imaginaries of modernity. In this register, modern futures are familiar both because they are closely linked to familial spaces and attachments and because they are *made familiar* through techniques operating on subjects' most intimate habits, capabilities, and desires.

Most of the conflicts around gender and family during these years have been forgotten in histories of the revolution. An exception is a controversy often mentioned in the scholarship, over the promulgation of the Iraqi Law of Personal Status on December 30, 1959. For the first time in Iraq's history, laws related to marriage, divorce, child custody, and inheritance were unified in a single code, brought under state control, and applied to all Muslim Iraqi citizens.[10] The most controversial provision was one that equalized intestate inheritance rights between male and female heirs. Other clauses restricted polygamy; abolished child and arranged marriages; and modestly increased women's rights in child custody cases. Scholars have often mentioned opposition to the law as a factor in the short-lived alliance of Shi'i and Sunni clerics with Arab nationalists that ensured the success of the first Ba'th coup in 1963 and thus the overthrow of Qasim's government and the assassination of Qasim himself. Yet few have devoted more than a sentence or two to explicating either the law itself or the struggle around it.

This book originated in an attempt to understand why the controversy over the 1959 personal status law became so pivotal during the revolutionary era, and what if any relation the conflict might have had to the Ba'thist rise to power. In other words, it was—and on some level still is—an intervention into the debate about what many have understood as the "failure" of the 1958 revolution.[11] During the course of my research, I became as interested in the shared discursive frameworks within which the controversy took place as I was in the points of dispute. For example, while the Ba'thist press published extensive critiques of certain clauses of the law, especially the equalization of inheritance rights, it framed those arguments in the same idioms—of economic development, social reform, and the care of children—in which the communist press framed its arguments supporting the same clauses. Moreover, most Ba'thist commentators, as well as many Sunni jurists, supported the principle of a unified family law under the control of the Iraqi territorial state. These groups shared a narrative with state officials, communists, and liberals that a nationwide homogenous law was necessary to produce stable conjugal families, and that such families were the foundation of the nation's sovereignty and development. Hence, contrary to the claims of some scholars that the personal status law itself was repealed after the 1963 coup, in fact the Ba'thist regime only modified two provisions, the equal-inheritance clause and the clause restricting polygamy. The rest of the law was left intact, contributing to the subsequent split between the new regime and Shiʻi clerics, who had wanted the entire law revoked.

The 1963 coup, which was in many ways driven by an alliance of anticommunist interests, was enabled by the fact that Qasim's regime had dismantled most of the popular organizations that might have defended it. The communists and other leftists could thus do little to save Qasim, or themselves, during the coup and the anticommunist bloodbath that followed. This has been often recognized in the historiography. But less attention has been paid to the widespread acceptance among Iraq's political actors during the revolutionary era that economic development and the social reform of Iraqi subjects trumped all other goods that may have been widely agreed upon in principle—including an end to military rule and its replacement with some kind of representative government—or to the ways in which this belief contributed to the demobilization of both the political party organizations and the urban and rural popular strata. As it happened, none of the parties that had come together in the United National Front would achieve its self-declared historical goal in Iraq: a socialist society for the ICP, a liberal democracy for the NDP, Arab union for the Baʻth and the Independence parties. But each of these parties would end up participating, in the name of its own imagined and perpetually receding future, in the expansion of the Iraqi territorial and militarized state into the intimate lives of Iraqi subjects.

In thinking these first three registers of "familiar futures" together, the chapters that follow refer to the modern political imaginary that Lee Edelman calls "reproductive futurism." This heteronormative discourse works to defer demands for political change in the present by placing on the "tiny shoulders" of the child the burden of embodying a political future that never arrives.[12] I will say more about my use of this concept below. Here I will just note that a reproductive futurist reasoning was familiar in Iraqi political discourse by the 1930s, and it flourished especially after the 1958 revolution. In many ways, its operations in this decolonizing context were less stable and predictable than Edelman sometimes seems to suggest in his own use of the concept. But its powers of moral unassailability were unquestionably strengthened in one particular way, which was through its inevitable imbrication with the emerging concept of the "developing" nation.

As Partha Chatterjee has noted, development was the 20th-century idiom through which all postcolonial states sought to secure their legitimacy.[13]

Like the child's future, and not unrelated to it, the nation's development was a politically unquestionable good in Iraq by the middle of the 20th century, the safeguarding of which could be, and often was, used as a trump card against any inconvenient demand for political change then and there. Edelman suggests that in the 20th-century United States, the figure of the child helped to create a boundary between acceptable partisan politics and enforced, through that very figure, sociopolitical consensus.[14] It seems to have been considerably easier for rulers of what came to be called "developing countries" in this period to declare, with straight faces, that partisan politics as such were a "waste of time," as state officials and even oppositional political party leaders in Iraq frequently did, especially but not exclusively in the revolutionary era.

There is a fourth register of the book's title, which stands outside of and often against the first three. More difficult to define than the others, instances of this register will flash up throughout the book. A critique of the 1959 personal status law made by the Shi'i jurist Muhammad Bahr al-'Ulum will serve to introduce it here. Unlike many Sunni jurists, Shi'i writers opposed not specific clauses of the new law but the very premise of a unified family code under the control of the secular state. In his critique, Bahr al-'Ulum suggested that the law only appeared to promote progressive change, while actually replacing the temporally and spatially dynamic Islamic systems of jurisprudence with legal stasis. In contrast to the open-endedness and nonterritoriality of Islamic law, the Iraqi personal status law required that "every judge in every generation" within Iraq's borders pass judgment according to its precepts.[15] This critique of the modern state for producing certain forms of temporal and spatial stasis, notwithstanding the claims of progressive time that always accompany such productions, is suggestive of Bahr al-'Ulum's grounding in a different kind of temporality, that of the Islamic discursive tradition.[16] Here change occurs over time in a way that links the past, present, and future, rather than sundering them through what Koselleck describes as the ever-widening gap in modern historical time between the "horizon of expectation" and the "space of experience." According to Koselleck, this gap is never greater than during modern revolutionary time, when the revolution "appears to unchain a yearned-for future while the nature of this future robs the present of materiality and actuality."[17] In the fourth register, which runs counter to the gap Koselleck describes, futures might be familiar because they are well known in the Iraqi context (Bahr al-'Ulum's conception of a non-static Islamic legal time is just one example) or because they are near or close futures, futures that might be realizable because they remain connected to the space of experience, rather than constantly receding along the horizon of expectation.

Historical Time and Sexual Difference

Scholars have theorized various ways in which the time of modernity, when conceived in all its fullness, is a paradoxically timeless time. The whole concept of the modern is predicated on a radical rupture with the past and on notions of perpetual newness and the linearity of a historical time stretching into infinity. Yet equally central to the production of modernity is its spatialization as a *place*, at which some (nations, races, classes) have *already* arrived. This "spatialization of time," intimately linked to global colonial relations, is what allows modernization and Westernization to work as synonyms in the first place.[18] The modern thus acquires a peculiar quality as both endlessly new and frozen, at least somewhere, in time. In the words of Kristin Ross: "[A]ll the possibilities of the future are being lived now, *at least for the West*: there they are, arranged before us, a changeless world functioning smoothly under the sign of technique."[19]

The changeless present of Western modernity relates both to the global historical time of colonialism and to the intimate experiences of modern technologies of political and social order. Koselleck and others have noted how the clock time and calendar time that measure modern homogeneous linear time, and that have come to dominate quotidian life with the rise of capitalism and the nation-state, are predicated on uniform duration and endless repetition. As these forms of time become the basis for modern experiences of governance, they come to mean "precisely not innovation or anything new but rather stability and routine both in the everyday and in the modes of organization of a political society. . . . [T]hrough repetition, precisely that which is new in it turns into the everyday and loses its meaning as new time."[20] I explore two institutions as particularly productive of modern experiences of timelessness: the nation-state and the conjugal family.

If the 1959 Baghdad women's march was framed as a sign of revolutionary new time, the discourse that envisioned modern women as guaranteeing the nation's development—and, conversely, non-modern women as blocking it—was not new. Modernizing reformers in Iraq, as in many other colonial and postcolonial contexts, had for several decades been constructing the "backward" indigenous woman, imagined to be sadly "trapped in the past," as a tragic symbol or even primary cause of her nation's backwardness. Increasingly seen as the dominant influence on the development of children, women—illiterate, superstitious, tied to biological rhythms of time—became objects of sympathy as well as concern for their role in the cyclical reproduction of the past with each generation, the pattern that seemed to block economic development and a sovereign future. One answer, in Iraq as elsewhere, had been to provide women with modern educations in feminine domesticity that would prepare them for a particular kind of conjugal and maternal life, one that would effect a decisive break with the nation's past and its diverse, messy, localized traditions and temporalities by reorienting its citizens toward what Benedict Anderson calls "homogeneous" historical time and the "limitless future" of the modern nation-state.[21]

In his well-known analysis of nationalism, Anderson argues that the modern sense of belonging to a nation depends on the learned capacity to imagine homogeneous historical time. The argument draws on Walter Benjamin's concept of modern homogeneous, or "empty," time as what makes possible the post-Enlightenment belief in "the historical progress of mankind."[22] In Anderson's extension of the concept, it describes the temporality of a modern nation as a discrete, organic, horizontal entity that moves ever forward in a uniform, linear fashion, as represented for instance in the visual timeline of a history textbook or the "meanwhile" of the modern novel. Anderson thus posits the modern nation-state, and not just mankind (as in Benjamin's analysis of the time of progress), as a central subject of this linear-temporal imaginary.[23]

I accept the basic premise that that the learned capacity to envision homogeneous linear-historical time is a condition of both the modern concept of progress and the modern sense of belonging to a nation. But this book complicates Anderson's argument in several ways. First, it considers how the actual movement of a subject—for example, a nation—through so-called homogeneous historical time is often imagined to be propelled by various forms of difference, including sexual difference. Second, it considers the way in which the "limitless future" that Anderson describes as integral to modern nationhood can sometimes work to defer rather than drive demands for change, and how gender shapes these logics of deferral as well.

Because modern feminine domesticity may seem to involve little change to women's status—they are still often expected to be at home—and because nationalists themselves often posit conjugal family life and domesticity as preserving the nation's authentic past, it is possible to see such discourses as primarily essentialist and backward-looking, ossifying patriarchal gender relations through the "invention of tradition."[24] But I propose that new dimensions of nationalism and sexual difference become available if we look at the deployment of such discourses as related instead to nationalism's forward-looking, future-directed sensibilities, its reliance on the political imaginary of reproductive futurism, imaginatively reinforced through new concepts of childhood and of generations to come. Biological reproduction is typically associated with notions of cyclical, rather than linear, time, and femininity itself is often imagined as a way of living in cyclical time.[25] But reproductive *futurism* is constituted by an interplay between cyclical-biological time and linear-historical time that is both modern and nationalist. For female subjects, as agents of reproduction, this interplay heralds new opportunities but also the consolidation of more formidable pressures. Having been finally freed from the past, the nation's women were henceforth to be trapped in its future.

In the reproductive-futurist imaginary analyzed by Lee Edelman, the "image of the Child" comes to shape "the logic within which the political itself must be thought." The fantasy of the child's innocence imposes "an ideological limit on political discourse as such"—who but a monster would stand against this innocence?—while the future the figure of the child embodies, but which no "historical child" is ever allowed to reach, becomes the "perpetual horizon of every acknowledged politics."[26]

The Child has come to embody for us the telos of the social order and come to be seen as the one for whom that order is held in perpetual trust. In its coercive universalization, however, the image of the Child, not to be confused with the lived experiences of any historical children, serves to regulate political discourse—to prescribe what will *count* as political discourse—by compelling such discourse to accede in advance to the reality of a collective future whose figurative status we are never permitted to acknowledge or address.[27]

The political rationality of reproductive futurism, while seemingly based on the valorization of change in its perpetual yearning toward the future, in effect compels a sort of political freezing of the present in the name of a child who never grows up and a future that never arrives. The figure of the child, writes Edelman, thus enacts "a logic of *repetition* that fixes identity through identification with the future of the social order."[28]

The framework of reproductive futurism resonates with concepts such as "patriotic motherhood" and "feminine domesticity" that have been used in many gender histories of the Middle East and that will also appear frequently in this book. But thinking about reproductive futurism as a hegemonic political imaginary of modernity helps to open up several aspects of these discourses that have not received much attention. One is the kind of disciplinary or depoliticizing work they can do, not only in the sense of "keeping women in the home" and out of politics—though often also that—but in the sense of centering a certain affective register of politics on an imaginary child as the embodiment of the nation's (equally imaginary) future. Another is the imagined timelessness of the modern domestic sphere, which is different from how the "traditional woman" or the "traditional family" is imagined to be rooted in the past. It is a qualitatively new kind of timelessness: hygienic, orderly, rational, safe, and reproductive of capitalism's *limitless* (that is to say, timeless) future.[29]

Sovereignty and the Social Order

Edelman does not consider whether "the social order" he refers to might have spatial as well as temporal contours. In contrast, I view reproductive futurism as an inescapably nationalist imaginary, one linked to a presumed isomorphism between a particular social order and a particular territorial nation-state. In both the pre-revolutionary and the revolutionary eras, the Iraqi state asserted its internal sovereignty through biopolitical and disciplinary interventions within the domain of the social. The word *sovereignty* in this book's subtitle thus points not so much to claims of external sovereignty and recognition by other states as it does to the internal production of sovereign power over human bodies within the state's borders and through its expanding social institutions and laws.[30] The production of internal sovereignty was a driving rationality of the promulgation of the 1959 personal status law, which reduced the jurisdiction of religious authorities, and expanded that of the territorial state, over the domain of the family. Again there were both ruptures and continuities with the pre-revolutionary era. The Iraqi state's sovereignty over its population had been asserted in part through the use of brute force, starting with the British deployment of airpower and other violent methods in the mandate period, and partly through forms of disciplinary and biopolitical power in the Foucauldian senses, especially from the 1930s on. I use "discipline" to refer to the minute and regular operations of power on human bodies through modern institutions such as schools and the military, the aim of which is to produce self-governing subjects, and "biopolitics" to refer to the regulation of the life and health of the national population.[31] The institution of the family is deeply invested in these two poles of modern power: the disciplinary and the biopolitical.

Most chapters of this book explore specific "crises" around which reproductive futurist discourses gathered in Iraq from the 1920s to the 1960s: the crisis of girls' education, the crisis of adolescent rebellion, the marriage crisis, even the agrarian crisis. Although strikingly similar crises were occurring in many other locations during this period, they were rarely if ever imagined as global crises; most were probably unthinkable as such. The nation-state was the bounded territorial space within which such crises occurred, and the future health and sovereignty of that nation-state were what they menaced. If they extended beyond the borders of the actually existing nation-state (Iraq, in my case), it was not to the world but to an imagined (e.g., Arab or Kurdish) future nation-state. But even this was extremely rare. After all, most of these crises could be addressed only through institutions territorially organized by the Iraqi state: a legal system, a school system, a health system, a national military, a land settlement system, and so on. The expansion of the state was not simply a response to preexisting social crises: in many ways, the crises were produced through the production of the state, and, conversely, the state was produced through the production and management of social crisis.

Jacques Donzelot's *The Policing of Families* explores how a core element in the emergence of "the social" in 19th-century France was the transformation of the family, which became the object of policing by the state at the same time as its members became subjects policing one another. In an argument that resonates in some ways with Edelman's, Donzelot writes that across otherwise salient political and ideological divides, and through this new realm of the social, "the family became the buttress at the foot of which all criticism stopped, the point of support from which demands were launched for the defense and improvement of the standard of living."[32] Thus, the social, which originally emerged "as a concrete space of intelligibility of the family," expanded into "a strange aquarium that has become, in a very brief period of time, the reality principle of our societies, the *raison d'être* of development, the proof that it has engendered, notwithstanding wars and pollution, a greater humanization."[33] In Donzelot's analysis, the policing of families operated differently for middle-class and working-class families. Both involved a "recentering of the family on itself," but for middle-class women it also meant an "alliance with the doctor." Through their role transmitting new hygienic interventions and knowledges, middle-class women were able to enter the public domain of the social in order to participate in the policing of lower-class families. The alliance between middle-class women and the doctor was also an alliance between the feminist movement and the state. For working-class families, this recentering of the family on itself worked differently, as their members were educated into policing one another.[34]

In Iraq, the urban/rural difference was central to almost all projects of reform, including those targeting family life. In the revolutionary era, one of the central controversies related to gender was over a rural literacy project launched by the League for the Defense of Women's Rights in 1959 and 1960. Rather than propagating effective techniques for the policing of rural families in the name of the child's and the nation's future, the communist women's literacy work was seen by Ba'thist and government critics as a symptom of "social promiscuity," to borrow Donzelot's term, threatening the political order.[35] Aspects of this conflict again echoed pre-revolutionary reform projects and discourses, such as land settlement programs that intervened in rural familial life in order to fix peasants on the land and prevent them from migrating to the cities. The interventions were always legitimated in the name of progressive change even as they worked to immobilize people in space.

Scholars critical of modernization theory and of what James Ferguson memorably called the post-1945 "development apparatus"[36] have tended to focus on one side or the other of this central problematic of development. They either criticize the universalizing logic of the apparatus or they criticize its particularistic, uneven logics. The latter critical trajectory was strong in the 1970s and 1980s, among scholars employing what is known as world-systems analysis and dependency theory.[37] Simply put, they argued that the development of some nations and the underdevelopment of others did not reflect those nations' different locations in historical time but rather were two sides of the coin of the global historical time of capitalism: industrial development in some places depended on the underdevelopment of other places. Starting in the 1990s, partly in reaction to these theories and also reflecting the "linguistic turn" or "cultural turn" in scholarship, the focus moved toward critiques of the universalizing narratives of development and modernization theory.[38] It has apparently been more difficult to keep both sides of the development problematic in the same theoretical frame, especially in ways that do not simply resort to a distinction between (universalizing) discourse and (differentiating) practice.[39]

Iraq and the Age of Development

The dawn of the global age of development is often located after World War II, with the founding of the World Bank, the United Nations and its development agencies, and the US Technical Cooperation Administration (President Truman's Point Four program). There were indeed important shifts in understandings of "development" around 1945, and it was at this moment that the territories and peoples of the globe were divided into two discrete categories: "developed" and "developing." But if the postwar concept of development has been the subject of substantial scholarly attention, the antecedents of this concept in the interwar period have been inadequately understood. Iraq is a particularly productive location for exploring those antecedents, especially concerning three problems related to development that run through this book. First, how did previously distinct notions—for example, the development of land and the development of humans—come to cohabit in a single concept? Second, how did development discourse often come to appear as an argument for temporal deferral, that is, for the opposite of what the word would seem to imply? Third, how did development discourse acquire its extraordinary moral force?

A number of recent scholars have argued that Iraq was somehow pivotal within the global history of decolonization and/or development in the interwar period. While colonized territories had been granted forms of independence by colonial powers before, through unilateral declarations or bilateral agreements, Iraq was the first state to be granted its postcolonial self-determination, or sovereignty, through a system of international law explicitly designed for that purpose.[40] Scholars who agree on Iraq's significance to some kind of historical shift in the operations of empire and sovereignty in the interwar period disagree on how the shift should be conceptualized. According to Toby Dodge, Iraq was the world's "first postcolonial state," but its "tortured birth" and later instability signified a failure of British officials to "accomplish what they had initially set out to do: build a liberal, modern, sustainable state capable of reshaping the lives of the Iraqi people."[41] Timothy Mitchell views the interwar British project rather differently, arguing that the production of self-determination was "a process of recognising (and in practice, of helping to constitute) forms of local despotism through which imperial control would continue to operate."[42] He concurs, though, on the significance of the Iraq experiment: "The most important site for producing this 'consent' to imperial rule was Iraq."[43]

Other historians have identified precocious shifts in understandings of "development" in British-occupied Iraq during and after World War I.[44] Priya Satia has even argued that "the modern notion of development did not begin, as is usually assumed, as a primarily post–World War II phenomenon in Africa, but earlier, in World War I–era Iraq where it underwrote fresh imperial conquest."[45] She argues that Iraq is where the British first introduced the "modern concept of development," which she defines as "a statist effort to use public investment for the avowed purpose of raising a colony into a modern nation state."[46] I also suggest that discourses and practices of development saw significant shifts in mandate-era Iraq, but my argument is different. The assertion of a singular and universalizing modern concept of development does not attend carefully enough either to the particular forms of British governance in Iraq or to the shifting, but still very multiple, meanings of "development" in this period. If mandate Iraq can be seen as a precocious subject of development, I suggest that this was related to how three previously distinct understandings of development started coming together there while still maintaining a productive difference from one another. The first understanding was the 19th-century colonial sense of development as the exploitation of a colonized territory's natural resources; the second was the notion of a people or nation as an organic entity moving through linear-historical time; and the third was the biopsychological imaginary of human development through particular delimited stages. Due to its vast oil and agricultural resources on the one hand and to its position in the League of Nations mandate system on the other, Iraq was an overdetermined space for the increasing entanglement of these three concepts of development in the interwar years.

In the next section, I lay out in some detail my own understanding of the various meanings and trajectories of "development" as they relate to Iraq, because this book is also an intervention in the scholarship on the global history of development and because there is still a considerable amount of confusion around the term, especially in studies of the interwar era. Here I focus on conceptions of development in the English language. In Iraq, it was predominantly British discourses on development that had to be translated into Arabic, Kurdish, and other local languages. In the chapters that follow, I will reference some of the Arabic terms that were conscripted into the project.

Development, Psychology, and the Mandate System

A striking characteristic of post–World War II development discourse, as numerous observers have recognized, was the way in which "development" had come to operate ambiguously or even simultaneously in transitive and intransitive grammatical senses. By 1945, it was often impossible to know whether the expression "the economic development of Iraq," for example, was positing Iraq as a subject developing or an object being developed.

According to H. W. Arndt, there were "two quite distinct channels through which the term 'economic development' entered English usage," one using it in a transitive and the other in an intransitive sense, and the two uses remained distinct through the interwar period.[47] In its transitive sense—that is, when it describes an action performed by some subject on some object—"economic development" appeared in colonial discourse starting in the mid-19th century to describe actions performed by a colonial power on a colonized territory in order to extract and exploit its natural resources. This usage of the term continued in colonial discourse through the interwar period—for example, in Lilian Knowles's 1924 *The Economic Development of the British Overseas Empire*, where it described "the hacking down of the forest or the sheep rearing or the gold mining which made Canada, Australia and South Africa into world factors . . . or the struggle with the overwhelming forces of nature which took shape in the unromantic guise of 'Public Works' in India."[48] This was also the sense used in British interwar legislation, such as the 1929 Colonial Development Act.

Meanwhile, in the other trajectory identified by Arndt, the intransitive use of development—that is, to refer to the self-propelled movement of a subject through time, with no grammatical object—acquired an economic connotation in the writings and translations of Marx. Aspects of Marx's conception of developmental time can be traced to Hegel and further back in the European intellectual tradition, but according to Arndt "it was Marx who gave development a specifically economic connotation." In the intransitive sense, "the birthplace of 'economic development' in English would seem to be the first English translation of Marx's *Capital* and the date 1887." Arndt quotes Marx's oft-cited statement that "[t]he country that is more developed industrially only shows, to the less developed, the image of its own future."[49] In this identification of countries as the subjects of economic development in the intransitive sense, one might see a harbinger of the nation-state as the subject/object of development in the dual sense that would become legible by 1945.

When "development" was used with an explicitly economic connotation in British mandate discourse on Iraq, it was in the first, transitive sense identified by Arndt. This conception was only starting to intermingle, toward the end of this period, with another strand in the genealogy of development, one that Arndt does not discuss: the development of a country or nation understood not as a territory, a state, or a container for an economy but as a *people*. It seems this may have been the understanding of development in which the transitive and intransitive senses first began to blur, around the turn of the 20th century—that is, well before it linked up with either of the economic uses identified by Arndt. It is also, I propose, what would give economic development the sense of unquestionable moral urgency that it would acquire by the end of World War II. Concepts drawn from the rapidly changing disciplines of biology and especially psychology were key here.

As is well known, it was Article 22 of the 1919 Covenant of the League of Nations that "introduced the concept of 'stage of development' into the literature of international organizations," and indeed into international law.[50] Article 22 referred to the development of "peoples," namely those living in the Allied-occupied territories of the Ottoman Empire and Germany's African colonies after the war, all of whom were to come under the mandate rule of one of the victorious powers. Its first clause stated, now infamously:

To those colonies and territories which as a consequence of the late war have ceased to be under the sovereignty of the States which formerly governed them and which are inhabited by peoples not yet able to stand by themselves under the strenuous conditions of the modern world, there should be applied the principle that the well-being and development of such peoples form a sacred trust of civilization and that securities for the performance of that trust should be embodied in this Covenant.[51]

The peoples in question were then arrayed across a three-tiered developmental continuum. Inhabitants of Iraq and other Allied-occupied regions of the defeated Ottoman Empire were designated immature peoples of "Class A," those in the final stage of development preceding emancipation and sovereignty, whose "existence as independent nations can be provisionally recognized subject to the rendering of administrative advice and assistance by a Mandatory until such time as they are able to stand alone." With the Class A category of immaturity, Article 22 inscribed into international law a "theory of tutelage of adolescent peoples in defined stages of development," granting "the benefits of self-determination for the sufficiently mature without its risks for the unprepared."[52]

Article 22's reference to the development of peoples did not necessarily suggest a universalizing modernization drive. Rather, it conformed to the doctrine of "development along native lines," which held that colonial policy should be to "intermeddle as little as possible with native institutions" in order to "develop the native peoples along the line of their own civilization."[53] This doctrine emerged in the 19th century but was given new theoretical substance in F. D. Lugard's 1921 *The Dual Mandate in British Tropical Africa*.[54] Lugard was a member of the Permanent Mandates Commission (PMC) of the League of Nations, and his book explicated the logic of mandatory power enshrined in Article 22. The dual mandate referred, on the one hand, to the exploitation of a territory's resources—that is, "economic development"—and, on the other, to the protection of the natives, or development "along native lines." The point of the theory was not that economic development and the development of the natives naturally worked in concert, as would come to be assumed in post-1945 development discourse, but the opposite: that they could harm each other if not kept separate. Unfettered economic development would exploit the native labor force to the extent that it would not be able to reproduce itself, ultimately harming economic development itself; unmanaged development of the natives would lead to unruly demands for popular sovereignty and for a share in economic development. As another member of the PMC explained: "The development of the mandated territories constituted for the mandatory powers a duty, alongside their other duty of securing the welfare of the natives. These two duties must be reconciled, and the two tasks must proceed side by side."[55]

In the interwar period, the doctrine of development along native lines, and the related policy of "indirect rule," became "the guiding principle of British colonial officials."[56] It reflected the increasing skepticism that colonized/colored people would ever develop along European lines, and was often an assault on the universalizing vision of progress. Lugard criticized what he saw as the disastrous earlier colonial attempts to universalize progress, purportedly most pronounced in India: "the results are with us to-day; liberty of speech and of the press degenerates to license; [and] well-meant efforts to accelerate the evolution of so-called democratic institutions are treated with contempt."[57] This shift was a global one, driving the British "dual policy" of "parallel development" for the European and native populations of Kenya; the institutionalization of apartheid in South Africa; new Jim Crow laws and projects of segregated schooling, such as the

Hampton and Tuskegee Institutes, in the post-Reconstruction US South; and the exportation of the "Tuskegee model" of "adapted education" to German colonies in West Africa.[58]

Scholars have recognized the connection made in this period between racialized ideas about the development of peoples and biopsychological ideas about the development of individual humans. But the tendency has been to see the connection as a metaphorical one, whereby the stages of the human life cycle are imagined as the stable, because imagined as biological, metaphors for the stages of development of peoples—rather than, for example, the other way around. In naturalizing developmental categories such as childhood, adolescence, and sovereign adulthood, the metaphor framework obscures how these categories themselves have histories and indeed were in significant flux during the period in which development was acquiring both its economic and its national connotations, that is, from the late 19th to the mid-20th centuries.[59] It also ignores what may be the strangest thing of all about the appeal of biological human development as a metaphor for national development in modernization narratives: that adulthood, sovereign or otherwise, is not in fact the final stage of the human or any other biological life cycle. Twentieth-century development discourse was built around the denial of death.

It was not, after all, the use of biological metaphors for envisioning the movement of a society through time that was new in this period. The 14th-century historian Ibn Khaldun, for example, had invoked the human life cycle as metaphor in his theory of historical time, in which a new civilization is born out of the conquest of an old one by nomadic invaders, develops into maturity, then weakens and declines before meeting its inevitable demise in the form of a new nomadic invasion. Numerous examples can also be found in the pre-Enlightenment European tradition. What was new about the use of the biological metaphor in modern development theory was that it ended with the attainment of healthy and sovereign adulthood, now implicitly envisioned as a permanent state, namely that of being "developed." This was a striking developmental imaginary, one that rejected continuous becoming even as it denied death.[60]

The influence of the 19th-century science of biology, especially evolutionism, on the new understandings of the development of peoples has been widely acknowledged.[61] But the role of the psychological sciences is virtually unexplored beyond passing references to turn-of-the-century recapitulation theory, which usually fail to situate that theory within the new social science discipline—psychology—that transformed it from its original evolutionary understanding.[62] In this theory, the historical development of "peoples" or "races" was seen as "recapitulating" the biopsychological development of individual humans, *and vice versa*. Thus, childhood and adolescence in this imaginary were not only stages of biological and psychological immaturity but also historically and racially primitive stages of development immanent to the temporality of every human psyche.

Like evolutionary theory, but against the belief in universal progress, psychological theory offered ways to normalize the "separate development" of different developing organisms toward different ends or futures, and could thus be mobilized to support the racial-scientific theories of development prominent by the turn of the century. But psychology also differed from evolutionism, for example in the space it opened up for notions of perverse or abnormal psychopathological development, including precocious or too rapid development. Employed on the plane of developing peoples or nations, this enabled some forms of anticolonial nationalism, and later communism, to be diagnosed as pathological forms of development, either because they were developmental deviations toward abnormal ends or because they reflected the abnormal demands of a subject to reach a stage of development before its time: the developmental pathology of precocity.

Even more than biology, then, psychology provided ways of thinking about how to intervene in a subject's development, such as in order to slow it down or to redirect it toward a future more proper to itself than the one it was pathologically striving for. Psychology could thus be used to detach development from universal notions of progress, including by imagining development as a kind of temporality internal to each developing subject. At the same time, it provided techniques of governance that could be applied to those racialized and gendered subjects who were located in the same stage of (under)development and moving toward the same kind of (agrarian or domestic) future.[63] Attending to the role of psychological categories in the history of development makes it difficult to ignore sex, class, race, and age as differences constitutive of that history.

It was the mapping of each of the world's "peoples" onto a particular territory or land during the late interwar and early postwar eras that enabled the peculiar linguistic convergence between the development of land and the development of a people, giving the latter a new transitive sense (a people that could be developed) and the former an intransitive one (a land that developed). By 1945, the "development of the Iraqi people" could be understood not only as compatible but as nearly synonymous with the "development of Iraq," and the former expression began to fade from view, having successfully transmitted its moral imperative.

The Narrative

The previous discussion of the interwar genealogy of development provides the background for Chapter 1, which takes a new look at British practices of governing Iraq in the occupation (1914–20) and mandate (1920–32) eras. British officials did not show much interest in state involvement in family reform, or in any other kind of biopolitical or disciplinary intervention in the Foucauldian senses. Instead, they relied on a combination of indirect rule— the production of zones of sovereignty for the rule of local despots, especially large landowning shaykhs[64]—and the notably direct use of corporeal violence, including hanging, whipping, corvée labor, and collective punishments such as bombing or burning down entire villages and cutting off water and food to recalcitrant towns. The chapter frames many of these practices as necropolitical, borrowing from Achille Mbembe, to mark their differences both from the modern disciplinary forms of power that have been the focus of much scholarship on the interwar Middle East and from what Foucault describes as the spectacular techniques of corporeal violence preferred by sovereign powers in premodern Europe.[65] As a means of achieving sovereignty by "exercising the right to kill,"[66] British necropolitical power in Iraq was implicated not only in immediate concerns over security but also in the production of Iraq as a bounded territorial space over which post-Ottoman sovereignty could be asserted and economic development, as the extraction of resources, carried out. The brute fact of corporeal violence was hardly exceptional in the history of the British empire. But in mandate Iraq it was shaped by new technologies of rule, especially airpower, and explained through emerging narratives of developmental psychology that drew from but were not identical to earlier colonial discourses on the childlike nature of non-Europeans.

Calls for the expansion of disciplinary and biopolitical techniques in the 1920s and 1930s came mainly from Iraqi nationalist elites, in opposition to British policy. Chapter 2 explores education and the military as key domains in which these struggles played out, mainly in this period over the bodies and minds of male youth. It engages especially with the writings of the Arab nationalist thinker and leading Iraqi education official Sati' al-Husri. In contrast to the usual scholarly concern with the (Arabist or Iraqist) *content* of nationalist narratives prevalent in Iraq's schools and military, the chapter traces how these institutions worked as spatio-temporal regimes to "synch up bodies and time" (to borrow a phrase from Elizabeth Freeman) and thus made a sovereign Iraqi future familiar even as it was temporally deferred.[67] It is not only that such regimes work on subjects' most intimate desires and capabilities but also that they work on them together, through shared temporal rhythms delimited by shared territorial borders. This indeed was the central conundrum faced by Arab nationalist policymakers such as al-Husri: how to produce Iraqi territorial sovereignty—which seemed to demand the cultivation of Iraqi subjects worthy of sovereignty, which in turn seemed to demand the expansion of Iraqi state institutions into every-day life—without binding those subjects to the sovereignty thus produced. They were well aware of the problem, even if they may have ultimately underestimated its scale.

The point, then, is not to minimize the role of Arabism in shaping an Iraqi national selfhood (quite the contrary, as will become clearer in the chapter), or to give the Iraqi state or Iraqi society more coherence than either had. Rather, it is to inquire into the widespread agreement in nationalist discourse around the very idea of an Iraqi society as the foundation of sover-eignty. Iraqi society became the "people" or the "self" around which interwar notions of sovereignty and self-determination coalesced. This was almost as true for Arab nationalists as it was for Iraqi nationalists—a divide that was not as salient in the interwar period as it would become later—in part because most Iraqi Arab nationalists viewed Iraq's territorial sovereignty as a prerequisite for future Arab political union and in part because they rarely defined that future union in territorial terms in the first place.[68] Against oppositional nationalist demands for Iraq's immediate independence, the Arabist discourse of mandate-era Hashimite officials—who depended on British power, even as they worked toward a phased independence—insisted that Iraqi subjects must be made worthy of sovereignty, and that this would take time. This Arabist and statist discourse envisioned precocious demands for Iraq's independence as symptoms of backwardness, not progress, and accused those making such demands of being both less modern and less Iraqi than those working toward a deferred sovereignty.

Chapter 3 turns to how, after Iraq's formal independence in 1932, reforming the family through the school became increasingly important. Even in the 1920s, when little emphasis was placed by either British or Iraqi officials on family reform, the struggle for sovereignty was intertwined with ideas about sexual difference and family life. The need for institutions such as schools and the military was often framed in terms of familial crisis: education and conscription would remove male youth, at least temporarily, from the harms of Iraqi family life. But it was only in the 1930s and 1940s, much later than in most places, that the Iraqi government implemented sustained, state-driven projects to educate girls, as the "mothers of the future," in modern practices of domesticity.[69] Yet rather than view the spread of public domestic education as a delayed repetition of a historical process that had already occurred elsewhere—which might suggest that there is little to be gained from studying it at all—I propose that this very peculiarity makes Iraq a productive context for examining pedagogies of domesticity in the late interwar and postwar periods. Discussions around state intervention in family life were explicitly informed by the concerns of that time, including the Great Depression, new directions in the social science disciplines, the rise of the United States as a world power, global decolonization, and the dawn of the age of development. The chapter explores how the curriculum implemented by al-Husri and his cohort was challenged by a new generation of education officials, a number of whom were educated in the United States. Influenced by the American conceptual vocabularies of pragmatism and adapted education, the new educators criticized the unified curriculum implemented by al-Husri's ministry, calling for a "differentiated curriculum" governed by the urban/rural difference and the male/female difference.

If the public school, the national military, and the family are all disciplinary institutions, their disciplinary effects are highly unpredictable. In the years around World War II, Iraqi officials were increasingly concerned that a crisis was brewing in the form of a new generation of educated youth who were taking up leftist ideologies. Chapter 4 looks at how generational affiliations produced largely by the expansion of public schooling—often in combination with extended family ties along intragenerational lines, that is, between siblings and cousins—worked to foster political mobilization within the underground but extremely popular Iraqi Communist Party (ICP). The widespread sense of generational crisis was expressed in three more specific crises prominent in public discourse during these years: the crisis of adolescence, the crisis of girls' education, and the marriage crisis. Efforts to intervene in and stabilize the stage of adolescence drew on new, globally circulating psychological theories, and conceptions of modern sexual difference and desire were key to these interventions.

Chapter 5 turns to family reform efforts on the Dujayla Land Settlement Project, founded in 1945 as the pilot project for a larger program envisioned to confront Iraq's agrarian crisis. The idea was to create a class of small "independent" or "family" farmers by distributing plots of newly irrigated state-owned land to some of the landless poor. The isolated nuclear family farm model used to design the settlement was based on US Cold War modernization and agrarian reform theory, which emphasized political stability at least as much as sustainable agricultural productivity. As it happened, the family farm design contributed to ecological and social catastrophe. The intensive agricultural methods on which the small farms depended, and the lack of infrastructure to sustain such methods, led to the rapid salinization of the soil. Meanwhile, the distance between the isolated homesteads precluded the pumping of clean water into them or even the use of a shared well for drinking water, fostering the spread of disease among settlers forced to use the same canals for their irrigation, drinking, and sewage needs. One of my arguments is that the nuclear family type, while failing to take hold as a widespread social reality in rural Iraq, nevertheless had significant effects on rural lives. By working as a kind of standardized grid for development operations, it materially altered agricultural practices and thus the land while making certain kinds of "family" relationships legible so that they could be worked on by techniques of governmentality.

In Chapters 6 and 7, I return to the controversies with which I began this Introduction, over women's mobilization and their role in social reform projects after the 1958 revolution. Chapter 6 explores the controversy over the rural literacy project launched by the League for the Defense of Women's Rights. I argue that the project was seen by state officials and Ba'thist commentators as violating the tacit terms of the alliance between the state and middle-class feminists to reform rural women and families. Rather than propagating effective techniques for the policing of families in the name of the child's and the nation's future, the communist women's literacy work was seen as a symptom of social promiscuity threatening the political order. This led not only to the shutting down of the program itself and the banning of the ICP daily newspaper *Ittihad al-Sha'b*, the widest circulating periodical in the country, but also to the legal prohibition of any teacher from an urban area so much as entering any of the rural regions of the volatile southern half of Iraq during the summer school vacation for any nonofficial reason.

Chapter 7 focuses on the post-revolutionary 1959 Iraqi personal status law. A primary aim of the law, according to the committee that drafted it, was to rectify a damaging legal situation that had fostered "instability in the life of the Iraqi family," and thereby to establish a foundation on which "the Iraqi family of the new era could be built."[70] The lawmakers traced the purported instability of Iraqi family life to the plurality of family laws themselves, as they were applied in shari'a courts according to different Islamic legal schools, as well as to what reformers saw as the failure of all the legal schools to foster stable conjugal families, for example by facilitating male unilateral divorce. Shi'i family law was often targeted for special attention due to its authorization of *mut'a*, or temporary, marriage.[71] Because it decouples heterosexual intercourse from permanent companionate marriage, reproduction, and the joint raising of children, one might say that *mut'a* marriage, in revolutionary Iraq, had no future. The attempts of the personal status law to make marriage more stable and permanent, while simultaneously making the conjugal home less permeable to strangers, were shaped by a reproductive-futurist drive to create a properly modern domestic sphere, where what Edelman calls the "logic of repetition" instituted by the modern fantasy of the child becomes a logic of timelessness pure and simple.[72]

This book's Epilogue explores a famous public monument in Baghdad built by the Iraqi artist Jawad Salim to commemorate the July revolution. In the early stages of my thinking about this book, I employed this monument as an illustration of the developmentalist and disciplinary reasoning underlying contemporary conceptions of time, sexual difference, and nationhood. This remains part of my analysis. But returning to Salim's work again and again over the years, supplemented by readings in a rich tradition of Arabic-language art criticism on the monument, I began to see the ways in which it also evokes multiple and heterogeneous conceptions of time, often drawn from the Islamic discursive tradition, that can be read as subversive of contemporary developmentalist reasoning.

A Note on Methodology and Sources

This is not a "history of" any coherent sociohistorical or conceptual subject (e.g., the conjugal family, feminine domesticity, the modern concept of development) moving through homogeneous historical time within a homogeneous national space. Each chapter draws on different types of sources and engages with what might be classified as different historiographical domains (social, cultural, intellectual, political, legal). The aim is to explore a number of different sociohistorical or discursive moments in mid-20th-century Iraq in which sexual difference and/or familial life were particularly charged objects of reform in the name of the nation's sovereign and developed future. It is also to show how such moments were not seamless or propelled by an ineluctable logic of power. They were usually attempts to contain or discipline oppositional forces of various kinds, they often ran up against modes of life not organized according to the future-oriented and child-centered logic of reproductive futurism in the age of development, and they met with varying degrees of success.

This methodological point is related to my use of sources. There is no denying the challenges of conducting research on a country that has been in a state of near-continuous war for almost four decades. But there are several reasons these challenges need not be exaggerated. First, the very limited state of scholarship on Iraq means that many available sources remain unexamined and many of those that have been examined remain open to alternate readings. Hand-wringing about missing sources might better be left to a time when more of the existing ones have been utilized. Second, if one is not looking for a coherent subject moving evenly through linear-historical time in the first place, then there are not exactly "gaps" in the archival record for the history one is writing. There are only clusters of sources around particular moments and particular problems, sources that in my case had sometimes already been collected in formal (but not necessarily state-assembled) archives and sometimes were the product of my own assembling of an alternate archive.[73]

Chapters 1 and 2 on the British mandate era—which were written last and with the aim of providing context for the later chapters—are based mainly on new readings of some familiar primary sources (British records, Iraqi and British memoirs, writings by Iraqi intellectuals) and on engagements with existing scholarship in English and Arabic. Chapters 3 through 7 are all based on original research conducted over many years and in many locations. Like other historians of Iraq, I have assembled an archive of sources scattered across three continents: Iraqi periodicals stored in partial collections in far-flung libraries; published Iraqi government records (the government gazette, journals of particular ministries); works by Iraqi intellectuals, including Islamic legal scholars; memoirs; oral interviews that I conducted; and British and US government archives. Many of the sources I used have not been previously examined in the scholarship; others I have reexamined to draw different conclusions. My research differs from much of the current historiography in other ways, three of which I note here.

First, in addition to the types of sources listed above, I conducted substantial research into global development expertise as it was employed in Iraq. Sometimes this was standard archival work, as in Chapter 5, which draws on the UNESCO archives in Paris to explore a joint pilot project of UNESCO and the Iraqi Ministry of Education that trained poor rural women on the Dujayla settlement in home economics. In other cases, it involved more genealogically oriented research tracing the sources and home-country context of foreign expertise itself. For example, Chapter 3 challenges common readings of the 1932 Monroe Report, which has been used widely as a source in histories of the Iraqi interwar education system. The chapter shows how the American experts who wrote the report were linked to segregated schooling projects for black youth in the US South and how, far from a transparent description of Iraqi schools, the report was an often almost verbatim repetition of earlier reports written by the same experts on schools from China to the Philippines to Mexico. Throughout the book, I engage in this kind of tracking back and forth between the Iraqi and contemporary Western contexts of development, a method that requires suspending the commonly held but rarely examined assumption that the West has been in a static state of modernity since the Enlightenment and/ or the industrial revolution and therefore that the meaning of modernization as Westernization in any subsequent historical moment requires no further inquiry.

Second, in my textual analyses of source material I challenge a divide that runs through much of the existing historiography on Iraq, that between political and intellectual history on the one hand and social history, especially of subaltern mobilization, on the other. From the 1932 Monroe Report to the 1945 Dujayla land settlement contract to the 1958 Agrarian Reform Law, development discourse was always a response to sociopolitical conflict in Iraq, whether the mass migration of the rural poor to Baghdad or the flocking of urban youth to the communist party, and thus always contained the imprint of such conflicts. The point, therefore, is not to suggest that the development apparatus was a closed or unidirectional projection of power but rather to illuminate, as Omnia El Shakry puts it, "the pressure that subalternity exerted upon dominant discourses."[74]

Third, I often engage with Iraqi intellectuals of the period under study not only as sources for exploring contemporary events and ideas but also as interlocutors around the theoretical problems with which this book is engaged. Questions of time, selfhood, and sovereignty were the explicit preoccupations of many of these thinkers, and grappling with their work has led me to rethink the arguments of this book on numerous occasions. Examples already mentioned are my engagement with the Shiʻi jurist Muhammad Bahr al-ʻUlum to consider how the 1959 personal status law was implicated in producing temporal and spatial stasis, and my explorations in the Epilogue of the artist Jawad Salim's uses of cyclical imaginaries of time in order to subvert the tendency of linear modernization narratives to open onto a universal and thus timeless future.

Another example, discussed in several chapters, is in the writings of the Iraqi sociologist ʻAli al-Wardi. In a series of books written in the early and mid-1950s, al-Wardi proposed a modified version of the Khaldunian narrative of historical time, arguing that much of Islamic history in general, and Iraqi history in particular, can be seen as a repeated struggle between "the people of the state" and "the people of revolution." A revolution occurs, under slogans of freedom and justice, but as soon as it succeeds, the former people of revolution begin their inevitable decline into corruption and injustice—since power is always corrupting despite people's best intentions—and a new people of revolution emerges. We must always oppose the current state, al-Wardi insisted, not because our longings for freedom and justice will ever be realized, but because it is the only way to prevent the state from becoming completely unjust. Engaging with the Khaldunian conception of cyclical time, as well as with earlier Islamic concepts of moral decline and revival, allowed al-Wardi to bypass what Jacques Derrida has described as the "tiresome" trajectory of every 20th-century secular political ideology toward its own version of "an end of history," and to warn his Iraqi readers, four years before the events of 1958, that "success is the grave of revolution."[75]

1

Sovereignty, Violence, and the Dual Mandate

DURING THE CELEBRATIONS of Iraq's entry into the League of Nations in 1932, the British foreign secretary expressed pride at having served "as representative of the country whose privilege it had been to guide the State of Iraq through the period of adolescence to the full status of manhood."[1] Like the discourse on Iraq's adolescence, the parallel one on its (non)masculinity had spanned the twelve years of the mandate. In May 1920, Acting Civil Commissioner in Iraq A. T. Wilson had announced to the Iraqi public the decision at the San Remo conference that Iraq would be placed under British mandate, and explained that the goal was to "train [the] charge" to "[fit] him to take his place in the world of men." Far from seeking to derail the process of maturation, the guardian would rejoice at "the growth of his ward into sane and independent manhood."[2]

It might be tempting to read the promise to guide the "ward into sane and independent manhood" as heralding the expansion of biopolitical and disciplinary forms of power, in the Foucauldian senses, into Iraq. Such a reading would expect British governance in Iraq to be concerned with intimately "conducting the conduct" of its colonial subjects.[3] Indeed, Antony Anghie has made an argument along these lines about the mandate system on a global scale, positing that it allowed international law and institutions "to address the unconscious, and thereby to administer 'civilizing therapy' to the body politic" of the state whose sovereignty was being formed, thus producing differences in "the most intimate and minute aspects of social life in mandate territories—native 'customs, traditions, manner of living, psychology, and even resistance to disease.'"[4] This argument suggests important links between changing psychological concepts, such as that of the unconscious, and the project to forge a system of legally sovereign nation-states out of the global colonial order. But it is less useful as an account of how mandate governance worked in and on Iraq, either at the level of the League of Nations or at that of British practices of rule.

The League of Nations was not institutionally present in mandate Iraq and did not intervene in the "intimate and minute aspects of social life" there, while British practices were usually more concerned with how to defer the expansion of modern disciplinary and biopolitical institutions than with how to accelerate it. David Scott has argued that there was a shift in the political rationality of European colonial power from the 16th to the 19th centuries, so that by the end of that period the task was "to produce not so much extractive-effects on colonial bodies as governing-effects on colonial conduct."[5] This shift was always uneven at best, and recent historians have shown how it was being at least partially reversed by the mid-19th century, as European powers moved toward models of indirect rule, usually meaning support for local despotic governments, and away from practices of direct rule more conducive to disciplinary projects.[6] In any case, British practices in mandate Iraq were usually concerned precisely with producing extractive effects on colonial bodies, their main aims—after security, or counterinsurgency—being the extraction of taxes in the short term and the guarantee of economic concessions in the long term, especially regarding control over the extraction of oil. The British neglect, and often active obstruction, of projects to produce governing effects on colonial conduct may be traced in part to the temporally constricted parameters of mandate rule; there simply was not enough time for such projects to bear fruit. It might also be traced to, and was certainly enabled by, a new technology of imperial rule that made the need for the intimate conduct of conduct less acute: airpower. In both ways, British mandate governance in Iraq may have been closer to later 20th-century imperial interventions than to 19th-century practices of colonial rule.

Mandate Iraq was the laboratory for the world's first large-scale imperial experiment in rule from the air. As British imperial historian Priya Satia notes, Iraq was "the only colony where airpower became a permanent instrument of imperial administration and policing. . . . It was in Iraq that the British first practiced, if never perfected, the technology of bombardment."[7] Airpower is not a disciplinary technique concerned with "the most intimate and minute aspects of social life," as Anghie posits the global rationality of mandate governance, nor is it a mechanism of governmentality that is "worried about the totality of the social, about an interconnected order of life," in Scott's words.[8] It is not a biopolitical technology at all, but a necropolitical one; it is "a means of achieving sovereignty" by "exercising the right to kill."[9] In this context, as this chapter will show, British discourse usually deployed the developmental category of adolescence not to call for intimate interventions into Iraqi psyches and bodies but, first, to argue for the deferral of Iraq's sovereignty and, second, to explain the use of necropolitical and other direct forms of corporeal violence.

The analytical models prevalent in the scholarship on colonial modernity in other Middle Eastern contexts are thus not always applicable to interwar Iraq. Omnia El Shakry notes that "the theoretical literature on subaltern studies has canonized the experience of 19th- and 20th-century British India as the paradigmatic example of colonialism."[10] For Iraq scholars, a similar point could be made about Egypt, the focus of some of the most innovative recent works on colonial modernity, subject formation, and gender in the Middle East.[11] Indeed, the history of British policy in Iraq is often narrated as a battle between the "India school" and the "Egypt school" of colonial thought, with the latter emerging victorious. While this narrative reflects the language of a contemporary colonial debate between those favoring "direct" and those favoring "indirect" rule, it also elides significant differences between the experiences of Egypt and Iraq under British governance. These include Britain's routine and institutionalized reliance in Iraq on necropolitical violence—most notably, air bombardment—not just as an exceptional punitive technique, to be employed when disciplinary and biopolitical methods failed, but as the primary means of imperial rule. British mandate policy did not attempt to reform Iraqi subjects through "concern with the individual body of the political subject" or "the institution of something resembling Foucaultian discipline," as Timothy Mitchell and Wilson Chacko Jacob, respectively, have argued of colonial rationalities in late 19th- and early 20th-century Egypt.[12]

The Dual Mandate and the Adolescent Stage of Development

This chapter takes a new look at British mandate rule in Iraq, both through new readings of some familiar primary sources (British records and Iraqi and British memoirs) and by putting existing scholarly works into conversation in new ways. Certain British technologies of violence in Iraq, especially airpower, have been explored extensively by scholars such as Satia, Jafna Cox, Toby Dodge, and David Omissi.[13] Other practices, such as hanging, whipping, and the use of corvée labor, have received less attention, especially in the English-language scholarship.[14] Similarly, some mandate practices of legal differentiation, such as the construction of the dual system of tribal and civil law, have been studied by Samira Haj, Noga Efrati, and others, while less attention has been paid to the British use of martial law or the mandate-era reversion from Anglo-Indian back to Ottoman civil and criminal law.[15] While extensive discussions of these underexplored areas of the historiography are beyond the scope of this chapter, I touch on them in the course of making my broader argument and to suggest avenues of future research.

Finally, historians such as Dodge, Peter Sluglett, and Orit Bashkin have documented Britain's opposition to the expansion of public education and a national military, typically central institutions for the operations of modern disciplinary power.[16] Indeed, Dodge argues explicitly that British mandate rule was not characterized by "disciplinary power," geographic "mapping," or "scientific quantification."[17] My research supports these claims about what British governance in Iraq did not do. But my framing of the productive operations of mandate rule is different from Dodge's account that British policy was riven by an ideological tension between "rational individualism" and "romantic collectivism."[18]

This chapter argues that British mandate governance in Iraq is more productively understood through the lens of the "dual mandate" theory. As explained in the introduction, the two sides of the dual mandate aligned with two prominent uses of "development" in British discourse during this period: "economic development" as the exploitation of a colonized territory's resources and "development along native lines" as the welfare and containment of the territory's native population. The point of the theory was not that economic development and the welfare of the natives were mutually supportive, as post-1945 development theory would claim, but that they would harm each other if not kept separate. Development along native lines was to be carried out through the principle of indirect rule. As British judicial secretary Edgar Bonham-Carter explained, the advantage of indirect rule in Iraq was that it "provide[d] a legislative machinery which should at least delay the premature introduction of representative institutions in advance of the need of the country."[19]

Indirect rule, it was hoped, would create the stability required for economic development, which primarily meant the creation of infrastructure to enable the exploitation of Iraq's agricultural resources, both by private

British agricultural interests and by the class of large landowning shaykhs whose power British policy worked to consolidate. It also meant securing concessions over Iraq's oil resources, though the outcome of this was often to defer, not to immediately develop, those resources. Nationalists often pointed critically to oriental secretary Gertrude Bell's comment that the British would like to see Iraq remain an agricultural country "forever," and as early as 1919, British officials referred to the "development of the country" to mean the securing of control over Iraq's oil.[20]

Development along native lines was intertwined with emerging psychological categories of development, such as the category of adolescence. The historically peculiar mandate system of semicolonial rule enshrined in Article 22 of the League of Nations charter was itself based on certain parallels between adolescence as a stage of psychological and national life. The concept of adolescence had taken its psychologized shape at the turn of the twentieth century as a racial-developmental category. In the 1890s and early 1900s, the American psychologist and "father of adolescence" G. Stanley Hall "popularized adolescent storm and stress and utilized a romantic idea of youth potential and problems that mandated increasing supervision of young lives."[21] These ideas were based on Hall's "recapitulation theory," which posited that individuals and races moved through the same stages of development. The newly psychologized and racialized category of adolescence was not simply an extension of earlier discourses on the immaturity or childlike nature of non-Europeans. While it clearly drew on such discourses, it was also constructed in the context of the global crisis of empire at the turn of the 20th century. Anticolonial insurgencies could now be read as symptoms of the emotional adolescent stage of development and of the psychological pathology of precocity. Thus, British mandate officials diagnosed precocious demands for independence as a symptom of Iraq's own immaturity, asserting that "political aspirations and the desire for self-government" were akin to the "wayward thoughts in any adolescent youth."[22] Coercive and violent methods of sovereign power employed on Iraqi bodies were framed as an appropriate British regression to the racially and psychologically primitive forms of Iraqi violence expressed in political insurgency.

Narratives of Iraq's national and psychological backwardness also included claims that Iraqi society lacked the developed forms of sexual differentiation associated with modernity. Since Iraqis, as a people and as individuals, had not successfully traversed the psychological stage of adolescence into mature adulthood, so the story went, they had not acquired modern aptitudes of masculinity and femininity or modern heteronormative desires. This discourse, like the one on adolescence, was deployed not to cultivate sexually differentiated and mature subjects but rather as evidence that Iraqis were not ready for modern forms of governance and thus to justify British regression to violence.

The British interwar policy of indirect rule did not contradict the so-called Wilsonian ideal of self-determination. Woodrow Wilson's Fourteen Points speech was partly a response to the declaration, three days earlier, by British Prime Minister David Lloyd George that the postwar settlements must respect "the right of self-determination or the consent of the governed," which was itself a response to Lenin's similar statement earlier.[23] Wilson's own statement, in his famous Twelfth Point, did not mention self-determination but rather asserted that the "Turkish portions of the present Ottoman Empire" were promised "secure sovereignty," but that the other, non-Turkish regions (including Iraq) were assured only of "an undoubted security of life and an absolutely unmolested opportunity of autonomous development." For these regions, sovereignty would be deferred to an unspecified future.[24] Development along native lines, or protecting the "security of life" and "unmolested autonomous development" of the natives, could be carried out through the principle of self-determination, which, far from seeking to accelerate the implementation of popular sovereignty, worked to indefinitely defer it. Everything, of course, hinged on the definition of the "self" of self-determination. As long as it was defined in racial terms—as it was, in Wilsonian, British, and League of Nations discourse—then any native despotic government, if run primarily by members of what in this period came to be called the "majority race" of the territory in question, could claim to represent and determine the national self.[25]

In addition to exploring the struggles over the timing of Iraq's sovereignty and development, this chapter looks at the "placing" of Iraq, that is, its production as a bounded territorial space within which sovereignty could be asserted—first by the British, then by a newly defined Iraqi self—and economic development, as the extraction of resources, carried out. Iraq has often been narrated as a colonial invention, beginning with its so-called artificial borders.[26] The point is usually made in reference to the country's religious and linguistic diversity, and is usually an attempt to explain its tragic history of dictatorship, war, and occupation in the late 20th and early 21st centuries, without which the artificiality of its borders would likely be as forgettable as that of the borders of most nation-states, diverse or not. But the artificiality narrative has been enabled by scholarly accounts that reify borders by depicting them as simple materializations of lines drawn on a map. Iraq's border formation, like that of all nation-states, was a drawn-out, violent process involving the production of both external and internal territorial sovereignty, a production that, moreover, had to be continuously repeated. Iraq's borders were the hard-earned, precarious, and yet notably long-lasting effect—not the foundation or starting point—of mandate governance. One aim of this chapter, then, is to defamiliarize the story of Iraq's formation after World War I. Moving away from the reification of maps and borders, as well as of ethnic and sectarian categories, it attends instead to how modern formations of sovereignty—including the production of law and of territorial borders—always occur through actions performed on human bodies, as "the site upon which sovereign violence always inscribes itself but also encounters the most stubborn resistance."[27]

An Emotion Like in Kind

The announcement of the San Remo decision that Iraq would be placed under British mandate was greeted by an anticolonial uprising, the 1920 Iraqi revolt that spread across large regions of the territory, especially the predominantly Sunni area northeast of Baghdad; Baghdad itself; and the Shi'i shrine cities and surrounding tribal regions of the Middle Euphrates. A 1925 report by the British high commissioner in Iraq situated the revolt within a global crisis of empire, namely the wave of anticolonial insurgency at the close of World War I. The Iraqi revolt only deepened concerns over excessive geographical mobility—of bodies, ideas, and arms—in a region devastated by war and famine and lacking defined borders.

In India the crisis came in 1919 and was followed by war with Afghanistan and risings all along the North West Frontier. Persia was for the time overawed by British troops . . . but in the beginning of 1920 the withdrawal of troops had begun and a wave of Anglophobia swept over the Persians. . . . To the north the Turks of Anatolia had revived. . . . Mustapha Kamal had begun his successful rebellion against the Sultan as a puppet of the English. . . . In Syria the government of King Faisal at Damascus had . . . been drawn into the anti-British current and had permitted encroachments along the Euphrates upon territories occupied by the British forces of Iraq. . . . Damascus was full of adventurous Iraqis eager to . . . sweep away British control from 'Iraq. . . . Egypt was already convulsed by agitation against the British Protectorate and serious rioting had taken place in November 1919. . . . Thus, from India to Egypt, the Eastern World lay in a welter of resentment against the policy of the British and their Allies. . . . 'Iraq, in the very centre of this vortex of hostile impulses, was especially affected by them.[28]

British authorities concerned with Iraq policy were thus worried not only about securing a pathway to India and control over the Persian and Mesopotamian oilfields, nor only about the power vacuum left by the defeat of the Ottoman state and the resulting uncertainty of borders and sovereignties in the region. They were also worried about the world-historical crisis of the British empire and about the need, in the entire region from India to Egypt, to "banish some of the theories that the Great War had produced."[29]

In addition to the anticolonial uprisings sweeping across Asia and Africa at the close of the war was the Russian revolution of 1917, the actual and potential effects of which were omnipresent for British officials. According to Satia, the fear of "the Bolshevik threat" trumped all other British concerns in Iraq.[30] The Bolsheviks had gained no little popularity by withdrawing Russia from the war against the Ottomans, publicizing the wartime machinations of the western European powers, and declaring their support for the self-determination of nations under colonial rule, months before British Prime Minister Lloyd George and US President Wilson discovered and proclaimed their own watered-down versions of that principle. Even before the Iraq revolt started, British officials were grappling with the problem of "itinerant mischief-makers," as Acting Civil Commissioner A. T. Wilson called them, wreaking havoc on what the British thought of as Iraq's northern frontier. "There were many such on the move in this period," he wrote, including "Bolshevik emissarries."[31] Anecdotal reports of strange occurrences, such as a wandering postwar troop of 1,800 soldiers who claimed to be "Bolsheviks not attached to any state" and who were said to have fought for a time on the side of the Iraqi rebels in Ramadi in 1920, did not help matters.[32] Moreover, it seems the problem was not limited to northern Iraq or the frontier regions; according to A. T. Wilson, the Bolsheviks also "seemed for a time to find a spiritual home in Karbala," in the Shi'i heart of the Middle Euphrates.[33]

Philosophizing about the "measures of punishment as well as of pacification" that British troops carried out in the fall of 1920, "after the fires of the rebellion had burnt themselves out," A. T. Wilson wrote:

Tragedy, according to Aristotle, purges the emotions through pity combined with fear. It excites emotion, only to allay it, and in the calm which follows the storm, the cure of emotional disorder is found. Milton regards it as a means of homeopathic treatment, a *Katharsis*, curing emotion by means of an emotion like in kind, but not identical.[34]

Wilson left to the reader's imagination what British troops might have done to cure Iraq's emotional disorder "by means of an emotion like in kind." But the measures are known to have included whipping, hanging, and the use of collective punishments such as bombing or burning down entire villages whose residents had participated in the insurgency, in addition to exile, imprisonment, land and property confiscations, and individual and collective monetary fines.[35] These were all well-practiced measures used by the British since the start of the occupation of Basra in 1914.

Anticolonial rebellions and violent suppressions of them were of course nothing new in the history of the British empire, though by 1920 new technologies of rule, especially airpower, were transforming how they played out. But it is also worth noting how shifting discourses, including the temporal imaginary of psychological development enshrined in the mandate system, helped to diagnose anticolonial resistance as a symptom of an emotional disorder internal to Iraq and its inhabitants simultaneously. In this imaginary, political conflict was never an expression of conflicting interests but rather one of conflicting historical and psychological temporalities. The British response was often not to try to bring Iraqis up to adult, rational British time—which would be feeding the very precocity that needed to be repressed—but rather to meet them in their own primitive, emotional time, by deploying "an emotion like in kind, but not identical." This discursive move made British violence illegible except as a mirror of the primitive violence of Iraqis, a mirroring that was faithful to the doctrine of development along native lines.[36] Indeed, British violence could be imagined as a sign of respect for native difference; as Royal Air Force (RAF) intelligence officer John Glubb explained, war was "romantic excitement" for tribal nomads in Iraq, and "tragedies, bereavements, widows, and orphans" a "normal way of life."[37]

Wilson had been standing in for High Commissioner Percy Cox, who returned to Iraq in October 1920, near the end of the revolt. Upon his return, Cox issued a public statement to the "tribes and communities" involved in the uprising, pleading for an end to the "misunderstandings" and insisting that he was "at a loss to know for what object tribesmen are at present fighting and would be glad if they would put themselves in communication with the nearest Political Officer."[38] This was a peculiar claim, and it was met with ridicule in Iraq, given the many written demands issued by the rebels to the British authorities and the many negotiations between the two sides over the course of six months. These had all failed due to the fact that Britain would not accept the rebels' primary demand: the evacuation of British troops and the "complete independence of Iraq" within "its natural borders," which they defined as stretching from north of Mosul to the Persian Gulf.[39] But Cox's statement should be read as a performative one: by hailing the insurgents as "tribesmen," it already announced that their demands would not be legible as rational goals. While adolescence often worked as a psychological category of temporal distancing, both tribe and sect performed similar work as historical categories of temporal distancing, and similarly justified British regression to an "emotion like in kind." Adolescence has fallen out of fashion as a category of this kind, but the other two continue to shape scholarly depictions of the 1920 revolt, often explained away as a "tribal uprising."[40]

According to another narrative of "misunderstanding" that continues to be repeated in scholarly works, especially those that rely mainly on British sources, it was the unfortunate official translation of the word "mandate" into Arabic that generated much of the Iraqi opposition to it in 1920.[41] But the translation of mandate in all official discourse was *intidab*, from a verb meaning "to delegate," which rather effectively transmits the opaque and euphemistic quality of the English word. Indeed, Wilson himself—who seems to have introduced the translation/misunderstanding claim, but only when addressing the British public—admitted elsewhere that *intidab* was chosen "for the sake of euphemy."[42] Perhaps when referencing an unfortunate translation, Wilson meant one of the other terms for the mandate that were in common—but not official—usage in Iraqi public discourse, such as *wisaya*, or "guardianship." Far from an instance of meaning lost in translation, this term reflected the saturation of global and local discourse on the mandate system with notions of immaturity and maturity, childish dependence and masculine sovereignty.

Moreover, while the 1920 revolt was sparked by the announcement of the San Remo decision, it was an uprising not only against the idea of British governance but also against the experience of it. A brief account of events in the Shi'i shrine city of Najaf under British occupation may help to illustrate local experience with British rule in a region central to the insurgency. Najaf had rebelled against the Ottoman government early in the war, partly to protect the Najafi conscripts who had defected from the army and were seeking refuge in their hometown, and was "completely self-governing" from 1915 to 1917. It was occupied by British troops near the end of 1917. Oppressive British taxes fueled resentment, which erupted into protests after a Najafi youth was stripped naked and publicly whipped by British troops. Things came to a head in March when a British military captain was killed. The British administration responded by surrounding Najaf with troops and cutting off its water and food supplies. Written protests from the town's religious leaders ("If you have no mercy for the men, we beg of you to take mercy on the women and children") had no effect.[43] British demands included the surrender of a list of suspects in the killing to stand trial in a British military court; the surrender of an additional one hundred Najafis for deportation to India as "prisoners of war"; and the payment of a collective fine in money and rifles by the town. After withstanding the water and food blockade for almost a month, the townspeople surrendered, rounded up those on the wanted lists, handed them over to the occupation forces, and paid the fine. Not surprisingly, though, the resentments continued, especially after the military court sentenced eleven of the detainees to death, while acknowledging that only two had participated in the killing. The eleven, who in Wilson's description "included some of the principal secular leaders of the town," were "duly hanged in public at Kufa on the morning of 25th May."[44]

An Amazingly Relentless and Terrible Thing

The 1920 revolt sealed the victory of indirect over direct imperial rule in Iraq. Even as British troops were violently suppressing the revolt, British officials were issuing promises that its primary demand—an independent Iraqi state free of foreign interference—was being fulfilled. The approach was similar to the one recommended by F. D. Lugard, the founder of the dual mandate theory, for dealing with rebellious natives: "thrash them first, conciliate them afterwards."[45] In fact, for a year after the revolt ended it was far from clear to many of the rebels that they had lost. One of their demands had been for a son of Sharif Husayn of the Hijaz—probably, Faysal or 'Abdullah—to rule as king of a sovereign Iraq. The British arranged for Faysal to be crowned in August 1921. He was given the conditional approval of the leaders of the 1920 revolt, including the Shi'i 'ulama' in the shrine cities; the condition was that he preside over a truly independent Iraq. By the summer of 1922 it was obvious that the condition was not being met, and many withdrew their support of Faysal. I will return in the next chapter to the sectarian discourses that emerged out of this conflict.[46]

Meanwhile, the revolt had revealed to some British authorities the potential of airpower not only as a counterinsurgency technology but as a revolutionary model of imperial rule, and they pushed successfully for reconfiguring British governance of Iraq around this insight. Indirect rule in mandate Iraq thus had distinctive features, some of which emerged out of the experience of the revolt. It included not only the development of a loyal native administration—the defining feature of indirect rule everywhere—but also the replacement of imperial ground troops not by an army of native soldiers but by an imperial air force, supplemented by small native levies organized along ethnosectarian lines. This decision was made at the 1921 Cairo conference and was instituted in 1922, when military command of the Iraq mandate was officially transferred to the British Royal Air Force (RAF). The experiment was called "control without occupation."[47]

According to Mohammed Tarbush's count, the RAF carried out 130 air bombing raids in Iraq from 1921 to 1932, or an average of almost one per month for twelve years in official peacetime, some of which dropped "ten tons of bombs, not infrequently resulting in villages being 'practically destroyed . . . the debris being completely burnt up by incendiary bombs and Verey lights.' "[48] In the sparsely populated rural areas of Iraq, airpower annihilated "the distances that otherwise kept nomadic tribes beyond the reach of any state's scrutiny," which, in the words of one British official, made it seem possible "to keep a whole country under more or less constant surveillance."[49] Satia writes that "air control was intended to work like the classic panopticon,"[50] and, indeed, T. E. Lawrence (aka Lawrence of Arabia) philosophized about airpower, in terms that sound oddly like those of Foucault, as producing "an intangibly ubiquitous distribution of force—pressing everywhere and yet assailable nowhere."[51]

But airpower also differs significantly both from the early modern forms of violence inflicted on criminal bodies in the public spectacles so memorably described by Foucault and from the more modern and dispersed forms of disciplinary power that work on the subject's everyday habits and desires.[52] One difference from both of these earlier practices is the greatly expanded distance between the point where power is discharged and the point of its impact on a target. The distancing and counter-biopolitical aspects of rule from the air could be disconcerting even to British officials. For example, the practice of numbering casualties within three discrete population categories—men, women, and children—was nearly impossible in situations where the human targets could not be clearly distinguished, especially when British ground forces were not present. Winston Churchill, perhaps not fully grasping the new challenge, objected to reports from Iraq that broke with tradition and estimated casualty numbers under the "comprehensive head of 'men and women.' "[53]

Churchill also claimed to be "extremely shocked" upon reading this 1921 report by an air force commander: "The 8 machines engaged in the attack broke formation and attacked at different points of the encampment simultaneously, causing a stampede among the animals. The tribesmen and their families were put in confusion, many of whom ran into the lake making a good target for the machine guns."[54] Churchill responded: "To fire wilfully on women and children taking refuge in a lake is a disgraceful act, and I am surprised you do not order the officers responsible for it to be tried by court martial."[55] The commander may have slipped in conveying the pleasure experienced by gunners firing on defenseless civilians trying to flee the air bombs. But that this mode of attack had become routine—and that it could elicit strange and new, if at times unsettling and even shocking, affects in British subjects—is supported by Gertrude Bell's account of an air force demonstration held for British civil administrators in Iraq.

The most interesting thing which happened this week was a performance by the R.A.F., a bombing demonstration. . . . They had made an imaginary village about a quarter of a mile from where we sat on the Diala dyke and the two first bombs, dropped from 3000 feet, went straight into the middle of it and set it alight. It was wonderful and horrible. Then they dropped bombs all round it, as if to catch the fugitives and finally fire bombs which even in the brightest sunlight made flues of bright flame in the desert. They burn through metal and water won't extinguish them. At the end the armoured cars went out to round up the fugitives with machine guns. I was tremendously impressed. It's an amazingly relentless and terrible thing, war from the air.[56]

British officials in Iraq grappled with how to account for the disturbing qualities of airpower as a necropolitical technology. They had little choice, since they had to respond to criticisms of its use in the British press and even among the very officials in London, such as Churchill, who had authorized its use to govern Iraq. One narrative posited that the killing of women and children, while certainly considered reprehensible in European culture, was not very upsetting to Iraqi tribesmen, who placed little value on women and children anyway. "They dread aeroplanes," conceded one official, "but do not seem to resent . . . that women and children are accidentally killed by bombs" dropped from them.[57] Another commander agreed that to Arabs, "women and children were 'negligible' casualties compared to those of the 'really important men,'" and Lawrence assured the British public that this was "too oriental a mood for us to feel very clearly."[58] Another narrative attributed the British killing of Iraqi women not to the difficulty of discerning targets from a distance or the routine practice of leveling entire villages but rather to the underdevelopment of sexual difference in Iraqi society. The air commander in Iraq responded to Churchill's objection to counting male and female casualties together by explaining that "in countries in which combatants and noncombatants and even the sexes could not be distinguished by visual markers, all casualties should be reported in 'bulk numbers' without details as to sex or age."[59] That Iraqi bodies were not sufficiently marked by sexual difference, at least from the air, helped to explain indiscriminate violence against them.

In official British policy, air bombardment was authorized for two reasons: external defense and internal security. Both of these turned out to be very flexible concepts, however. Lack of internal security was often described as a vague absence of "law and order," and often meant little more than a community's failure to pay taxes, as with the massive bombing of the tax-evading Bani Huchaim tribe on the Middle Euphrates in 1924.[60] While officials denied publicly that revenue collection was a motive for the bombings, private British reports made little effort to hide that motive. A typical report noted that "with the subsequent bombing of Al Budur, Bani Sa'id, and al Qatran towards the end of the year, law and order reached a satisfactory level, with the consequent payment of revenue and obedience to dictates of Government."[61] Another stated even more bluntly: "Revenue collection and keeping of the peace are one or part of the same thing. If sufficient force is available to keep the peace, revenue has only to be asked for, and if there is sufficient authority to make the tribes pay revenue there is no disorder."[62] Debates in Britain about the costs of Iraq's occupation had led to an agreement at home that those costs must be borne by Iraqis, which was another motivation behind the shift to rule from the air. The policy would substantially reduce the costs of military operations, as measured in British pounds as well as British lives. It would also make it easier to extract the costs of British administration from Iraqi bodies, especially in otherwise hard-to-reach rural areas. In these areas, it was hoped, select demonstrations and occasional reminders of the new technology would be sufficient to shock and awe rural communities into paying their taxes, without the need for too many repetitions of the "amazingly relentless and terrible thing" that was airpower.

The two official justifications for airpower, defense and security, align with what some theorists call "external" and "internal" forms of modern territorial sovereignty. But since the bombing raids were employed to help establish Iraq's territorial borders, it is often difficult to determine which form of sovereignty they were exercising. For example, while bombings in the northern and southern frontier regions (near the borders with Turkey and Najd) were usually claimed to be fulfilling the first legitimate aim, that is, external defense, most of the bombs in both cases—as Iraqi critics often pointed out—were dropped inside Iraqi territory and on Iraqi subjects. After all, neither Iraq nor Britain was officially at war with any of Iraq's neighbors. Conversely, when reasons of internal security were given for a bombing campaign, these could be difficult to distinguish from concerns about external defense, such as when bombs were dropped on those the British considered to be Iraqi subjects harboring subversive attachments to Turkey. Bombs dropped on Kurds were usually attributed to internal security precisely because they were meant to persuade the targets that they belonged to Iraq and not to Turkey or a Kurdish territorial state. Rather than exercising two distinct forms of sovereignty, then, the bombing raids were helping to produce the very distinction between what—and who—was external and internal to Iraq.

The Firm Rock of Native Laws and Customs

As Dina Khoury has noted, British officials in Iraq not only tolerated but seem to have actively fostered a judicial system, or rather a judicial field, in which a "bewildering array" of overlapping laws and jurisdictions contended.[63] This was partly a process of producing multiple zones of sovereignty within the Iraq territory in accordance with the principles of indirect rule and development along native lines. The British revenue commissioner in Iraq explained in 1919: "We must recognise that it is primarily our business not to give rights to those who have them not, but to secure their rights to those who have them."[64] This would be done, in the words of the judicial secretary, by laying down "the fabric of justice" upon "the firm rock of the native laws and customs of the people."[65]

The Tribal Disputes Regulation was introduced in 1916, during the occupation of Basra; it was instituted for all of occupied Iraq in 1918, and then as the law of the state in the 1925 Iraqi constitution.[66] The system was an explicit reversal of the legal modernization begun by the Ottoman government, which for example had instituted a separation of powers between the executive and judicial branches. Henry Dobbs, who drafted the Iraqi tribal code, explained:

In Turkish times the executive was entirely divorced from the judicial power and all offenders, even the wildest tribesmen, were tried before the regular courts. Tribal customs . . . by which tribesmen naturally settle their disputes and terminate their blood feuds, were ignored and these wretched and ignorant men were forced into the strait waistcoats of a rigid and, to them, incomprehensible judicial code.[67]

The tribal code eliminated this culturally insensitive separation of powers, giving near absolute power to those the British designated as tribal shaykhs, to settle disputes and levy taxes. Defenders of the code argued that "the tribal [guest-house] is a better training center for citizens than the coffee-shop,"[68] and that the system was more efficient than maintaining a government bureaucracy to deal directly with individual rural subjects. As Dobbs pointed out, the mandate government had not been established to "go through the population of Iraq with a fine tooth comb."[69] It was, however, willing to back up indirect rule through notably direct air bombardments of peasants and nomads who refused to pay taxes or otherwise resisted the authority of their landlord shaykhs.[70]

On the one hand, the tribal code, which was inherited from British practice on the Indian North West Frontier, cautions against aligning direct and indirect rule too tightly with the Indian and Egyptian models of imperial rule, with the latter purportedly triumphing in Iraq. Colonial power in India and everywhere else had always worked through a combination of direct methods and collaboration with local elites. On the other hand, the tribal code itself, while justified by reference to indirect rule, also instituted a mechanism for a very direct form of British authority. It gave the British political officer the power not only to refer tribal defendants to the shaykh or tribal council of his choice but also to convict and sentence defendants after reviewing the findings of the shaykh. The sentences that the political officer could pass included fines, imprisonment, internal exile, and whipping. The political officer and the courts also had the authority to transfer any defendant from the civil and criminal court system to the political officer to enforce the tribal code, simply by designating that person a "tribesman." Since most Iraqis could be discovered to have some kind of tribal affiliation or ancestry, and since the code gave the British political officer and ultimately the high commissioner the authority to determine "whether any person or is or is not a 'tribesman,'" the tribal law did not remain confined to rural space but infiltrated urban space as well.[71] It was thus used by civil authorities against urban political insurgents, including participants in the 1928 protests against Zionist leader Alfred Mond and in the 1931 Baghdad General Strike.[72]

While the British military administration had initially, during the occupation of Basra, abolished Ottoman law and replaced it with the Iraq Occupied Territories Code, based on Anglo-Indian law, this policy was later reversed and Ottoman civil law reinstated, except in cases where a specific law had been abolished or amended by a new one.[73] Criminal law, in the form of the Baghdad Criminal Procedure Regulations and the Baghdad Penal Code, was likewise an amalgamation of Ottoman law with Anglo-Sudanese-Egyptian law.[74] These decisions may have been related to the discovery of some useful Ottoman laws, at least as translated and interpreted by British authorities. Examples reported in various sources include laws criminalizing gatherings with a "political intent";[75] the banning of trade unions and imprisonment of laborers for going on strike;[76] and the deportation of political detainees—up to 600 at a time—to India, Iran, or the infamous British penal island colony of Henjam.[77]

None of these were unusual as British imperial practices. What is noteworthy for my purposes is that the reversion to so-called Ottoman law was ostensibly part of the shift to indirect rule, a peculiar notion given that the Ottoman authorities were gone and it was British authorities who were applying the law. It was only legible at all according to a temporal reasoning that associated indirect rule with the laws of the past. In Iraq, the "order of colonial rule" was not quite established "in terms of its difference from the arbitrary violence of the past," as Timothy Mitchell has argued of Egypt.[78] Rather, colonial rule in Iraq announced its own mobile capacity to regress to the violence of the past, in the interest of development along native lines.

Finally, civil and criminal law, Ottoman and otherwise, was regularly subordinated to martial law. Since the British mandate administration was built on the military administration established during the occupation, martial law was foundational to Iraq's formation as a state, and was regularly invoked, as "emergency law," by Iraqi governments through the 20th century. In mandate Iraq, then, what Mitchell calls the "zones of exceptionality" extended over almost the entirety of the law.[79] The mixing and matching of tribal law, Ottoman civil and criminal law, Anglo-Sudanese-Egyptian criminal law, and British martial law was highly productive for the mandate administration, in ways that certainly stretched the concept of indirect rule.

The Prevailing Vice of the Country

In 1929, Britain's annual report to the League of Nations on the Mandate of Iraq criticized a new regulation of the Iraqi Ministry of Education banning the use of corporal punishment in secondary schools and restricting it to six "blows on the hand" in primary schools. The report's authors seem to have been genuinely alarmed by the measure, which they warned "may well prove to be a national calamity. In the towns especially some form of discipline that acts quickly, painfully, and irrevocably is badly needed."[80] Two years later, the last British advisor to the Ministry of Education, Lionel Smith, resigned his position, in part to register his government's protest against the ongoing refusal of Iraqi officials to permit corporal punishment in secondary schools. "Parental discipline, which is, if not weak, at any rate very spasmodic in this country, has received a still further set back [*sic*]. . . . It is most regrettable that in a country where passions are strong and even primeval, no corporal punishment is allowed except in Primary and Elementary Schools and then is limited to 6 blows on the hand. Other forms of punishment cannot be regarded as substitutes, as they are revocable and involve the element of time."[81] Yet, Iraqi officials and the public more broadly continued to insist that "Iraqi schoolboys were of too sensitive a nature to be exposed to anything so brutal as corporal punishment."[82]

Smith then proceeded directly into a discussion of the "prevailing vice" purportedly widespread in both secondary schools and the country at large:

It would not be reasonable to expect the schools to be free from what is sometimes called the prevailing vice of the country. It is like an endemic disease, and has its ups and downs. A year ago it was certainly increased by a large importation of bicycles. A free ride at the expense of a senior person furnished the bribe and the opportunity. Again the first visit of an Egyptian dramatic company . . . led to a demand for ready cash on the part of schoolboys, and one way of raising this cash was by hiring out their persons according to a regular tariff. I risk mentioning these things partly because I have reason to know that they are true.[83]

The vice in question was obviously male homosexuality, which British officials believed was an endemic disease of Iraqi society that could occasionally swell to epidemic proportions. Notwithstanding Smith's claim that he was taking a "risk" in raising this issue, he was drawing on well-established narratives of British colonial officials in Iraq and elsewhere. In 1921, British education advisor Jerome Farrell claimed to have never witnessed a situation in which moral education was "so utterly lacking and so urgently needed as in the middle classes of the urban population of Iraq, where after the age of puberty an inveterate dignity allows to few the indulgence of more vigorous hobbies than tea-drinking and gossip in public, and in private certain unmentionable indoor sports."[84] He advocated moral education techniques in boys' schools that included not only corporal punishment but also team sports and cold showers.[85]

British officials' preoccupation with the "unmentionable" vice of Iraqi schoolboys—which they managed to mention often enough—and their discourses on adolescent discipline both worked to place Iraq in a certain temporal relation to Britain. First, as Leela Gandhi has explained, a narrative with roots in "the allied Victorian disciplines of evolutionary biology, social anthropology, and sexology" had since the late nineteenth century identified the Orient as a "sotadic zone" where "homosexuality thrived without social constraint."[86] In this evolutionary discourse, higher civilizations were those in which the "secondary sexual characteristics" were most fully developed, resulting in an "acute sexual dimorphism" that became the motor of historical time, leaving behind what Sir Richard Burton, in his 1885 translation of the *Arabian Nights*, called "Le Vice" that was still the primary distinguishing characteristic of the sotadic zone.[87] By 1908, Iwan Bloch's *The Sexual Life of Our Time, in Its Relation to Modern Civilisation* could declare as "obvious . . . that the whole of civilisation is the product of the physical and mental differentiation of the sexes, that civilisation has, in fact, to a certain extent a heterosexual character."[88]

Second, British officials associated nationalist mischief with Iraq's youth, on both a national plane of temporality (Iraq as young) and an individual one (Iraqi youth as troublemakers). As we have seen, the belief that a nation traversed the same stages of life as the human, including the recently discovered and critically important one stretching between dependent childhood and sovereign adulthood, was foundational to the mandate system itself. On the plane of individual development, British officials opposed the premature expansion of public secondary schools in Iraq because they feared it would produce nationalists.[89] While there were only four such schools (all male) in 1923, Britain's report to the League of Nations that year recommended that they be reduced to two, since "in this country it is neither desirable nor practicable to provide Secondary education except for the selected few."[90] A recurring argument was that graduates would not find jobs, but this was continuously interwoven with discourses of moral and political danger posed by the very coming together of adolescents in the space of the school. As British education advisor F. B. Riley wrote, Iraq's youth "wish to promote, through the schools, a raging campaign of patriotic propaganda."[91] In a country where "parental discipline" was "sporadic" and "passions" were "primeval," the immature passions inherent to the culture at large were most dangerous where the primeval but increasingly independent psychological stage of adolescence came into contact with modern forms of schooling and the solidarities and mobilities thus engendered, without the tempering effect of a mature indigenous adulthood.

Yet British officials were not simply trapped inside their own tautological metaphors. Just as those metaphors were attempts to manage the historical crises of colonialism, the categories they deployed were dense fields of colonial and anticolonial contestation. The controversy over corporal punishment erupted in the 1920s not as a fantastical extension of the logic of Article 22 in British minds but as a direct consequence of the political mobilization of adolescent schoolboys in Baghdad. In 1927, British officials recommended its use on students who had protested the political firing of a secondary school teacher, a suggestion Iraqi officials declined. The British report to the League of Nations that year complained that "public opinion seems to accept it as axiomatic that no student should be regarded as responsible for his actions. . . . No one seems to reflect what a disastrous effect such an assumption is bound to have on the training of young citizens."[92] When students protested in 1928 against the visit of Zionist leader Alfred Mond, however, British pressure on the Iraqi parliament led to an ordinance permitting the use of twenty-five lashes on any student under eighteen years of age "who participates in an illegal gathering or disturbs the peace."[93] The law was met with widespread public opposition, a movement that succeeded not only in getting it annulled but also in the promulgation of a new law banning the use of any corporal punishment against secondary school students for any reason.[94]

Exploiting the Riches of Our Country

When the first Iraqi parliament convened, in 1925, King Faysal announced:

Now that we have banished the confusion and anxiety that clouded our future, we can encourage companies to use their capital to cooperate with us in exploiting the riches of our country. . . . Once the issue of the borders with our neighbor Turkey has been resolved, and the world is convinced that there is genuine peace in the Middle East, there is no doubt that our country's share of the efforts of businessmen and technicians will be very great. The question of demarcating the northern border was and remains our primary concern . . . upon which rests the future of our country in its entirety. . . . Once we have established the foundations of the country's political situation, we must focus completely on economic matters such as agriculture and commerce. . . . There is no political independence without economic independence.[95]

High Commissioner Dobbs reported the convening of parliament to London in similar terms: "Thus 'Iraq has now attained the first stage of her development. . . . It only remains for her frontiers to be fixed . . . before she can apply for admission to the League of Nations and take on the full status of an independent State."[96] The hope was that "with her frontiers fixed, foreign capital will no longer be shy of investment, irrigation will increase, the valuable cotton crop will be substituted for the less valuable wheat and barley and the operations of the International Turkish Petroleum Company, if on a scale anything like that anticipated, will pour money out upon the land."[97]

The tenuous alliance between British officials and members of the Iraqi nationalist elite through most of the mandate period was based largely on their agreement about the importance of border formation, a prerequisite of Iraq's claims to territorial sovereignty and of its entry into the League of Nations. As Fadil Barrak observed, Iraq needed Britain because it was "a weak state born surrounded by hostile states . . . every politician in Iraq knew this regardless of his personal leanings."[98] Similarly, Husayn Jamil recalled that even "the students and youth"—a synonym for oppositional nationalists in the 1920s, among whom Jamil counted himself—eventually realized that "the politicians" were working within the "realm of the possible" in understanding that Iraq "did not have an army that could protect its borders,"[99] though it might have been more accurate to say "that could create its borders." When Iraqi and British officials talked about "neighboring" states violating the territorial "sovereignty" of "Iraq," it must be understood that in most cases that sovereignty did not yet exist, even on paper, since the borders had not been mutually recognized by the authorities on both sides, let alone by the international community. Acquiring that recognition was a shared interest of British and Iraqi officials. As Faysal put it, "Iraq's life could only be realized through the demarcation" of its borders.[100] The fixing of the borders was important not only for Iraq's sovereignty but also in order to secure foreign capitalist investment, a recurring theme in British and Iraqi government discourse. It was, after all, difficult to attract such investment before the state could claim internationally recognized sovereignty over the territory in question.

The most significant border question in Iraq's formation was the one with Turkey. The British army had occupied the Ottoman province of Mosul three days *after* the signing of the armistice that ended World War I in the Middle East—that is, when Britain was not at war with the Ottoman Empire. First the Ottoman and then the Turkish state thus naturally refused to recognize the legality of the occupation and, by extension, Mosul's incorporation into Iraq. Mosul was of great importance to all concerned for many reasons, not least of which was its vast oil reserves. As a confidential memo by the Middle East Department of the Colonial Office in 1922 noted: "There is no doubt that there are considerable deposits of oil, particularly in the Mosul vilayet, though the exact quantities still remain a matter for surmise. . . . What is relevant to the present purpose is the desirability of keeping within the British sphere of influence what may prove to be one of the most important oil-fields of the future."[101]

The Turkish Petroleum Company (later renamed the Iraq Petroleum Company), in which British interests had a controlling share, claimed that it was given a concession over all oil exploration in Baghdad and Mosul provinces by the Ottoman government just before the start of the war. This claim was highly contested, as it was based solely on a memo promising to lease the concession to the company once all the conditions were worked out, which they never were due to the outbreak of the war. Opponents of the deal—including, initially, the US government and US oil interests—rejected the TPC's claim that this promise, which specified no conditions whatsoever, constituted the concession itself. Indeed, some British officials acknowledged privately that "an obligation to grant a concession on terms to be arranged does not really amount to very much."[102] The US government's objection was based not only on the concession's shaky legal foundation but also on the US principle of the "open door," which held that the territories of the defeated states in the war should be open to exploitation by companies from any victorious state and not just those of the mandate power. In the end, the TPC agreed to give US oil interests a one-quarter share in the company, and "little more was heard about the Open Door after that."[103]

Once the objections of the United States and a few other players were put to rest, the Mosul dispute was ultimately resolved by the League of Nations, which in 1925 sent a commission to tour the province and ascertain whether its residents wanted to be part of Turkey or Iraq. The British air force bombed pro-Turkey communities in the borderlands until the eve of the commission's arrival, at which point the administration rounded up leading pro-Turkey activists and detained them for the duration of the tour; villages were again bombed after the commission's departure, reportedly as punishment for expressing pro-Turkey sentiments.[104] The League recommended that the province be given to Iraq, on the condition that the Iraqi government agreed to extend the British mandate by twenty-five years, with the caveat that the League could agree to end it earlier by admitting Iraq as a member state. There was controversy in Iraq over this condition, but most members of the nationalist elite agreed that the importance of Mosul forced them to accept it. King Faysal asserted that the Mosul question was "a life or death matter for our beloved country," and invoked futurist discourses to stifle discussions of present sovereignty: "Is it right for us, at this juncture, holding in our hands the future of the coming generations, to regress to the past, leaving anarchy and bloodshed behind us? . . . . Are we permitted to act recklessly with the future of our country?"[105]

British mandate governance, as I have been arguing, was focused on security, or counterinsurgency; on the extraction of taxes from Iraqi subjects; on the production of Iraq's territorial sovereignty; and on what was known in British colonial discourse as economic development: the creation of infrastructure to enable the exploitation—or at least control over the exploitation—of Iraq's natural resources. Development as the exploitation of resources would be driven mainly by private capitalist investment. The role of the British government was to establish the conditions that would enable development, including security, infrastructure (transportation, communications, and irrigation), and a legal regime conducive to foreign investment. As a 1922 memo explained: "Schemes of agricultural development must depend largely on private enterprise, and no money for such enterprise is likely to be forthcoming unless there is some assurance of settled political conditions such as the British connection alone can secure."[106] Ensuring these conditions did involve efforts to make a labor force available for development, but not primarily through education. In fact, British opposition to the expansion of the public school system was partially justified by reference to the need for economic development. Over-education would not only produce unemployment among a "class productive of political agitators" but would also diminish the number of willing manual laborers in Iraq, with "disastrous" results, since "the labour of every available workman is required for that economic development of the country which stands between it and bankruptcy."[107]

Economic development as capitalist development needs to be qualified in a few other ways. First, control over Iraq's resources by foreign companies did not mean those resources would be developed in the near future; it could well mean the opposite. As Mitchell points out, foreign oil companies active in Iraq in the 1920s were more interested in deferring the exploitation of Iraq's oil than they were in developing it, as a way to protect their oil interests elsewhere by ensuring that prices would not be driven down by the flooding of Iraqi oil onto the world market.[108] Second, British mandate policy reinforced systems of sharecropping and forced labor. As is well known, tribal shaykhs who were loyal to Britain in the uprisings that marked Iraq's formation were rewarded with large land distributions, tax exemptions, and absolute juridical power over their tribespeople/tenants through the tribal code.[109] These estates operated mainly through relations of sharecropping, not wage labor. Moreover, the use of compulsory or corvée labor was a regular British practice in Iraq, and a source of both popular and elite opposition. The latter stemmed from the fact that labor extracted by the British administration was labor that could not be extracted by landlords. British officials sometimes acknowledged the difficulties that compulsory labor caused for their rural elite allies: as a 1918 British report put it, "the landlord class has naturally suffered much" from the forced labor regime.[110]

Compulsory labor was restricted in interwar British colonial policy and in the regulations of the League of Nations mandate system, but it was not prohibited. Besides the use of prison labor, which was "extensively employed on road-making, excavations, dyke building, demolitions and the reclamation of land inundated by floods," there were two mechanisms through which labor could be forced.[111] The first worked through the principle of development along native lines, which could be used to argue that British authorities had limited authority over "native" labor regimes, including the use of corvée labor by native landlords. The British did find it necessary to inform tribal landlords who employed such labor on large-scale irrigation projects that they could not force laborers to "work for nothing and at the same time provide their own tools, food and shelter" at the worksite, a fairly limited injunction.[112] The second mechanism permitted the direct use of forced labor by British officials for "works of public utility as determined by the law or ordered by the Government."[113] While this type of compulsory labor could not be unpaid, the pay rate was determined solely by the government, which employed this labor for projects such as dredging rivers, draining swamps, and building roads and railways—that is, for what were at the time called "development projects." That these projects were considered to be "public works" did not mean that the finished products belonged to the public. For example, the independent Iraqi government would later have to purchase the Iraq railways, which were built partly by Iraqi corvée labor, from Britain at current value, using tax money extracted from Iraqi subjects.[114]

Iraq was not unique. Other European empires and mandates also relied on compulsory labor in the interwar period, a practice authorized by League of Nations policies enabling its use for colonial "development-on-the-cheap."[115] For my purposes, what is worth noting is the increasing interwar conflation between the legitimate use of compulsory labor and government-managed "development projects." Works built by government-conscripted corvée labor were, by definition, in the public service, and thus officials could counter any opposition to such labor with moralizing narratives. Already in 1920, acknowledging in a report to London that British use of corvée labor was one cause of the revolt, Wilson asserted that "the Arab would rather risk a flood, an act of God, than do heavy work on flood banks."[116] Similarly, British military captain James Mann complained of the "gross use of the word 'exploitation' to cover what anyone except an incurable romantic would call 'development.'"[117] Since "development" in colonial discourse up to this time actually meant the exploitation of land and other resources, Mann's comment hints at the increasing moralization of development itself, as it came to be attached to the notion of "public works and services." Development—even when it still meant the mundane colonial work of exploiting a territory's natural resources—was acquiring its strange power to authorize, at least to "anyone except an incurable romantic," what could not be authorized for any other reason.

2

Determining a Self

IN 1921, THE FORMER OTTOMAN education official Sati' al-Husri arrived in Baghdad from Cairo on the invitation of King Faysal, with the
mission of heading up an Iraqi public school system that would foster
Iraq's gradual independence from Britain.[1] Shortly after his arrival, al-Husri
recalls in his memoirs, he met with Gertrude Bell, British oriental secretary
in Iraq, who cautioned him: "Everything must proceed in stages." Al-Husri
replied: "True. But stages can be traversed quickly."[2] This exchange attests
to the shared temporal imaginary of British and Iraqi mandate officials,
who concurred that Iraq was moving toward phased independence through
delimited stages of development, as well as their divergence over the pace of
that trajectory. Controlled acceleration of Iraq's progress toward a sovereign
future was al-Husri's nationalist and pedagogical project, against the British
mandate project of indefinite deferral.

This difference would put al-Husri repeatedly at odds with British
authorities during the mandate era, including on the corporal punishment controversy discussed in the previous chapter. When British education advisor Lionel Smith consulted al-Husri, the latter explained that
he opposed corporal punishment in schools, because "beating students
does not influence their thoughts . . . and does not work to create discipline in their souls [or selves/psyches, *nufus*]."[3] For nationalist educators
such as al-Husri, the repetition of slower-acting disciplinary mechanisms
would work on the emotions, bodies, and minds of youth in order to
insert them into a stable, linear, and forward-moving temporal regime.
They were not interested in quick-acting punitive techniques to repress

rebellious young bodies but in the making of strong, nationalist bodies over and through time, not only to serve in the nation's army and fuel its economy—though these goals were certainly present—but also precisely to rebel against British rule.

Throughout the mandate period, British officials resisted the expansion of public primary and secondary schools, or even the reopening of all the Ottoman schools that British occupying forces had closed during the war. As Bell admitted, "our neglect of education is making Iraqis say we are keeping them backwards on purpose."[4] With the limited resources they devoted to education, British authorities supported a differentiated and class-based system that aimed to produce civil servants loyal to Britain. It also included some agricultural and vocational training, but since funding for education generally was minimal this was not extensive. The public primary system was divided into two types of schools, one for urban children that prepared them for secondary school and careers in civil service and the other for rural children that provided a terminal education. The British also provided funding for private Christian and Jewish schools.[5]

Iraqi nationalist elites struggled against the British neglect of disciplinary institutions, especially schools and a national military. Exploring aspects of that struggle, this chapter engages especially with the writings of al-Husri, who served as Iraq's director general of education from 1922 to 1927 and from the mid-1920s on was also a well-known proponent of the emerging philosophy of Arab nationalism. While al-Husri's nationalism, including its influence on Iraqi education, has been the subject of considerable scholarly interest, his many writings on pedagogy and psychology have received less attention.[6] This neglect is related to how Iraq's political and intellectual history has often been viewed as a struggle between two competing nationalist visions: Arabism and Iraqism.[7] Less attention has been paid to the ways in which Arabism in Iraq developed within the framework, and shaped the history, of the Iraqi territorial state.[8] In the mandate period, many of Arabism's leading proponents, including al-Husri, were officials of the Iraqi state, and viewed that state as the legitimate agent for producing subjects worthy of national sovereignty. Even in his memoirs, written several decades after becoming a leading Arab nationalist spokesman, al-Husri asserted that the demarcation of Iraq's borders was one of Faysal's biggest achievements.[9] Faysal and other Hashimite officials knew that they needed Britain to establish Iraq's borders and could not have created a "unified Iraqi state" without Britain's help.[10]

Al-Husri himself often insisted that the content of the curriculum was less important than the pedagogies used in the classroom and the unity of the curriculum as a whole.[11] His project was to both expand and homogenize the Iraqi public school experience, against the restricted and differentiated system established by British occupying forces during World War I and the first years of the mandate. Ensuring that all Iraqi students at the same grade level were studying the same subjects would produce what al-Husri called "unity of consciousness." In his reforms, he drew on concepts from the emerging discipline of psychology, as did British mandate officials in their opposition to the same reforms. The difference was that al-Husri insisted on the right of Iraqi youth to develop through the range of psychological stages to arrive at a fully conscious and independent adult selfhood, against what he saw as colonial misuses of psychology to arrest the development of "the children of the colonies" at earlier stages.[12] Al-Husri thus engaged the discipline of psychology in the interest of strategically asserting a reasoning ego, which involved educating the emotions during each stage of development.[13]

Arabism and the Iraqi State

The framework within which al-Husri was working as an Iraqi state official meant that the "unity of consciousness" the schools were producing was a territorial Iraqi one. Elizabeth Freeman argues that modern institutions such as schools and the military work as "chronobiopolitical regimes," producing shared bodily and affective experiences through participation in shared temporal routines. "People are bound to one another, engrouped, made to feel coherently collective, through particular orchestrations of time. . . . Manipulations of time convert historically specific regimes of asymmetrical power into seemingly ordinary bodily tempos and routines."[14] But these routines, under modern nation-state governance, also involve manipulations of space: national belonging is produced through both the temporal and the spatial ordering of bodies. This was the conundrum of an Arab nationalist curriculum deployed within the bounded territorial space of Iraq, a conundrum that al-Husri grappled with over the course of his career but was unable to resolve.

As some of the most theoretically sophisticated formulations of Arabist thought in this period, al-Husri's writings help to illustrate how Arabism, regardless of the intentions of its promoters, was not only compatible with but highly productive for the formation of an Iraqi territorial nation-state. The construction of Iraq as an "Arab state" was the work of both British and Iraqi officials, and was consistent with the emerging interwar concept of the nation-state as a territorial entity inhabited by one "majority race" and a flexible number of "minority races." The notion of "majority race" entered international law, as well as Iraqi law specifically, with the 1924 Treaty of Lausanne, which established the terms for severing Iraq and other Mashriq states from the Ottoman Empire/Turkey, including the terms of citizenship for the new nation-states.[15]

In the 1920s, the emergence of Iraqi Arabism was shaped by the struggle between oppositional nationalists, who demanded Iraq's immediate independence, and state-aligned nationalists such as al-Husri, who worked for the phased implementation of that independence. In other words, the Arabist imaginary that emerged among the latter group was constructed not only against British rule and external enemies on Iraq's borders but also against oppositional Iraqi nationalists, who were increasingly envisioned as threats to the nation-building project in both spatial and temporal terms. Spatially, they were imagined as foreigners to Iraq; temporally, they were imagined as backward and antimodern. Somewhat paradoxically, then, this discourse accused those who were demanding a speedier path toward Iraqi sovereignty of being less modern, and less Iraqi, than those advocating a more gradual one.[16]

Arabist discourse thus engaged in temporal and spatial distancing moves that sought to construct some Iraqi lives as worthy and others as dispensable and to produce foreigners both within and without Iraq's territorial borders.[17] When a strong and explicitly anti-Arabist Iraqi nationalist movement emerged, especially from the 1940s on, it was in many ways a response to this exclusionary imaginary of Iraqi Arab identity. At stake in the decades-long struggle that ensued between Arabism and Iraqism were not only the future territorial borders of the nation-state but also, and perhaps far more consequentially, the imagined boundaries of sovereign Iraqi selfhood. The "sovereign prerogative," as Hansen and Stepputat write, "is to declare who is an internal enemy."[18]

Before turning to al-Husri's educational reforms, and his writings on pedagogy and psychology that help to frame them, the next section looks at the context of sociopolitical contestation that shaped both the reforms and the emerging philosophy of Arabism in Iraq. While the details of the historical narrative presented in the section are not particularly controversial, and are familiar especially within the Arabic-language historiography, it diverges from accounts that explain this period of Iraqi history primarily through the categories of sect and tribe.

Subjects Worthy of Sovereignty

In the fall of 1922, the program of the new government ministry formed under Prime Minister 'Abd al-Muhsin al-Sa'dun pledged to pursue the fulfillment of the "Iraqi people's desires" for "the independence of the Iraqi country and its nationalist [*qawmiyya*] sovereignty within its original borders." The program used two different Arabic words for "nationalism," *qawmiyya* and *wataniyya*, framing both as contributing to the formation of Iraqi sovereignty. It promised that the government would employ "active means" to

strengthen *watani* and *qawmi* sentiments [and] cultivate the sons of the people mentally and morally according to the highest religious principles, fight every idea or movement that disturbs the peace or that is opposed to *watani* and *qawmi* hopes . . . and enable the revival of projects that have been neglected for ages, such as developing the land, the towns, and the roads, following the most modern methods.[19]

The repetition of the *watani* and *qawmi* pair did not indicate that the terms were interchangeable but rather that Iraqi territorial nationalism and Arab nationalism were mutually constitutive. *Wataniyya* already contained its meaning of territorial attachment—territory/homeland (*watan*) is linguistically built into the term—but had not yet acquired its negative connotation of *iqlimiyya*, or regionalism. *Qawmiyya*, which linguistically refers to any loyalty to a people, or *qawm*, was somewhat more flexible than it would become later, but already in official Hashimite discourse it typically had an Arabist connotation.

The spatial framework of the program's vision of a future "*qawmiyya* sovereignty" is clear: Iraq, namely, "within its original borders."[20] This assertion of territorial sovereignty was connected to the project of economic development, that is, of "the land, the towns, and the roads." The program's temporal framework was less clear, as it took the form of a deferred promise. In pledging to "pursue the fulfillment"—and not necessarily to fulfill—the "Iraqi people's desires" for "the independence of the Iraqi country," the program committed the ministry not to end the British mandate but rather to change the very people who desired independence, through the use of "active means" to strengthen their "*watani* and *qawmi* sentiments" and "cultivate" them "mentally and morally according to the highest religious principles." The people's "desires" (for Iraq's independence) were those that had been expressed during the 1920 revolt and continued to be expressed by the oppositional nationalist movement, which demanded the immediate nullification of the mandate and the evacuation of British troops from Iraqi territory. In the months before the formation of Sa'dun's ministry, this movement had indeed been "disturbing the peace," as the statement suggests. The "*watani* and *qawmi* sentiments," on the other hand, were those disciplined (rather than oppositional) forms of nationalist attachment that had to be cultivated before sovereignty could be fulfilled. It was not that Iraqis had to learn to desire sovereignty but that they had to be made worthy of it.

The external context for the cultivation of a pedagogical Arabism, or *qawmiyya*, related to the project of excising Iraq from its Ottoman past and Turkish neighbor. British officials had deployed Arabist discourse to this end since the occupation of the Ottoman provinces of Baghdad and Basra during the war, for example to justify changing the language of public schools from Ottoman Turkish to Arabic overnight, which in turn was used to shut down many schools due to a sudden lack of qualified teachers.[21] The internal context related mainly to the conflict over the Anglo-Iraqi Treaty and the status of the mandate. Al-Sa'dun had been selected as prime minister by Faysal and the British high commissioner because he had pledged to crack down on the wave of protests against the treaty and the mandate that spread across the country in the summer of 1922. Understanding the Arabist discourse that took shape in 1920s Iraq requires understanding the split that developed among the forces that had united in the 1920 revolt, a split that became increasingly irreconcilable in the summer and fall of 1922, just as Sa'dun was issuing his government's ministerial program and al-Husri was implementing his first curricular reforms. While this divide has sometimes been viewed in sectarian terms, as a Sunni-Shi'a conflict, that narrative cannot account for the timing of its flare-up in 1922, not to mention the participation of people from both sects on each side. Nor was the primary conflict a spatial one, that is, it was not about demands for an Arab versus an Iraqi nation-state. Both sides claimed to be fighting for Iraq's independence, and many members of both camps had some notion of a possible larger future Arab state or federation. Rather, the main conflict was temporal: those I refer to as "oppositional nationalists" demanded Iraq's immediate independence from Britain, while the "official nationalists" worked within the terms of the mandate and therefore toward a deferred sovereignty.

For the first year after Faysal's crowning in August 1921, the nationalist movement forged during the revolt was fairly quiet, since its leaders, both Sunni and Shi'i, had given Faysal their conditional support.[22] The conditions, laid out explicitly by nationalists in Baghdad and by the Shi'i *mujtahid*s who supported the revolt, were that he preside over a truly sovereign Iraqi state under a representative government bound by a constitution. By the summer of 1922, the conditions had not been met; many of the original rebel leaders thus withdrew their support of Faysal and renewed their opposition to the British occupation and mandate.[23] A key factor was the announcement of the Anglo-Iraqi Treaty in June 1922. Contrary to the demands of oppositional nationalists, the treaty did not include any text nullifying the mandate.[24] Protests broke out immediately in three areas that had been critical to the 1920 uprisings: Baghdad, the Shi'i shrine cities, and the surrounding tribal regions of the Middle Euphrates. In Baghdad, the minister of trade and well-known nationalist leader Ja'far Abu Timman resigned in protest. A month later he and other leading oppositional Baghdadi nationalists—including leaders of the Nahda and Watani opposition parties and the editors of newspapers that had published their demands—were arrested and incarcerated on the British prison island colony of Henjam in the Persian Gulf.[25]

Meanwhile, in the Middle Euphrates region, the leading anti-British tribal shaykhs sent telegrams to King Faysal and High Commissioner Percy Cox, which were reprinted in the opposition papers before those papers were closed down. One statement addressed to Cox recalled "the British government's promises to the Iraqis to establish a democratic constitutional government under an Arab king, according to which the Iraqi nation of all the different classes supported His Highness Faysal as its king," and demanded the immediate abolition of the mandate. It also demanded that Faysal negotiate with the British foreign ministry, as befitted an ally, not with the minister of colonies, "which contradicts the principle of complete independence." Finally, it asserted that "the nation has the capacity to manage its affairs."[26] Cox reported that "the Middle Euphrates is on the verge of an uprising and all signs are that it is no less dangerous than the one these same elements stirred up in 1920." He dispatched the Royal Air Force to bomb the rebels.[27]

After the repression of the nationalist movement in Baghdad and the rural regions of the Middle Euphrates, the main organized opposition was in the Shi'i shrine cities, especially Najaf and Kadhimiyya. The 'ulama' could not be packed off to Henjam as easily as secular nationalists in Baghdad, nor could their homes simply be bombed as was the approach taken with members of rural tribal communities. They thus took the lead in protests that broke out in October 1922 when the government announced plans to hold elections for the constituent assembly.[28] In November, the three leading *mujtahids* issued fatwas calling for a boycott of the elections, since "the goal of the nation from the foundation of the Arab Iraqi government [with Faysal's crowning in August 1921] has been the complete independence of the state and the absence of any foreign control over it. . . . This has been proclaimed by all the [elements] of the nation."[29] Fatwas and other statements by the leading Shi'i *marja'* in Iraq, Mahdi al-Khalisi, were directed to "the entire Iraq nation [*umma*]" and noted that "the allegiance we pledged to Faysal as king of Iraq was conditional. . . . [H]e has violated these conditions and the Iraqi people now owe him no allegiance."[30] Al-Khalisi also linked the boycott to the invocation of emergency law, the suppression of the press, the exile of political opponents, and the bombing of women and children.[31] Given the mandate government's use of such techniques, "participating in the elections . . . is harmful to the future of Iraq" and is prohibited to Muslims.[32] While the Shi'i 'ulama' were the main leaders of the boycott movement, Iraqis of all sectarian backgrounds participated in it.[33]

The solution to the problem of the rebellious 'ulama' was the brainchild of Prime Minister Sa'dun, who introduced a law authorizing the deportation of anyone holding a foreign passport. Most of the Shi'i 'ulama' held Iranian citizenship, some because they descended from Iranian families or came from Iran themselves, others because it had been a common method for religious men to gain exemption from Ottoman military conscription. Through this method, al-Khalisi and other leading 'ulama' were deported in 1923.[34]

This was the context of the emergence in the Iraqi public sphere of an Arabist discourse directed not against the Ottoman Empire or Turkey but against local oppositional nationalists, including the Shi'i 'ulama'. These were now accused of threatening "the Arab cause."[35] The newspaper *al-'Asima* called for "a campaign against the foreigners [*dukhala*] who have no connection to Iraq," and demanded "that the government prevent anyone who is not Iraqi and Arab from interfering in the nation's affairs."[36] It asserted that the leaders of the boycott movement were "Persians" who were "not loyal to

Arab nationalism or the independence of Iraq." In fact, their goal was "to eradicate Arab nationalism from the territory of Iraq [*rubu' al-Iraq*]."[37] As several scholars have noted, these alleged foreigners were often discredited through the term *shu'ubiyya*, a reference to a "medieval literary movement that valued Persian culture," and which in Iraqi Arabist discourse would come to "signify anything that was anti-Arab . . . from homoerotic poetry to communism." But it was "most commonly used to cast doubts on those who upheld a territorial Iraqi nationalism rather than a Pan-Arab one."[38]

Paradoxically, then, while the Shi'i 'ulama' and other oppositional nationalists were demanding Iraq's immediate independence from Britain, they were accused of trying to undermine Iraq's sovereignty. The minister of justice explained the deportations by asserting that "the government will employ legal means to prevent any attempt to deprive the nation of its representational sovereignty."[39] Similarly, an official government statement asserted: "The government is attempting to deliver lawful power to the true representatives of the people . . . but a band of foreigners with no connection to the Arab cause . . . is disrupting the elections, based on fabricated assertions of Islamic law. . . . They are standing in the way of the people's path to realize the power that is theirs to enjoy."[40] Another article accused the 'ulama' of being "simple-minded" and of not understanding modern science, the "history and psychology of the people, or even the borders of their nation."[41]

History and Territory

Sometime between his departure from Istanbul in 1919 and a speech he gave in Baghdad in 1923, al-Husri developed a concept of Arabism, or what he usually called "Arab unity," based on the contention that language and history were the two most effective nationalist bonds for Arabic speakers living in the former Ottoman Empire. What distinguished these bonds was that they enabled a sense of national belonging across generational time that did not depend on ties of blood (family, tribe, race).[42] Over centuries of rule by others, al-Husri explained, the Arab nation (*al-umma al-'arabiyya*) had preserved its language and thus its life, since language is what "connects the past to the future" by connecting the generations to one another.[43] But the nation was currently missing the other foundation of sovereignty, a shared historical sensibility that would enable its members to situate "the past in relation to the future."[44] Language was a nation's "life" or "spirit" while history was its "personality," "memory," or "consciousness."[45]

While al-Husri's transition from an Ottomanist to an Arabist has often been seen as an ideological rupture or even contradiction, what is more remarkable about his philosophy of nationalism is its consistency across the historical rupture of the collapse of the Ottoman Empire. In 1913, as his biographer William Cleveland notes, al-Husri had already posited France and Germany as the two paradigmatic cases of how nation (*millet*), state (*devlet*), and territory or homeland (*vatan*) came to be aligned in the modern period. In France, the nation-state-territory convergence was the product of "history and will," while in Germany, it was the product of history and language. What made "will" a factor of unity in France but not Germany was that the former possessed a "tradition of a great state" asserting sovereignty over a territory.[46] As an Ottomanist, al-Husri asserted: "We cannot accept the concept of the Germans because language is the least of the ties which bind the Ottomans to one another."[47] Fortunately, it was not necessary to resort to language, since the Ottomans, like the French in the 18th century, possessed the "tradition of a great state" asserting sovereignty over a territory, which meant that *vatan*, or homeland, could be the basis of Ottoman belonging. In contrast to the French, 19th-century Germans prior to unification had "no tradition of a great state" and thus "no unity of will" or capacity to love a German homeland. They therefore had to resort to the tie of language to produce a sense of national belonging.[48]

After the defeat of the Ottoman Empire in World War I, Arabic speakers found themselves in a situation similar to that of 19th-century German speakers, that is, lacking the will to unity that the tradition of a state can provide. Throughout his life, al-Husri vehemently rejected all theories of national belonging based on bonds of blood. This meant that another bond had to be found, one operating below the plane of consciousness—Arabs after World War I were clearly not conscious of themselves as a nation—but above that of familial or racial ties. He had already identified the solution for precisely this circumstance, taken from the 19th-century German model: the bond of language. France was the most useful model for Ottomans before the war, Germany for Arabs after it.

It is not clear how fully developed al-Husri's Arabist thought was in 1922, when he implemented his first overhaul of the Iraqi primary school curriculum. But the Arabist content of that curriculum has often been exaggerated by scholars.[49] Cleveland, for example, asserts that new curriculum specified "that the history of other nations should be studied in the early courses only as it related to Arab history."[50] In fact, it directed that other national histories be introduced only as they related to "the history of Iraq and the history of the Arabs."[51] Rather than asserting the primacy of Arab nationalism, or *qawmiyya*, over territorial Iraqi nationalism, or *wataniyya*, the curriculum repeatedly paired the terms "*qawmi* and *watani*," again not as synonyms but as symbiotic forms of nationalist attachment. Thus, it declared that the goal of teaching history in primary school was to strengthen "*qawmi* and *watani* feelings in the minds of students."[52] Teachers were instructed to focus on "the history of Iraq, the history of the Arabs, and the geography of Iraq."[53] Arabism, it bears noting, was a specifically nonterritorial form of nationalist attachment in the curriculum: Arabs had a history, while Iraq had a history and a geography. In later years, while the history of other nations could be added, the teaching of history should still focus mainly on "Iraq in particular and the Arabs in general." Students would learn "the history of the *watan*" and "the past of the *umma*," defined more precisely as "the history of the Iraqi country" (*al-bilad al-'iraqiyya*) and "the history of the Arab nation" (*al-umma al-'arabiyya*).[54]

History as a discipline and a sensibility was arguably more central to al-Husri's curriculum than any particular Arab or Iraqi content associated with it. This was a project of cultivating the capacity to imagine linear-historical time, in the sense analyzed by Benedict Anderson.[55] The curriculum instructions directed teachers not to make students memorize names and dates except to the extent "necessary to understand the flow of history [*sayr al-tarikh*]."[56] History was about "comparing past and present conditions," and recognizing "the differences and similarities between the various past generations."[57] Al-Husri was an uncompromising modernizer, for whom the capacity to apprehend historical time mattered only to the extent that it oriented subjects toward a future. History is "a dynamic motive force propelling us toward a new future," but "becomes harmful when it takes the form of an enticing force calling us backward. We must not view the past as a goal that we are moving toward and that we strive to return to."[58] The sole purpose of the past is to function as "the continuous wellspring of the future."[59]

Al-Husri himself asserted that the most important feature of the curriculum was not its content but that it was unified for all public primary schools, and would thus foster "unity of consciousness" among Iraqi schoolchildren.[60] The British system, which as al-Husri pointed out was imported from British-occupied Egypt, had divided primary education into two types of schools that differed in the length of their programs, in their curricula, and, usually, in their location in either urban or rural space. The primary schools were located mainly in urban areas; their programs took six years and were designed to prepare students for entry into secondary school. Their curriculum was geared largely toward producing civil servants loyal to Britain and thus focused on Arabic, English, and translation skills. The elementary schools, which were mostly rural, offered four years of what was considered a terminal primary education, and focused on agricultural and other manual skills.[61]

This dual system, in al-Husri's analysis, reflected a colonial approach to schooling that aimed to exploit the bodies of the colonized without "awakening the spirit of revolution [*ruh al-thawra*]" in their souls. The colonizer's solution for maintaining the crucial split between schooling and revolution was "learning without education."[62] Al-Husri criticized the dual system for tracking children into their future vocations from the time they entered primary school. But his belief that schools should produce unity of consciousness was not primarily about equality of economic opportunity. It was not even primarily about teaching students the same content regardless of the class to which they belonged or the environment in which they lived. Rather, it was about teaching them the same content *at the same time*. For al-Husri, the modern system of national age-graded schooling produced unity of consciousness by organizing the nation's children in time both diachronically and synchronically. On a diachronic plane, it regulated each individual child's linear progression from one age and grade level to the next, thus aligning psychological and biological time with national time. On a synchronic plane, it ensured that children at the same grade level within the national territory were studying the same subjects and performing the same routines at the same time of day as all other children at their grade level. It was especially this second, synchronic, function of the age-graded modern school that the British dual education system violated.

Thus, al-Husri's 1922 curriculum did not attempt to add fifth and sixth grades to the rural schools but instead mandated that the first four grades would follow the same curriculum across all schools.[63] Rather than adding more academic subjects to rural schools, moreover, al-Husri's first curriculum removed them from the first four grades of urban schools. It focused less on language skills than the British primary school curriculum had, especially in the first four grades but also overall. Periods devoted to English were reduced from 35 to 18 total periods, now all taught in the fifth and sixth grades, and the time devoted to translation in the British curriculum was eliminated altogether. Moreover, despite scholarly claims that al-Husri's 1922 curriculum expanded the study of Arabic language and history, in line with his conception of these two bonds as the foundation of national belonging, in fact it reduced the periods devoted to both subjects. Arabic language was reduced from 62 to 48 total periods, and the study of "geography and history" from 21 to 19 periods.[64]

Educating the Emotions

Over the 1920s, al-Husri developed his ideas about language and history as the twin foundations of national belonging. His Arabist thought drew, as has often been noted, on 19th-century German romantic philosophers of nationalism. But it also engaged with more recent imaginaries drawn from the discipline of psychology. Language was the nation's unconscious, while history—or, more precisely, a shared historical memory—was its consciousness.

Every nation has a consciousness [shu'ur], just as every individual person does. . . . The consciousness of any nation consists of the historical memories that are particular to it. A nation that preserves its language and forgets its history is like an individual who has lost consciousness or is immersed in sleep, or like a sick person in a catatonic state. He is still alive, but his life has no value unless he awakens from his sleep and regains the consciousness that he had lost for a period of time.[65]

I have translated al-shu'ur here as "consciousness," but the Arabic word also carries the sense of sentiment or feeling. It thus does not align with the concept of conscious mind as reasoning ego, for which al-'aql would have been a more obvious choice. My translation is based on al-Husri's opposition in this quotation of al-shu'ur to sleep and other forms of nonconsciousness, as well as to his use elsewhere of the term al-la-shu'ur for "the unconscious" in the psychological sense.[66]

Keeping in mind the dual linguistic sense of al-shu'ur as both consciousness and feeling or sentiment is useful for understanding al-Husri's pedagogical conception of history. Sometimes history appears to exist within the people, as a kind of semi-repressed memory that can be restored to full consciousness. "When I say history, I do not mean the history recorded in books. . . . I mean the history that lives in the psyches [or souls, nufus], which is known to the people's minds and is captured in their traditions."[67] Yet history must also be instilled in the people through pedagogies that shape not only their conscious minds but also their unconscious feelings. While there may be some tension between these conceptions, what they share is an association of historical consciousness with sentiment rather than reason, reflecting al-Husri's emphasis on shaping students' affective attachments.[68] Thus, the 1922 curriculum did not mandate the particular historical content or nationalist narrative to be transmitted to students; instead, it invited teachers to select events in Arab and Iraqi history that would "stir the imagination of students" and "arouse their emotions."[69]

With the time opened up by the reduction of academic subjects, other subjects were expanded and two new ones added: music and "moral and civic information." Al-Husri asserted that these subjects had been neglected in the British curriculum, "despite their enormous importance in nationalist pedagogy [al-tarbiya al-wataniyya]."[70] The curriculum instructed teachers to choose music that would "arouse nationalist sentiments in the heart, incite action and joy in the soul, and organize the movements" of the body.[71] The study of moral and civic information was similarly intended to "arouse moral sentiments in [students'] hearts."[72]

By neglecting these subjects, al-Husri continued, British officials had ignored one of the most basic principles of modern schooling: that effective pedagogies work primarily on the level of the unconscious, the emotions, and the bodily senses and habits, with the aim of generating certain kinds of conduct or action. The concept of "learning through feeling is the most important of our pedagogical principles."[73] Categorizing the forces that shape human conduct into "thought, emotion, and habit," he asserted that effective ethical pedagogy, or moral education (al-tarbiya al-akhlaqiyya),[74] worked on all three forces: thoughts were shaped through pedagogies of persuasion, emotions through association with others, and habits through the repetition of action. But the three were not equal in their influence on conduct or, therefore, in pedagogical priority: "Emotions and habits are the most important; thoughts and ideas have less influence," and anyway, "they are bound by the emotions."[75]

While often considered one of the most "secular" Arab intellectuals of his time, al-Husri was interested in how Islamic ethical pedagogies might be employed to help form modern moral subjects. Indeed, he believed that the knowledges and practices of ethical self-formation in classical Islam prefigured some of the discoveries of the modern science of pedagogy. But he also believed that these practices were an almost lost Islamic art. He thus commissioned the publication of textbooks and educational handbooks for the public that would update the classical ethical concepts in a language that 20th-century students, parents, and teachers could understand.[76]

The 1922 curriculum instructions directed teachers of religion to focus on ethics/morality (*akhlaq*) and avoid "giving detailed information [on Islam] that exceeds the students' capacity." Al-Husri's main critique of Islamic educators was that they did not understand basic psychological principles, especially the concept of developmental stages. In Iraq's schools, classes on Islam were taught by those trained in Islamic institutions, and thus "with no sound pedagogical direction." The study of religion could not take a "pedagogical form" if those teaching it had not studied the "science of psychology and the principles of pedagogy." As an example, he criticized a primary-school religion textbook, written by an Iraqi Islamic scholar, which explained that fasting during Ramadan includes avoiding "enjoyment below the navel," a statement al-Husri found highly inappropriate for children. Similarly, religion teachers did not understand "the principle of age-grading in education" and thus taught "the same material using the same methods" to all of their classes throughout the day, without regard for the students' different ages.[77] Both examples violated the central principle of the modern school as a regime regulating childrens' moral, physical, and psychological development according to their biological age. As al-Husri wrote, the principle of age-graded education was the "most important characteristic that distinguishes schools today from those of the past."[78]

In 1911, as an Ottoman educator, al-Husri had participated in a famous debate in Istanbul with the sociologist and future Turkish nationalist Ziya Gökalp, on the relative usefulness of the disciplines of psychology and sociology in shaping a modern school system, with al-Husri championing the virtues of psychology and Gökalp those of sociology. Al-Husri argued that psychology offered better tools for developing individuality, independence, and agency, while sociology threatened to inhibit those sensibilities by promoting conformity to the group.[79] He carried aspects of this commitment to fostering independent and reasoning subjects into Iraq. Thus, the 1922 curriculum instructions noted that schools should "avoid making the students obedient listeners only; but rather are concerned with making them thinking actors, by accustoming them to attention and observation, guiding them toward evaluation and judgment during each lesson."[80]

Al-Husri was highly attuned to what he saw as colonial (mis)uses of psychology to promote obedience among the colonized. He identified a major trend of education theory in his time, which he associated with the European colonial mentality, of invoking the psychological theory of the unconscious to argue that most students should be denied intellectual forms of education, since psychology had located the intellect within the hopelessly feeble conscious mind. Al-Husri agreed that modern education must work on students' emotions, habits, and bodies, but if it was restricted to such work it would produce mindless subjects resembling machines or animals rather than thinking citizens of a sovereign nation. And this was what colonial approaches to education, newly invigorated by what al-Husri saw as their misuse of the psychological theory of the unconscious, had always aimed to do.

An example of al-Husri's development of this argument is his 1928 critique of the French psychologist and sociologist Gustave Le Bon, whose writings had been widely translated into Arabic and were extremely influential in the Arab world.[81] Al-Husri targeted Le Bon's central pedagogical theory that the purpose of education is to "transform the conscious into the unconscious." The pedagogical practice that Le Bon developed from this theory was, in al-Husri's words, "to repeat and repeat" until the thing becomes a habit and part of the unconscious. Al-Husri found Le Bon's criticism of mental memorization techniques "strange," given that Le Bon's own methods involved nothing more than "physical memorization" to inculcate an unthinking habit, leaving no room "for the strengthening of alertness, independence [istiqlal], and character" in the student. According to al-Husri, Le Bon had simply dressed up the old colonial interest in exploitation as a modern theory of the unconscious. Everyone now agrees, wrote al-Husri, that most of our actions are driven by the unconscious and by habit rather than by the conscious mind. Yet it does not follow "that the teacher must rely solely on habit and the unconscious." On the contrary, the teacher's primary responsibility is to help the student "develop a psyche governed by reason," and not to turn him into "a machine or an animal." In addition to transforming the conscious into the unconscious, then, schools must "transform the unconscious into the conscious"; the point of education is to "strengthen the conscious mind," not make it disappear.[82] Since Le Bon's pedagogical philosophy was designed to serve French colonialism, al-Husri argued, its aim was simple: to keep the children of the colonized from rebelling.[83] He pointed out Le Bon's well-known argument that the psyches of Arabs and other non-Europeans were fundamentally (that is, racially) different from the psyches of Europeans, and that the former thus could not simply be educated into catching up to the latter. Indeed, Le Bon's philosophy was an example of how psychology could be employed to call for racialized theories of divergent development. Given the colonial racism on which Le Bon's educational theories were based, al-Husri found their popularity among Arab intellectuals of his time puzzling.[84]

Social Morality

In the late 1920s and the 1930s, al-Husri gradually modified his views on the pedagogical priority of psychology over sociology, increasingly asserting the importance of sociological insights for forming moral subjects, and especially moral Arab subjects. He argued that the kinds of morality required after "the most recent wars," and in modern militaries, are different from those of the past.[85] This and other factors called for the formation of a "social" rather than an individual morality among the "sons of the nation," a morality that must be active, not passive.[86] More generally al-Husri insisted that Arabs were in particular need of sociologically derived insights, because Arabs tend to be more "individualistic" and less "social" than people in the West.[87] What the Arab character "most requires is a 'social education' that strengthens and develops in his *nafs* [soul, psyche, self] the spirit of cooperation, obedience, and sacrifice, ensuring his success not as an individual standing on his own but as a person serving his nation, too."[88]

The assertion that Arabs are more individualistic and less social than people in the West may sound strange today, when the same civilizational opposition is frequently made in reverse. But it was a recurring claim of Arab intellectuals from the late 19th century to the 1960s.[89] This period corresponds to a shift in dominant European and American thinking on subject formation and social order, from 19th-century liberal visions of society as a "collection of autonomous individuals, each equipped with a free will," toward Progressive-era conceptions of society as "a social body."[90] Marwa ElShakry has similarly noted a "growing disillusion with liberal individualism" and a "new focus on social cooperation" in Arabic writings of the early 20th century.[91]

Al-Husri traced the overly individualistic psyches of Arabs to the condition of women and the family in Arab society. "The seclusion of women creates a particular social structure that blocks the strengthening of social activity, in the same way that the cellular membrane surrounding a seed blocks the penetration of life into it."[92] The solution for al-Husri was simply to remove youth from their antisocial families for as long as possible. Young children, unfortunately, had to be returned to their mothers each day, but adolescent boys and young men could be separated for longer periods of time, through compulsory military service. This was precisely the aspect of military training that ultimately made al-Husri declare it even more important than the school. "The school removes the individual from his private home and original family for only a few hours per day, then returns him," while "the barracks . . . demands his complete separation from his original family and private life, forcing him to live with his peers in a new environment, for a long period of time."[93] There is "no doubt," al-Husri wrote, "that separating the young man from his private environment . . . has a deep influence on his psyche [*nafsiyya*]."[94]

If the role of schools was to shape the psyches of children (*nafsiyyat al-atfal*), that of the barracks was to shape the psyches of young men (*nafsiyyat al-shubban*).[95] To succeed in its efforts to construct a "modern social order," the Iraqi government should require every male to join both of these institutions, "in a particular stage of his life, passing through the school in his childhood and through the barracks in his young adulthood."[96] This would address one of the nation's gravest problems, namely that "the spirit of individualism is strong among us, while the spirit of sociality is still weak in our souls."[97] The school and the barracks would remove youth for increasing durations from their families, local attachments, and heterogeneous temporalities and enable them to identify with a larger entity, the nation, moving in its own time.

During the last years of the mandate, nationalist officials had unsuccessfully pushed British authorities to implement universal military conscription in Iraq. But in 1934, a law of universal military conscription was passed. Al-Husri declared it "the most important event in the Arab East" that year, because it made the Iraqi army "a nationalist tool, drawing its power from all the classes of the *umma*."[98] Even while situating the new law within the "Arab East," al-Husri celebrated it as a victory for *wataniyya*, not *qawmiyya*. The Iraqi army, he wrote, "can obviously not be truly nationalist [*wataniyyan*] unless it is based on universal military service, in which all citizens participate."[99] Again, military service was necessary "for strengthening the spirit of *wataniyyat* as well as that of public interest."[100]

The military, as Elizabeth Freeman argues, is the "perhaps the nation's most explicit form of synching up bodies and time."[101] But, like other chrono-biopolitical regimes of the nation-state, the military also synchs up bodies in space, and thereby produces not only particular kinds of bodies but also particular spaces.[102] As far as its connection to nationalist belonging was concerned, even al-Husri envisioned the role of the military barracks as a victory for *wataniyya*, love of homeland.

In the years following independence, and parallel to the introduction of military conscription, the Ministry of Education introduced al-Futuwwa, a system of military training for male secondary school and college students.[103] The word *al-futuwwa* concisely captured the driving principle of the institution: the nationalist cultivation of masculine discipline in young men. Literally translated as "youthful masculinity," the word had been applied in various ways throughout Islamic history, including to Sufi practices and brotherhoods, artisanal guilds, young men policing urban quarters, and knightly institutions of the 'Abbasid court. "As a concept, al-futuwwa is contradictorily capacious, accommodating notions like chivalry, courage, generosity, and brotherhood, as well as thuggery, banditry, criminality, and depravity; furthermore, it might signify a warrior, an ascetic, or a gift."[104] In 1924, a proposal had been made to use *al-futuwwa* as the name for the Iraqi Boy Scouts, which al-Husri rejected because the "Scouts was not limited to adolescents [*al-fityan*] but also included young boys [*al-sibyan*]." But in the 1930s, "the word *al-futuwwa* was found to be highly fitting" for military education in secondary schools.[105] In 1939, a law was passed making participation in al-Futuwwa compulsory for all male secondary school and college students.

Some scholars have suggested that al-Futuwwa, and other military-masculinization projects in the 1930s, had a powerful and unidirectional effect on impressionable Iraqi schoolboys.[106] But this elides the ways in which such projects were always already situated within sociopolitical and generational conflicts in Iraq. Orit Bashkin has pertinently posed the question of how the Iraqi public as well as students and teachers in schools actually responded to the militarization of boys' education, and her research points to resistance in both spheres.[107] Moreover, there are clear references to existing conflict in the text of the al-Futuwwa law itself and the discourses of its supporters. The law stated that its goal was to "accustom adolescent boys [*al-fityan*] to the roughness of life, increase their tolerance for hardships and sacrifice, and cultivate the military spirit and qualities of masculinity and chivalry that will habituate them to a love of order and obedience."[108] The driving force behind al-Futuwwa was the Arab nationalist Sami Shawkat, who served as director general of education from 1931 to 1933 and continued as an official and advocate of al-Futuwwa in later years. He wrote that the purpose of the 1939 al-Futuwwa law was to address "the nation's current affliction with psychological weaknesses and spiritual vacillations." These he linked to the dissolution of "our family environment and social life," which "used to be guided by a spirit of obedience for the old and affection for the young." But the spread of coffee shops and cinemas, along with the increasing disinterest of Iraqi adults in family life, had led to a growing generational divide: "These were the reasons that drove the Ministry of Education to implement al-Futuwwa." Moreover, the institution's stabilizing effects were expected to reach beyond the schoolboys themselves: "Each of the 100,000 students who will be trained in al-Futuwwa is in contact with at least ten people in the society—a mother, a father, relatives, friends, and others—so that this military spirit and moral order will reach no less than one million souls in our Iraqi society."[109]

While Shawkat's diagnosis of the nation's "affliction" identified the family as a cause, this was a different reasoning from the one that posited the family as a stagnant space of tradition blocking development. A problematic dissolution of family life had been identified, a weakening of intergenerational ties that were presumably once a source of stability. This had created, parallel to a decline in the "spirit of obedience," a crisis of morality, which was also a gender crisis. Shawkat stated that the primary aim of education was "the formation of morals, especially the morals of masculinity."[110] The increasing moralization of both education and masculinity was not just about producing strong male bodies for the national army but also about producing heteronormative citizens, as is clear from Shawkat's concern for the reform of girls' education as the flip side of al-Futuwwa. Such reform must recognize what "science has proven," namely that a woman cannot reach full "mental, psychological, and physical" maturity unless she marries and has children; on the contrary, she often ends up with "nutritional, nervous, uterine, and even mental illnesses." Shawkat marveled that "before these scientific facts and eternal laws, whose aim is to protect the race . . . human reason cannot but stand humbled and amazed."[111]

Masculine Time and Feminine Space

Al-Husri's pedagogical and nationalist philosophy had several implications for the schooling of Iraqi girls in the 1920s. First, during his
tenure as director general of education from 1922 to 1927, the official
public school curriculum for girls was identical to that for boys. This was
consistent not only with his advocacy for the education of women, but
also with his view that unity in the curriculum would produce unity in
the nation. Al-Husri would later support, in response to criticism on this
front, greater differentiation of the curriculum on the basis of sex. However, he insisted that such differences should apply only to the "details,"
for example by adding home economics classes for female students; they
should not affect the "fundamentals" of public education, which should
remain the same for boys and girls. Most importantly, al-Husri insisted
that male and female students should progress through the school system
according to identical temporal rhythms of intellectual development and
bureaucratic order. Thus, he sharply criticized a proposed curriculum
reform in 1931 that had girls and boys in intermediate schools studying
different subjects at different grade levels; for example, modern history
in the girls' schools would be studied in the second year and Arab history in the third year, while in the boys' schools the two subjects would
be taught in reverse order. Al-Husri insisted not only that girls and boys
must study the same core subjects but that it was a national imperative
that they study them at the same time.[112]

It would thus seem that, in some ways, al-Husri's conception of the
historical time of nationhood was gender-neutral. Yet his writings on Arab
youth and Arab history consistently constructed the universal national citizen, and thus the subject of national pedagogy, as male.[113] It is his emphasis
on the military that attests most clearly to this: "Military life is a life of
movement and toil. It strengthens the spirit of movement and activity in
the young man [shab], and accustoms him to the roughness of life and the
endurance of hardships, through which he develops habits of masculinity
[al-rujula] and perseverance."[114]

Moreover, despite al-Husri's insistence that morality is rooted in "social
life,"[115] which was stunted by the dominant family structure in Iraq, he did
not wage any large-scale campaign to reform Iraqi familial life through the
schools, and he often seemed pessimistic or apathetic about proposals for

such reforms. For example, the primary school "Moral and Civic Information" curriculum, which al-Husri wrote and which was supposed to teach students about family relations and civic duties, dispensed with the first of these in a summary fashion that hardly concealed the author's disinterest.

The physical and spiritual ties that bind the members of a family together are obvious and do not need a great deal of explanation but the ties that bind individuals with their nation and government are not by themselves clear. The teacher should therefore take special care to bring them out and show what duties devolve on individuals in view of these ties.[116]

In the 1930s, as we will see in the next chapter, al-Husri's critics would use this passage of the curriculum to argue that his school system had ignored the ways in which backward families, and backward women in particular, obstructed the formation of modern subjects.

Indeed, al-Husri never seemed able to explain, or was never very interested in explaining, how the stagnant feminine space of the family was to be brought into the progressive masculine time of the nation. His lack of interest in or optimism about the possibility of effective family reform, combined with the essential masculinism of his conception of national citizenship, probably has some relation to the fact that neither the rising enrollment of female students nor the numerical increase in female schoolteachers was matched by an equivalent rise in the number of new schools for girls under his leadership.[117] Some of his critics would use this discrepancy to argue that the expansion of Iraqi public education for girls in the 1920s was fueled from below by popular demand rather than from above by genuine government support. In any case, for the new generation of Iraqi educators that emerged in the 1930s, the elimination of the stagnant familial space at the heart of the nation, and its replacement by modern, future-oriented spaces of domesticity and femininity, would be indispensable for forming modern selves and thus for realizing the promises of sovereignty and development.

3

The Gendering of School Time

IN 1932, THE YEAR IRAQ BECAME formally independent, a team of US educators from Teachers College of Columbia University toured the country on the invitation of the Hashimite monarchy. The final report this commission authored—commonly known as the Monroe Report after the commission's director, Paul Monroe—criticized the Ministry of Education for a range of purported failings. Drawing on American pedagogical vocabularies of "learning by doing" and "adapted education," it called for differentiating the Iraqi public school curriculum according to the different "environments" in which children lived. Two differences were of particular concern: the urban/rural difference and the male/female difference. A central critique was that the curriculum was "uniform for [all] schools, whether urban or rural, whether boys' schools or girls' schools, throughout the kingdom."[1] The report recommended that rural boys' schools place more emphasis on agricultural education and girls' schools on home economics, in the name of the "economic development" of Iraq's natural resources and the "development of a national consciousness" among its youth.[2]

Criticizing what it posited as the sex-blindness of Iraqi education, the report recommended that girls be taught "domestic science and domestic art, home-making, the proper care of children, and similar matters, subjects which now receive little or no attention in the curriculum."[3] It also called for an expansion of female education, especially at the primary school level.

These recommendations are made because the Commission believes that the life of a community or a people cannot be enlightened and modernized without the adequate education of its girls and women. To expect a modern school to translate scientific knowledge into the habits and customs of a people without the education of women is a vain hope. Nor can social life be modernized when the school instructs in one set of ideas and the home in another.[4]

This passage highlights a temporal paradox that runs through the report. On the one hand, the report's reasoning recalls Uday Singh Mehta's description of liberal discourse as one "in which experience is always viewed and assessed from a future point. It is on account of this futural perspective that one can know, or claim to know, the experience's future history, its process of gestation into another stage of life."[5] In the 1930s United States, compulsory education in domesticity was a fact of life for all female students in the public school system; for US educators advising foreign governments, it was thus a sine qua non of becoming modern anywhere. The authors of the report gave no indication that, for all they knew, compulsory home economics education for girls might just be a phase the American school system was passing through on its way toward less knowable modern futures. Rather, they asserted it as an indispensable component of what being modern meant. What made the remarkable confidence of this temporal perspective possible was that it aligned precisely with a spatial perspective; Iraq's future was intimately familiar to the commission members as their own present.

On the other hand, the Monroe Commission was clear that Iraq's future might and indeed should look very different from the present of the United States. As some Iraqi critics observed, the report said almost nothing about industrialization, for example, while it had a great deal to say about the importance of keeping rural Iraqis in rural areas, including by cultivating their desires for agricultural labor, "which has always been the chief means of support of the people of this ancient land."[6] A similar reasoning related to sexual difference is expressed in the assertion in the passage just quoted that it was through female students that public schools would "translate scientific knowledge into the habits and customs of a people." This was not a call for girls to study the modern scientific disciplines in school, as was true of some late 19th- and early 20th-century discourses advocating the education of companionate wives for middle-class men. Rather, it was about teaching girls, especially lower-class girls, habits of living that may have derived from "scientific knowledge," but that had already been translated by experts into practices compatible with the "habits and customs" of the people. Thus, the report discouraged overly "academic" forms of education for girls, as well as for rural boys, which might awaken unrealistic desires for change.

Some of the Monroe Report's recommendations generated considerable controversy in the Iraqi public sphere during the first years of independence. An early charge was led by Sati' al-Husri, who saw striking similarities
between the report and earlier British mandate policy, especially in its recommendation to reverse the expansion of secondary education. He also
questioned the proposal to reorient rural boys' schooling around agricultural
education, which, he argued, deviously misidentified the central obstacles
to economic development in Iraq. There were indeed echoes between the
report's recommendations and earlier British critiques of "bookish" types
of education in Iraq, which had usually been invoked to argue for strictly
vocational schooling for the lower classes.[7] But the report was also shaped
by American pedagogical theories that were related but not reducible to
calls for vocational education.

The Monroe Report was the opening salvo in a conflict that pitted al-
Husri and his cohort of ex-Ottoman Arabists in the Ministry of Education
against a new generation of Iraqi educators, many of whom were trained in
the United States. By the end of World War II, the latter group was perfectly
poised to lead the Iraqi school system into an era marked by the expansion of
American influence and by the dawning of the global "age of development"
with the Bretton Woods Conference that founded the World Bank in 1944; the
establishment of the United Nations and its development organizations, including UNESCO, in 1945; and President Truman's Point Four speech promising
US technical assistance to Western-aligned "developing" countries in 1949.
The new Iraqi educators were supported in many of their proposals by US
commissions and international development teams that arrived in Iraq, starting
with the Monroe Commission in 1932, and appearing with great regularity
by the 1950s, often on the invitation of the new educators in their capacity as
ministry officials. These groups included the American Council on Education
in 1949; the World Bank in 1952; the University of Bradley Mission from 1953
to 1956; Arthur D. Little, Inc., in 1956; and the US Technical Cooperation
Administration (Truman's Point Four program), as well as various UN missions, such as those of UNESCO and the Food and Agricultural Organization
(FAO), from 1951 to 1958. The postwar commissions consistently repeated
the Monroe Report's claim that the Iraqi public school curriculum was not sufficiently differentiated by sex, and recommended that female students from the
primary through the secondary levels, and in many cases at the college levels,
be required to take more courses in home economics, a field developed in the
United States in the late 19th century that had originally targeted rural women.[8]

From 1932 to 1958, the Ministry of Education reshaped significant aspects of the Iraqi public school experience around sexual difference, by revising curricula, textbooks, exams, and teacher training programs, as well as by constructing new schools. In what might seem to be a paradox, the differentiation of the public school curriculum by sex was paralleled by the expansion of coeducation in Iraq at the primary and postsecondary levels during these same decades. A girl entering the public school system in 1926 was certain to study in a school populated only by other girls, but it seems she was almost equally certain to follow the same course of schooling as a boy at her grade level. A girl entering the system in 1956 might or might not find herself in a coeducational primary school, but either way she would follow a mandatory female-only official curriculum for about 20 percent of the time she spent in that school. It was as if the more girls mixed with boys, and women with men, in the public sphere, the greater became the impetus to produce differences in their learned modes of thinking and acting.

In tracing the gendering of Iraqi education during these decades, this chapter draws on the writings of Iraqi and American educators, many of whom were directly involved in Iraqi education policy. The Hashimite school system was the workplace of many of Iraq's most powerful intellects and influential writers. In part, this was due to the effective abandonment of the Ministry of Education by British authorities and its takeover, only a few years into the mandate, by nationalists of varied leanings.[9] As Orit Bashkin notes, the ministry was not only a vast "employer of writers, journalists, poets, and novelists" as policymakers, administrators, inspectors, and teachers, but through its publications, which often represented a vibrant range of opinion, it became an "important power in the public sphere," quite apart from its influence on schoolchildren.[10]

Feminine Domesticity

The emergence, starting in the late 19th century, of modern feminine domesticity or "patriotic motherhood"[11] has been studied by many historians of the Middle East and is one of the most theoretically dynamic branches of the field. A seminal work in this area, Beth Baron's 1994 *The Women's Awakening in Egypt*, showed how a "new ideology of domesticity" emerged in late 19th-century Egypt that involved a shift "from the father to the mother as the central figure in shaping the child. . . . The mother was no longer just a vessel for bringing an infant into the world but a critical influence on the child's early life." The new emphasis on motherhood coincided with a "greater interest in child development" in general.[12] Today, few historians would dispute what Omnia El Shakry describes as a "fundamental shift" around the turn of the 20th century, across the region, "in which mothers came to be responsible for the physical, moral, and intellectual development of children within the nexus of a nascent nationalist discourse."[13]

This chapter begins from the premise that, if modern interventions into domesticity are geared largely toward producing "children worthy of modernity,"[14] as Afsaneh Najmabadi writes, it might be pertinent to ask just what qualities make a child worthy of modernity in the first place, how these qualities might differ across time and space, and what effects such differences might have on constructions of feminine domesticity in particular contexts. From the 1930s through the 1950s, discourses and techniques of domesticity in Iraq spread far beyond the urban middle-class domains that have been the focus of most scholarship on domesticity in the region.[15] I view such interventions as more than symbolic or metaphoric tropes used by nationalists in their struggle for sovereignty.[16] That is, I take my sources' assertions that the (re)education of Iraqi women and the reconstitution of the Iraqi family were critical to the future of the nation as more or less genuine statements of contemporary understandings of the relation between sexual difference, historical time, and national sovereignty. It is this very relation, rather than something else it might stand for, that I explore in what follows. Of course, I am not arguing that family metaphors are not important in nation-building projects. Moreover, most women's historians would likely agree that even explicitly metaphorical uses of gender categories in nationalist discourses (e.g., the nation as a mother) can be productive of changes in interpersonal relations and modes of life.[17] I am only suggesting that there might be other questions to ask about affiliations of domestic practices and spaces with sovereign futures, and that trying to work "along the archival grain" of sources on gender and family, in addition to working against it, can open up affective registers and other dimensions of such discourses that may otherwise remain unavailable.[18]

My research indicates that mandatory female education in home economics emerged later in Iraq than in many other locations. It became a nominal requirement for girls in primary school only in 1928, and was not effectively instituted on a nation-wide level in public primary schools until the 1930s and in secondary schools until the 1940s.[19] This difference relates both to British mandate policies of "control without occupation" and to the ideological and pedagogical proclivities of the Arabist officials who ran the school system in the 1920s, as explored in Chapters 1 and 2, respectively. But rather than view the spread of domestic education from the 1930s to the 1950s as a delayed repetition of a process that had already occurred elsewhere, I suggest that this peculiarity makes Iraq a productive context for examining shifts in notions and practices of feminine domesticity during the late interwar and early postwar eras.

Making the World Safe for Nation-States: Paul Monroe and Adapted Education

The Monroe Report has been widely used as a source in histories of Iraq. Its observations have often been read as transparent descriptions of Hashimite schools in 1932, and its recommendations have been often interpreted hastily, and rather cheerfully, as promoting "the inculcation of democratic ideals" and of "equal opportunity" in Iraqi education.[20] One reason for this is that scholars have tended to sympathize with the report's criticisms of "rote memorization" and its calls for "active learning" and "education for real life."

Situating the report within its American and global contexts raises questions about these readings. Members of the Monroe Commission had for several decades advocated the export to the world's newly decolonizing nations of the "Tuskegee model" of education, developed in segregated schooling projects for black youth in the post-Reconstruction US South, and the report's descriptions of Iraqi schools are strikingly similar to Monroe's earlier accounts of school systems from Mexico to China to the Philippines. The frequently uncritical reception of the report by historians may point to what Robert Vitalis has identified as a central blind spot in analyses of American activities abroad in the 20th century, namely around "the rich tradition of racism in American life." It is only by forgetting this tradition, Vitalis argues, that historians can produce exceptionalist narratives that the United States is "empire's antithesis" and that Americans "learn[ed] early" to be good citizens.[21]

Paul Monroe was a leading theorist of "adapted education," the philosophy that school systems should be adapted to the economic, cultural, and psychological stage of development of the communities they serve. In 1917, he had directed the education team of the Commission of Inquiry established by Woodrow Wilson to prepare US officials for the postwar negotiations; he was assigned to analyze "the problem of education in the backward countries," especially the Arab regions of the Ottoman Empire then under Allied occupation. One of his tasks was to explore education as a sphere "in which the United States may find some possibility of assuming direction."[22] Monroe was an obvious choice. Besides his status as a leading Progressive educator, he had experience in missionary work in the Middle East and East Asia, and in 1913 had led educational missions to the Philippines and China for the US government and the Rockefeller Foundation, respectively. In his memoranda for the inquiry, Monroe formulated "a fundamental American understanding of the relationship between education and the social reconstruction required in so much of the world."[23]

Monroe spent the interwar years working to spread this understanding across the globe. "From virtually the conclusion of the Armistice of the First World War to the middle of the Second World War, Monroe was in motion, crossing the seas and driving through the deserts, carrying the messages, elaborated and improved, of course, that he had developed for the pre-Versailles peace process."[24] He was equally busy at home, where he served as advisor for the Near East Relief committee and, in 1930, helped transform it into the Near East Foundation.[25] In 1923, he founded the International Institute at Teachers College of Columbia University, with the dual aim of training American missionaries in cross-cultural educational methods and foreign students in American pedagogical theories.

Monroe's interwar writings continued to hone his ideas on education "as the means of raising backward nations to full membership in the family of nations."[26] This interest was an extension of his earlier focus on the expansion of education to the lower classes in the United States. In 1913, he identified a monumental shift in understandings of education among "advanced" peoples. "Throughout at least the entire modern period education was either considered as the means of perfecting or of disciplining the individual or it was held to be the best means of getting on in the world."[27] Both conceptions of education—the "liberal" and the "practical"—were made obsolete by a new understanding of education as "a social art."[28] The expansion of public education to the lower classes had become necessary because "the stability and development of our political institutions depend on the education of the masses as well as that of leaders. . . . In no less degree does the same hold true of economic development."[29] This shift had made the old debate between liberal and practical approaches to education irrelevant. Education was now always both; it was "liberal," even for "the masses," because it not only provided vocational schooling but also ensured "the social, political, vocational, aesthetic, and moral adjustment of the child for normal participation in society." And it was practical in that even classically liberal, or intellectual, forms of education were now "measured not in the old terms of criticism of life [but] in the new terms of contribution to life."[30]

In his work abroad, Monroe was interested in the role public schools could play in the formation of stable nation-states in a future envisioned to follow the end of the European empires. In 1920, he noted the increasingly global importance of the discovery that modern national culture is "an artificial product and can be manufactured. The process of this manufacture is by education."[31] The diffusion of the nation-state form around the world required the production of citizens with nondisruptive nationalist sensibilities, a process that was fraught with danger. Education, wrote Monroe, "is the only means by which the world can be 'made safe' for the national type of organization."[32] It could do so through adapted education, or "adjustment to the actual life and needs of the community, to the culture of the people," since "the cultural system and the educational process conform to distinctive principles or laws peculiar to the given stage."[33] He warned of the dangers of transplanting a school system from one society to another if their stages of development were different. Thus, he criticized the "Americanization" of youth belonging to "ancient cultures" abroad, which "may have a decidedly deleterious effect economically and may even make for social and intellectual instability."[34]

For countries in what he called the "primitive" and "transitional" stages of development, Monroe argued for "industrial education," or pedagogies to instill the sensibilities required for manual labor, whether industrial or agricultural. Industrial education had emerged in the US South as the model for the Hampton and Tuskegee Institutes. The idea was that "blacks should be trained for a life of manual labor and should stay away from studies that were too 'bookish' and academic."[35] Needless to say, it was a controversial theory in its home country. In the words of W.E.B. DuBois: "The white world wants the black world to study 'agriculture.' It is not only easier to lynch Negroes and keep them in ignorance and peonage in country districts, but it is also easier to cheat them out of a decent income."[36] These controversies do not appear in Monroe's reports on schooling in the decolonizing regions of the world, where, according to him, "the education of a Hampton or a Tuskegee, not that of a New England college or high school, is needed."[37]

When Monroe cautioned against the "Americanization" of schooling in the decolonizing world, it must be understood that he was speaking against its New England-ization, not its Tuskegee-ization.

The International Institute at Teachers College was funded by the General Education Board of the Rockefeller Foundation, which also funded the Hampton and Tuskegee Institutes. Hampton was a popular site of fieldwork for the foreign students at Teachers College, who "were especially encouraged to learn from the Southern experience what might be applicable to the situation of their homelands."[38] One of the other three American members of the Monroe Commission was Edgar Wallace Knight. He specialized in the education of black children in the South, was on the board of trustees of the Hampton Institute, and was well known in the United States for his critiques of Reconstruction and his advocacy of segregated schooling, Jim Crow laws, and the disenfranchisement of black Southerners.[39] It should not surprise to find that much of the Monroe Report's reasoning was oriented not toward universalizing an American middle-class experience but toward reproducing existing patterns of uneven development, both globally and within the territory of the nation-state.

If adapted education was one theoretical tradition shaping the Monroe Report, another was the pedagogical philosophy of pragmatism often associated with John Dewey, who taught at Teachers College until his retirement in 1930. I often use the term "pragmatist" to describe the approaches of the new Iraqi educators, although some of the concepts they employ align more precisely with philosophies of adapted or industrial education. The term is appropriate both because many Iraqi educators affirmed the importance of pragmatism to their intellectual development and because the central concepts they repeatedly invoked—such as "education for real life," "learning by doing," and "child-centered curriculum"—are associated with pragmatist thought the world over. As education theorist Thomas Popkewitz notes, pragmatism was employed in diverse ways across the globe in the interwar era, not all of which are "necessarily traceable to Dewey as the original author."[40] But wherever it appeared, pragmatism functioned "as a cultural thesis about modes of living" and was imbricated in "cultural narratives about who the citizen and the child are."[41]

Here I will just note how, according to Popkewitz, pragmatist educators charged both schools and mothers with the task of interiorizing scientific reasoning—now understood as the capacity to plan for the future—in children. Through this interiorization, the child would become a "learner and problem solver who acts toward future goals." Rather than a set of specialized knowledges to be learned by the nation's future technocrats, as science was understood throughout the 19th century, science in relation to pedagogy was now understood as synonymous with reason: "to practice science was to be reasonable and reason was what science provided." Science taught the capacity for "rational planning directed to the future" and thus became a pedagogy that "places individuals in time." From its 19th-century conception as knowledge, science was transformed into "a process of enacting life."[42]

Education for Development

Along with the University of Chicago, Teachers College was the institutional heart of the global pragmatist movement in education. The Iraqi monarchy, like many other governments around the world, forged agreements with Teachers College in the late 1920s and 1930s to cosponsor some of the country's top college graduates to pursue advanced degrees at the institution. The students signed agreements to return to Iraq after receiving their degrees and to work for the Ministry of Education for a specified number of years. Among the Iraqi students completing their doctoral work at Teachers College in 1932, under the direction of Paul Monroe as dissertation advisor, was Muhammad Fadil al-Jamali, the only Iraqi member of the Monroe Commission and the author of the report's chapter on Bedouin education. He was appointed director general of Iraqi education in 1934, two years after receiving his PhD, and would later serve as Iraqi prime minister. Al-Jamali and Matta Akrawi, who also earned his PhD degree from Teachers College and would serve his own stint as director general of education, led the movement to integrate American educational philosophies into the Iraqi school system, in direct and often very public conflict with Sati' al-Husri. In 1936, they would succeed in pushing al-Husri out of the Ministry of Education altogether.[43]

The global expansion of pragmatism, and kindred philosophies of education for real life emerging in Europe, was fueled by the global economic depression, which was transforming the landscape of public schooling and driving the search for new approaches that emphasized the relationship between national school systems and the health of national economies and polities. In Iraq, as in many other predominantly rural countries, the depression played out largely as an agrarian crisis and was marked by widespread rural revolts and migration to the cities. During the 1930s, as Omnia El Shakry writes of the same decade in Egypt, the peasantry became "central to the social-scientific research agenda," as reformers sought to manage the effects of the increasingly "antagonistic relationship between peasants and land-owners, which crystallized in the figure of the undisciplined rural subject."[44] In Iraq, the situation was exacerbated, especially in the southern regions, by the vastly unequal system of land distribution that had been consolidated, in the interest of stability, by British and monarchical policy.[45]

For the new educators, the primary mission of public schooling was what in the 1930s was often called "economic reconstruction." Al-Jamali argued for this reconceptualization of education in his Teachers College dissertation on Bedouin education in Iraq, which was published as a book in 1934. He wrote that of the three main problems facing the school system—"economic reconstruction, nationalism, and morality"—the first "presents the greatest challenge to education."[46] Iraq, he wrote, "has recently attained recognition from the world as an independent country," and yet, "its rich natural sources are idle. Its people are mainly poor, sick, ignorant and idle. . . . The reconstruction of the country by the efforts of its own natives is the hope of every intelligent Iraqi [and] calls for the work of brains and hands."[47] The Monroe Report similarly asserted that the task of public schooling was "to bridge the chasm which now exists between a modern form of government on the one hand and a retarded and more or less undisciplined people on the other."[48] Pedagogies should "develop among the people a larger measure of individual initiative and enterprise that will enable them to undertake for themselves the development of the resources of the country rather than waiting for the government . . . to do this for them."[49] For example, the report notes that existing apprenticeship practices for training Iraqi youth in the manufacture of local handicrafts "do not lead to economic develop-ment and enrichment of society in general."[50]

Differentiating the Curriculum

If economic development was now the goal of public schooling, the curriculum had to reflect that aim. A central concern of the new educators was the curriculum's "uniformity," which al-Husri considered a hard-won nationalist achievement. In a bold and direct swipe at al-Husri himself, Akrawi asserted in his Teachers College dissertation that the "primary school regulations, the course of study, the methods of teaching, inspection, ex-amination and textbooks are all directed towards one end: uniformity, or as

one of the protagonists of the system prefers to call it: 'the unity of education.'"[51] Against this uniformity, the reformers advocated particular kinds
of difference: some were beneficial to the nation and others were harmful.
They shared al-Husri's concern that British policy had fostered sectarianism in Iraq by funding Christian schools to produce civil servants loyal to
Britain.[52] Difference of the positive type would fuel economic development
rather than sectarian fragmentation. Thus, the curriculum for a child living
in a reed hut in the southern marshes and engaged in the raising of water
buffaloes should differ from the curriculum for a child growing up in an
urban industrial community.[53]

In response to critiques that these proposals echoed those of earlier
British calls for vocational education, some pragmatists insisted that the type
of differentiation they advocated was not synonymous with occupational
specialization or social stratification. The point, they argued, was not to
teach students particular crafts or bind them to particular future vocations,
but rather to create new kinds of citizens, confident in their ability to shape
their immediate environment.[54] But there were many ambiguities in pragmatist proposals for differentiated education. The reports of international
experts, from the Monroe Commission to the UN reports of the early 1950s,
emphasized the importance of agricultural education to Iraq's development
and were often unequivocal that the point of such education was to keep
rural youth in rural areas. As the Monroe Report explained:

The materials of instruction [in the rural school curriculum] should be selected carefully
with the view of training rural boys into healthy, productive and useful citizens to whom
rural life is attractive and significant. . . . [This] will increase among rural youth respect for
manual labor and the desire to have a part in the basic economic activities of agriculture
which has always been the chief means of support of the people of this ancient land.[55]

In a series of open letters to Paul Monroe published in the Iraqi press, Sati'
al-Husri conceded that some curriculum differentiation might be useful, especially for female students, but vehemently opposed the radical forms of
differentiation recommended in the report. He argued that they would deny
the majority of Iraqi children any form of intellectual education, reflecting
a colonial approach to schooling that aimed to undermine the struggle for
sovereignty by discouraging students from thinking critically about their situation.[56] Al-Husri recalled a meeting he had with the Monroe Commission
members, during which they asked him: "Don't you believe that implementing agricultural education in village schools will lead to a great agricultural

renaissance?" According to al-Husri, he replied, "I don't believe that at all," and explained that an "agricultural renaissance" depended on many things outside the purview of the Ministry of Education, such as new land laws and irrigation systems, and that it was "unreasonable" to expect one to occur simply through the training of village boys in the latest farming techniques. Pointing out that public schools in Iraq already engaged students at every level in agricultural education, he insisted that such education was important for "its pedagogical value, not its economic outcome."[57]

Probably the most formidable obstacle to implementing a differentiated curriculum, according to the reformers themselves, was that manual laborers in Iraq did not want to send their children to school in order to become manual laborers. This problem was often blamed on "traditional Arab views" of disdain for manual labor and of education as a means to a "white-collar" job. Akrawi wrote:

> This traditional view of education has been handed down through the ages to the present generation of Iraqis and Arabs and makes both teachers and parents put undue stress on subject matter in the schools. We can see its effects in the fact that many a parent looks with suspicion at such things as physical education, manual training and the like.[58]

Al-Jamali agreed that educational reform would have to grapple with the fact that "many of these parents have a clear aim in mind in sending their children to school. Their aim is that their children may eventually be engaged in 'white-collar' jobs."[59] But reform must take place, since the government was perhaps "going too far in patronizing the public," with the result of educating future nonproducers.[60]

Arguments for differentiating the curriculum by sex emerged out of a similar logic, but with some differences. Akrawi proposed five public school curricula in Iraq: for urban, rural, tribal, mountain-dwelling Kurdish, and female students.[61] Among several striking aspects of this proposal is that one kind of difference—that of being female—not only overlaps with but trumps every other kind of difference, so that urban, rural, tribal, and mountain-dwelling Kurdish girls would all follow the same curriculum. It turned out that differentiation itself was sex-specific, applicable only to male students. According to Akrawi, this was because female students were likely to be future homemakers and thus their environment and the materials they worked on were the same, regardless of where they lived, an explanation that arguably belies his insistence that curriculum differentiation was not about tying youth to future vocations.[62]

While Akrawi's proposal contained a higher degree of differentiation than many pragmatists advocated—notably in its separation of the curricula for Kurdish and Arab rural male youth—the notion that female education should be uniform while male education was differentiated was a recurring theme in pragmatist and, later, development discourse. Thus, in the early 1940s, reformers launched a campaign to modify the secondary school curriculum, which was divided into literary and scientific tracks in both boys' and girls' schools. For boys, the reformers proposed increasing the differentiation from two to four tracks, corresponding to science, mathematics, literature, and social science. At the same time, they proposed eliminating differentiation altogether in the girls' schools, so that female secondary students would all follow the same curriculum, oriented toward domestic and child-raising skills. Both proposals were temporarily instituted and then revoked, apparently in response to public protest.[63] Nevertheless, they remain a striking example of the gendered nature of pragmatist education for real life. While in al-Husri's world view, the feminine-governed household represented particularity, fragmentation, and attachment to local difference, in the pragmatist vision it promised to be a homogenizing force, the one universal environment found in every corner of the nation. But this national uniformity would be produced through the difference of sex.

Changing the Subject of Schooling: The Child-Centered Curriculum

In the pragmatists' view, education was not about transmitting knowledge from one generation to another, which they were fond of denigrating as "stuffing children's heads with facts."[64] Instead, it was about developing the whole child—mentally, physically, and morally. Akrawi wrote:

The giving of information can under no circumstances be considered the fundamental aim of primary education. The aim can be nothing less than the reconstruction of the whole life and behavior of the child along lines that will lead to his physical, psychological and social moral growth. Information in order to be functional and useful must be translated into action.[65]

Thus, in opposing "bookish" education, the pragmatists were not simply—contrary to al-Husri's assertions—calling for vocational schooling. They were also drawing on insights from the emerging discipline of psychology, including those related to the stages of child development.

Popkewitz writes that for pragmatists:

Designing the interior of the child entailed a new materiality of time. The child was located in the history of development, growth and learning. . . . Childhood was given chronological ages and developmental stages. The idea of individual differences and changes in body and mind gave the child a progression that could be mapped and administered through purposeful, orderly and goal-directed actions.[66]

In Iraq, a major pragmatist criticism was that the primary school curriculum was organized according to subject matter instead of according to the stages of child development. Each teacher was an expert in a particular subject, and taught that subject to all grade levels, rather than being an expert in a particular age of childhood who would teach all subjects to the same grade. The result was "an over-emphasis on subject-matter. With every teacher considering only the teaching of his own subject little attention is paid naturally to character education. Individual knowledge and care of each child is relegated to the background."[67] In addition, schools taught too much information in each subject, and at too "academic" a level for young children.[68] Each subject was taught according to the rational and method-ological traditions of the discipline from which it was derived, rather than according to the disciplinary knowledges of child psychology and develop-ment. Pragmatists often opposed the terms "logical" and "psychological," treating them as synonyms for the old and new approaches to learning. For example, Akrawi wrote that teaching in the Iraqi primary school "is logical, following the organization of science, rather than psychological to suit the mentality of children."[69]

The new approach called for the slowing down of time in the primary school classroom, as part of the temporal lengthening of childhood itself and the suppression of precocity. The primary school should avoid the "anarchy of those who rush time by teaching the greatest quantity of material in the shortest possible time."[70] The overly academic nature of the primary cur-riculum was connected by many pragmatists to a more general ignorance about children in Iraqi society. Because Iraqi teachers and mothers did not understand the psychology of children, so the argument went, Iraqi children did not act like children. Akrawi complained that they did not even *look* like children. He wrote that they affect an "assumed air of seriousness" and a "grown-up look" on their faces, attitudes that are "unlevel, unnatural and stifle their spontaneity." And even their spontaneous behavior was too adult-like, including, for instance, a "very common use of profane language."[71] If

Iraqi children did not appear to live their childhoods the way that American psychologists said that childhoods should be lived, the problem was that Iraqi adults did not understand what a child is.

One implication of the growing importance of psychology as a social science discipline was a greatly heightened interest in the earliest stages of human development. Of course, al-Husri had devoted his life to the education of the nation's children, and had based the Arab nationalist dream on it as well. But he was concerned most of all with adolescents and young adults (*shabab*). The pragmatists were far more interested in preschool children than he was, and they also argued for the strong prioritization of primary over secondary education. Indeed, al-Husri compared the Monroe Report's recommendations, rather convincingly, to European colonial policy in this regard. While it was widely, and correctly, believed that the British had feared secondary education in Iraq because they thought it would produce nationalists,[72] the pragmatists insisted that their own argument for privileging primary education was based on the discovery by modern psychology of the importance of the child's earliest years. Unfortunately for their argument, the Monroe Report had explicitly warned against the continued expansion of secondary education in Iraq, since "we have a very definite impression that a surplus of academically prepared youth will become a menace to the political stability of any country. In several countries of the Orient such a situation is now quite obvious."[73]

Al-Husri penned a devastating response to this ill-fated passage of the Monroe Report in one of his open letters to Paul Monroe. "Do you believe that 'political stability' is in the best interests of any country under any circumstances? Could you enlighten us on just which countries of the Orient have fallen into political or social troubles due to their surplus of educated citizens?"[74] Al-Husri argued that countries under the control of colonial or other powers that did not rule in the nation's interests were best served not by stability but by revolution (*inqilab*). Only a government that ruled "in light of the genuine aspirations of the nation" could credibly claim that political stability was in that nation's interests, and such a government would have nothing to fear from educating its citizens beyond the age of early childhood.

I will concede to you that a surplus of educated citizens may lead to instability in the first type of political situation, but I believe you will concede to me that this is not the kind of stability that is in the genuine interests of the nation. . . . You are no doubt aware that most countries of the Orient have come under the rule or influence of European states.[75]

Finally, al-Husri chided Monroe by pointing out that, "as you know," the number of students enrolled in intermediate schools in Iraq in 1932 barely exceeded 2,000, the number at the preparatory level of secondary school was under 300, and the total number of secondary school graduates since the Iraqi state was established had not yet reached 700. By way of comparison, "if secondary education had expanded in our country at the rate it has expanded in yours, the number of our secondary school students would now be 125,000."[76]

Paul Monroe's earlier reports on other education systems provide some support for al-Husri's suspicion that the commission was recycling preexisting narratives in its evaluation of Iraqi schools and students. During tours of the Philippines in 1913 and 1925, Monroe had observed a "hostility toward all forms of manual work" and toward "trade and agricultural schools" among the local population, and warned of the "social and political discontent" fueled by the over-availability of secondary education.[77] In 1916, we find him reporting on the "prejudices of the Latin American people against trade and industry," and applauding efforts to reduce the number of "educated men with no other outlet for their activities than political agitation."[78] In 1922 and 1926, he was commenting on the total "inadequacy" of the Chinese inclination toward "literary education," and the challenges posed by China's overly politicized students.[79]

Notwithstanding its suspect affinity with European colonial policy, the pragmatist emphasis on early childhood education was also based, at least in part, on the different understandings of child development and psychology outlined above. These understandings, like the other aspects of pragmatist pedagogy examined here, would have special implications for the schooling of Iraqi girls. In a 1938 radio address on "the child and the nation," al-Jamali asserted that "modern psychology has established definitively the importance of the first years of the child's life and its influence on his spiritual, moral, and mental life in future ages."[80] Thus, mothers need education to raise healthy children. "The ignorant mother, no matter how noble her feelings and how well-intentioned she is about raising her child, will not be able to fulfill the responsibilities that healthy child-raising demands of her; motherly instincts in humans are not enough to raise a child, as they are in animals." According to al-Jamali, this was especially a problem among the poor.[81]

Against al-Husri, the pragmatists insisted that interventions of public institutions such as schools and the military would never be enough, because they simply came too late in the child's life. Akrawi criticized al-Husri's 1922 primary school curriculum for "moral and civic information" for not taking seriously the school's role in reforming family relations. "Aside from certain stereotyped notions about the love of parents, brothers and sisters, and about society, there is little in the course to stir the thinking of the pupil about his family life and about his social environment."[82] For the new educators, the elimination of the stagnant familial space at the heart of the nation was essential to the cultivation of healthy citizens, in part because they saw the earliest years of childhood as critical for the child's future development. Deviations during this stage, usually due to some failing of the mother, were difficult if not impossible to correct later. In these arguments, a central aim of school reform itself was thus the reform of the family.

Learning by Doing, or the Activity-Based Curriculum

A final difference in the approach of the new educators was their emphasis on activity-based learning. They criticized current pedagogies in Iraqi classrooms for being too "academic," "scholarly," or "bookish." Related complaints were that students were "passive" while the teacher was "active"; teaching was "oral" rather than "activity-based"; and learning was about "memorization" rather than "problem-solving." Al-Jamali wrote:

The present curriculum lacks direct bearing on the social and economic life of the people to-day. It is mainly literary and non-practical. . . . There is a maximum of inert memory work and a minimum of activity and thinking. There is a maximum of imposing orders on children from without and a minimum of developing individual initiative and group planning. With such an educational machinery at work there should be little wonder if the product were a group of nonproducers dependent on the government for their livelihood.[83]

The pragmatists regularly mixed criticisms of "literary" or "academic" education with criticisms of "inert memory work," as if the two things were self-evidently identical. But there was a coherent reasoning running through such arguments. They consistently advocated pedagogical techniques that motivated students to "activity," by which they usually meant physical activity to cultivate a habit or capability, and classroom experiences that related to real life, by which they usually meant either habituation to modern hygienic practices or training for future manual labor (agricultural, industrial, or domestic). As the Monroe Report put it: "The village or farm boy particularly learns by seeing and doing. His best education can not come from books. . . . Schoolroom work of an academic character should have a definite place, but a subordinate one."[84]

The disparaging of memorization, and the championing of an activity-based approach in its stead, did not necessarily signify an attack by the forces of democratization and individualism on authority and despotism.[85] How teaching practices based on an active, real-life approach could be employed to foster a different *kind* of discipline among children is vividly illustrated in the following observation by a mission of the American Council on Education, which toured Iraq in the mid-1940s under the direction of Akrawi.

In one village school first-grade children were being given a practical lesson in the use of soap; those whose use of it was ineffective were sent back to the water tap to clean their hands and faces. The Commission found this a refreshing departure from the predominantly academic and detached-from-life atmosphere of the schools.[86]

The problem with the typical Iraqi classroom was not so much that children were being controlled by their teachers, but that they were being controlled in a nonproductive way, one that did not compel them to *action*.

As a pedagogical technique, memorization has not fared well with pragmatists in any country, and Iraqi educators saw it as the cause of many harmful effects. First, it was viewed as passive rather than active and therefore as damaging to the development of the child's agency. A 1951 UNESCO report explained that since the current "methods of learning" in Iraq were based on memorization, students "do not appear to have opportunities of acquiring a sense of individual responsibility through the exercise of their own initiative."[87] Memorization was regularly linked to "verbalism," or "oralism," which was associated with idleness. A regularly recycled narrative was that Iraqi education was derived from "the traditional Arabic mullah school," where students "memorized religious lore in a monotonous and repetitive manner. Traces of this verbal technique are still obvious in many primary schools."[88] According to al-Husri, the campaign against verbalism reached the point that some Iraqi enthusiasts of "practical pedagogy" (*al-tarbiya al-faʿila*) suggested that whenever a student asked the teacher a question, the teacher should tell the student to look it up in a book—to which al-Husri responded in exasperation that asking a teacher a question was not inherently less valid as a means of knowledge-seeking than asking a book the same question.[89] But for many pragmatists, speaking and listening hardly counted as activity. The UNESCO report commented that in Iraqi classrooms "there is little activity on the part of the children apart from incredibly quick oral response."[90] Similarly, the Monroe Report criticized "the existing type of school work which . . . results for the most part in verbal knowledge alone [and] contains very little which leads to the formation of moral habits." Pedagogy in Iraq was concerned solely with students' intellectual development while failing to recognize "that, after all, the sole purpose of intellectual development is the more rational direction of conduct."[91]

In some ways, the contrast between verbalism as damaging and reading as healthy might seem contradictory to parallel attacks on the overly bookish curriculum. And indeed, well into the 1950s development experts would express ambivalence about the spread of literacy in Iraq, which they considered essential to effective governance but also potentially dangerous, especially in light of the spread of communism. But beyond this political ambivalence, there was arguably a continuum drawn in pragmatist forms of reasoning between passive and active experiences of learning, which placed speaking, listening, and memorization on one end and physical activity and habit formation on the other, with reading somewhere in between. No pragmatist educator would have seriously advocated that the school system tolerate the production of illiterates, and few phrased the new philosophy in terms quite as vulgar as those of an infamous 1952 World Bank report, which proposed the transformation of Iraq's existing "book schools" into "work schools."[92] But it was a characteristic feature of all the educators I am labeling "pragmatist" to argue that literacy was secondary to the formation of healthy habits and the "more rational direction of conduct." As the Monroe Report commented, in less inflammatory terms than those used by the World Bank: "sane, healthy and illiterate children are more fortunate than anemic and unhealthy youth who can read and write."[93]

Another way of thinking about pragmatist abhorrence for memorization is to ask whether the capacity to forget may have become a virtue to be cultivated in children. Popkewitz argues that *action* in pragmatist thought was understood in a very specific sense as action linked to "temporal sequences geared to the future." The agentive sensibility cultivated by activity-based pedagogies was one that experienced everyday life as "planned events in regulated time, with *the past discarded as a hindrance* to the progress of the future."[94] The interiorization of agency in this conception involved the capacity to distance oneself both from one's past and from local identifications. The need for the agentive, future-directed citizen moving through linear time to forget local temporalities, affiliations, histories, and narratives might help to explain how certain techniques of cultivating memory skills were seen by pragmatist educators not only as useless or a waste of school time but as actively damaging to the child's capacity to interiorize agency.

In pragmatist theory, the "cosmopolitan individual" was one who had learned how to "actively intervene in his or her own development and thus guarantee the progress of the nation."[95] This reflected a dual conception of reason as "both an object of public scrutiny and a private inner mode of conduct to order everyday life." It was concern over this latter facet of reason—its quotidian interiority in relation to both mental and bodily habits—that drove the search for pedagogical techniques to redesign "the interior of the child who would 'reason' and become a reasonable citizen."[96] Popkewitz's analysis of pragmatist pedagogy is useful in part because it emphasizes aspects of the American conception of reason in the late 19th and early 20th centuries that derived from but were also distinguished from earlier Enlightenment forms of rationality. These differences were connected to the sociopolitical disorder caused by the crises of capitalism in this period and the related emergence of the concept of universal compulsory education. Educators searched for pedagogical techniques that would help "eliminate the dangers of those who challenged the search for order and harmony." Inserting the child into temporal stages of development helped to "render the characteristics of the child . . . amenable to government."[97]

Schooling and Sexual Difference

The pragmatist advocacy of an activity-based curriculum had a number of implications for female education. First, it shaped approaches to the actual study of home economics. Those with a more "academic" conception of schooling might also advocate domestic education for girls, as al-Husri ultimately did, but they were more likely to view home economics as what US historian Rima Apple calls a gendered form of "liberal arts education."[98] This implied a broad-based academic education for women in addition to training in domestic skills. The idea was partly to produce modern companionate wives for middle-class men. It was also linked to the conception of science as discrete bodies of knowledge—rather than a "process of enacting life"—and the related notion that women had to acquire knowledge of the hard sciences in order to effectively manage a family. Al-Husri recalled an

Iraqi educator who had quipped that girls needed only to be taught "house-cleaning-ology" and "cooking-ology" (*kansulujiya wa-tabakhulujiya*), and countered this "demagogy" with the argument that

the usual methods of cleaning and cooking in the country were completely contrary to the principles of health, and in need of development and reform on a scientific basis; the housewives of the future needed to know these principles of health that were not possible to really understand except by learning something of physiology, just as the mothers of the future needed to know many things about the best methods of raising children, and the correct understanding of these methods required knowing not a few things about the facts of psychology.[99]

Al-Husri's belief in women's need for a broad scientific education was one basis for his contention that proposals to make the girls' curriculum "fundamentally different" from that of boys "could in no way be justified. . . . The differences between the curriculum of the girls' and boys' schools must be limited to matters that are relevant to the special circumstances of girls. . . . It is not reasonable for the studies to differ from one other in substance."[100] Proponents of an activity-based curriculum felt differently, often advocating a more vocational understanding of home economics. An article on home economics in *al-Mu'allim al-Jadid* explained:

We live in a scientific age in which experiment and experience prevail, which respects machines and manual labor, and which has made these the pillars of modern science. . . . The practice of material and manual housework and its study in schools is not considered a strange or lowly affair in this age. . . . In this age, development [*al-tatawwur*] pervades all fields of work.[101]

A second way that the emphasis on activity-based learning shaped girls' education was that it increased reformers' interest in what were understood as female-specific skills. Women were often seen as inherently more attuned than men to the nonintellectual, activity-based process of conduct formation that lay at the heart of pragmatist pedagogy. The Monroe Report explained:

The fixing of habits by training is always a more fundamental process in education than the imparting of ideals through instruction, more fundamental than training in the skills of reading, writing and arithmetic, which is practically all that the conventional school does. These statements do not ignore the fact that in Moslem lands women and girls receive a very fundamental training in customs, habits and moral conduct. But the fixing of proper habits by training is far more effective in directing the education of boys in the home than is the formal education given through the school. Hence the importance of educated women for the home.[102]

The belief in women's ability to teach healthy habit formation—or as the Monroe Report put it, to "translate scientific knowledge into the habits and customs of a people"—was also the basis of the recommendation in the UNESCO report that more Iraqi women be hired to teach outside the home in primary schools for boys.[103] Advocacy of a sex-differentiated curriculum should thus not be seen necessarily as an effort to confine future female citizens to the home. Whether they became "teachers, physicians, social workers, public health nurses, physical education specialists," or housewives, schoolgirls were seen by pragmatist educators as the means through which modern subjects would be formed.[104]

The dual effects of the activity-based curriculum on the education of girls—the partial reconceptualization of home economics as vocational training on the one hand and the revaluing of women for their presumed capacity to shape agentive citizens on the other—had complex implications. Within the Ministry of Education in the 1930s and 1940s, home economics was explicitly classified as a type of vocational education, parallel to the other three types—agricultural, commercial, and industrial—that were designed for boys. Thus, starting in the 1930s, specialized "vocational" secondary schools were built for all four types. Yet home economics was unlike the other three in important ways, not least in that, by the mid-1940s, it was taught to all Iraqi girls at every age and level of public schooling, not just to those in the special vocational schools. Contrary to the claims of some reformers, the sex-differentiated curriculum clearly aimed in part at enabling and disabling particular vocational skills and therefore futures. But it also aimed at enabling and disabling certain capabilities, motivations, habits, social behaviors, and mental approaches to problems. This process of enabling and disabling was a process of constructing gendered citizens. Clearly, a girl's sex determined her future vocation in a way that a boy's sex did not, at least not by itself. But the vocation in question was also different from other vocations. It was frequently depicted as timeless, a product of nature as much as history, which is why its future relevance could be assumed for all girls in spite of the widely felt acceleration of historical time and unpredictability of modern futures.[105] It was synonymous with modern femininity itself—not just a set of technical skills or disciplinary knowledges but a whole mode of being in the world, prior to and constitutive of the mode of being known as citizenship.

The Gendering of School Time

The years 1932 and 1952 marked two turning points in which the ministry committed to redirecting its efforts to orient female education around domestic skills. In both years, the project involved collaboration between Iraqi officials and foreign experts. The shift in 1932, and the general trajectory of home economics in the school system until the mid-1940s, focused mainly on girls in primary school. The 1952 campaign targeted female students at the secondary and higher education levels, and will be examined in more detail in Chapter 4.

In primary school, the sex-differentiated curriculum was built partly through increasing the time and overhauling the content of "drawing and manual arts." This subject existed prior to the interventions of the pragmatists, but became one of the focal points of their interest as it seemed the most amenable to a child-centered, activity-based, sex-differentiated pedagogy. In 1928, it was allotted a total of eleven periods in the six years of primary school, and these decreased as the pupil progressed from first to sixth grade.[106] It was seen primarily as a way to develop motor skills in young children.[107] It constituted less than 7 percent of the time a child spent in primary school, which placed it sixth behind Arabic, math, geography and history, English, and religion.[108] In the 1930s and 1940s, this subject became increasingly differentiated by sex as its time in the schedule steadily lengthened. For girls, it covered "needlework and embroidery, knitting, and making such things as doilies, aprons, and baby clothes. They also learn how to wash and clean clothes, polish windows and furniture, and prepare the tea table," in addition to "other home economics subjects." Boys worked with "colored paper, cardboard, plasticine, straw and palm leaves, and wood, making toylike things, leading to more useful objects later."[109] By the 1945–46 school year, drawing and manual arts comprised twenty-two periods of primary school, third behind Arabic and math, and its time increased rather than decreased as the pupil advanced from first to sixth grade. Rather than teaching young children motor skills, it now seemed designed in large part to produce sexual difference as the child developed. The additional time in the curriculum was created by reducing the periods of Arabic, English, geography and history, and religion. Besides math, the only subjects whose allotted time was not affected were the other three activity-based, real-life subjects privileged by the pragmatists: object lessons and hygiene, civics and morals, and physical education and singing. The last of these was also differentiated by sex, so that an Iraqi girl now followed a female-only curriculum for approximately 20 percent of the time she spent in primary school.[110]

Home economics at the secondary school level developed in two different ways, neither of which had much impact on the lives of most Iraqi schoolgirls until the mid-1940s or even early 1950s. One was the foundation of home economics secondary schools as vocational schools parallel to the academic secondary school system and open to female graduates of primary school. The first of these was established in Baghdad in 1932 with an enrollment of 53 girls. Its main function was to train teachers for the girls' primary schools, a role that became even more important as these schools expanded their home economics curriculum.[111] In 1946, its mission was modified to encompass the "dual purpose" of producing teachers and "intelligent homemakers," and in 1952, the mission was modified again so that the school's aim was "first and foremost" to prepare future homemakers.[112] The school—at least in official discourse and actual curriculum—thus moved further and further away from the concept of vocational training for feminine occupations outside the home and toward the notion of homemaking as the primary vocation for which the school existed. Yet it is clear that no more than a tiny fraction of future Iraqi homemakers were expected to attend this school, and in that sense officials could not have been very optimistic about its impact on society as a direct form of vocational training. Moreover, whatever the school's mission might claim, its graduates remained in high demand as primary and intermediate school teachers and as recruits for the higher teacher training colleges and the Queen 'Aliya College for women.[113] The modifications in the school's mission thus represented a discursive and political shift that also had effects on the content of girls' education, rather than any real change in the likely futures of its graduates. In the early 1950s, additional vocational home economics schools were established in numerous Iraqi provinces to supplement the one in Baghdad, and between 1952 and 1958, the number of students attending these schools increased more than tenfold, from 236 to 2,528.[114] In 1953, their number of yearly graduates began to exceed that of the women's primary teacher training institutes, the other main source of female teachers for Iraq's elementary schools, and by 1955, it exceeded the combined total of the women's primary and secondary teacher training institutes.[115]

The second way home economics was introduced into the secondary school system, starting in the 1940s, was through the modification of the girls' curriculum in the regular ("academic") secondary schools. Curriculum

revisions in 1940 and 1943 added two mandatory periods in home economics per year for the three years of intermediate school and the two years of
preparatory school, in both the literary and scientific tracks. They covered
"sewing, embroidery, knitting, cooking and home cleaning in a more developed form than in the previous years."[116] As in primary school, the curriculum became more differentiated as the student advanced through the grade
levels. In addition to the two core home economics courses now required
for all five years of secondary school, girls at the preparatory school level
(the final two years of secondary education) were required to take additional
specialized courses. Those in the scientific track took two periods covering
medical aspects of child care and hygiene, while those in the literary track
took four periods in child psychology and development.[117] The new classes
on home economics and child care in the girls' science curriculum were
particularly controversial, since most of the female students in the scientific
track were preparing for public exams to enter college science programs, in
competition with boys who did not have similar requirements.

At the higher education level, the Queen 'Aliya College for women in
Baghdad, established in 1945, overhauled its curriculum starting in 1952,
changing its areas of specialization from literature, chemistry, social work,
geography, history, and physics to home arts, education, English, fine arts,
and secretarial work.[118] The proponents of the change justified it in part
by pointing to the fact that most of Iraq's postsecondary institutions were
coeducational, and by this time women were studying alongside men at
the colleges of arts and sciences, fine arts, chemistry, law, engineering, and
economics.[119] Thus it was argued that women who wished to specialize
in academic subjects could enroll in one of those colleges. Yet it had long
been recognized that many Iraqis would not send their daughters to a coeducational college, which was why Queen 'Aliya had been established in
the first place. Throughout the late 1940s and 1950s, the majority of Iraqi
women pursuing higher education were enrolled either at Queen 'Aliya or
the women's higher teacher training college, and slightly more at the former
than the latter.[120] These were also the two main sources of teachers for the
girls' secondary schools.

Foreign, especially US, advisors had enough influence on the gendering of the Iraqi school experience from the 1930s through the 1950s
that it became standard in bureaucratic narratives of the "history of Iraqi
education" to assert that much of the impetus behind the shift had come
from them.[121] Nevertheless, the primary motivations were local, and they

were increasingly political as much as economic. In particular, the ministry's 1952 campaign to expand home economics requirements at the secondary and higher education levels was driven by the growing sense among officials that the female education system was not only failing in its primary mission of schooling future mothers capable of raising agentive and governable citizens, but that it was having a rather contrary effect: producing a generation of educated Iraqi women who were *resistant* to marriage, domesticity, and motherhood, and who evidently believed that they could better serve the nation's interests by overthrowing the existing political order than by learning how to efficiently manage a household. A clear subtext, and often the explicit context, of many of the discussions around the "crisis of girls' education" in these years was the deepening political unrest of Iraqi society, especially the widespread popularity of the Iraqi Communist Party among youth.

4

The Stage of Adolescence and the Marriage Crisis

A 1948 ARTICLE IN THE Ministry of Education's journal, *al-Mu'allim al-Jadid*, sounded what by then was a familiar warning.

Psychologists agree that the secondary level of education corresponds to the most important and the most dangerous stage of development [*al-numu*], which these psychologists call the stage of adolescence [*al-murahaqa*] or the stage of youth [*al-shabab*]. This is the stage of transition from the age of childhood to the age of maturity. . . . It is characterized by a multitude of problems and a confusion of ideas. . . . If those traversing this stage do not have people whose mission it is to provide them guidance and direction . . . the consequences will be dire and the future unknown. The stage of adolescence is a stage of revolution.[1]

The disturbing political implications of the association of adolescence with revolution could be quite explicit. Two years earlier, an article in *al-Mu'allim al-Jadid* had criticized the history curriculum for teaching the 1789 French Revolution in secondary school, precisely when the student was "traversing one of the most critical stages of his life—the stage of adolescence. It is no exaggeration to say that this is itself a stage of revolution." By "stuffing students' heads with the events of the French Revolution at this critical stage of their development," secondary schools were fomenting a "psychological revolution" (*thawra nafsiyya*) in the souls of Iraqi youth that, even if repressed for the moment, "will inevitably explode one day."[2]

As elsewhere in the postwar world, the growing concern over adolescence as not only a psychologically precarious but also a politically revolutionary stage of life was frequently connected to the emergence of sexual desires after puberty. A 1954 article explained that during this stage the individual "lives in a world full of dreams, fantasies, and illusions because of the emergence of sexual instincts." Great care must thus be taken "lest the boy or girl go astray, develop psychological complexes, and become a danger to himself and his society." Political, social, and sexual deviances in adulthood could all be traced back to unresolved psychological complexes in adolescence, which explained the proliferation in Iraq of individuals afflicted with "strange concepts" and "moral and sexual perversity."[3]

There were continuities as well as ruptures between these and earlier narratives. Already in the 1920s, as we have seen, British officials had linked the political and the sexual mischief of adolescent Iraqi schoolboys. And of course the mandate system itself was based on connections drawn between national development and human psychological development that located both Iraq and Iraqis in an adolescent stage. Recapitulation theory, along with the newly psychologized concept of adolescence that it helped shape, was from its inception a means of managing the global historical crises of colonialism and race relations in the early 20th century. Both colonial and anticolonial discourses in Hashimite Iraq were thus inevitably riven with the tensions, homologies, and incommensurabilities of the spatio-temporal category of adolescence, which was simultaneously normalizing and constitutively conflictual.

While British mandate and independent Hashimite narratives on adolescence were both rooted in the global psychologization of human life in the 20th century, there were differences, linked to the transformation and expansion of psychology as a discipline over the intervening years. In 1935, Sati' al-Husri wrote that "our century has been called the age of the child," but "the coming age will be the age of youth" (al-shabab), whose education now "requires at least as much commitment as that of children, if not more." The growing conviction among "intellectuals and scientists" that "the years of true moral education are not the years of childhood but the stage of youth" was rooted in the discovery that "many psychological instincts do not emerge until after puberty" (al-murahaqa), and that whatever "moral education that can be taught in childhood may be obliterated under the torrent" of such instincts.[4] In the 1920s and 1930s, al-Husri and other educators still used al-murahaqa primarily to mean the event of puberty, but by the 1940s it came to refer more frequently to "adolescence" as an extended stage of life, partially displacing the terms al-shabab (youth) and al-fityan (juvenile). As

Omnia El Shakry notes for Egypt, the new use of the word worked to distinguish educational literature engaged with the latest psychological theories from "the more popular writings of the mainstream press" that continued to employ the older terms, reflecting the increasingly central role played by psychology, across the globe, "in processes of adolescent normalization."[5] By the mid-1940s, adolescence had been "reconfigured as a psychological stage of social adjustment, sexual repression, and existential anomie."[6] El Shakry connects the uses of adolescent psychology in Egypt partly to the mass student demonstrations of the 1930s. Psychology helped construct adolescence "as both a collective temporality and a depoliticized individual interiority," opening up space for "collective politicization" to be replaced by "individualized psychology."[7]

In El Shakry's study, the adolescent subject of such interventions was "most often male."[8] In this chapter, I focus on the female adolescent subject as a concern of reformers in postwar Iraq. Many warned that managing the turbulence endemic to the stage of adolescence was at least as critical for females as males, if not more so.[9] These concerns were linked to other moral and sexual crises prominent in postwar discourse, including the marriage crisis, an antipathy to conjugal life that had purportedly reached alarming dimensions among Iraqi youth of both sexes and all classes, but especially among educated youth in urban areas. If adolescence was when developmental deviations were most likely to occur, marriage was a stabilizing temporal milestone, evidence of the successful traversing of this volatile stage.

The intertwined crises of adolescence and marriage shaped the expansion of home economics requirements for female secondary school and college students in the postwar era. In the 1952–53 school year, the Ministry of Education launched its most comprehensive campaign yet to restructure the schooling of adolescent girls around their sexual difference, with the aim of preparing them for the demands, and orienting them toward the pleasures, of future conjugal life. As with the interwar reforms of the girls' primary school curriculum, the postwar overhaul of the curriculum for female secondary school and college students drew on pragmatist vocabularies of "education for real life" and "learning by doing." They were also driven by Cold War concerns around the spread of communism and by the emerging body of global economic development expertise.

A New Generation? A Note on Terminology

The years from 1932 to 1958 were marked by urban and rural revolts, several military coups, and a few halfhearted attempts to revise the Iraqi-British treaty of independence of 1930, none of which seemed to satisfy the country's increasingly politicized and mobilized population. Urban youth played a prominent role in political protests throughout these years; student demonstrations in Baghdad sparked the two most famous uprisings of the period, the 1948 Wathba and the 1952 Intifada, and many participants in both events were teenagers.[10] Young people, especially students, were also the dominant force in the underground but, by the late 1940s, extremely popular Iraqi Communist Party (ICP).[11]

From the perspective of leading Iraqi education officials, something clearly went wrong with public schooling in the late interwar and early postwar years. Rather than molding a broader nationalist elite in those officials' own image, Iraq's schools seem to have produced a generation of leftist activists who self-identified as their staunchest opponents. But the schools did not do so only by producing a "class" or "generation" of overeducated and underemployed graduates, which has been a dominant explanatory framework. This explanation cannot fully account for how Iraqi students themselves, especially at the secondary level, were mobilized during these years, often at great personal cost. The somewhat unidirectional narrative additionally offered by Hanna Batatu—in which students were radicalized by their teachers, in part through the ICP's strategic infiltration of the teacher training colleges—also has limitations.[12] More suggestive is Orit Bashkin's inversion of this causal logic: it was the "radicalization of students" in postwar Iraq that "produced radical teachers."[13]

There were ways in which secondary schooling itself—and not just the content of the curriculum, the radicalization of teachers, or the underemployment of graduates—contributed to the phenomenon of youth insurgency in late Hashimite Iraq. Some of these factors were local while others resonated across the postwar globe; needless to say, Iraq's elite classes were not alone in confronting various "problems" of youth in this period. Youth insurgency was everywhere influenced by local and global struggles over decolonization, and was enabled by the expansion of public secondary schooling, which had greatly deepened the political capacities of generational affiliations. This, of course, was partly what British mandate officials in the 1920s and US advisors from the 1930s on had warned incessantly against.

The notion that there are "groups of people related horizontally to one another in terms of demarcated periods of linear history" is, as Lisa Rofel writes, a modern feat of imagination. That these groups "can be attributed shared experiences and characteristics makes sense only when the modernist idea of progress—of always overcoming and surpassing that which came before—appears and takes hold."[14] But I would add to Rofel's account that the emergence of horizontal generational affiliations is not only an imaginative process but also an institutional one. The expansion of national school systems actually produced "shared experiences and characteristics" among many individuals of the same age in the process of producing their capacities to imagine that they shared them.

This framework may help elucidate my use of terms such as "youth" and "generation," which are often uncritically linked to modernization-as-Westernization narratives. References to a "new generation"—which in Iraq scholarship is sometimes called the "young *effendiyya*"—often seem to relate more to identifying a "Westernized" segment of the population at a particular moment in time than they do to defining other kinds of generational change.[15] For example, there is considerable evidence that a sociopolitical and generational rupture of some importance occurred in Iraq during and around World War II, from the Rashid 'Ali coup and consequent British invasion in 1941 to the partition of Palestine and the Wathba rebellion in 1948. This is generally accepted by historians of Iraq—and for that matter by Iraqis, who still refer to "the generation of '58" to describe the now elderly cohort that came of age after World War II and is often seen as the driving force behind the 1958 revolution. For the category "generation" to be useful for an understanding of the country's history that does not simply reinscribe that history within a modern/traditional (or, worse, Western/traditional) binary, it needs to take such ruptures as defining. That is, "generation" should describe an age cohort that has some affiliational characteristics and sensibilities beyond those that would seem to apply to any Westernized segment of any non-Western country at any historical moment. Otherwise, "the new generation" and "the young *effendiyya*" become just more ways of spatializing time, making those who are Westernized by definition "new" and "young."

Familial Ties and Youth Insurgency

It is often assumed that family bonds work against schools and other modern public institutions that are often said to promote horizontal identifications, and that families will thus function as brakes on political mobilization. This assumption is based on the notion of the family as a conservative or traditional institution that binds its members to one another through vertical ties.[16] Yet familial bonds and networks can work horizontally within as well as vertically across the category of age, or any other category for that matter. Communist politicization in Iraq often traveled through extended-family networks, as a number of scholars have noted.[17] While more research on this is needed, I suggest that intragenerational kinship bonds in particular—that is, those between siblings and cousins—may have often worked as relays both for the dissemination of leftist political ideas and sensibilities and for the consolidation of a broader self-identification of the nation's youth, especially literate youth in urban areas, as an age cohort. Family structures in postwar Iraq, rather than being simply undermined by the broader, extrafamilial generational alliances produced by schooling and print culture, were often reworked by and integrated into those new alliances. The mobilities generated by this intermixing of different social relationships fueled Iraqi officials' increasing sense of a "family crisis" that threatened the political order and their well-laid plans to forge a stable path toward sovereignty and development.

In Iraq, as elsewhere, the spread of compulsory public schooling was partly a response to the politically mobilizing capacities of intergenerational alliances, including familial ones. As Donzelot writes of 19th-century France, universal compulsory education was part of a broader "normalization of the adult-child relationship" that sought "to reduce the sociopolitical capacity of the [laboring] strata by breaking the initiatory ties that existed between children and adults, the autarchic transmission of skills, the freedom of movement and of agitation that resulted from the loosening of ancient communal constraints."[18] It was "a struggle against these popular enclaves that allowed for autonomous ties between the generations."[19] The aim was not the destruction of the family but rather its "autonomization . . . with respect to the old allegiances and networks of solidarity,"[20] that is, its reorganization and privatization around the conjugal couple and the education of children. Public schooling thus aimed in part at the undermining of intergenerational forms of affiliation and of class-based mobilizations. But by mid-century it had unintended, even if frequently predicted, consequences around the world: namely, the rapid spread of political mobilizations along the axis of age.

Bushra Perto and Mubejel Baban, two young leaders of the communist women's league at the time of the revolution with whom I conducted interviews in 2007 and 2008, both denied, independently and adamantly, that the public schools they attended in the 1940s and 1950s had any influence on their politicization. Their memories were of a generationally defined political milieu, in relation to which school administrators and teachers were, almost by definition, the enemy. Only when I mentioned that many Iraqi teachers in this period were known to be communists did Perto remember, with apparent surprise, specific teachers she had known as a student who were, or were rumored to be, communists.

Perto and Baban also told very similar stories about what *were* the main avenues of their politicization, namely, sibling bonds and private reading. To my question about whether she first learned about politics at school, Perto responded:

No. It was not the influence of the schools [that led me to] politics, nothing of that sort. It was my brother's influence on me, to turn to politics. I have an older brother, six years older than me, and I was very friendly with him, he looked after me, really . . . since I was very young. He was inclined to a political atmosphere. And he used to collect, I remember, pictures of personalities—you know, prime ministers, ministers, I don't know. And I was a very small child [*laughs*], not even in primary school . . . and he was telling me: "This is so-and-so, this is so-and-so." And asking me always: "Who's this?" You know, examining me. And because I liked my brother very much, I was following him a lot. . . . He was telling me all about things, and so I had that in mind, you know, all these politics. And the first time I heard about communism it was from him.[21]

The next step in Perto's self-narrative of politicization was a journey into reading, via a conspiratorial relation with a leftist bookseller in Kirkuk.

I was passing through the suq and I saw—I [already] had in mind things about communism—and I saw some books . . . and I began to go there and take books from [the bookseller], borrow them, because I could not buy them. My father would not—he would see them, you know. So I took the books; I would read them, hide them, read them, and then take them back.[22]

Baban narrated her own introduction to politics, at age eleven or twelve, in strikingly similar terms.

The thing is, my eldest brother, he had TB, and they had to send him to Lebanon. . . . Lebanon was the place where cultured people lived, poets and thinkers and everything. It seems he met very left-wing people there. He stayed a year. When he came back—that was '46, something like that—when he came back, he came back with huge boxes of books. He used to give them to us: "Read! Read!" [*Smiles and mimics handing books out to a crowd*]. . . . This was after the Second World War, all the democratic ideas flourished and people started reading and reading and knowing what was going on in the world.[23]

Perto's and Baban's narratives of politicization both point toward the early formation of sensibilities, through sibling bonds of love, that oriented them toward leftist thought. This was followed by the development of more re- fined political sensibilities through reading, which had nothing to do with the official curriculum but which did presuppose their literacy, a capability that both girls owed to the public school system. The practice of reading was believed by many members of this generation to be a special and revered Iraqi pastime. According to a well-known Arabic saying of the mid-20th century: "Cairo writes, Beirut publishes, Baghdad reads." Uttered in Egypt or Lebanon, the aphorism may have connoted a friendly teasing of Iraqis for the supposed backwardness of their literary production sector. But in Iraq, it was repeated with pride.[24]

The political mobilization of both young women, nevertheless, did occur through Baghdad's secondary schools and colleges, where they joined underground communist student organizations in the early 1950s. The school system was important to the functioning of the male wing of the party, but even more so to its female wing. As Batatu writes, secondary schools and colleges "were the chief springs that fed the female contingent of the party."[25] Baban joined a party cell at her secondary school in Bagh- dad. Perto became an official party member as a student at the college of chemistry; at her girls' secondary school, she recalls, she had "only ten or fifteen" friends who were communists.[26]

In 1952, female members of the ICP established a women's "popular front" organization, Rabitat al-Difa' 'an Huquq al-Mar'a (League for the Defense of Women's Rights), known locally as al-Rabita or the League, which mobilized the existing women's branch of the ICP to recruit mem- bers both inside and outside the party. The driving force behind the group's formation was Naziha al-Dulaimi, a gynecologist in Baghdad. It seems that she used her medical practice to recruit women into al-Rabita, including Mubejel Baban, who met al-Dulaimi when she went to the communist doctor's office, escorted by her brother, for a medical issue.[27]

The 1952 Intifada, which shook the regime to its foundation, involved large sections of the population. But students provided the initial spark, in the form of a protest against an unpopular dean at Baghdad's coeducational college of chemistry.[28] Bushra Perto was a leader of the demonstration that sparked the Intifada and one of two students expelled from the college of chemistry as a consequence.[29] In the crackdown that followed the uprising, emergency law was once again declared, political prisoners rounded up, censorship of the press tightened, and a "police mentality" came to dominate all government institutions, including and perhaps especially the schools.[30]

As discussed in Chapter 2, the interwar period had already seen the introduction of mandatory military education for boys in public schools. In the post-Intifada years, military training became an openly punitive method for rehabilitating politically transgressive youth. Male secondary school students exhibiting leftist sentiments were incarcerated in military boot camps for the summer; repeat offenders were expelled from school and conscripted directly into the army. Once there, they were soon discovered, perhaps not surprisingly, to pose an even greater threat than they had in school, and military leaders demanded funding for special camps to keep them segregated from the other soldiers.[31]

As the military camps for male leftist students expanded, the Ministry of Education instituted summer work programs for female secondary school students. These aimed to channel the free time of adolescent girls into social work rather than politics by involving them in "campaigns for the protection of morals" or sending them into rural areas to teach literacy and provide "social guidance" to women, such as those on the Dujayla Land Settlement Project examined in Chapter 5. It was hoped that these activities would improve girls' physical health and cultivate a sense of responsibility toward "the society and the nation." If the government could "build the social character of the female student," it would make the next generation of Iraqi women "aware that the nation was in dire need of them."[32]

The Crisis of Girls' Education

In September 1953, a year after the Intifada and the foundation of al-Rabita, *al-Muʿallim al-Jadid* devoted a special issue to the perceived crisis of girls' education in Iraq. As one article explained the problem:

For a quarter of a century we have forgotten, or have pretended to have forgotten, the difference between the woman and the man. . . . The result is that we have given the Iraqi woman a masculine education. . . . She has now forgotten that she is a woman . . . and a class of women has appeared in Iraq who despise cooking, housework, and child-draising. . . . We have made women bad at marriage and motherhood.[33]

Historically speaking, the argument had a few holes. As it happened, it was in September 1928—exactly one quarter of a century earlier—that a sex-differentiated curriculum was *introduced* at a national level in Iraq's school system, with the addition of the first official home economics requirement in girls' primary schools. Moreover, by 1953, no female student in Iraq's primary or secondary public school system was receiving a "masculine" education. Only when she reached the college level could an Iraqi woman receive the same public education as her male counterpart, and even then only outside of Queen 'Aliya College and the women's higher teacher training college, where most women at this level were enrolled. But the issue was obviously not about historical research. It was about the radicalization of youth in the postwar era, and the sense that this trend was at least as prevalent and potentially even more dangerous among female youth.

In contrast to articles on most other topics in the ministry's journal, *al-Mu'allim al-Jadid*, those on the perils of adolescence almost always went to the trouble of spelling out both the female and male Arabic forms of nouns for students. A 1954 article, titled "Tilmidhat wa-Talamidh al-Madaris al-Thanawiyya wa-Awqat al-Faragh" (Female and male secondary school students and free time), insisted on the need to regulate the extracurricular time of girls and boys (*fatayat wa-fityan*). The author explains that at a time when "education has become an art derived from psychology, and scientists and educators have delimited the stages of life in order to fulfill each person's educational needs, the stage of adolescence" has been recognized as "one of the most important and most dangerous" stages of development.[34] The article criticized both the school system's "lack of concern with the stage of adolescence" inside the school and its failure to regulate the "free time" (*awqat al-faragh*) of students outside of school by filling it with activities "to cultivate the minds, bodies, and souls of girls and boys."[35] The age-horizontal identifications fostered by schooling and the postwar spread of print culture and other forms of entertainment, especially the cinema, had combined to facilitate dangerous mobilities for adolescents once they exited the schoolyard. The author made the familiar critique of the "strictly theoretical education" purportedly provided in Iraq's secondary schools, calling for an end to their "social and cultural isolation" by engaging students in extracurricular social service projects.[36] Covering all his bases, he attributed to Aristotle the notion that "the aim of education is to help people utilize their free time in the best manner"; reminded his readers that, in the view of religion, "idle hours are Satan's hours"; and explained that the most "fundamental principle of secondary education" in the developed nations was to teach youth "the best way of using their free time," which was why the "modern" American high school was so interested in the extracurricular activities of its students.[37]

Other commentators asserted that managing the psychosocial turbulence of adolescence was even more critical for girls than for boys. 'Abd al-Rahman al-Bazzaz called on the government to monitor "all of the social and cultural activities" of youth, including the films, books, magazines, and "pocket novels" they consume, since they all have "an active influence in shaping the mind of a boy or a girl." But this was especially true for girls, "because every girl is a potential mother [*umm muhtamala*] and as such she will become the cornerstone of social life. . . . She will instill morality or depravity in her children . . . and thus controls the fate of the coming generations."[38] Al-Bazzaz contrasted *al-ta'lim* (education or knowledge) with *al-tathqif*, the latter connoting pedagogical cultivation with a more moralizing and civilizing orientation. It was the latter type of education, based on "spiritual guidance and refined morals," that Iraqi women needed, if schools were not to simply "increase the confusion and backwardness of the society."

I do not know which is more beneficial to our society today, and which is more graced with good values: an illiterate village woman who has preserved her natural beauty . . . and has a sense of duty toward her home and her village; or an educated, made-up woman who is not guided by any moral standards, who thinks it is her right to blindly imitate the Western woman and to achieve complete freedom, who enjoys smoking, drinking, gambling, and staying up late, and who frequents every locality with no decency.[39]

The school system must immediately reorient female education around moral character development, al-Bazzaz warned, since Iraq's current "band of educated women" (*al-nafar min al-mut'allimat*) was on the verge of becoming a "social calamity" (*baliya ijtima'iyya*).[40] The spread of communism in girls' secondary schools was more a context than a subtext of the article; al-Bazzaz blamed "materialist philosophies" for propagating the notion among schoolgirls that "acknowledging a woman's femininity" was a "sign of reactionism and backwardness," an effort to "enslave" women and "destroy her rights."[41]

In the 1953 special issue, and in other articles in *al-Mu'allim al-Jadid* in the early 1950s, proposals to address the crisis of girls' education were actually diverse and creative, ranging from greater attention to religious study to new classes in sex education.[42] But in the end, the ministry's primary solutions were oddly familiar: more differentiation on the basis of sex in the curriculum, and more attention to real-life instead of academic learning in girls' schools. Thus, even the curriculum in the vocational home economics secondary schools was now discovered to be too academic, and a new one was drafted, "with the aim of reducing the hours of theory and increasing the hours of practice, so that the graduate of this school is first and foremost a housewife."[43] In fact, as discussed in the previous chapter, this and other changes to the girls' education system had been introduced in 1952, a year before the publication of the special issue, which thus appears to be more of a post facto justification of the reforms than a set of proposals to confront a newly discovered crisis.

Religious Morality and the Marriage Crisis

If the activity-based curriculum was now embraced with greater enthusiasm than ever, the oft-repeated pragmatist ideals of fostering curiosity and independent thinking were now seen to have gone too far, at least for female students. This approach had produced a generation of Iraqi women who "love adventure"—much like the United States of America loves adventure, one writer suggested.[44] The challenge was how to teach women stability and sobriety in moral and political life while also teaching them flexibility and openness to change in everyday mentality. One solution was to join the discourse of pragmatism with that of cultural authenticity. Thus, Minister of Education 'Abd al-Hamid Kazim asserted in 1957 that the point of modern schooling was "to organize the individual's natural motivations" and "to build a whole, developed [mutanami] character," but that the character Iraqi schools sought to develop was "an Arab Islamic Iraqi character." Educators should look to their own history for tools to build that character, rather than relying solely on the advice of "foreign delegations."[45]

One of the ironies is that Western pedagogical approaches were now blamed for the purported focus on academic rather than real-life learning in Iraq's schools, which had filled girls' heads with frivolous and/or rebellious notions. Al-Bazzaz called for overhauling the female secondary school curriculum around home economics by arguing that while a detached-from-life type of learning might work for the advanced nations (al-umum al-raqiyya), whose citizens had the luxury of pursuing knowledge for its own sake, it was dangerous for the developing countries (al-duwal al-nashi'a). "The theory of knowledge for knowledge's sake, education for education's sake, art for art's sake . . . might be appropriate for some of the advanced countries . . . but it is not appropriate for us today."[46] Yet this reasoning echoed decades of criticism of the Iraqi school system made by Western experts, and was deployed for the same purpose: to argue that an Iraqi girl's education should be determined by her sex and focus on domestic and child-raising skills.

In a similar vein, some articles in the 1953 special issue proposed the expansion of Islamic education in public schools to instill morality in female students. "We need to give the religious sphere sufficient attention in order to root out these reckless tendencies that have taken hold of the minds of female students."[47] These calls were accompanied by careful disavowals of Islamic pedagogies that were inattentive to the production of sexual difference and inappropriate for a developing nation. In their introduction to the special issue, the editors invoked the familiar refrains that modern schooling must avoid repetition, memorization, and "learning by heart," all well-established codes for criticizing Islamic pedagogies. These practices were not merely useless but actively harmful for a nation seeking development, because they "killed [students'] capabilities" and worked to create "a dependent, weak generation [*jil ittikali mutakhadhil*] unable to stand on its own feet in the battlefield of life."[48] What a developing nation needed were moral pedagogies to foster young people's "physical and psychological development [*al-numu al-nafsani wa-l-jusmani*] according to the differences between the two sexes."[49]

The crisis of girls' education was related to the "marriage crisis" (*azmat al-zawaj*), in response to which the Ministry of Education launched a "campaign against singlehood" (*muharabat al-'uzuba*). Besides the expansion of home economics requirements in girls' schools, proposals included higher taxes on single adults, family law reform to counter "the anarchy of divorce and polygamy," national contests and prizes for mothers, and uses of print media, the cinema, and religious institutions to promote the joys of conjugality.[50] The marriage crisis discourse was prominent in debates around the need for a unified national family law, which culminated in a draft law presented to the Chamber of Deputies in their 1946–47 session.[51] This law was not passed, but it formed the basis of the 1959 personal status law promulgated after the revolution.

The term "marriage crisis" or its equivalent in other languages, used to describe a perceived society-threatening antipathy to marital life, has appeared as a preoccupation of reformers across a wide range of historical contexts, from 15th-century Saxony to 19th-century Russia to the

21st-century United States.[52] But the heyday of marriage crises was undoubtedly the 20th century, when their number seemed to correspond pretty closely to the number of nation-states and nationalist movements on the planet.[53] Despite the apparently global reach of the 20th-century marriage crisis phenomenon, that is, each particular crisis seems to have unfolded strictly within its own territorial borders, as if marriage and the nation-state had become so intertwined that the concept of a "global marriage crisis" would be nonsensical.

In her work on the 1930s marriage crisis in Egypt, Hanan Kholoussy reads increasingly prevalent condemnations of "bachelorhood" less as genuine concerns over marital life than as metaphorical discourses invoked "to critique larger socioeconomic and political turmoil and to envision a postcolonial nation free of social ills."[54] In Iraq, the campaign against singlehood was also seen by reformers as necessary for true political sovereignty and economic development, and it may well have had little relation to an empirical increase in the number of single adults in Iraqi society, as Kholoussy suggests in the case of Egypt. But it does not seem on those grounds to have been very metaphorical. Rather, its aim was to *normalize* marriage, to transform singlehood from an exceptional state that some people live in by choice or circumstance into a psychological deviance and a social problem.[55] This is why the campaign was waged most concertedly by the Ministry of Education rather than any other ministry. It was not the aim of these reformers to encourage students to marry; on the contrary, the expansion of secondary schooling depended on delaying marriage beyond the age of adolescence. But it was their aim to cultivate in youth the desires and capabilities required for the future construction of conjugal, monogamous, child-centered families and thereby to stabilize the temporal stages of both psychological and national development.

Home Economics in the Age of Development

The 1952 Intifada and the ongoing popularity of communism among Iraqi youth constituted one context of the overhaul of the female secondary school curriculum in the 1952–53 school year. Another was the emerging global field of economic development expertise. An article in the 1953 special issue of *al-Muʿallim al-Jadid* on girls' education explained: "Today education is considered a means of forming the new life. . . . Education itself is a productive economic activity. It is through education that individuals, and likewise the nation, can combat poverty and achieve a high standard of living."[56] The article described two spheres of national economic life: the public sphere of the man, based on production, and the domestic sphere of the woman, based on consumption. Education must be centered on the differences between the sexes and on these different needs of a modern society.[57]

Recognizing the role of sexual difference in economic development, the government had already invited the Food and Agricultural Organization (FAO) of the United Nations to send an expert in home economics to suggest improvements in the girls' secondary school curriculum. The 1952 FAO report produced by this expert repeated the argument made by the Monroe Commission twenty years earlier, that the Iraqi school system was not sufficiently differentiated by sex, and recommended the qualitative improvement and quantitative expansion of home economics in the girls' curriculum. Thus, either ignoring or oblivious to the fact that female students were already required to study home economics at every grade level, it proposed that

the curriculum for girls' schools should not be patterned on that designed for boys but should be suited to their special needs in life. It should provide them with a broad general education and also fit them for homemaking. Part of their schooling should therefore deal with subjects such as food, clothing, shelter, family relationships and child development.[58]

While it is not unusual for foreign experts to discover their particular area of expertise to be lacking in the country to which they are sent, the report also suggests a shift in the dominant conceptualization of home economics in the postwar period.

For underdeveloped countries like Iraq, the most important topics subsumed under the category of home economics after World War II were hygiene, nutrition, household budgeting, the psychological development of children, and consumer sciences. A more detailed FAO report two years later, in 1954, explained:

The present [home economics] programs in [Iraqi] secondary schools emphasize only needlework and child care and very little attention is given to the broader fields of nutrition and family feeding, household management and family economics, the physical, mental and emotional development of children, household furnishings and equipment and textiles and clothing. Provision needs to be made by the Government of Iraq for the inclusion of this training in the elementary and secondary schools and in selected institutions of higher learning.[59]

One aspect of the shift was a conceptual reorientation of women's household labor from the sphere of production to that of consumption. Thus, while the current secondary school home economics curriculum in Iraq, established in 1943, covered "sewing, embroidery, knitting, cooking and home cleaning," the FAO now recommended that "more attention be given in schools to clothing selection, dress design and textiles, and that less emphasis be placed on embroidery."[60] The education of intelligent female consumers in the selection and purchase of manufactured textiles should be based on the "results of research conducted in universities, government departments and industries [in the United States, Canada and Europe] on fibers and fabrics, textile finishes and textile strength etc along with courses on art principles and design."[61]

In addition to recommending changes in the content of home economics education, the FAO proposed a dramatic expansion of the mandatory time devoted to it, especially in secondary schools. Specifically, the 1952 report recommended that girls in Iraq's preparatory schools, in both the literary and scientific tracks, be required to study home economics for 20 percent of the time they spent in school, up from 6 to 7 percent of the current curriculum and from 0 percent ten years earlier.[62] This is a remarkable proposal, especially given the controversy in the early 1940s over the addition of *any* home economics requirements to the female preparatory school curriculum, especially in the scientific track, where most students were preparing for higher education in competition with boys who did not have similar requirements.[63] It is difficult to imagine how its implementation would not have impacted an Iraqi girl's chances of scoring high enough in the public school examinations to enter one of the country's science colleges, all of which were coeducational.

The author of the report, Ava Milam, was the dean of the School of Domestic Science and Art at Oregon Agricultural College, and something of an American home economics missionary during the first decade of the Cold War. Prior to arriving in Baghdad, she had helped establish programs in China, Korea, the Philippines, and Syria. She worked in Iraq for several months in 1951 and 1952, visiting primary and secondary schools and serving as a consultant for Queen 'Aliya College, before writing the report. Curiously, she later claimed in her memoirs that the female educators she worked with in Iraq faced opposition from "conservative" male officials who "violently opposed" teaching subjects such as political science to women.[64] Milam may be referring to an earlier (nonviolent) public debate over the content of a political science textbook, which preceded and had nothing to do with her work in Iraq. In any case, writing for an American audience in 1969, the author neglects to mention that her own primary recommendation to the Iraqi government in 1952 was to significantly *reduce* the study of academic subjects, including political science, for all girls in Iraq's secondary schools. In the intervening years, the American second-wave feminist movement had launched its attack on sex-based home economics requirements in public schools, which would be banned by law in 1972 with the passage of Title IX. Between Milam's 1952 report and her 1969 memoirs, then, neither the use of women's status to index a nation's progress and modernity nor the relative locations of Iraq and the United States on the resulting spatio-temporal map of the world had changed. What *had* changed were the dominant American conceptions of progress and modernity. This is how, looking back in 1969, Milam could simply suggest—without needing to explain—that her work in Iraq in 1952 had the effect of expanding academic educational opportunities for Iraqi women, the exact opposite of its actual intent as well as its actual effect.

In the end, the 1952 FAO proposal was never fully implemented, at least in part because it required a large increase in the number of female secondary school teachers qualified to teach home economics, and this target was not reached prior to the 1958 revolution.[65] But Milam and other FAO experts were involved in the initial stages of the post-1952 project to expand home economics requirements in Iraq's schools.

Disciplinary and Revolutionary Time

The notion that the nation's development depended on blocking the proliferation of psychological deviances through the cultivation of modern sexual difference may have received its most controversial elaboration with the 1954 publication of *Wu'az al-Salatin* (The sultans' preachers) by the prominent Iraqi sociologist 'Ali al-Wardi. The book attributed the development of Western nations in part to the regulated mixing of women and men in the public sphere and the consequent low rate of homosexuality in those nations, and the underdevelopment of Arab societies to the segregation of women, which had led to a prevalence of both male and female same-sex practices. In any society that "secludes women, there will be a proliferation of sexual deviances such as sodomy, tribadism, and the like," since "when nature is blocked from reaching its goal . . . it must strive toward it by a deviant path." Al-Wardi asserts that deviance is a social law and that "it will appear inevitably in any society that segregates women from men."[66]

As Afsaneh Najmabadi has shown for Iran, projects to cultivate modern sexual difference were also projects to cultivate modern sexual desire, as "the heteronormalization of eros and sex became a condition of 'achieving modernity.'"[67] These discourses were somewhat different from those of European and American social science writings since the 19th century that had produced the homosexual as "a species," in Foucault's famous words. In Iraq, as in Iran, "modernists were optimists; they imagined that sex-gender heterosocialization ... would redirect men's sexual desires away from young males onto females, and that women, once satisfied by the heterosexualized men, would have no reason to turn to other women."[68] Yet sexual deviance was also seen in Iraq as an individual pathology caused by unresolved psychological turmoil in adolescence. That this turmoil originated in the social structure did not mean that its effects were easily reversible in adulthood, since, as al-Wardi writes, habits and values "buried in the unconscious do not disappear quickly, and perhaps stay with the person until the day he dies."[69]

Being a social law, al-Wardi continues, sexual deviance is immune to moral persuasion. The sultans' preachers of the book's title are those "who think they can prevent deviance with words and admonitions."[70] Ignoring the discoveries of Freud and other psychologists that "preaching only affects the conscious mind," while human conduct is guided primarily by "unconscious drives rooted in psychological and social conditions," they fail to understand that "neither religion nor conscience" can control desire.[71] When a person does try to abandon his habits through the power of "will, thought, or reason," he instead develops a psychological complex, a split personality, produced by the gap between his morals and his actions.[72]

Al-Wardi's argument helps to clarify the particular directions taken by many Iraqi reformers' disavowals of existing Islam even as they sought to mobilize a renovated Islam for the cultivation of modern sexual difference and desire. These disavowals can be grouped into two lines of critique. First, reformers from al-Husri in the 1920s to al-Wardi in the 1950s attacked what they saw as the scholastic preoccupation of Islamic thinkers in their time with abstract texts, ideas, and speech that worked only on the planes of reason and the conscious mind, rather than on those of the body and the unconscious, and were therefore ineffective. Second, they criticized Islamic pedagogies such as memorization and the "blind" practice of rituals, which *did* work on the planes of the body and the unconscious and *were* effective, namely in producing mindless fanatics dependent on external authority rather than modern, self-disciplined subjects with developed interiorities. The problem for these reformers was thus not that Islam in their time concerned itself strictly with the soul, or perversely with the body, or that it was understood as a collection of ethical pedagogies rather than a set of private beliefs.[73] It was that it failed to provide "education for real life," which meant (1) life that would contribute to the nation's future sovereignty and economic development; and (2) life that moved in its own discrete time through specific psychological stages of development and according to the differences between the two sexes.[74]

Al-Wardi's comparison of "Arab" and "Western" pedagogies centers on how they shape morality and deviance. The Islamic kuttabs produce nothing but "false dignity."[75] But al-Wardi's preachers included all "Platonic" educators, religious and otherwise, who try to change human nature by preaching moral ideals. In fact, "all of our thinkers today" do this, "whether their education is modern or traditional," which is why "the new generation mocks" them all.[76] By failing to relate to the child's real life and relying instead on moral admonitions, public schools had contributed to the flourishing of an ungovernable "children's society" in the alleys of Iraq's cities.[77] Modern Western pedagogies, by contrast, are based on the principle of letting students "dance, play, and laugh, in order to draw their passions into the light of day," where they are easier to influence, rather than leaving them to fester in the darkness.[78] Al-Wardi was particularly impressed by the innovative practice in American colleges of official chaperoned dances, where students' "natural" heterosexual desires can be drawn out and educated under the supervision of their teachers.[79] Left to itself, "difference" leads to anarchy, but inserted into certain spatio-temporal regimes, it fuels positive renewal and change. Indeed, in "modern sociological thought," motion is not a deviation—it is stasis that is a "deviation."[80] If homosexuality is both index and cause of a society in stasis, or deviation, heteronormativity—formed by the education of adolescent desires through their insertion in heterosocial spaces of pedagogy and the developmental time of psychology—is not only a requirement of but the very engine that drives the historical time of national development.

In some ways, al-Wardi's argument resonates with the modern political imaginary that Lee Edelman calls "reproductive futurism," in which history becomes meaningful through the "world-making logic of heterosexual meaningfulness," and politics is "a name for the temporalization of desire, for its translation into a narrative, for its teleological determination."[81] In this discourse, it is the figure of the child that structures "the logic within which the political itself must be thought" and secures the orientation of all politics toward a congenitally receding future.[82] But there were also differences, including the anticolonial one. Al-Wardi—like al-Husri and many other Iraqi intellectuals of the Hashimite era—was highly attuned to and critical of the deferring, depoliticizing, and colonizing moves of certain discourses of progress. He writes: "The preachers of religion have been replaced by the preachers of progress . . . one yelling 'Forward!' and the other 'Backward!' and both trying to paralyze people from solving their actual problems, which are neither ahead of nor behind them."[83]

Al-Wardi's sociological interventions did aim in part at stabilizing the nation's development through pedagogies of heteronormativity, but not at freezing the political present in the name of a child who never grows up and a future that never arrives. This tension in his work sometimes manifested as an ambivalence about the relation between youth and political insurgency, an ambivalence that was also common in the writings of al-Husri. Both thinkers called for modern forms of disciplining adolescents at the same time that they celebrated youth as subjects of anticolonial insurgency. As I have argued elsewhere, concepts of youth and adolescence in the writings of anticolonial intellectuals could never have been simply a repetition or re-enactment of Western discourses about youth, for the simple reason that they were differently located within the global spatio-temporal recapitulation narratives aligning national, racial, and psychological development.[84]

I will explore al-Wardi's conceptions of revolutionary time in more detail in Chapter 7. Here I will just note how this ambivalence about youth and political insurgency sometimes overlapped with another that runs through his work, between religion as a disciplinary system and as a set of practices for cultivating revolutionary sensibilities. For him, the revolutionary potential of religion was especially immanent in Iraqi Shi'ism. Commenting that British mandate officials had also recognized this potential, especially after they confronted it as an actuality in the 1920 rebellion, he writes that they, and Iraqi officials after them, attempted to spread secularism in the country in order to weaken the revolutionary religious sentiments of the southern Shi'i regions, only to discover that their actions would instead create the most revolutionary "new generation" of youth in the Arab world. Thus, "while in Iraq there used to be one sect with a revolutionary inclination, now all of the sects are mixed together willy-nilly in revolution."[85]

5

The Family Farm and the Peculiar Futurist Perspective of Development

ONE OF THE WORLD'S FIRST postwar development projects involving multinational expertise was the Dujayla Land Settlement Project in Iraq, established in 1945. Exploring both the failures and the productive effects of this project reveals a paradox at the heart of development's orientation toward the future. One failure was a form of rapid ecological destruction, salinization of the land, which the planners knew from the beginning threatened the entire project and for which technical solutions were often asserted to be available. Another was the devastating proliferation of disease at Dujayla, a problem for which technical solutions had been made practically impossible by the design of the settlement itself. Among the project's lasting effects were the reconstitution of several thousand rural lives and an expansion of technocratic expertise in both Iraq and the emerging body of international development agencies that identified the family, and women in particular, as a target of rural modernization programs. The paradox I explore is thus the process by which rural families and individual lives at Dujayla were transformed in the name of a distant and universal developed future, while the deterioration of the land and of the settlers' bodies continued along its rapid and unsurprising course to block even a modest local future for those same families and individuals.

Dujayla was designed according to a family-farm model based on early US Cold War modernization and agrarian reform theory, which was oriented toward political stability at least as much as sustainable agricultural productivity, especially in the face of growing nationalist and communist movements in the region.[1] As it happened, the family-farm design of the settlement played a significant role in its two primary failures. The intensive agricultural methods on which the small farms depended, and the lack of a drainage infrastructure to sustain those methods, led to the rapid salinization of the soil, while the distance between the isolated homesteads made it impossible to pump clean water to them, or even to build a shared well for drinking water, fostering the spread of disease among settlers forced to use the same canals for their drinking, irrigation, and sewage needs.

The abysmal failure of the Dujayla Land Settlement Project by nearly every conceivable measure, which a mere two decades after its foundation was contested by no one, has relegated this early flagship experiment in development to the dustbin of world history. But I propose that Dujayla need not be understood merely as an aberration from what were purportedly more successful development projects that followed it, or as a tragic series of beginners' mistakes, as it was ultimately framed in the assessments of the international agencies that played a part in it. It can also be viewed as an amplification of certain trends in early development practice that were to persist in subtler and more "effective" ways in later projects. Andrew Zimmerman has commented that development failures "do not merely give the lie to liberal ideology: they reveal its truth."[2] In many ways, and not least of all in relation to gender and family reform, Dujayla might be seen as the *reductio ad absurdum* of postwar development thought.

Remaking Rural People

According to Darwish al-Haidari, director general of agriculture in Iraq, the Dujayla settlement was "the first project of its kind in the Arab Middle East and the forerunner of a large scale social experiment."[3] Established by the 1945 Law for the Settlement and Cultivation of the Lands of Dujayla (commonly known as the Dujayla law), it was the first in a series of postwar projects that aimed to create a class of small independent landowners in Iraq, by settling landless peasants on underexploited *miri sirf*, or state-owned, lands.[4] In 1951, the law was extended to establish other settlements, grouped under the Miri Sirf Land Development (MSLD) program.[5] Most of the lands, including Dujayla, were located in Iraq's "irrigation zone," the fertile but rain-deprived plain between the Tigris and Euphrates rivers, and had been recently opened to agriculture by the building of large dams and irrigation systems. After the completion of the Kut Barrage, "the showpiece of the government's agricultural and irrigation effort,"[6] water from the Tigris was diverted into the Dujayla Canal, "to convert the semi-desert into 164,000 acres of flow irrigated fertile farm land." The large landowners of the area attempted to "lay hands upon it" by claiming previous occupancy, and in the end the government gave them 76,000 acres, or nearly half of the newly irrigated lands, at the cost of US$5.60 per acre. The remaining 88,000 acres were set aside for the Dujayla Land Settlement Project.[7]

The Dujayla and other MSLD laws reflected a growing interest in developing Iraq's rural areas and population that had gained force in Iraq after formal independence in 1932.[8] These laws aimed not just at the more efficient extraction of resources but also at the reconstruction of rural lives. By the end of World War II, the interest in "the rural question" appeared in the discourses of all government ministries and political parties, and in periodicals, books, novels, and poems across the ideological spectrum. One of the more widely read works on the topic, Ja'far Khayyat's 1950 al-Qarya al-'Iraqiyya: Dirasa fi Ahwaliha wa-Islahiha (The Iraqi village: A study of its conditions and reform), which won a book of the year prize from the Iraqi Academy, explicated a familiar refrain: that "the countryside is the main cause of the whole nation's backwardness," and that it is "governed by the three maladies of the Third World: poverty, ignorance, and disease."[9] Only through an all-out "war" on the "three maladies" could the state hope "to revive the countryside and awaken the village from its deathly slumber."[10] Of the three maladies, however, government projects tended to target ignorance, identifying it as the main cause of the other two. Matta Akrawi, who was trained at Teachers College of Columbia University, explained in an earlier lecture in Baghdad:

The illiterate . . . is not one who is ignorant only of reading and writing. The illiterate is one who is ignorant of his homeland and his nation, ignorant of his patriotic duties and responsibilities. The illiterate is one who has no moral character, who does not know how to behave in a socially acceptable manner and how to live an orderly family life [ya'ish 'isha 'a'iliyya munazzama]. The illiterate is one who does not know how to protect his health or how to earn his daily bread or how to struggle on his own behalf in the battle of life using the most modern and healthy methods.[11]

The increasing urban concern over governance of the rural population was fueled by agrarian revolts and the growing slums of rural migrants in urban areas, especially Baghdad, both of which were responses to increasingly exploitative landlord-peasant relations. Eighty-four percent of peasants migrating to the cities in this period came from Iraq's central and southern regions, the focus of the MSLD program.[12] As one land settlement expert explained: "Excessive migration results in disturbing the harmony of the society, reducing [the people's] income, lowering the standard of living, and disturbing the balance of the population . . . in different parts of the country."[13] The MSLD program was in no small part a response to rural people who were, as Iraqi writer Baqir Muhammad Jawad al-Zujaji put it, "voting with their feet" on the state of national agriculture.[14]

Iraq and the Global Age of Development

The Dujayla settlement was thus launched in 1945 as an Iraqi attempt to cope with some very Iraqi problems. But by the early 1950s, it had attracted the attention of some of the new international and US agencies that were laying the foundation of the global age of development, including the United Nations Educational, Scientific and Cultural Organization (UNESCO), the UN's Food and Agriculture Organization (FAO), the Ford Foundation, and the US Technical Cooperation Administration (TCA), which administered Truman's Point Four program. Much as Iraqi officials conceived of Dujayla as the flagship project of the larger MSLD program, leading planners in these agencies saw that program as a laboratory for the planned development of the world's underdeveloped regions.

There were several reasons Dujayla and subsequent MSLD settlements were regarded by many as an attractive development laboratory. Located 135 miles southeast of Baghdad, Dujayla was part of a "table-flat, dry, treeless plain"; left to its own devices, its "rich alluvial soil is almost barren because of the scant 6-inch annual rainfall," but when properly watered, it "blooms like a Garden of Eden."[15] For Westerners, and perhaps especially for Americans, this reference was more than a metaphor. It drew on the secular trope of ancient Mesopotamia as the "cradle of civilization," but it was also linked to the increasingly widespread Western belief that hidden somewhere on the currently desertified plains of Mesopotamia was the actual geographical site of the biblical Eden.[16] Both narratives gave Iraq "special relevance" in the West as a "fallen cradle of civilization where development would hail a new age of miracles."[17] President Truman himself proclaimed that if the Tigris and Euphrates were developed, there would be "a revival of the Garden of Eden that would take care of thirty million people and feed all the Near East."[18]

Moreover, the image of a vast, underexploited, underpopulated, and fertile land resonated with Americans' view of their own country's history, at a time when anti-collectivist Cold War discourse was breathing new life into the 19th-century American construction of "the self-sufficient farmer as the ideal citizen."[19] The revival of this ideal appeared both in popular American discourse and in the field of technical expertise that grew up around the Point Four program, which designated agrarian reform as the core principle of US-supported development schemes in the Third World, the main battleground of the Cold War by the early 1950s. On the Western side of the Cold War divide, land reform, or agrarian reform, meant the creation of "independent" or "family" farms, preferably while avoiding the confiscation of large landholdings, a sensitive issue given the centrality of private property to Western Cold War discourse.[20] Nathan Citino explains: "Cold Warriors identified land reform as key to America's economic and political goals. Wider distribution of landownership would result in more egalitarian societies immune to radical subversion."[21]

When US officials took notice of Dujayla, they hailed it as "one of the most important and largest scale efforts by a Near Eastern Government to encourage and assist peasants to become owner-operators of family-sized farms."[22] The first US official to visit Dujayla, in 1951, was Norman Burns of the State Department's new Bureau of Near Eastern, South Asian, and African Affairs (NEA).[23] Burns effused that the purpose of the Dujayla law, "like our own Homestead Act of pioneer days," was to provide "for the transfer of state-owned lands to small independent proprietors upon condition of occupancy and use." Dujayla thus

points the way toward a possible solution of the crucial land tenure problem that underlies many of Iraq's political and economic difficulties today. . . . The development of a class of small individual proprietors would fundamentally alter the social-economic structure of the Iraqi population and would, if experience in other countries is a guide, give Iraq the kind of progressive stability that the Middle East needs.[24]

Like many other officials, Burns framed the value of producing a "class of small individual proprietors" less in terms of increasing agricultural productivity than in terms of fostering "the kind of progressive stability that the Middle East needs."

Finally, these narratives were fueled by a growing appreciation of the magnitude of oil revenues that would be available to the Iraqi government for development projects, especially after the renegotiated oil treaty of 1952.[25] The government earmarked 70 percent of this revenue to the Development Board—founded in 1950 but reorganized after the new treaty and subsumed under the Ministry of Development—"to use in programs that would raise the standard of living of the average Iraqi."[26] Western and multinational agencies could thus bypass the thorny question of providing direct financial aid for Iraq's development and focus exclusively on "technical assistance," the core policy laid out in Truman's Point Four speech.

By the early 1950s, this convergence had produced a powerful narrative of Iraqi development exceptionalism. As a Ford Foundation expert explained:

Among the underdeveloped countries of the world Iraq is one of the most fortunate, in her possession of a unique combination of attributes: (1) Significant unused resources. . . . (2) A population small in comparison with those resources. . . . Finally, (3) a large source of foreign exchange in the form of oil revenues, with which Iraq may purchase the capital goods and technical assistance necessary for economic development. . . . Other countries [in the oil-rich Middle East] . . . have one or two of these attributes, but no other has all three.[27]

The enthusiasm is understandable: here was a Western-aligned government ruling over a predominantly poor, rural population in a territory with vast agricultural potential that could actually afford to pay for its own development projects. There could hardly be a more ideal setting for demonstrating to a world increasingly riven by Cold War divisions the viability of the emerging US-led field of Western development expertise. These specialists imagined Iraq as a vast territorial laboratory of raw materials—undeveloped natural and human resources—made available to their experimental interventions through a felicitous convergence of circumstances. For their part, Iraqi officials were well aware of the narrative of their country's development exceptionalism, and helped cultivate it in their requests for technical assistance. As al-Haidari wrote in a report to the FAO: "Iraq possesses the potentialities and the means to promulgate a program of Development, a fact rarely found in most under-developed countries."[28]

Producing Family Farms

In 1950, the Iraqi government issued a statement that the promotion of "small family farm ownership" would guide all future agricultural expansion undertaken by the state.[29] This followed the recommendations of US and UN advisors, who asserted that the size of each plot on the land settlements "should be based on the area which a family can effectively handle under intensive cultivation."[30] It was hoped that this family-based model of land distribution would foster the individual settler's initiative and rationality, encouraging him to stop "wast[ing] time" and "to manage his property and market his produce wisely."[31]

The whole notion of designing, planning, and ultimately producing a class of small independent landowners is inconceivable outside of certain notions about the relation of sexual difference and family structure to agrarian development. But historians have tended to uncritically accept and reproduce a familiar discursive slide in the textual sources, from the terms "independent farmer" to "individual farmer" to "family farmer," as if those modifiers were self-evidently interchangeable. Thus, the slide is allowed to obscure just what it should reveal: that a "dependent" male sharecropper or pastoral nomad becomes a modern "independent" farmer not only as a result of his new and truly individual title to land but also—and just as importantly—by virtue of his legally consolidated control over a woman and children in an often newly defined "family."

The process of selecting Dujayla homesteaders from among the "fifty thousand land-hungry fellahin" who applied for the initial 1,200 tracts of land illustrates this process quite clearly.[32] The committee created by the Dujayla law to oversee the project established a few criteria that helpfully eliminated 47,200 of the applicants from eligibility in a single stroke: the would-be settler must be from the Dujayla province or surrounding areas; he must have previous farming experience; he must be married; he must have at least one child; he must be over eighteen but under fifty years of age; he must never have been convicted of a crime; and he must produce a medical certificate of freedom from incurable infectious diseases.[33] The formulation of these explicit criteria left no doubt of the underlying, semi-implicit one, namely that he must be a "he." Together, they established a legal baseline for what kind of human could conceivably count as an individual in the production of a class of individual farmers in Iraq. Yet in order to be eligible for land ownership, this healthy and civil male candidate for individuality and independence had to promise to settle on that land in the company of at least one woman and one child, and he had to be young to middle-aged himself—that is, an identifiable head of household in a nuclear family, regardless of his current status in what may have been an extended family household. Elders and other extended kin were not banned from Dujayla in the law; their presence was simply not legible in it. And if some were to happen along nonetheless—as in fact thousands would—their very illegibility would ensure their legal and economic powerlessness in the new relations of property and family enacted by the law and the committee.

Settlement of the winning applicants at Dujayla started in 1945, the year the law was passed, with eighty-five families, and within a decade all 1,200 tracts of land had been settled. Each homesteader was provided with 100 dunums (62.5 acres) of "land free of rent and other charges upon occupancy." If he (along with the other members of his family) successfully cultivated the land for ten years, he would receive full legal title to it, without cost, subject to the condition that he "may not sell or otherwise alienate it to any other party for another 10 years after registration" of the title.[34]

In the meantime, the settler's independence was seriously circumscribed through the rules of the settlement contract. He was required to build "from his own resources . . . his farm dwellings for his family and helpers, stables for his corn, etc. according to design by the committee." The committee would "determine the location and number of houses [on each plot] as well as the time period within which construction shall be completed on the units."[35] The settler was required to build his own irrigation ditches joining his plot of land to the larger canals. The committee determined what crops the settler would grow, and how many dunums of land he would devote to each crop. Finally, no settler was "allowed to leave his land or absent himself for more than five days without notifying the responsible officer."[36]

On the ground, there were factors not envisioned in the law, the contract, and the committee's regulations that limited their power to fully determine settlement life. One of the most intractable had to do with pre-existing class relations. The contract required that settlers be free of debt to their previous landlords, which most of them accomplished by obtaining credit at high interest from the merchants of nearby Kut, an exchange that left them deeper in debt than ever by the time they arrived on the settlement. Since a settler's crops were always mortgaged before they were planted, this problem would continuously undermine the ostensible project of fostering his "initiative," including his capacity to rationally market his produce. Other factors obstructing the orderly execution of the plan included the experiences and preferences of the settlers, the shifting advice of the experts, interference from neighboring landowning shaykhs, irrigation and drainage problems, and, last but not least, the land itself. For instance, the contract specified that each settler was to devote two dunums of land to the cultivation of cotton, a cash crop the production and export of which was encouraged by US policy, and a cotton ginnery was accordingly built on the settlement. But the soil did not cooperate; it was "too heavy for cotton, and no cotton [was] grown."[37]

The construction of settler homes also seems to have frequently deviated from the plan:

Actually, one sees a wide variety of houses while driving through the project; some have window frames opening to the public view, with bars for protection; other[s] have no opening to the outside and open only onto the enclosed courtyard. Within the courtyard there is a great variation in the number of rooms and the quality of the accommodations. It seems to depend largely on the financial status of the settler.[38]

It also depended on the number of people who actually settled on the plot: "Part of the deviations seen were undoubtedly caused by the presence of several families living on a single plot of land." Most plots had at least one additional "family," usually described in the literature as that of the "hired assistant or sharecropper," who upon closer inspection often turned out to be the legal proprietor's brother and his household. When the assistant farmer "belongs to the family of the settler, he and his family are likely to live within the compound, which is therefore more crowded. . . . Otherwise, his hut is likely to adjoin the outside wall of the compound or to be located indiscriminately in the areas between the compound and the canal."[39]

It would be a mistake, however, to conclude that such "facts on the ground" determined life on the settlement, and that the plan was therefore ineffectual. One stark example of the plan's power to shape life on the settlement was the layout of farms in units of four, each group one kilometer from the next, and the consequent absence of village life. In fact, villages had been deliberately excluded from Dujayla. The "four-corners" settlement pattern, it was hoped, would "save the fellahin much time in going to and from their fields and avoid the unsanitary congestion of villages."[40] The distance of the four-farm clusters from one another—as well as the deliberate practice of settling a family from one of four different tribal groupings in each corner—was also intended to "reduce public security requirements" and enable "the Government [to] control the settlers' activities."[41] The model of isolated family farms was intended to reduce both the mobilities and the political capacities of the rural poor.

While it is often difficult to hear the voices of settlers in the sources pertaining to Dujayla, on the question of the four-corners settlement plan they come through indirectly. Sattareh Farman, a UN home economics specialist working at Dujayla, reported:

The settlers are deprived [of] group living and they deeply feel the need for a typical Middle Eastern community life which is centered around a shop, a coffee house and other rural social organizations. Since these settlers have been recently imported from the various communities and villages this absence of group living tends to affect their social pattern of life.[42]

Of course, affecting the settlers' "social pattern of life" was the explicit goal of the settlement plan. Yet a US expert similarly wrote:

Unaccustomedly segregated into "4 corners" settlements, families miss village sociability and recreation facilities. No adequate recreational outlets exist—individual center tea houses, like the schools, are often four or more muleback miles from outlying farms. This distance limits demonstration farm activities as well, and prohibits the cross-fertilizing influences of discussion.[43]

Not only did the settlement pattern thus erect formidable barriers to familiar leisure activities for the settlers, it hindered even the social interventions of the specialists.

Perhaps most remarkably of all, the four-corners settlement plan proved counterproductive to the aim most often invoked in its defense: improved sanitation and hygiene. The reason was not difficult to foresee. One American critic explained: "The settlement pattern also precludes the costly piping of pure water into each dwelling. Farmers rely upon the all-purpose irrigation ditch for water, purifying it for drinking with chemicals."[44] In fact, most settlers could not afford water-purification chemicals and did not use them. Moreover, the plan not only precluded the piping of clean water into the homes, but even the digging and use of a shared well for drinking water, such as could be found in any settled Iraqi village.[45] Thus, while experts continued to rail against "peasant ignorance," which was purportedly responsible for the stubborn use of unclean water, the settlement plan itself—which prioritized the creation of isolated family farms over all other development considerations—guaranteed that homesteaders would have no access to any other water source.

Development workers at Dujayla were painfully aware that the lack of villages was a hindrance to social-reform interventions.[46] Indeed, the four-corners plan was a source of controversy throughout the life of the project, and some future land settlements in Iraq would be based on model villages rather than isolated homesteads. But that the plan remained a model for some future settlements in spite of all the known problems associated with it speaks to the importance of the role land settlement was expected to play in reducing rural capacities of mobilization. The attempt to fix settlers on isolated family farms resonates with what Michael Cowen and Robert Shenton posit as the "agrarian doctrine of development" favored by postcolonial regimes across the globe in this period. The overall orientation of the doctrine, the authors argue, was not to foster the capitalist development of agriculture at all.[47] Rather, it was to contain the sociopolitical disorder effected by already existing capitalist development. The function of state-promoted land settlements based on the model of small family or independent farms was to absorb a "relative surplus population" in the countryside, making it responsible for its own subsistence and keeping it away from the cities. Thus, "family farms were 'independent' only in so far as the family farm regulated its own disposition of labour effort."[48]

This is a useful preliminary framework for making some sense out of what otherwise seems to be a pattern of puzzling decisions made by the planners of Dujayla. But in treating the family farm as a given and unitary subject (which, for example, regulates "its own" labor effort), rather than as a porous, shifting, and semi-malleable complex of unequal social relationships, Cowen and Shenton too fail to explore the implications of agrarian development doctrine for different members, and nonmembers, of the family unit on which the small landholding was based. Their analysis also does not address the active process by which, in postwar Iraq at least, government and development agencies *worked* to make members of the family farm responsible for their own subsistence, through social interventions in their everyday practices.

Fundamental Education

In 1950, the Iraqi government invited UNESCO to establish a "fundamental education center" at Dujayla; the agreement was signed in 1951.[49] "Fundamental education" was a UNESO project to educate rural poor people in underdeveloped countries who had not received formal education. In the words of the head of the UNESCO team in Iraq, A. B. Trowbridge, fundamental education "is what the words imply: education of a people to improve by their own efforts their living conditions by getting down to fundamentals. . . . In other words, health, home economics and education must all be the concern of Fundamental Education."[50] The project at Dujayla would teach rural people "the knowledge and skills necessary for good use of their material resources, for home-making, for literacy and for the development of their community life."[51] UNESCO's role was to establish a project on the settlement to demonstrate fundamental education in action, while teaching its principles to Iraqi trainees sent by the Ministry of Education.

The main difference between fundamental education and regular education, an article in *al-Mu'allim al-Jadid* explained, was that the former must work to "correct the deficiencies in the individual who has not had the chance to be educated in school."[52] One of the core deficiencies identified in those who lacked formal schooling was their relationship to time. The initial UNESCO report assessing Dujayla as a pilot site explained:

In formal schooling much emphasis is given to history. It is not often realised that apart from this acquiring of knowledge, there is the question of attitude. Those with . . . a background of education and historical sense differ profoundly from the peasant in their attitude to past, present and future, towards cause and effect. . . . The educated man is, or should, be more objective; he can see time as a sequence. He can study the past and visualize a different future. But the peasant . . . seems to carry the past within him. It thus becomes woven with the present. He cannot look ahead, and does not realize the steps which have brought him to his present position. . . . He is so much more the incapable of seeing the path ahead and the sort of effort required.[53]

UNESCO did not propose to teach Dujayla settlers academic subjects such as history, however. Fundamental education drew heavily on pedagogical vocabularies of education for "real life" and "learning by doing," which, as discussed in Chapter 3, were also seen as inculcating in students an openness to change and the capacity to "see time as a sequence." The techniques of fundamental education, explained the editors of *al-Mu'allim al-Jadid*, "rely on real life, going beyond the walls of the school to the fields and communities, using methods that help [students] accept new ideas, not those based on pure theory or on recitation and rote memorization . . . and that are compatible with what modern Iraq is striving towards."[54]

Since the 1990s, a body of scholarship has emerged that critically examines development projects in the postwar era—especially in Latin American studies but with important works also on sub-Saharan Africa and East and South Asia. A number of these works have argued that postwar development projects worked through the "rendering technical" of development problems, thus attempting to remove such problems from the domain of politics and producing development as what James Ferguson called an "anti-politics machine."[55] In his classic formulation of the rendering-technical argument, Arturo Escobar argued that Truman's Point

Four program and other early development projects focused on the transfer of modern technology to underdeveloped countries, without realizing "that such a transfer would depend not merely on technical elements but on social and cultural factors as well."[56]

My research on Dujayla supports, in some ways, the critique that postwar development projects worked through various logics of depoliticization. However, at Dujayla they did not do so by rendering development problems technical in quite the way that process has often been described. The core principle of what came to be called technical assistance (TA) in this period was not the transfer of agricultural or other technologies from developed to underdeveloped countries. It was the transfer of *technical know-how* by sending experts in a variety of fields, including education, health, agriculture, and home economics, to intervene in the daily lives, habits, and practices of poor people in the target underdeveloped country. It should be remembered that the concept of technical assistance, as laid out for example in Truman's Point Four speech, was opposed not to social or cultural reform but rather to direct financial assistance to governments. In postwar Iraq, foreign technical assistants were far more likely to be trained in the social sciences than in the hard sciences, and this tendency was not specific to UNESCO. In 1952, the highest number of foreign TA personnel working in Iraq across all development agencies specialized in education (thirty-one), followed closely by health and hygiene personnel (twenty-eight); agricultural specialists came third (twenty). Much smaller numbers provided expertise in categories such as water resources (twelve), public services (seven), housing (five), economic development (three), mineral resources (two), and industry (one).[57] While UNESCO was the agency designated to run the pilot fundamental education project at Dujayla, and is thus the focus of this chapter, other foreign development agencies, including those associated with the US Point Four program, ran similar projects on other MLSD settlements in Iraq.[58]

The attention to social reform was consistent with the dominant mood in global development theory, which shifted in the 1950s "toward nonmaterial factors—psychological, behavioral, political."[59] In 1958, US modernization theorist Daniel Lerner asserted that "the problem of stimulating productivity" was no longer seen by "economists and other professional observers" as a fundamentally technical problem, but rather a "psychological one."

Here the political and sociological problems of the Middle East become intertwined with its economic problems. . . . What is required there to "motivate" the isolated and illiterate peasants and tribesmen who compose the bulk of the area's population is to provide them with clues as to what the better things of life might be. Needed there is a massive growth of *imaginativeness* about alternatives to their present lifeways. . . . The issue, in fact, was joined several decades ago. There is a large and growing preoccupation with modern lifeways and major efforts to adapt them to the Middle Eastern situation.[60]

A similar preoccupation ran through the writings of the US-trained Lebanese modernization and agrarian reform theorist Afif Tannous, who was the "leading promoter of land reform in US Middle East policy"[61] and influenced projects in Iraq and elsewhere in the region. Tannous stressed the "essential need," in any agrarian reform project in the Arab world, "for the social scientist to be actively implicated in the program from the beginning. Otherwise, any project of technical aid will run a grave risk of being disrupted, and possibly wrecked, by the ignored forces of local culture, or of creating in the long run more problems than it will have solved."[62]

A new department, the Division of Fundamental Education, was established within the Iraqi Ministry of Education to work with UNESCO on building first the pilot project at Dujayla and then the nationwide program. The division's director, Fu'ad Jamil, explained that fundamental education went "hand in hand" with the "concept of small landholding."[63] Education professor Muhammad Husayn Al Yasin similarly wrote that the purpose of fundamental education was "to work to solve the agrarian problem on the basis of small landholdings distributed to the cultivators, in a way that will assure their stability and well-being and arouse their self-confidence, while at the same time helping to foster innovation and increased production."[64] And the editors of *al-Mu'allim al-Jadid* explained that Iraq's fundamental education program would "enable citizens to achieve industrial, social, and economic progress" by fostering their desire "to acquire the type of knowledge that will help them reform and improve social conditions, and . . . to utilize their free time to increase and diversify production."[65]

The underlying aim of all foreign technical assistance at Dujayla was to produce "independent"—that is, nondependent or self-sufficient—farmers. This meant precisely not providing them with technology or any other material they could not pay for. Members of the UNESCO team were acutely aware of their mandate to cultivate capacities of "self-help" in settlers, and worried constantly that their services might instead foster a "debilitating" reliance on "charity."[66] As one of them explained, the objective was to teach rural people how to "meet [their] immediate needs while utilizing materials and facilities available [to them] rather than depending upon expensive and outside imports."[67] Thus, we "try very hard not to make them dependent on us."[68] The director of the UNESCO children's schools at Dujayla fretted that providing free lunches in school without requiring the children to raise the livestock, grow and harvest the vegetables, cook the meals, set the table, and wash the dishes afterward would produce "spineless dependence on Government or other charity," and the children were accordingly required to do all those things.[69] Trowbridge explained:

Always we try to think how we can help them without giving out as charity the many items they need. . . . The families need practically everything—cloth, shoes for the children, medicines, soap, even food. But we dare not give out gifts of these items for there would be no end to this charity, nor would it solve their problems. . . . All plead for medicine, which we cannot give out except in small quantities.[70]

Conversely, the team rejoiced at any sign that settlers were "realising that self-help is the only solution to pull them out of their low living standards."[71]

Domesticating Women

A branch of development-critique scholarship has looked at issues of women and gender in development, but it has focused almost exclusively on the post-1970 period. In fact, a common refrain in the feminist "post-development" literature is that from 1945 to 1970, the Western "gender stereotypes" dominating development discourse provided a "rationale for ignoring women," and thus that the "issue of women and development entered the development discourse in the 1970s."[72] This is therefore the point at which most critical feminist scholarship on women, gender, and development begins. Even in the rare studies that recognize the early development preoccupation with teaching home economics to poor rural women, this itself is somehow read as evidence of a *lack* of interest in women. For example, Escobar correctly observes that postwar development theory in organizations such as the UN and USAID was based on a "division of intellectual labor: agriculture for men, home economics for women." Yet he then concludes, inexplicably, that this division demonstrates "the invisibility of women in rural development programs."[73] One might wonder in this case why the US and Iraqi governments and UN organizations bothered devoting so much time and money to home economics education for women, especially within rural development programs. In short, when it comes to women, scholars critical of early development projects have too often been content with prescriptive and dismissive critiques based on what they think those projects should have done (gotten women out of the house into paid employment), rather than producing critical historical analyses of what they in fact did. The assumption that there is nothing more to be said about home economics campaigns other than that they aimed at "keeping women in the home" is based on the assumption that both "women" and "the home" are self-explanatory, that they are transhistorical categories.[74]

In November 1951, the first member of the UNESCO team arrived in Iraq, a specialist in home economics from Canada named Margaret Hockin.[75] Her report recommended that the team begin by carrying out a study of home conditions at Dujayla, in order to identify existing "patterns of inter-personal relations within the family and the community." The home visits should use "directed conversations" to extract "facts related to the daily life and work of the women, including evidence of established ways of performing work and those which appear to be most (least) resistant to change."[76]

In 1952, the "second phase" of the project was launched with the arrival of four new UNESCO experts. They included two sisters from Mexico, Noemi and Enriqueta Lopez, specialists in home economics and health, respectively, who had worked on a similar project in Mexico. Their mission at Dujayla was threefold: to establish a school for girls, focused on home economics; to establish a women's health clinic; and to carry out home visits to educate female settlers in modern practices of family care and home management. The Lopez sisters worked with four young Iraqi women who served as translators and trainees, and in 1954 were joined by a home economics expert from Iran, Sattareh Farman.[77]

As the original UNESCO report on Dujayla explained, the creation of a girls' school was necessary because

the young girls must have a program of home economics in which their mothers will take pride; this special schooling in home economics should be compatible with a modi-fied but immediate improvement of home conditions so that the new habits learned at school or clinic will not be lost when they leave school and are subjected to whole time family influences [sic].[78]

The director of the UNESCO team later proclaimed that the girls' school was "our biggest accomplishment" and that "if we did nothing else, this little beginning of education for girls was a wedge into the backward school provisions of Dujaila." Indeed, if the school did not become permanent, "our efforts will have been wasted."[79] Similarly, Al Yasin asserted that the UNESCO girls' school was the Dujayla project that most "inspires optimism and confidence in the future and the capabilities of the people of the coun-tryside" and best illustrates how settlers could "become capable of adapting to the work of development and growth and of marching side by side with the people of the cities in the domain of life."[80]

The home visits were launched under the direction of Noemi Lopez, assisted by the Iraqi trainees. The hope was that "if we could educate at least one woman in every home, she would be capable of influencing her family and improving its living conditions."[81] They gave advice on "housework, sanitation, hand work and home industries (knitting of socks, cutting out and sewing of garments, etc.) to women and children."[82] They also provided some vaccinations, but the health aspects of the home visits focused pri-marily on teaching "cleanliness of person, house and farm yard," including modern techniques of "washing clothes and babies."[83] When it seemed at the start of one year that no female Iraqi trainees would be sent to Dujayla, Trowbridge lamented: "If we cannot get women [trainees] some serious thinking must be done for the whole future program in Iraq. . . . Why make plans for Fundamental Education centers in all the liwas if we cannot foresee staffing any of them with women workers?"[84]

According to the UNESCO reports, Dujayla women were not that interested in the foreigners' advice on family issues. But they avidly sought out health services and advice. The women's health clinic run by Enriqueta Lopez with the help of Iraqi trainees was reportedly frequented by an aver-age of fifty to sixty people per day, as "farmers and their wives [rode] in from great distances" to "receive treatment as well as the education which always accompanies Miss Lopez' work."[85] In a translated article published in *al-Mu'allim al-Jadid*, the Lopez sisters wrote:

Our objective was to guide and direct [the inhabitants], with the aim of enabling them to solve their family problems by themselves. But it became clear to us that they would not be convinced of the importance of what we were asking them to do in this regard, unless we focused first on providing them with what they most urgently needed. We knew it was in our capacity to respond to these demands of theirs, and in that way to earn their trust and support for our [other] aims. . . . These poor and ignorant people were in dire need of health education above all else.[86]

Similarly, Enriqueta Lopez told the *Iraq Times*, in an article on Dujayla titled "Iraq Builds its Future," that "treating their urgent pains and fears is only the first step to making friends of them; and making friends of them is only the first step to educating them into habits of cleanliness and commonsense."[87]

The narrative in which foreign development workers stumbled upon health care as the first step toward earning the trust of settlers, especially women, was a recurring one. Warren Adams, who conducted fieldwork at Dujayla as part of his PhD dissertation at Berkeley, similarly wrote that "although medical clinical work was not originally planned [at Dujayla], it soon became obvious that one of the primary local concerns was along medical lines. As a way of developing interest and following, the [UNESCO] team found itself engaged in medical work, for which it acquired a wide reputation among the settlers."[88] Yet most of those who "found" themselves providing medical care to settlers, such as Enriqueta Lopez, were health specialists who had been sent by UNESCO for that purpose. Margaret Hockin's initial proposal for Dujayla had noted that

health services (educational and clinical) will be welcomed in the area and represent such an important and natural approach to the education of women that, in the initial stages at least, all other educational programmes should be based on these services. Homemaking education . . . is obviously dependent upon health services and will be radically handicapped, if not rendered totally ineffective, unless such are provided.[89]

Indeed, the health-care technique, notwithstanding its regular rediscovery by development workers on the ground, was a core principle of postwar development doctrine. A 1958 article in *Middle East Journal* on Iraqi village life, written by an anthropologist working in Iraq on a Ford Foundation grant, explains the reasoning:

If a hospital or dispensary were set up with the sole object of curing villagers it would have a minimal effect in bringing about the social change which is the ultimate goal of any rural development program. If, however, the hospital or dispensary were looked upon as an opening wedge in village development and took upon itself some of the functions of an educational institution it might very well have some of the far reaching effects desired. . . . Thus the medical facility must, at first, function as a dispensary to treat disease, a school to modify understanding of the peasants, and a police force to insure that minimal standards are being practiced.[90]

The main point of the health-care discovery narrative seems to have been the insistence that the provision of medical care was always *only* the first step, that it was not offered for its own sake but as the opening wedge of social and cultural development: first a dispensary, then a school, and finally a police force.

Despite UNESCO's prioritization of health care, health problems at Dujayla remained the source of endless suffering for the settlers and endless frustration for the development workers. It was often observed that the treatments provided by Enriqueta Lopez at the women's clinic were usually ineffective, since "once cured, the people will certainly be contaminated again within a few days or weeks by drinking the polluted water from the canals."[91] The combination of the widely scattered plots and the lack of a proper drainage system made sanitation problems practically impossible to solve. The poverty and indebtedness of the settlers meant that most could not purchase chlorine pills, which UNESCO offered for sale rather than giving away.[92] The scarcity of wood and other fuel meant that most settlers could not afford to boil their drinking water.[93] The lack of drainage ditches meant not only the ongoing salinization of the soil but also that the latrines built by UNESCO were useless due to the ever-rising water table.

The campaign to build latrines was a dismal failure, for the water level is so close to the surface that about 1½ meters down water begins to collect in any hole dug. The results are not impressive when a latrine is built, and the farmers say: "I will build a latrine if you tell me to, but I shall [then have to] move my house a kilometer away." We can scarcely blame them for feeling this way, and all we can do is tell them not to use the canals as latrines.[94]

But the other option available to settlers, using the fields as latrines, was not much better. Due to the high water table and the fact that the same canals were used for irrigation and field drainage, both human and animal waste in the fields found its way into the canals soon enough.

Technical awareness of the structural problems posed by the settlement plan was thus ever-present for development workers. Certainly it was common knowledge among both settlers and technocrats at Dujayla that the diseases from which most of the inhabitants and their children suffered—especially bilharzia, trachoma, and malaria—were spread by the irrigation canals. As Trowbridge wrote: "Most of the sicknesses come from drinking impure water, direct from the canals, the only water there is."[95] Adams similarly noted that the settlers "are forced to drink and use the canal water, with all of the incipient infection. The settlers themselves are well aware of the fact that they get Bilharzia from the water of the canals, but they have no other alternative."[96] Yet it is typical in development writings on Dujayla for the explicitly stated knowledge that the settlers are "well aware" of the source of the problem to be soon forgotten, and for the spread of disease to be blamed, once again, on rural ignorance. Thus, Adams writes later in the same work that the diseases found at Dujayla are the "common rural ones of

Iraq" such as bilharzia, tuberculosis, malaria, and trachoma, and that "most of these are diseases are associated with ignorance, poverty, and filth."[97]

Unlike other development programs, Trowbridge wrote, fundamental education attempted to "deal simultaneously with the several *causes* of social ills, trying to heal them at the *sources*. . . . Our mission would try to see what caused undernourished bodies and what can be done about it."[98] Despite all the formidable technical obstacles to health and hygiene that development workers at Dujayla couldn't help but notice, what they found to be the ultimate sources and root causes of the many diseased bodies on the settlement were not political, economic, environmental, or technological conditions but local human ignorance and underdevelopment, especially of women. The production of independent farmers at Dujayla meant the production of farmers with healthy bodies and citizenly sensibilities who would neither flee to the cities nor be dependent on the government for assistance, much less look toward larger political or socioeconomic reform. And an "independent farmer" was by definition a "family farmer," in part because he had a wife who could be mobilized, via techniques of modern domesticity, to cultivate the family's economic, psychological, and bodily nondependence. After all, "healthy bodies would not need extra feeding at school nor would they be prone to be tubercular."[99] Development problems at Dujayla were indeed rendered technical, in the sense that they were rendered amenable to the interventions of specialists applying new knowledge techniques. But an examination of the techniques that were most strongly prioritized, in both theory and practice, shows how they were also rendered social, and in particular how they were rendered feminine.

The Time and Space of Development

The perpetual return to "ignorance" as an explanation for diseased rural bodies was integral to the very temporality of development, in which neither the historicity of rural lives nor that of their environment (houses, canals, soil, microbes, etc.) was truly legible. When the foreign technical assistants arrived at Dujayla, what they found were the very problems they had been trained to solve.

Three out of four [settlers] suffered from bilharzia, a debilitating water-borne disease characterized by slow bleeding, and other diseases were also rife. *This was where the team had to start*; out of health activities would come not only confidence in the team but an interest in clean water, clean bodies, better homes and food, even reading and writing.[100]

The temporality of development required that the team of experts start at what for them was the beginning: rural ignorance of modern health and hygiene precepts. This, in turn, predisposed them to forget, over and over again, the fact that the settlers' bodies, habits, and lives were powerfully shaped and in important ways determined by the settlement itself.

What I want to suggest is that the 1945 Dujayla law and settlement plan fostered this conceptual separation of people from their environment and the simultaneous reconfiguration and dehistoricization of each. As the legal property grid of the individual landholding became the spatial grid of the four-corners settlement plan and then the social grid of the family farm, into which humans were inserted, it was hoped that new relationships between people and the things around them would be enabled—relationships that would be spatially fixed but temporally malleable. The application of the nuclear family grid at Dujayla was part of a larger modernizing project in Iraq that demanded the production and fixing of space—including stabilizing the course and flow of the two great rivers, expanding the area of cultivable land, settling nomads and their herds of animals, and introducing intensive methods of agriculture on small, fixed-size plots. That is, setting the nation into dynamic temporal motion toward a developed future was seen to depend on the construction of new kinds of spatial immobilities, especially for peasants, nomads, women, and the rural nonhuman world.

As Samera Esmeir has argued for legal reforms in colonial and semicolonial Egypt, the Iraqi land settlement laws were part of a process of "binding the living to the state," in part by fostering a "renewed relationship" between humans and nature.[101] But producing a boundary between the human and the inhuman was not driving rationality of these laws, as Esmeir argues of positivist Egyptian law in the early 20th century. Rather, they produced complex hierarchies of human and nonhuman kinds through gradations of inclusion and exclusion. On the one hand, they aimed to create a new kind of rural Iraqi citizen, the independent farmer, with some similarities to the universal figure of modern law posited by Esmeir. But they did so by embedding him in legal, social, and spatial grids that depended on and produced—rather than excluded—other human kinds, including wives, children, extended-family kin, and seasonal wage-laborers.[102] Rather than distinguishing primarily between citizens and noncitizens, or between the human and the inhuman, the settlement laws distinguished between humans who were independent and those who were dependent. Among those designated as dependent, they further distinguished between those whose dependence was seen as a problem to be overcome and those for whom it was a quality to be reinforced and naturalized. Transforming the problematically dependent male peasant into a modern independent farmer demanded both his liberation from those upon whom he was dependent—landlords, extended kin, the government—and the production of new subjects who would be dependent upon him. This, in turn, involved the production and regulation of rural space and of the nonhuman elements within it.

Over the past few decades, scholars of agrarian family history outside the industrialized West have tended to agree that the narrative of the rise of the nuclear family is of little relevance to their work. In one of the classic critiques, Joan Smith and Immanuel Wallerstein wrote that "this image of the family, as perpetrated by world social-science, has been an obstacle to our understanding of how households have in fact been constructed in the capitalist world-economy."[103] But I have suggested that the rise of the nuclear family is much more than an image perpetrated by world social science, in part because world social science does not stand outside the reality it claims to describe, and thus cannot be simply isolated and pushed aside as an "obstacle to our understanding" of that reality. The modern nuclear/conjugal family model need not be understood simply as the telos of a universal historical process, the empirical realization of which scholars would then set out to prove or disprove in this or that location. Rather, it can be seen as a legal, social, and spatial grid that makes certain kinds of "family" relationships legible so that they can be worked on by technologies of governmentality and development. At Dujayla, the nuclear family grid seems to have had limited success in unraveling extended family bonds or in producing recognizably bourgeois familial sentiments among the rural poor—nor, in the end, did it foster the capitalist development of agriculture in Iraq. But it nevertheless played a powerful role in the remaking of both time and space for those whose lives had become enmeshed in a development apparatus, while providing planners with an identifiable point of entry—the rural housewife—for projects of reform and improvement.

The Collapse of the Dujayla Laboratory, the Propagation of the Dujayla Technique

As it happened at Dujayla, the outcome of all these plans to fix people, animals, plants, water, and land in certain legal and spatial grids was a social and ecological catastrophe. Not only did the model of isolated nuclear family farms contribute significantly to the spread of human disease on the settlement, but the lack of a drainage infrastructure led to the rapid salinization of the soil. As Kamil Mahdi writes, all the "efforts and expenditure [at Dujayla] were dissipated by the failure to tackle the salinisation problem."[104]

Salinization was not an unanticipated consequence of development, a popular theme in the scholarship. Like the larger land salinity crisis throughout the newly irrigated regions of Iraq, the causes and mechanisms of the process occurring in the soils of Dujayla were well known, as was its technical solution. As one observer noted in 1951: "If extant blueprints are not immediately translated into a comprehensive drainage scheme, all cultivated soil within the project will salt up. The lands settled first have less than three years of grace left."[105] But the blueprints were not implemented, and by 1954, just as forecast, the "minimum subsistence requirements of a family could no longer be met and the settlers started to abandon their farms."[106] Things continued to decline after the 1958 revolution. In 1965—the year that the first settlers, according to the original Dujayla law, would have obtained free and clear title to their farms—an Iraqi government study of one of the settlement's sections showed that only 12 percent of its original 351 farm units were operated by the original homesteaders; the others either lay idle or were managed by tenants after the settlers had left. Only 25 percent of the plots still had any residences on the unit.[107] Five years later, "the whole settlement had reverted to the original extensive form of sheep husbandry."[108]

The UNESCO team was long gone by then, but its members witnessed the early effects of the soil disaster. Already in 1953, Trowbridge was reporting that some of UNESCO's own agricultural "demonstration plots" on the settlement had become little more than demonstrations "of the heart break known to many Dujayla farmers whose land is becoming salted and unproductive." Yet in the very next paragraph he proclaimed: "Our whole farm program now 'speaks with authority' and the younger generation of future farmers are learning much of value, perhaps to pass it on to their parents."[109] Not even the heartbreaking agricultural failure of Dujayla could undermine the UNESCO director's faith in its success with inculcating new values and habits in the nation's "future farmers." To the extent that this was the aim of fundamental education, it did not seem to matter much whether the farmers in question had any local future on the settlement.

For the Iraqi Hashimite monarchy, needless to say, Dujayla cannot be seen as anything but a failure. Whether its primary objective is understood to be the capitalist development of agriculture or to be what Cowen and Shenton posit as the aim of the "agrarian doctrine of development," namely to exclude rural social disorder from urban areas by "locking up population in the countryside,"[110] the Dujayla experiment, and the larger Miri Sirf Land Development program from 1945 to 1958, clearly did not work. Yet this failure does not exactly signify the ineffectiveness of the development techniques for which the settlement and its inhabitants served as a laboratory. In addition to the project's indelible effects on thousands of rural lives, and unknown numbers of rural deaths, many Iraqi trainees at Dujayla became leading technocrats involved in later development projects, including the ongoing reform of rural and urban family life, while lessons learned on the settlement were taken by the foreign specialists to new locations.

Meanwhile, the failure of the Miri Sirf Land Development project further fueled the discontent and the oppositional movements that the government had hoped it would help stem, along with the momentum of the political parties that claimed to represent those movements. After settling with the Hashimite regime in July 1958, these actors would embark on a far more thoroughgoing national project of agrarian reform, the need for which was widely seen as central to the need for the revolution itself and struggles over which would drive much of the sociopolitical upheaval in Iraq during its revolutionary era. As controversial as the development project was in many ways, it was based on a familiar model of settling landless peasants on independent family farms, in which landownership was conditioned on the family members' amenability to technical interventions in their daily lives. It also featured an equally familiar insistence on the need to demobilize the rural population. Unlike specific historical governments, then, modern technologies of governmentality and development thrive on failure. As Peter Miller and Nikolas Rose point out, failure is what motivates the propagation of more expert interventions for programming healthier bodies and happier futures. If government is a "congenitally failing operation," governmentality "is characterized by an eternal optimism that a domain or society could be administered better or more effectively, that reality is, in some way or other, programmable."[111]

6

Revolutionary Time and Wasted Time

ON THE MORNING OF JULY 14, 1958, twenty-four-year-old Mubejel
Baban, who like many Baghdadis during the summer months was sleeping
on the roof with the rest of her household, woke early to the cries of her
baby. She and the wife of her husband's brother descended the stairs of their
father-in-law's house together. While nursing their infants in the kitchen,
they heard a sudden explosion. Mubejel exclaimed: "It's the king's palace!"
Her sister-in-law laughed. "You dream," she replied.[1]

Indeed, Mubejel Baban had often dreamed of such an event. But on
that morning she had other reasons to suspect that the commotion was
coming from the palace. Like many members of the Iraqi Communist Party
(ICP), she and her husband had received a secret notice on July 12 calling
for "great vigilance" and conveying the party's directives in the event of "a
sudden emergency or in complicated circumstances," given the "critical
posture of affairs" and "the possibilities of evolution from one moment to
another."[2] They did not know exactly what to expect or when, but they knew
to expect something soon. The Free Officers of the Iraqi military who were
at that moment overthrowing the Hashimite monarchy, established thirty-
seven years earlier under British mandate rule, were not communists. But
they had been in contact with the ICP along with the other political parties
that joined in 1957 to form the United National Front: the liberal National
Democratic Party (NDP) and the two Arab nationalist parties, the Ba'th and
the Independence Party. The strategy of the ICP—the most popular and
well-organized political party in Iraq, albeit entirely underground during

the monarchical period—was to bring its thousands of members and supporters into the streets at the first sign of the coup.

Mubejel left her baby with the family and rushed out of the house with her husband. Half a century later, she would still remember it as the "best day of my life."[3] In Hanna Batatu's description:

Members of the party began issuing from their homes or underground hideaways. The movement increased from minute to minute until, about 8:00 a.m., the whole active following of the party was on the streets. Nationalists of all hues had also come out. Before very long the capital overflowed with people—*shargawiyyas* [hut-dwellers] and others—many of them in a fighting mood and united by a single passion: "Death to the traitors and agents of imperialism!" It was like a tide coming in, and at first engulfed and with a vengeance [Prime Minister] Nuri's house and the royal palace, but soon extended to the British consulate and embassy and other places. . . . When in the end, after nightfall, the crowds ebbed back, the statue of Faisal, the symbol of the monarchy, lay shattered, and the figure of General Maude, the conqueror of Baghdad, rested in the dust outside the burning old British Chancellery.[4]

The young monarch Faysal II, the crown prince 'Abd Allah, and the prime minister Nuri al-Sa'id were killed, as were the other royal family members living in the palace. But resistance to the coup was astonishingly flimsy by all accounts. After years of repressing opposition movements, using ever more brutal means including mass detentions for political crimes, the systematic use of torture, and the killing of political prisoners, in the end the Iraqi Hashimite monarchy collapsed, as historian Uriel Dann put it, "like a house of cards."[5]

Scholars agree that the outpouring of people into the streets of Baghdad on July 14 had "a tremendous psychological effect. It planted fear in the heart of the supporters of the monarchy, and helped to paralyze their will and give the coup the irresistible character that was its surest bulwark."[6] It was also a factor in discouraging the United States and Britain from intervening immediately in the course of events inside Iraq.[7] Instead, they set themselves the more limited short-term objective of containing revolutionary expectations within Iraq's borders. Thus, on July 15, US troops landed in Lebanon, already destabilized by a political crisis of its own, and on July 17, British troops arrived in Jordan to bolster the understandably nervous Jordanian royal branch of the Hashimite family.[8] By then, the Iraqi monarchy had been abolished and replaced by the Republic of Iraq, which was being recognized by more of the world's governments every day, starting with the United Arab Republic and the countries of the socialist bloc.

Women, Revolution, and the Social Domain

On January 1, 1959, Mubejel Baban and several thousand other women convened for a march through the streets of Baghdad, ending at the Ministry of Defense. The march was organized by the communist popular front women's organization, Rabitat al-Difa' 'an Huquq al-Mar'a (League for the Defense of Women's Rights), commonly known as al-Rabita or the League. The women were protesting the monarchical regime of "the time gone by"—agents of which they held responsible for the attempted Rashid 'Ali coup in December as well as the recent killing of a member of the Popular Resistance Forces (PRF), a civilian militia established to protect the government against counterrevolutionary forces and filled with enthusiastic young leftists of both sexes. Among the protestors were "the widows of the martyrs, who fell in Baghdad streets during various patriotic uprisings, or those who died in prison." Another contingent was of female PRF members bearing arms. Some carried a portrait of leading Free Officer and Iraq's new prime minister, 'Abd al-Karim Qasim, while others waved portraits of martyrs or placards calling for the "immediate execution of the traitors and plotters."[9] The organizers sent an appeal along the same lines to Qasim:

Do you recall the atrocious crimes against our sons in the prisons of Baghdad and Kut [and] on the people of Haj, Basrah, Kirkuk, Mosul, Najaf and elsewhere. We, the deceaseds' mothers, will never forget any of the black days of those traitors. Nor shall we ever forgive them. . . . We, the women of Baghdad, will keep the fire burning in our hearts until we see the traitors' bodies hanging from the gallows. The blood of our martyrs exhorts you, Karim, to carry out the death sentences passed on the traitors by the People's Court.[10]

The women's vengeful and bloody demands seem to have bemused at least one observer, a US diplomat who quipped in his report to Washington that this was "an interesting stage in the emancipation of Iraqi women."[11]

Other reports downplayed or simply ignored the march's demands and focused instead on the purportedly unprecedented nature of a female public demonstration in Iraq and/or the Arab world. At the end of January, the *Illustrated London News* published a letter to the editor from the Iraqi Ministry of Development asserting that "the women of Baghdad, some 50,000 including students, doctors, teachers, housewives, etc. took part in the first female demonstration in the country in support of the present government."[12] And a July 1959 article in the communist *Iraqi Review* proclaimed: "It was the first demonstration of its kind in the history of the whole Arab people. It was greater than words can express. The streets were silent. . . . Never before had the Iraqi people witnessed such an event."[13]

The reimagining of the women's march reflected the post-revolutionary expansion of the domain of the social, often through the mobilization of women and around the care of children ("doctors, teachers, housewives, etc."). While these discourses and practices were not new, the first few years of Qasim's regime saw an unprecedented range of new social reform laws and institutions, primarily targeting the urban and rural poor. As a government publication asserted in 1960: "The social domain [al-midan al-ijtima'i]—which received no attention from the governments of the time gone by—has received the greatest share of attention and care" from the new government since the day of the revolution.[14] In this chapter, I explore the work of expanding the social domain, and the simultaneous deferral of popular sovereignty or democracy into an ever-receding future. Even as political parties engaged in serious and sometimes violent conflict over other questions, they converged on the need to create a stable political space in which capitalist economic development could unfold. The newspapers of all the main parties stressed the need to combat "lethargy" or "stagnation" in the economy as a whole and/or in the bodies and minds of the country's laborers. The word often used for this condition was jumud, literally "a frozen state."[15] At the same time, many agreed on the need for the "suspension"—tajmid, "freezing," from the same root as jumud—of various kinds of political mobilization in the present. In other words, the overcoming of economic stagnation or jumud was frequently seen as depending on the enforcement of political stagnation or tajmid.

These social reform projects were shaped, to quote Jacques Donzelot, "by a decisive alliance between promotional feminism and moralizing philanthropy."[16] Members of the communist women's league, the main feminist organization in 1950s Iraq, cooperated with government agencies to provide health services for women and children and literacy and vocational training for poor women. All of Iraq's major political parties and newspapers produced narratives supporting the necessity of women's work in the public domain of the social. Yet, in revolutionary Iraq, the alliance between the state and feminism was far from a seamless one. It was riven with the same social and political instabilities that it had been formed to address and with new ones that it created. Starting in mid-1959, and

accelerating considerably in 1960, the consensus on the role of sexual difference in the revolutionary and developmental project unraveled, both
revealing and fostering deep divisions in Iraqi society over questions of
sexual equality, family law, and women's political activism.

The unraveling occurred through several specific conflicts as well
as through the intensification of a broader gender crisis discourse. One
conflict was over the December 1959 promulgation of the personal status
law, and especially over its clause mandating sexual equality in inheritance
rights. Another was a controversy over a literacy program for rural women
launched by the communist women of al-Rabita in the summers of 1959
and 1960. The basic conflict over the personal status law is well known in
the historiography on the revolution, though key aspects of it have often
been misrepresented, as I will show in Chapter 7. The struggle over the
literacy program, to be explored below, has to my knowledge not been
examined in the literature. But it was a central political battle in Iraq from
mid-1959 through the end of 1960, expressed in a fiery war of words in
the communist, Arab nationalist, and liberal press as well as in several
violent confrontations. Ultimately, it was used by Qasim's regime to justify
banning the ICP daily newspaper *Ittihad al-Sha'b*, the widest circulating
periodical in the country.

The communist women's literacy program was seen by both the
government and anticommunist political parties, especially the Ba'th, as
violating the tacit terms of the alliance between the state and middle-class
feminists to "familialize the popular strata," to again borrow Donzelot's
phrase. Rather than propagating techniques for the "policing of families"
in rural areas, the project was seen as exacerbating forms of "social promiscuity" and the "mobile networks of solidarity" that threatened to further
destabilize Iraq's fragile post-revolutionary rural order.[17] This conflict—in
the context of the broader gender crisis discourse, especially as it played
out in the struggle between communists and Ba'thists—linked the regime's
efforts to depoliticize oppositional urban activists with the campaign to
demobilize the rural and urban subaltern classes. One aim of this chapter
is thus to challenge the narrow focus in most histories of Iraq's "revolutionary era" (1958–1963) on the political and ideological battles between the
regime and the political parties, which usually do not elucidate how these
conflicts related to the widespread subaltern mobilizations, both urban
and rural, that recurred throughout this era.

Revolutionary Time

A British official working in Baghdad on July 14 later wrote, under a pseudonym, that "the Revolution, when it came, corresponded so closely to the opinion that had formed before, that everything that happened seemed, in its turn, to be what one had already been taught to expect."[18] This and many other sources, both foreign and Iraqi, attest that Mubejel Baban's sister-in-law had identified a somewhat deeper phenomenon when she teased Mubejel for dreaming the revolution that had in fact already begun. The widely reported experience of the revolution as déjà vu was based on many Iraqis' recognition of it as a "future past,"[19] which was paradoxically the grounds on which it could be imagined as the inauguration of a new time. Al-'ahd al-ba'id or al-'ahd al-mubad—"the time gone by" or "the bygone era"—quickly emerged as the primary designation for the monarchical era. Yet in order to be identified as revolutionary time, the coup had to inaugurate a series of other events whose outcome was already known. Each of the four parties in the United National Front had a different vision of the future-past revolution. For the NDP, it inaugurated a truly national sovereign space for the flourishing of liberal democracy and capitalist development. For the ICP and the Arab nationalist parties, it was the first stage in a longer historical process with different ends: for the former, it was the anti-imperialist and bourgeois phase of the two-stage revolution leading to socialism; for the latter, it was the political prerequisite of Iraq's union with the larger Arab nation.

The central political battle in revolutionary Iraq is often seen to be the one between the communists and the Arab nationalists. The nationalists sought Iraq's unification with other Arab regions, and in particular with Jamal 'Abd al-Nasir's United Arab Republic (UAR), created earlier that year through a merger of Egypt and Syria. The communists argued against immediate union, on the grounds that uniting different Arab economies, which were moving in different times, would inhibit the economic development of the slower-moving entities. The result would be an exploitative, semicolonial relationship rather than the emergence of viable, independent bourgeoisies capable of leading their respective nations to the next historical stage.[20] While this was the ICP's main public explanation, its position against union was also related to 'Abd al-Nasir's war on the communist movement in the Arab world and to the fate of first the Egyptian and then the Syrian communist parties under his rule. The ICP also had concerns about the ethnolinguistic basis of Arab nationalist identity and its implications for Kurds and other minorities in Iraq, who formed an important constituency of the party.[21]

As is well known, one of Qasim's main strategies was to play the Arab nationalists and the communists off each other, more or less successfully for a while, and then not.[22] But on the question of Iraqi state sovereignty and territoriality, he was consistently aligned with the ICP and the NDP against the Arab nationalists. Article 1 of the temporary constitution, promulgated thirteen days after the revolution, asserted that "the Iraqi state [al-dawla al-'iraqiyya] is an independent republic possessing complete sovereignty [dhat siyada kamila]," while Article 2 stated that "Iraq is a part of the Arab nation [al-umma al-'arabiyya]."[23] As Qasim liked to point out, the order of the articles was not an accident.[24] They also did not contradict each other; rather, they identified Iraq as a state, or *dawla*, with sovereignty over a territory and the Arab nation as a community, or *umma*, a term that has no necessary territorial implications. Qasim argued against union with the UAR by asserting that while Iraq's constitution declared it "part of the Arab nation," it was "part of the whole, not part of a part."[25]

Despite their differences, the parties agreed on certain conditions that the new regime would have to fulfill in order to maintain the legitimacy of July 14 as the long-awaited revolution. Achieving the primary twin goals of sovereignty and development involved specific expectations, such as abolishing the monarchy, declaring a republic, terminating British control over Iraq's affairs, implementing a land reform program to break the stranglehold of the large landholding class on the country's development, and demonstrating advances toward industrialization. There were many ideological conflicts within the ICP, as well as several public shifts in its relation to Qasim's government. But for most of the revolutionary era the party saw its role as assisting the state in producing the conditions that would enable the "national bourgeoisie" to develop a national industrialized economy.[26] As ICP members Zaki Khayri and Su'ad Khayri later wrote: "All of the national forces realized that political independence could not be defended without removing the causes of economic dependence, so the platforms of every party included freedom from foreign monopoly capital and the development of the national economy [tatwir al-iqtisad al-watani]." Like the other parties, then, the ICP focused on "encouraging national industry and national capital."[27]

The parties further agreed on the need for state intervention to implement legal and social reforms aimed at constituting the kinds of subjects that development required. Qasim's minister of finance Muhammad Hadid later explained that July 14 "became a revolution, not merely a military coup, by virtue of its achievements in the domain of national liberation, social reform, raising the general standard of living, and unleashing the capacities of the people."[28] None of the parties that had come together in the United National Front would ever achieve its designated main historical goal in Iraq, whether liberal democracy, a socialist society, or Arab union. But the general agreement on the state's role in social reform meant that Iraq's political parties, even as they were not fully allowed to operate or to participate in democratic elections, contributed to the expansion of the Iraqi territorial and militarized state into the intimate lives of Iraqi subjects.

The "primary slogan" of the ICP during these years was "the defense of the republic." This slogan was consistent with the Soviet line that communist parties in decolonizing countries should form an alliance with the anti-imperialist segment of the national bourgeoisie. It also aligned with the Soviet tendency to support stable regimes with nonaligned orientations rather than promote communist revolution from below in such states.[29] Many Iraqi leftists have criticized the ICP's insistence that capitalist development under Qasin would serve some imagined shared national interest, rather than subjecting workers to greater exploitation. Former party member Yeheskel Kojaman writes that in its effusive pronouncements on the capacity of the bourgeois government to spread general prosperity throughout the country, the ICP "forgot just one minor detail: that in Iraq there was this thing called capitalism." Kojaman goes on to criticize the slogan "defending the republic," noting that it violated the first requirement of any political slogan, which is that it must have an "end" (nihaya). But there is only one conceivable "end" to the slogan of "defending the republic," and that is "the end of the republic that was supposed to be defended."[30]

Other Iraqi intellectuals have observed that the dominant mode of political reasoning in Iraq, starting in the Qasim era, has been to invoke the divide between past and future, progress and reaction, revolution and counterrevolution, to justify whatever claim is being made. Appealing to this divide has contributed to the perpetuation of military dictatorships in the country and the ongoing deferral of democratic institutions.[31] This discourse indeed permeated public discourse in the Qasim years. To invoke one of countless examples, a 1959 article in the Marxist-leaning journal al-Muthaqqaf used it to justify violence against the counterrevolutionary class, which "does not express the revolutionaries' spirit of revenge or thirst for blood but rather the strong dedication to the revolution's future." The article presents some of the revolution's enemies as members of the former ruling class, while others are presented as those who simply cannot keep up with history: "Some fall behind the revolution's rapid march, and others retreat, until in the end they are with the enemies of the revolution."[32] They can then be eliminated without undue moral difficulty, as people already without a future.

The League for the Defense of Women's Rights

The public presence of communism after the revolution was shaped largely by the popular front organizations the party had established in the early 1950s, especially the Partisans of Peace, the Federation of Democratic Youth, and the League for the Defense of Women's Rights (al-Rabita). As Charles Tripp writes, by 1958 these groups "were not simply fronts for political parties, but represented attempts by a wide variety of Iraqis to establish a voice for hitherto neglected sections of society. Nowhere," he continues, "was this more the case than in al-Rabita."[33] Like the other communist front organizations, al-Rabita had operated more or less underground during the Hashimite era. On July 14, it declared its public existence by sending a cable to Qasim expressing its "solidarity with the revolutionary government" and asserting that "all its members and the rest of the women of Iraq stand united behind the Premier and the Government."[34] In March 1959, the group announced that it had 20,000 members; a year later, it reported a membership roll of 42,000.[35]

Before the revolution, al-Rabita had three slogans: defending women's rights, defending motherhood, and defending childhood. After July 14, it added a fourth, which took precedence over the others and was identical to the main slogan of the ICP: defending the republic. Toward this end, the group launched door-to-door campaigns to gather signatures from women on various causes while educating them in the "importance of defending the republic." Some petitions expressed support for actions the government had taken, such as passing the land reform law; others pressured it in areas where it appeared to be wavering, such as on Iraq's withdrawal from the Baghdad Pact. According to the communist press, al-Rabita members "entered one house after another in order to explain the importance of the revolution and its gains. . . . The cities and the rural areas were divided into so many regions and localities, and there were so many committees for each region and locality . . . that everyone [in Iraq] heard and came in contact with these groups."[36] The campaigns had enough impact to be mentioned regularly in telegrams to the US State Department from the US Embassy in Baghdad. "Girls from Erbil (100 signatures) express solidarity with the Prime Minister, call for the crushing of plots. The Agrarian

Reform Law was supported by the Women of the League for the Defense of Women's Rights in Mosul."[37] During a demonstration against the US-sponsored Baghdad Pact, two delegations stopped by the embassy to deliver petitions: the first, from the Partisans of Peace, had 655 signatures; the second, from al-Rabita, had 2,780. "The girls presenting it to the Embassy said signatures were obtained on a house-to-house campaign."[38]

Another indication of al-Rabita's visibility in the Iraqi public sphere can be found in a remarkable pair of telegrams from the US Secret Service in Baghdad to the State Department in July 1959. The first telegram mentions, somewhat dismissively, comments by Qasim concerning women's rights: "[The] last third of speech [was a] rambling discourse which touched on the following: Women's rights are under consideration and women [may] share in government responsibility before July 14."[39] But someone in the secret service seems to have reconsidered this part of Qasim's speech, finding it less "rambling" than described in the first telegram and in fact rather alarming from a US Cold War perspective. The second telegram concludes that if Qasim was really planning to appoint an Iraqi woman to a senior government post then he was also, in all likelihood, planning to appoint a communist, since "among women currently active on local scene it would be difficult [to] find one not far left." Thus, the second telegram predicts: "Qasim may designate woman Communist such as Women's Rights League President Dulaimi."[40] Four days later, Qasim announced his new minister of municipalities, Naziha al-Dulaimi, a card-carrying member of the ICP and a founder as well as the current president of al-Rabita. She was the first female government minister in Iraq's history and the only ICP member appointed to the cabinet under Qasim.

Much of al-Rabita's work was related to defending its two explicitly social slogans, defending motherhood and defending childhood, which it saw as integral to its primary political slogan of defending the republic. As al-Rabita member Rose Khadduri put it, there was a strong connection "between work to eliminate social diseases and the question of protecting national independence."[41]

Wasted Time

In April 1959, Qasim gave a speech on the problem of *jumud*, or stagnation, in which he asserted that "the colonial states and reactionary elements are always trying to foster *jumud* in the country . . . so they can destroy it using its own people." The aim was to "to keep the people in its place . . . and not to arose its movement for the sake of development [*al-tatawwur*]. Productive work, marching in the caravan of freedom, demands the destruction of *jumud*. Thanks to God . . . we have been able to overcome *jumud* and to overcome the past and crush it."[42] A few months later, on the first anniversary of the revolution, Qasim proclaimed that Iraq had the resources to defeat "poverty, ignorance, and disease," but whether it did so would depend on increased production. He explained that the government had done its part to protect laborers and peasants from naked exploitation, by passing the 1958 land reform law and the 1959 labor law, and now asked these groups to fulfill the revolution's mission of development. Qasim called on "my brothers the workers and peasants" to

make mighty efforts to strengthen [the nation's] riches, because the struggles of the workers and the loyalty of the peasants are necessary to create an abundant flow of capital and ensure the well-being of the people. . . . The worker does not labor only for wages but is also guided by the standard of increasing production and by the sincerity of his love of work. . . . As for my brothers the peasants, after we have distributed land to them . . . I ask from them sincerity and dedication in increasing production and providing food to the sons of the nation, who are their brothers. The peasant who neglects his work neglects the production of nourishment for his people. . . . [Thus] we will not waste our time but will devote it to work.[43]

The context of Qasim's preoccupation with *jumud* and wasted time in the spring and summer of 1959 was an economic crisis that officials linked to a decline in labor productivity. This in turn they attributed both to lethargy in the bodies of workers and to labor disturbances, including strikes in the cities and peasant-led land appropriations in the countryside. State officials, along with NDP and Ba'th leaders, accused the ICP of exploiting workers and peasants by fostering dissent and thereby obstructing economic development.[44] The ICP was indeed involved in the wave of peasant and worker mobilization sweeping the country in the first half of 1959. After communists helped thwart an attempted Arabist coup in Mosul in March, the government had acceded to some of the party's demands, including recognizing the right of peasants to form associations. By the end of May, 2, 267 out of a total of 3,577 peasant societies were under communist control, and they began pushing the government to implement more comprehensive land reform. Meanwhile, all fifty-one trade unions in the General Federation of Trade Unions were in the hands of communists.[45] The ICP began making demands for direct representation in government by pointing to its widespread support among the popular organizations.

But already by May the regime was pushing back. That month it passed the Criminal Ordinance Law, which outlawed the propagation of "political and 'demagogic' ideas against the republic." On July 18, it announced the dissolution of the Federation of Trade Unions, arrested its members, and confiscated its documents. In September, the monarchical-era Martial Law Ordinance was reestablished, abolishing freedom of expression, and all peasant societies were declared illegal on the basis that they had not been approved by provincial governors. Finally, in January 1960, the Association Act prohibited all political parties, trade unions, and societies from operating without government approval. The ICP's application to continue operating was rejected. These actions were a clear assault by Qasim's government on the ICP, but they were also an assault on increasing labor unrest in the cities and the countryside.[46]

In May, at the height of the ICP's bid for a share in government, Muhammad Hadid—a leading NDP figure and a major Iraqi industrialist as well as Qasim's minister of finance—proclaimed the voluntary "freezing" (*tajmid*) of the NDP's political activities and encouraged Iraq's other political parties to follow suit.[47] This pronouncement was not supported by the other leading NDP figure, Kamil al-Chadirchi, and led to a split in the party, with Hadid and his faction forming the National Progressive Party. The call was also publicly rejected by the ICP. But if the ICP declined to suspend its political activities, it did retreat from fostering subaltern mobilization, after a sudden about-face and change of leadership in the fall of 1959. In fact, the party went further than withdrawing from labor unrest, at times actively working to subdue it.[48] The ICP was soon helping to resolve workers' "problems and disputes with the businessmen" though "friendly and constructive means," and denouncing "the saboteurs and infiltrators" who had chosen to "drag the workers into strikes." It also announced "comparatively good results" for the "intricate task" of "the settlement of disputes in the countryside," in the interest of "safeguarding the Republic and backing the patriotic authority for the accomplishment of Agrarian reform."[49] In October 1959, when communists led a demonstration in support of Qasim after he was wounded in a Ba'thist assassination attempt, they carried placards such as "More Grain for Your People, Brave Peasants!" and "Produce More, O Valiant Workers!"[50]

Neither the government's crackdown nor the ICP's about-face put an end to worker unrest; there were numerous strikes and other labor protests throughout 1960 and 1961.[51] The ICP participated in some of these, albeit "half-heartedly."[52] Its main labor-movement work that year was to try to retain its influence in the unions, a losing battle due to rigged union elections and large-scale arrests of communist workers.[53] Meanwhile, the party continued to publicly support Qasim, appealing to the need for "stability" and to give the regime time to build "the new life" promised by the revolution. As it explained in December 1959:

The road towards stability is the road of providing the conditions and circumstances that facilitate the task of the patriotic authority towards the new life. It requires from all the loyal patriotic forces and elements inside the patriotic government and outside it to fight patiently and persistently . . . in order to establish the favourable ground for ensuring [that] stability.[54]

The notion expressed in this passage that a new life had been inaugurated by the revolution, yet needed state intervention to secure it, was widely shared. An editorial in the NDP newspaper al-Ahali, published during the 1960 cement workers' strike, noted that the party was "scientifically studying the reality of our society and its capacities for development" in order to "treat its sicknesses and backwardness" and thereby overcome its "stagnation" (jumud).[55] Another al-Ahali editorial explained that a central goal of the revolution was to "protect the national economy" and increase production, but that Iraq "lacked the necessary capabilities" for industrialization, a legacy of the "backwardness and neglect of the time gone by." Building those capabilities required cooperation "between industrialists and workers" and efforts from the government to "build a society capable of growth, development, and flourishing" (al-numu wa-l-tatawwur wa-l-izdihar).[56]

In the first half of 1960, Qasim lightened up on the Arab nationalist parties as part of his crackdown on the communists. Permitted to start publication again, the Ba'thist newspaper al-Hurriyya responded to the cement workers' strike by calling on "heroic workers" to ignore "the opportunistic elements" (i.e., communists) who want to "exploit your powers," and reminded them that "the republic needs your labor and dedication, your patience and your sacrifice." The statement suggested that workers adopt the slogan "Increase Production and God Will Grant Us Victory."[57] Two weeks later, at the height of the strike, an article asserted that it was through faith in God, his Prophet, and the Day of Judgment (a day on which, after all, "money is of no use") that "the sons of the nation" would learn to exert "their money, their spirits, and their souls." Paradoxically, given the Ba'th Party's struggles with Qasim and its ideological opposition to Iraq's perpetuation as a nation-state, the party deployed discourse similar to that of the NDP and the ICP in calling on the Iraqi state as the arbiter of conflict and the guarantor of law and order. The same article asserted that a shared morality, which it linked to Islam, would "dissolve special interests," so that the people could become "a single body and a single spirit." But the power of faith would be ineffective if not backed by the "power of order," which would ensure stability and eliminate "anarchy," and which could only be secured by the "rule of law."[58]

Political leaders of varied leanings converged on a narrative that, as *al-Hurriyya* put it, the primary cause of the nation's "backwardness" (*ta'akhkhur*) was its people's failure to struggle "for a better future" and their loss of a spirit of "self-improvement" (*al-islah al-dhati*).[59] Similarly, as the (at that time) pro-Qasim and leftist Shi'i literary journal *al-Najaf* explained, the true "enemies of the revolution" were the agents of "the time gone by" who had "destroyed the spirit of development [*ruh al-tatawwur*] in the people."[60] The Ministry of Education's journal, *al-Mu'allim al-Jadid*, warned that all of Iraq's "great revolutionary achievements and social and economic projects" would have limited effects if not accompanied by the "building of strong morals" and the fostering of diligence in "cultivating and developing the self" (*tathqif al-dhat wa-tanmiyatiha*) among members of the "rising generation."[61] The solution, in the words of Qasim's minister of education Muhyi al-Din 'Abd al-Hamid, was to manage the welfare of every Iraqi through every stage of the human life cycle, by "encircling this individual in complete care from the moment he opens his eyes."[62]

The Care of Children

On June 1, 1959, a celebration of World Children's Day was co-sponsored by al-Rabita and the Ministry of Health. Among other prizes, a cash award was given to the Iraqi woman with the largest number of living children (seventeen). The parents "said that they are happy to have this big family, not only to contribute to the development of society [but also] to be able to defend the Democratic Republic, with a bigger number of faithful soldiers." A photo of the family accompanied the article, with the caption "The Happiest Mother in the Republic."[63]

The government used the occasion to announce a new "law for the protection of childhood." The law's preamble explained that "the child is the nucleus of the coming generation on which stands the future of the country."

Since the nation's future rested on the shoulders of the child, it was the government's duty to ensure that "every child has a chance" to develop "mentally, spiritually, morally, and socially."[64] The text identified three institutions responsible for the care of children, essentially defining what I have been calling the "domain of the social": the family, the government, and "social organizations." It then distributed the legal obligations of caring for children among them. It was the duty of the parents to "defend the child against oppression and exploitation, protect him from sickness, and create an environment of warmth and material welfare." The government was responsible for providing primary education to every Iraqi child, to ensure the "development of his character" (*tanmiyat shakhsiyyatihi*), and for creating institutions for children who were disabled, delinquent, orphaned, or whose families had otherwise failed in their obligations. Communicating between the family and the government was the task of the social organizations, which would "cooperate with official authorities in the duties of caring for children, and guide the family . . . in its responsibilities toward its children."[65] These guidelines thus extended the 1958 Law for Social Institutions, which had established the legal framework for such organizations, making the government responsible for creating public institutions and working with private ones to care for, incarcerate, and/ or rehabilitate the needy and delinquent. These included institutions for the mentally ill and physically handicapped; shelters and rehabilitation houses for "repentant prostitutes"; and reformatories for "the care, life, subsistence, and education" of orphans and juvenile delinquents.[66]

The care of children was also a focus of the government's housing projects to resettle both the urban and rural poor. When introducing the 1958 Agrarian Reform Law, Qasim asserted: "We have found that agrarian reform is the basic foundation of social reform."[67] The typical model village established as part of the implementation of this law included an elementary school and medical clinic for mothers and children as well as a school to teach girls and women "domestic arts" and child-raising techniques, a day-care center, and a fenced-in public playground for children.[68] The leftist journal *al-Muthaqqaf* explained that the role of the teacher in the model village schools was to reform rural children, "cleansing their minds of the defects of the time gone by."[69]

The regime acquired much of its legitimacy through these projects, distinguishing itself from the monarchy through its attention to health, education, and other social services as equally important to the nation's development as "economic planning," if not more so. The budget created by Qasim's Ministry of Finance thus altered the ratio of oil proceeds that had been allocated to these two spheres from 30/70 in the "time gone by" to 50/50 after the revolution. As Minister of Finance Hadid explained the decision: "investing in the individual person [al-insan] is no less important than material investments in economic projects, even recognizing [the latter's] importance to economic development [al-tanmiya al-iqtisadiyya]."[70]

The alliance between the state and the leftist women of al-Rabita was forged through the production of the social domain. In addition to World Children's Day, al-Rabita and the Ministry of Health cosponsored celebrations for Health and Hygiene Week, which gave awards to the "cleanest mother and cleanest child, and the cleanest restaurant, coffee shop and hotel."[71] Al-Rabita worked on more extensive social reform projects as well, cosponsoring some with the government, and received government funding for some of its own projects.[72] It opened maternity clinics for pregnant women and new mothers that provided free medical services as well as hygienic information on "the best ways of promoting their own health and that of their children and families." It also launched its own vaccination campaigns and, according to the communist press, "was responsible for the [smallpox] inoculation of 70,000 persons."[73]

Gender Crises and Rural Disorder

In February 1959, Qasim issued a "directive to women teachers" in secondary schools:

The old regime had left us coquetry and immodesty which were the social aspects of the old regime though they are far from virtue and sound morality and are not conforming to the movement of progress and the spirit of liberated nations. . . . We appeal to this conscious vanguard to be a good example to their students in order that the schools produce men of science and education and good women, and not be beauty parlors where time is wasted.[74]

In suggesting that girls' schools were beauty parlors where time was wasted, the statement draws on familiar constructions of certain female activities as decadent and Westernized in the wrong way, while simultaneously employing the temporal-distancing move that locates them in a past time.[75] But there is more going on in this directive. February 1959 saw the beginning of Qasim's crackdown on the ICP, which would be stalled only temporarily in March after the attempted coup in Mosul. Since the ICP was particularly popular in Iraq's colleges and secondary schools, both male and female, these spaces were important targets of the crackdown.

The statement also reflected broader anxieties around what was going on in female-only spaces, interwoven with a newly invigorated "marriage crisis" narrative. In March, the president of the People's Court, Colonel Fadil 'Abbas al-Mahdawi, in one of his famous digressions from the trial at hand, criticized "the traditions among the womenfolk to hold at-home parties for other women," urging middle-class women to spend their free time instead helping "their sisters among the poorer classes."[76] In May, al-Mahdawi launched his own campaign against singlehood in Iraq, arguing that women should not remain single beyond the age of twenty-five and men not beyond thirty, since "in our great republican regime, we need to increase the population. As we have said, in a few years' time, the population of Iraq should reach 10,000,000."[77] Al-Mahdawi's concerns were not limited to the pronatalist argument that Iraq was underpopulated; he also asserted that singlehood as such was "harmful" to Iraqi society, because it led inexorably to "sexual and mental diseases."[78]

An article in *al-Najaf* likewise identified female spaces, especially among the lower classes, as a problem. The segregation of women, especially those who were "uneducated," had "created a foreign body within the body of the nation, a closed world within the society that does not interact with it and leaves no trace except for a negative influence." Women should be educated to provide "social services" in addition to contributing to "the realm of family life." The article asserted that "the problem of the Iraqi woman" was an important cause of the disturbances in Iraqi society, and was thus becoming a central concern of "social reformers in our country today." Remarkably for a journal based in Najaf and associated with some Shi'i 'ulama', given the coming controversy over the personal status law, the article called on the government to institute legal reforms addressing the marriage crisis, which was a "grave problem that the Iraqi society is suffering from, connected to women," as well as "a source of anxiety in the souls of individuals, both men and women, and a cause of instability in the society."[79] The author called on the government to take measures, including enacting legislation, "to lift the barriers standing in the way of marriage and to facilitate an increase in the marriage rate." The article hastened to add that "our aim is not to do anything contrary to the nature of our religion or foreign to our nation," but rather "to remove the layers of grime from our customs and traditions."[80]

The most serious controversy related to women's activities may have been over the communist women's literacy project. Al-Rabita had launched a literacy program for rural women "to raise the level of social and national consciousness among the masses," for the sake of the "rising generation."[81] By July 1959 it reported that it had graduated more than 7,000 rural women from its schools, which were staffed by female volunteers, primarily leftist schoolteachers and secondary school students.[82] Al-Rabita leader Rose Khadduri noted that the program taught women not only how to read and write but also "the meaning of freedom, the meaning of family life, the meaning of peace, and other such concepts."[83]

But al-Rabita soon found itself in a "fight against social prejudice and official obstruction in some parts of the country."[84] Over the summers of 1959 and 1960, its literacy schools across the central and southern rural regions of Iraq were shut down by the commander of the First Division of the Iraqi Army, responsible for the military governance of those areas, which comprised seven of Iraq's fourteen liwas, or districts. Some young female volunteers were arrested and delivered to their parents, who were instructed to prevent them from returning to al-Rabita activities. The commander, whose action was not opposed by Qasim despite an extensive campaign in the communist press, claimed that the program had "deviated" from its mission by pursuing "partisan" activities, and asserted that "an honest illiterate is better than an educated provocateur."[85]

Al-Rabita denied the charges, insisting that it was

a democratic organization, not a partisan one, and the curricula of the schools did not include anything except what concerns women in household and educational affairs. . . . We ask you to reverse this injustice . . . and return to women the light of knowledge and education which was denied them during the time gone by.[86]

While al-Rabita repeatedly attempted to legitimate its program through widely accepted narratives on the necessity of women's work in the social domain, these failed to have the desired effect. Instead, the project was seen by government officials and the anticommunist press as violating the precept that development work be conducted through purely social—that is, apolitical—methods. Rather than functioning as a relay in the "antipolitics machine" of development,[87] the encounter between urban middle-class leftist women and poor illiterate rural women was seen as a threat to post-revolutionary stability.

The military commander of the southern regions followed up the closing of the literacy classes with an order that no teacher from an urban area was permitted to so much as enter any of the rural areas in the seven liwas for any nonofficial reason, and declared it a "crime" to combat illiteracy in those areas, which as *Ittihad al-Sha'b* pointed out comprised "half of Iraq."[88] The shutting down of al-Rabita's literacy classes, as well as those of the communist-affiliated Federation of Democratic Youth and the teachers' union, became a major public conflict. *Ittihad al-Sha'b* ran numerous editorials and articles condemning the action, to which the commander responded by banning the newspaper itself, prohibiting its "purchase or circulation" in the same seven liwas. This was the first step toward *Ittihad al-Sha'b*'s permanent shutdown in 1961. Unwilling to abandon the slogan "defending the republic" by criticizing the top levels of the government, the editors of the paper appealed publicly to Qasim, "who has always affirmed his respect for freedom of the press," and asserted that the commander's actions "contradicted the spirit of the historical stage we are passing through," but to no avail.[89]

Al-Rabita's literacy project received the bulk of attention, but its other social programs did not go unnoticed in the crackdown. In December 1959, the government announced that all organizations with a "relation to public health," whether public or private, would henceforth report directly to the Ministry of Health and require its approval for their activities. Such organizations, especially those "working in the rural areas," were directed to attend a conference sponsored by the ministry to "discuss their roles."[90] There is little doubt that this decision was made with the rural health activities of communist women in mind. In the midst of these controversies, *Ittihad al-Sha'b* began posting notices denying the "rumors" being spread in the "reactionary newspapers" maligning the "nationalist character" of al-Rabita and the morals of its members. These included the false accusation that al-Rabita had refused to participate in the 1960 World Children's Day celebrations.[91] The rumors in question were published mainly in the Ba'th Party press, as the deepening gender crisis became a central node in its struggle with the ICP.

The crisis also shaped the increasingly violent street war between communists and Ba'thists. *Ittihad al-Sha'b* began publishing notices of verbal and physical attacks on women known for their political activities, often as they were entering or exiting girls' schools. In December 1959, as one of many examples, it reported an attack on students attending a girls' home economics school, by a "gang of riffraff" who verbally abused and physically assaulted the girls. When the students reported the attack, the school's director rebuked them rather than the attackers, though the latter were "known for their criminal acts of sabotage."[92]

In a 1960 editorial, the Ba'thist *al-Hurriyya* made a statement similar to Qasim's earlier one, questioning the "wasting of time" by middle-class women who should focus on social work.

We must understand the meaning of the freedom that we want for the women of our republic. What we have meant by it has always been opposed to aristocratic trends and fashions; we do not want it to be a form of amusement for women to enjoy in their free time. We want it to be a noble mission that the Iraqi woman will use to solve her social problems and to raise the level of the women of the republic, culturally, socially, and in the domain of health, so that the woman in Iraq will stand with her brothers in the Arab nation and with the women of the world to spread honor and dignity.[93]

Ba'thists linked communism both to the sexual promiscuity they perceived among European communists and to the anti-Arab *shu'ubiyya* movement of the 'Abbasid period, which according to *al-Hurriyya* had "promoted equality in wealth and women, anarchy, and the dismantling and destruction of the family structure and the teachings of religion."[94] During its campaign against the cement workers' strike, *al-Hurriyya* accused the communists of "destroying the bonds of family, friendship, and community . . . and kindling the fire of class struggle."[95]

For its part, the ICP, which often found itself on the defensive on these issues, published a lengthy article in *Ittihad a-Sha'b* to combat the recent accusations in "known newspapers" that "twisted" the writings of Marx and Engels in order to make the communists appear "licentious." The article explained that "communism is the enemy of prostitution" and that it calls for monogamous (*wahdaniyya*) marriage built on "the basis of shared love and complete equality."[96] The ICP also accused Arab nationalists of destroying family life, as when it launched a campaign to free female political prisoners in the UAR who had been arrested in a broader roundup of Syrian communists by 'Abd al-Nasir's government. *Ittihad al-Sha'b* asserted that "for the first time in the history of the Arab peoples, an Arab government is engaging in the destruction of the institution of the family," by imprisoning women "for no reason other than their leadership of the movement to liberate their country and because they are defending democracy and peace."[97] Al-Rabita issued a statement to 'Abd al-Nasir calling for the "liberation of the female detainees in the prisons of the UAR," asserting that they had been "removed from their homes and tortured in the offices of the security services and prisons," that their children had been "deprived of the warmth and protection of motherhood," and that "millions of Iraqi women condemned these barbaric acts."[98]

Qasim gave the opening speech at the second annual conference of al-Rabita, in March 1960, as he had the previous year, but this time he dropped a bombshell. "Until now the League was known as the League for the Defence of Women's Rights. Today, this name is gone and is replaced, in accordance with your wishes, by another name—the League of the Iraqi Woman or the League of Iraqi Women." Qasim's next sentence contained less ambiguous instructions about which part of the change was to be "in accordance" with al-Rabita's wishes: "Sisters, if you wish to use the singular form you will then call it the League of the Iraqi Woman. If you want to use the plural form then you can call it the League of Iraqi Women." He went on to explain that since women in Iraq had achieved their rights, they no longer needed to defend them. "In the past you were defending the rights of women. Now you are defending the rights of the homeland. Along with your brothers, the men of the Republic, you are now defending the homeland and struggling for the preservation of the gains of the victorious Iraqi Revolution."[99] Qasim thus invoked the primary slogan of both the ICP and al-Rabita, "defending the republic," in order to remove any hint of politics from the very name of the organization. On the closing day of the conference, members voted to change its name to the League of Iraqi Women.

The Domain of the Social and the Eternal State

Qasim's insistence that the Iraqi state was the static, stable, and permanent framework of territorial sovereignty was a recurring theme in his speeches. He often asserted that the army intervened on July 14 because it had no choice, but once it did, "our free and eternal [*khalida*] republic burst forth into history."[100] The nature of the Iraqi state and people as eternal was often contrasted in his speeches with that of the individual as ephemeral. "Among our goals is collective rule and the end of individual rule . . . because the people [*al-sha'b*] is the absolute sovereign [*al-sayyid al-mutlaq*]. . . . The individual is ephemeral, whatever his age, and the people is eternal [*baqin*]."[101] Qasim's government used the term *al-sha'b* exclusively for the Iraqi people, and reserved other terms, such as *qawm*, to refer to Arabs or Kurds.[102]

If Qasim referred frequently to the eternal nature of Iraqi sovereign statehood, the popular sovereignty suggested in his reference to the Iraqi people as the "absolute sovereign" was always a deferred promise. In July 1959, he announced that political parties would be allowed to operate openly starting in January 1960 and that elections would follow. The promise was not kept; Qasim's regime, like many other postcolonial governments around the world, to quote Andrew Sartori on India, "endlessly deferred the actual realization of national-popular (subaltern) sovereignty through its subordination to, and absorption into, a statist, elitist politics of national development."[103] In this chapter, I have suggested that the absorption worked in part through the purportedly apolitical work of expanding the social domain. The communist women of al-Rabita often found themselves in the middle of the tensions and contradictions of this situation. Providing significant amounts of free labor for the state's social reform projects, and committed to the ICP slogan of defending the republic, they failed to convince Iraq's anticommunists that their work was apolitical. That work instead became enmeshed in many controversies, perhaps most directly when the women ventured into the volatile southern rural areas of Iraq in the summers of 1959 and 1960. The ways in which Iraq's ongoing agrarian crisis—manifested in limited agricultural productivity and in widespread sociopolitical disorder in the countryside—shaped the events and outcome of the revolutionary era has been insufficiently explored in the scholarship. The banning of urban teachers from entering the rural southern regions, as a way to shut down the communist literacy project, and the censorship of *Ittihad al-Sha'b* for its coverage of that conflict, themselves point to a deliberate campaign to limit the flow of information from rural to urban areas that still affects our understanding of the revolutionary era.

By early 1963, the Ba'thists were able to build a fragile and very temporary alliance of anticommunist interests that was nevertheless strong enough to forestall widespread opposition to their coup long enough for it to succeed and for Qasim to be overthrown. Qasim's regime had been increasingly isolated internationally and regionally, due partly to his threats against Kuwait. His war against the Kurdish national movement, which included aerial bombardments, had further eroded his popularity inside Iraq and led to some of the most direct criticisms of him ever made by the ICP.[104] Qasim had also paved the way for the success of the unlikely gathering of interests that enabled the coup, by destroying most of the mass political organizations that might have defended him, apparently believing that the important balance of power to maintain in his divide-and-conquer strategy was that between the central party organizations, which he left more or less intact.[105] But the ICP had never had any power beyond that which derived from the popular organizations that supported it; the party could thus do little to protect Qasim—or itself—on February 8, 1963. This has been widely recognized by historians, and indeed the ICP had desperately pointed it out to Qasim on numerous occasions. Yet the emphasis on the political and ideological struggle between the central party organizations continues to dominate the scholarship, thus analytically repeating Qasim's mistake.

The Ba'th regime, and the Arab nationalist governments that followed it, never united Iraq with any other Arab countries, the aim that was purportedly their central political difference with Qasim and with the communists. But these governments did continue the practice of military rule, justified through a revolutionary discourse of "blowing up the old world" in the name of the future, a discourse that Fawzi Karim asserts has been produced by all of Iraq's regimes and many of its intellectuals since 1958.[106] The reach of the state into intimate life continued to expand, in the name of producing subjects worthy of sovereignty and capable of economic development. By the 1980s, the Ba'thist state's interest in the care of children and the policing of families through the domain of the social had become a nightmare for many Iraqi adults, as children were mobilized by teachers and other social authorities to inform on the political statements and activities of their parents.[107]

This chapter has implicitly suggested that gender studies based on the assumption of a public/private divide that can be mapped onto constructions of sexual difference may not be that useful for analyzing the modern state's construction of the social as a domain that bridges the public and private spheres while also being deeply implicated in the production of modern forms of sexual difference. Nevertheless, the private domestic sphere was also seen by Qasim's regime and most of Iraq's political parties as demanding social intervention and reform. The next chapter turns to the conflict that emerged out of that intervention.

7

Law and the Post-Revolutionary Self

ON DECEMBER 30, 1959, the Iraqi government promulgated the Law of Personal Status, hailed in the liberal and communist press as a major step forward for Iraqi sovereignty, the Iraqi family, and Iraqi women. Among its most widely noted provisions were the equalization of intestate inheritance rights for male and female heirs, the restriction (but not abolition) of men's right to polygamy, and the fixing of the legal age of consent for marriage at eighteen years for both sexes. But the law's significance derived from more than its content. It was the first time in Iraq that Islamic "personal status laws"—regulations concerning marriage, divorce, and inheritance—had been codified in a unified body of law under the purview of the state. It was also the last area of law applicable to Iraqi Muslims to undergo this process, since civil, commercial, and criminal branches of law were codified by the Ottoman state during the 19th century. The new law did not apply to Iraq's Jewish and Christian minorities, who continued to maintain their own family laws.

The 1959 personal status law occupies an interesting position in histories of the 1958 revolution, the rise of the Ba'th after 1963, and the emergence of Islamic political opposition movements during the 1960s and 1970s. On the one hand, scholars have accorded it no small significance by suggesting that the controversy it provoked helps explain the coalition of forces that ensured the success of the 1963 Ba'th coup.[1] Historiography on the late 20th-century Sunni and, especially, Shi'i opposition movements in Iraq has likewise identified the 1959 personal status law as a factor in their emergence.[2] On the other hand, few historians have devoted more than a sentence or two to analyzing the law's content or the conflict it produced.

Moreover, with the exception of recent work by Noga Efrati, scholars' interest in the legislation seems to have steadily declined over the past fifty years, notwithstanding the emergence of women's and gender history as disciplinary subfields during that time.[3] One explanation is that the forms of reason driving the controversy are imagined to fall along simple modern/ traditional lines, and thus its basic contours are assumed to be always already known: the law's supporters stood for women's rights and liberal equality, its opponents for male privilege and religious tradition. But an examination of the law and the ensuing controversy reveals a more complicated picture.

The law's provisions do not always follow a consistent logic, which was most likely a result of the diverse individuals, representing diverse Iraqi constituencies, who sat on the drafting committee. But if there is an overall reasoning guiding the provisions, it is not coherently framed as an expansion of "rights," nor for the most part do the provisions extend the concept of equality before the law. Rather, they were guided primarily by the aim asserted in the statement of objectives appended to the law: namely, to repair a damaging legal environment that had generated "instability" in the "life of the Iraqi family," and thereby to establish "the foundation on which the Iraqi family of the new era" would be built.[4]

The reference to "instability" in the Iraqi family seems to have connoted several things. First, it pointed to how different Muslims in Iraq were governed by different Islamic family laws, a situation that was often said, perhaps paradoxically, both to fuel sectarianism and to tempt Iraqis to change their sect or legal school at will (e.g., based on whichever inheritance law most appealed to them). Second, it referred to the instability, indeterminacy, and opacity (to civil bureaucrats) of Islamic law itself, which was uncodified and thus frequently open to juristic interpretation and to change over time and space. Third, it referred to the temporal instability of the family, caused by the ease of unilateral male divorce in all schools of Islamic law and by the Shi'i institution of *mut'a*, or temporary, marriage. Fourth, it suggested the family's spatial instability, its porosity to the outside world, reflected on the one hand by the household's openness to those outside the nuclear unit—extended kin, servants, wet nurses—and on the other hand by the embeddedness of its members in broader social networks, to the detriment of the conjugal bond and the care of children. Thus, while the legislators' solution was to institute a uniform code that would also, in its content, foster stability, its provisions in fact worked to stabilize certain kinds of interpersonal relationships and to destabilize others.

While the statement itself does not provide a definition of "instability" in the family, it does account for its origins, namely the lack of "a unified law bringing together, from the opinions of Islamic jurists [*fuqaha*'], the [shari'a] rulings on personal status that are agreed upon and are most appropriate to contemporary welfare." To state the causal logic even more baldly, it was the "multiplicity of juridical sources and the diversity of rulings" on matters of personal status in Islam that had "made the life of the Iraqi family unstable."[5] Criticism by modernizing reformers of the pluralism, complexity, and open-endedness of Islamic jurisprudence was nothing new. Since the 19th century, it had been endlessly deployed to argue for codification of areas of the law other than personal status law, and indeed similar critiques are familiar to the process of modernizing and rationalizing legal systems the world over.[6] What is interesting about the statement's reasoning is that it makes the pluralism of the Islamic legal system the *cause* of instability in the Iraqi family.

In establishing a correlation between the diversity of Islamic laws that had been categorized since the 19th century as "personal status" or "family" law—a categorization that joined previously disunited opinions, texts, and rulings relating to childbirth, custody, marriage, divorce, bequests, and so on—and the instability of the interpersonal relationships governed by those laws, the lawmakers also established a correlation between a unified national family law and the construction of stable families worthy of the revolutionary era. In place of a multiplicity of laws governing a multiplicity of relationships subject to spatial difference and temporal change, the personal status law was to lay the foundation for a unified system governing a timeless institution based on a fixed relationship: the monogamous conjugal couple. It was also to lay the foundation for the everyday life of each member of this institution—man, woman, and child—encouraging, for each of these, certain ways of spending time and discouraging others. This effort to reconstitute everyday time reflected the lawmakers' aim of creating, as the statement of objectives put it, not only a stable family life but also a "society stable in its rights and its duties."[7] Along with the other revolutionary-era social reform projects examined in the previous chapter, the law would help encircle the post-revolutionary self in a complete system of care, from the cradle to the grave.[8]

The society hailed by the statement was unambiguously an Iraqi territorial one, just as the family it referred to was an Iraqi family. A central reasoning of the law was to submerge the diverse religio-legal spaces inhabited by Muslims in Iraq into the homogeneous legal space of the sovereign

nation-state. But, as I have shown throughout this book, the production of a
certain kind of homogeneous space also involved the production of differences
within that space: almost all of the law's provisions distributed rights to Muslim
Iraqi citizens on the basis of sex, while the law as a whole distributed rights on
the basis of religion. Notably, given its relationship to Iraqi territoriality as well
as its subsumption of family law under the sovereignty of the state, the law
was supported in principle by many leading Arab nationalists and by many
Sunni commentators, as were most of the actual law's individual provisions.
This support has been missed in most scholarly works on the revolution, which
have portrayed the controversy as one between the secular state and Islamic
authorities generally, exploited opportunistically by the Ba'th, and which have
often inaccurately stated that the personal status law in its entirety was revoked
after the 1963 coup. In fact, the Ba'thist regime modified only the equal inheritance and polygamy clauses, leaving the rest of the law intact.

If the law was guided by an effort to eliminate some of the heterogeneous
practices of Islamic systems of jurisprudence—a project supported by many
Sunni thinkers—it was not driven by an impulse to undermine Islam as a
source of national morality and Iraqi identity: quite the contrary. The statement of objectives does not conceal the lawmakers' consternation that the
pluralism of family laws in Iraq had led "certain interested persons to make a
sport of the law and the principles of the shari'a by changing their religion or
legal school [*madhhab*]."⁹ This concern over insincere religious conversion in
the text of what is often considered the final step in the secularization of Iraqi
law is striking. I will argue that the law's promulgation is more productively
understood as part of a process by which religion was equated with morality as
both were displaced to the private sphere of state-regulated familial relations.
This was not a process of undermining religion but of remaking it.

Finally, this chapter explores more comprehensive critiques of the
law produced by Iraqi Shi'i jurists, who questioned the very legitimacy
of a unified personal status code under the control of the secular state. It
focuses especially on a 1963 book by the Shi'i *mujtahid* Muhammad Bahr
al-'Ulum. Conceptions of time in its relation to law in Bahr al-'Ulum's
arguments are complex, but can be grouped into two basic lines of thought.
On the one hand, he asserted that the 1959 personal status law was incompatible with the unchanging nature of the shari'a. On the other hand,
he argued that the law temporally and spatially immobilized legal *practice*
by obliterating differences in the five living schools of Islamic law, fixing
laws and legal authorities to a particular time and place, and "closing the

gates of *ijtihad*" or independent juristic reasoning, as well as the gates of *taqlid*, or the follower's emulation of a living *mujtahid*. The temporality of the shari'a laid out in these arguments was not static, although the law derived from unchanging principles. Rather, it was shaped by the dynamic temporality of Islamic legal schools as discursive traditions and by more specific Shi'i legal practices.[10]

The last section of this chapter uses these critiques to reflect more broadly on the temporality of the modern sovereign state and its law, which in the case of post-revolutionary Iraq sought to enable one form of change (economic development) through the production of other forms of stasis. Concepts of sexual difference, the care of children, and the conjugal family were once again key to this process. The fixity of the modern state and its law constituted a rupture not only from earlier practices of Islamic legal schools as nonterritorial discursive traditions but also from earlier Islamic understandings of the state, or *al-dawla*, as cyclical and ephemeral. Turning to a 1962 work on Ibn Khaldun by the Iraqi sociologist 'Ali al-Wardi, I invoke another way of understanding historical time.

Private Morality and the Self-Governing Subject

According to a standard modernization narrative of legal secularization and rationalization, Islamic laws were gradually removed from the domain of religious authorities in the modern era, codified into unified bodies of law, and brought under the control of the secular state. The last legal category to undergo the transformation was that of personal status law, often glossed as "family law," and the reason commonly given for the delay is that this area of law was regarded by Islamic authorities as the untouchable heart of the shari'a. Thus, for pragmatic reasons, legal reformers in the 19th-century Ottoman Empire concentrated on reforming commercial, civil, and criminal law, leaving family law alone. Only in the 20th century, so the story goes, did states acquire the confidence, or the power, to begin encroaching on the domain of Islamic personal status law, with greater or lesser success depending on the respective strength of secular and religious authorities in each national context.

This narrative has been challenged in recent years. One of the most important critiques, by Talal Asad, contests the notion that the shari'a was simply "restricted" to personal status law in this period and that the reason for the exceptionality of family law was that it was seen by Muslims as the "heart of religious doctrine and practice." Asad argues that the concept of "family law"—and indeed of "the family"—was unknown in Islamic legal discourse prior to the 19th century, and that both concepts were constructed through the judicial transformations of that era. The formation of the dual legal system in 19th-century Egypt thus did not simply leave family law to the domain of Islam but rather constituted both "family" and "religion" as belonging to the "private" sphere, where religion was assigned the role of fostering a healthy national morality through the regulation of family life. "It is in this context that 'the family' emerges as a category in law, in welfare administration, and in public moralizing discourse. The family is the unit of 'society' in which the individual is physically and morally reproduced and has his or her primary formation as a 'private' being." The shari'a thus reconstituted "is precisely a secular formula for privatizing 'religion' and preparing the ground for the self-governing subject."[11]

Article 1 of the 1959 law asserts that its provisions are drawn from the shari'a, as well as from the personal status laws of "other Islamic countries." It further specifies that in cases where no provision of the law is applicable, judgment shall be made according to "the Islamic shari'a," without naming any particular school of law. Article 2 states that the present code shall apply to all Iraqi citizens with the exception of those covered by a "special law."[12] This clause has generally been interpreted as meaning that Christians and Jews in Iraq would retain their own personal status laws.[13] It presents some difficulty to the familiar narrative that the law was, as legal scholar J.N.D. Anderson claims, a "sacrifice of sectarian principles on the altar of national unity."[14] No doubt many Christian and Jewish authorities appreciated the right to maintain their own family laws. Yet the exclusion of these communities from the personal status law seems to fly in the face of the revolutionary project to unify the law for all Iraqi citizens and of the ubiquitous nationalist criticism of Britain and the monarchy for dividing the nation by inserting different Iraqis into different legal regimes.

One explanation is that Iraqi national identity or selfhood was constructed as Muslim, against the Christian/Jewish Other, communities that had been increasingly associated with the European colonial powers despite their deep Iraqi heritage. This project would be furthered on the one hand by the forging of a more unified identity from among the various Muslim sects and legal schools, and on the other hand by the exclusion of Christians and Jews from full national citizenship, both of which are forms of reasoning the personal status law seems to participate in. In addition to the exclusion of non-Muslims from the law itself, some of its provisions restrict their rights more than can be justified by any claim of remaining true to the shari'a. Most notable is a clause prohibiting the bequeathing of real property to someone of a different religion. Since the law applies only to Muslims, the clause presumably only means that a Muslim cannot bequeath property to a non-Muslim, and in fact it specifies that the prohibition applies even if the laws of the designated legatee would allow that person to bequeath property in the other direction. By contrast, other provisions in the law permit bequests from an Iraqi citizen to a foreign national on the condition that the law of the foreign national permits reciprocal bequests. According to Anderson, the clause banning the bequeathing of property to non-Muslims has no historical basis in any school of Islamic law, which, at the most, makes religion a bar only to intestate inheritance, not to testate inheritance or voluntary bequests. Anderson simply notes that the provision is "strange"—as indeed it is if, as he argues, the personal status law is to be interpreted as a "sacrifice of sectarian principles on the altar of national unity."[15] If, however, the law is understood as part of the construction of Iraqi sovereign selfhood as Muslim, and the hardening of religious difference as part of that construction, it appears less strange.[16]

The Iraqi Family of the New Era

The remainder of the law, following Article 2, consists of the actual codes related to marriage, divorce, child care, and inheritance. The presentation of the provisions in this order reflects the new type of family envisaged by the legislators. The term "personal status law"—a category that derives not from the shari'a but from 19th-century European law[17]—is most commonly defined as "family law," but this is not quite accurate. It does not cover all codes regulating family relations; it excludes laws on incest and adultery, for example, which fall under criminal law. More useful is a definition proposed by Muhammad Bahr al-'Ulum in his 1963 critique of the Iraqi code. The category of "personal status law" includes all codes that govern "the relationship of the individual with his family [usratihi]," and more specifically those that govern the temporal stages of the individual's life within the family—from his appearance as a fetus to his death and beyond it (the distribution of his property and debt).[18]

Indeed, the substantive provisions of the 1959 Iraqi law can almost be read as a temporal narrative of a normative human life—except that they begin not with conception or with birth but with marriage, the act that founds the modern conjugal family. This choice reflects the law's orientation not only toward regulating the life cycle of the individual human—as Bahr al-'Ulum understands the category of personal status law in its appropriation within Islamic law—but also toward regulating the life cycle of a particular kind of family. Unlike the extended family, this family is easily narratizable for the simple reason that it has a beginning: the individuation of the conjugal couple from the spouses' previous social contexts. The necessity of making such narrative choices already illustrates the relevance of Brinkley Messick's insight that codification of the shari'a is *always* a transformation of the shari'a, regardless of how closely the new codes might be said to adhere to Islamic legal precepts.[19]

Article 3 defines marriage as "a contract between a man and a woman," the aims of which are "to establish the bond of a shared life and to beget children."[20] This definition resonates to a degree with Islamic law, which also views marriage as a contract; legal rulings on marriage have thus often worked through analogy with other instances of contract law. The marriage contract in Islam likewise has two authorized aims, one of which is procreation. But here the overlap ends, since the second legitimate purpose of marriage in all schools of Islamic law is sexual pleasure. The concept of marriage as the foundation of "a shared life" is historically unknown in Islamic law, though of course the conjugal couple as the basis of modern family life was a familiar understanding in Iraq by this time.[21] The absence of sexual pleasure as a legal aim of the marriage contract is consonant with long-standing Western conceptions of the institution, both Christian and secular. Yet its omission from the 1959 law, and the addition of "the bond of a shared life" in its place, are so far from historical Islamic understandings of marriage that their failure to generate significant commentary from Islamic scholars opposed to other aspects of the law is worth noting.

In Shi'i law, moreover, sexual pleasure has historically been the only authorized purpose of *mut'a* or temporary marriage. The word *mut'a* actually translates as "pleasure," though the terms *zawaj al-mut'a* or *nikah al-mut'a* have conventionally been translated into English as "temporary marriage" rather than the more direct "pleasure marriage." This form of marriage, which is not recognized in the four Sunni schools of law, consists of a contract between a man and a woman for a specified period of time, which might be one hour or ninety-nine years.[22] While procreation is not a legitimate intent of the parties to a *mut'a* contract, children conceived during the contracted period are considered legitimate. Since, at least historically, Shi'i law has explicitly banned procreation as a purpose of *mut'a* marriage,[23] and has implicitly banned the creation of a shared life as such, it would seem that the definition of marriage in Article 3 of the Iraqi personal status law would fail to legitimize *mutʿa* marriages. As Iranian Shiʿi scholar Muhammad Jaʿfar Jaʿfari Langarudi explains, marriage in Islamic (i.e., Shiʿi) law "cannot be defined as an agreement for the establishment of a family or household between a man and a woman, because that does not include *mutʿa* marriage . . . [sexual] intercourse is the *raison d'être* of marriage."[24]

A detailed analysis of the law's provisions is beyond the scope of this chapter.[25] In the following paragraphs, I focus on a few clauses that raise some questions about the common view of the law as oriented toward the expansion of rights, before turning to the responses to its promulgation in the Iraqi public sphere.

The divorce provisions are among those most often portrayed as moves toward sexual equality, that is, toward restricting the rights of men and/or expanding the rights of women to divorce. But to the extent that they have much coherence at all, these provisions are more accurately seen as governed by the law's definition of marriage: "a contract between a man and a woman, the legitimate aims of which are to establish the bond of a shared life and to beget children." They thus restrict irrational divorces made in the heat of passion, while facilitating those based on the already effected dissolution of a "shared life" for the couple (e.g., the prolonged absence of the husband), their inability to produce offspring, or the danger that a marriage poses to women or children.

The provisions on divorce begin with a section on *talaq*, or unilateral divorce initiated by the man. In all five schools of Islamic law, a man may divorce his wife, without stating a reason, by proclaiming a formula (e.g., "I divorce thee"). On the third pronouncement, the divorce becomes irrevocable. The schools differ over whether the three statements must be separated by a span of time, whether they can be conditional (i.e., based on the wife's future actions or inactions), and whether the formula is effective when uttered under certain physiological or mental conditions, such as intoxication, rage, or jest.[26] The personal status law retains the man's right to *talaq*, while adopting from among the legal schools the opinions most restrictive of the conditions under which the pronouncement is valid. In brief, *talaq* is valid if the man intended for it to be valid and if he was in full control of his mental capacities when making the statement. These restrictions on *talaq* were welcomed by women's rights advocates and Western legal theorists. The latter had long been horrified by the legal validation, and in some cases irrevocability, of divorce statements made by men under the influence of alcohol or in moments of anger or jest. Anderson, for example, departs from his usual neutral tone when noting that the 1959 law limited "the appallingly wide scope previously accorded to pronouncements of unilateral repudiation of their wives by Muslim husbands."[27]

Talaq is clearly an instance of male privilege in a patriarchal legal system. Yet comments such as Anderson's do little to enlighten us on the legal reasoning establishing the conditions under which *talaq* is valid. Islamic opinions that enforce statements of *talaq* uttered by a drunk, enraged, or mocking husband do not exactly protect men's rights, since their sole legal effect is to deny the man's right to revoke the statement later. Rather, they reflect the broader ethical and pedagogical orientation of Islamic law, the norms of which include refraining from intoxication, losing control of oneself, and saying things one doesn't mean. In the personal status law, this is replaced by a far greater concern for stabilizing the conjugal bond. Contrary to Anderson's description, the law's provisions on *talaq* did not limit the "scope" of men's divorce pronouncements, since a man who actually wanted to divorce his wife was still entirely free to do so. It would be more accurate to say that they expanded the scope of men's rights to make and then rescind pronouncements of divorce at will.

They also, as the law's advocates often pointed out, protected a woman from suffering the consequences of rash, abusive, or drunken statements uttered by her spouse. The assumption in liberal discourse was always that the wife would not want the pronouncement of *talaq* to be enforced. Given the precarious status of divorced women in Iraqi society, this may have often been the case. Yet it is certainly not the only possible scenario, especially since women retain more rights under the *talaq* form of divorce, in terms of maintenance and the deferred dower, than they do under any other form in Islamic law. The very nature of *talaq* as regulated private communication suggests that some women might sometimes have some agency in producing the conditions that lead to its fulfillment, to say nothing of its appearance as a dispute between two parties in a court of law.[28] In any case, even granting that the new provisions may have offered legal protection for some women, it is difficult to conceive of them on that basis as an expansion of women's rights, since the woman's will is simply not under consideration in either the relevant provisions of the Islamic legal schools or those of the personal status law.

In a striking provision with no direct parallel in the shari'a, the law requires that a woman breastfeed her own infant unless a physical illness prevents her from doing so.[29] The Islamic legal tradition that the clause gestures toward relates to the conditions under which it is permissible for a woman who is not the child's mother—that is, a wet nurse—to suckle an infant. The majority opinion—that of the Ja'fari (Shi'i), Hanafi, Hanbali, and Shafi'i schools—is that a mother is not required to nurse her own infant unless there is no one else available to do it, that is, if the child would otherwise die. The Maliki school does mandate that a mother nurse her infant except under certain circumstances, though these circumstances are more lenient than those of the personal status law: they exempt a woman who has been divorced by the baby's father from any requirement to nurse their child as well as any woman for whom breastfeeding would be "dishonorable" or "shameful." Not surprisingly, the Malikis also allow the sole exemption permitted in the personal status law, that of mothers who are ill or deficient in breast milk.[30]

The breastfeeding provision clearly cannot be interpreted as an expansion of women's rights, nor can it be explained away as a concession to patriarchal Islamic law. Not only does it reject the majority opinion in Islam that nursing is not an obligation of the mother unless the child's life is at stake—which, between the Ja'fari and Hanafi schools, in fact represented an overwhelming majority of Islamic jurists in Iraq—but it deviates from all legal schools in order to devise a new, more restrictive law. The provision does, however, reflect the modernizing drive to expel those who are strangers to the nuclear conjugal family from the home, and especially from the care of the children inside it. Beth Baron has shown how wet nurses were increasingly constructed in 19th- and 20th-century Egyptian nationalist discourses as foreign, to both the family and the nation, and thus dangerous.[31] Similarly, in Jacques Donzelot's analysis of philanthropic campaigns in 19th-century France, wet nurses were among those "mobile elements" of the household who had to be excluded so that "the children might be immobilized within it."[32]

In addition to family stability and individual rights, the statement of objectives promises the Iraqi woman in particular something more: the protection of "her familial independence" (*istiqlaluha al-'a'ili*).[33] This somewhat curious expression could be read as referring to a woman's independence, as an individual, within her family. But the law institutes a notably conservative reading of shari'a law in relation to a woman's autonomy vis-à-vis her husband; most significantly, it mandates that she is not allowed to leave the home without his permission.[34] It thus seems more likely that the expression refers to the independence of the conjugal family itself, promising to protect it from the intrusions of strangers, whether wet nurses or elder members of the patrilineal extended family. It is not the rights of the individual Iraqi citizen that the personal status law advances so much as the individuation of the conjugal couple from the spouses' other social contexts. Within the domestic space inhabited by that unit—which is now designated as "her" family—the wife is accorded a number of powers, especially in relation to the care of her children. But the law also codifies her husband's absolute power over her interaction with the outside world, while simultaneously working to exclude that world from her home.

A few clauses in the personal status law were indeed oriented toward the expansion of women's rights and of sexual equality. The most notable is Article 74 on intestate inheritance, by far the law's most controversial provision, its innocuous presentation notwithstanding. The text simply states: "The provisions comprised in articles 1187–1199 of the Civil Code shall govern the determination of who are the heirs and what share in the estate they shall take, whether in regard to real or personal property."[35] The articles in question originated in the Ottoman Land Law of 1858 and related solely to the inheritance of leaseholds on state lands. In neither that law nor the monarchical-era Iraqi Civil Code that was partially derived from it did the articles apply to the inheritance of private property, whether real or personal. Nevertheless, officials could and did respond to the opposition they knew would be forthcoming from defenders of the shari'a by pointing out that the articles on inheritance of leaseholds on state land had not, in the century that had passed since their promulgation, produced any memorable dissent from Iraq's 'ulama'.[36] The main implication of these articles is that they gave female and male heirs equal shares of the property governed by intestate inheritance, whereas in all schools of Islamic law a female inherits one half the share of a male in the equivalent position. In the personal status law, as in Islamic law, the rules of intestate inheritance govern a minimum of two-thirds of the deceased's estate. The other one-third may be bequeathed—that is, may be given through testate inheritance—according to the will of the testator, though there are differences among the schools over whether this part can be bequeathed to the heirs who automatically receive portions of the estate through the rules of intestate inheritance. Thus, Article 74 would apply to at least two-thirds of all inherited property in Iraq, and probably much more than that, since many people did not invoke their right to testate inheritance.

Responses to the Law: Communists, Ba'thists, and the 'Ulama'

The communist League for the Defense of Women's Rights, or al-Rabita, was one of the main proponents of the 1959 personal status law. Female lawyers from the group sat on the drafting committee and al-Rabita's president, Naziha al-Dulaimi, was also involved. The Iraqi Communist Party (ICP) itself followed the committee's work with interest, and took pains to prepare Iraqis for the law's promulgation. On November 6, 1959, less than two months before the law was published in the government gazette, the ICP daily *Ittihad al-Sha'b* published a special report titled "Marriage and Family Life in the Soviet Union." Its title notwithstanding, the essay is an explication of Soviet family law (not "life"), and in particular of provisions in that law that happened to also be provisions of the Iraqi personal status law that was soon to be announced. These include the fixing of the age of consent to marry at eighteen years for both sexes; the outlawing of polygamy (in the Iraqi law, polygamy would be restricted but not banned); limitations on divorce; legal preference for the mother in child custody disputes; and the requirement of state registration of marriages and of medical certificates verifying the prospective spouses are free of disease.[37]

The article helps explain why the ICP considered family law reform a critical issue, even in the midst of Iraq's volatile revolutionary situation. Soviet marriage law bestows on marriage "the protection of the state," and "frees the individual from the bonds of class, nationality, sect, and any other bonds that were originally inherited." It allows the state to "prevent harmful marriages, such as marriage to a person with an infectious or genetic disease that could affect the health of the children." Marriage is "the first phase in the formation of the family [*takwin al-usra*], and in the raising of children. . . . This calls for the creation of legal relationships, in addition to social relationships, between spouses, children, and parents." Under the section on divorce, the article further explains that "questions of marriage and the formation of the family are not private questions that the state is not allowed to intervene in; rather, they are social questions that states must intervene in to regulate [the family's] affairs and ensure its continuity . . . and to prevent any mockery of this sacred bond." The article directs its most forceful critiques against "despotic traditions," such as arranged and child marriages, that had been especially prevalent in the "southern and eastern" regions of the USSR.[38]

The main difference between the article's description of Soviet family law and the coming Iraqi personal status law related to women's work outside the home. The article notes that Soviet law ensures a woman's right to leave the home without her husband's permission and to work outside the home. The Iraqi law, when promulgated two months later, however, would mandate that a woman is not allowed to leave the home without her husband's permission. It is likely that this was a controversial aspect of the law within the drafting committee, given, for example, al-Dulaimi's belief in the importance of women's right to work outside the home.[39]

Another lengthy explication of the communist position on the law was published in *Ittihad al-Sha'b* on August 8, 1960, by which time the controversy was in full swing. This was the text of a recent lecture in Baghdad by Ahmad Jamal al-Din, a lawyer and founder of the ICP, titled "Personal Status and the Rights of Women." Jamal al-Din defined personal status as "a component of public status [*al-ahwal al-'amma*]" and the bonds related to it as "a component of social bonds [*rawabit ijtima'iyya*]" organizing family relations. The family "stands on the foundation of marriage."[40]

Jamal al-Din then produced a historical narrative of the Iraqi family that explained why marriages in Iraq so often ended up in court. In the early age of Islam, jurists had struggled commendably for a "unified [family] law for all the people." But the different legal schools gradually developed, and their family laws became more and more divergent. During the classical and Ottoman eras, marriages were arranged, and spouses were not allowed to meet before the wedding night. Marriages were contracted solely for pleasure (*mut'a*), wealth, or power. Since the spouses were strangers to one another, the marital household was full of "trouble and misery," which naturally had a "significant effect on the children who would live within it." This necessitated the creation of laws that did not try to impose marital permanence upon the people, that is, laws facilitating the separation of the spouses so as not to prolong their misery. Family laws deteriorated further under the British occupying forces, who "divided the people into various groups, on the basis of sect and religion, and each sect or group was given special laws . . . in order to build a solid foundation for colonialism, which could never have survived otherwise." The promulgation of the 1959 Iraqi personal status law marked nothing less than "the end of religious and sectarian division in our country."[41] In this narrative, the historical trajectory of marriage from a contract of pleasure and property to one of companionship and the care of children, and from an ephemeral and impermanent institution to a stable and lasting one, precisely parallels the historical trajectory of Iraq from internal sectarianism and foreign exploitation to full political sovereignty and economic development.

Leaders of the Ba'th Party were apparently split over the personal status law. Batatu reports that the equal-inheritance clause was repealed after the 1963 coup while one of the party's leading figures, 'Ali Salih al-Sa'di, was in Cairo, since he had warned that repeal would "lead to a split" in the coalition behind the coup and that the world would not be able "look upon us as a progressive regime."[42] Nevertheless, the party's newspaper, *al-Hurriyya*, was publishing articles as early as 1960 supporting every provision in the 1959 law *except* the equal-inheritance clause and, sometimes, the polygamy one. This position seems to have helped consolidate the party's alliance with some of the country's leading Sunni 'ulama', which was much stronger than the tenuous coalition with Shi'i 'ulama' it would form just prior to the coup.

In May 1960, *al-Hurriyya* published a statement from the qadi of Basra, Shaykh 'Ala' al-Din Kharrufa, that he had sent to Qasim, the minister of justice, and the interior minister. "Muslims welcomed the personal status law as a leap forward on the path of reform and of the unity of Muslims," Kharrufa asserts. But, he continues, they were "surprised by Article 74, which equalizes inheritance rights between the man and the woman and is a clear violation of the word of God." Kharrufa declares that if Qasim would repeal the equal-inheritance clause, the Iraqi personal status law would be "the greatest law that has appeared in Iraq or in the rest of the Islamic countries," and he states that all its provisions, with the exception of the inheritance clause, were compatible with the shari'a.[43]

The primary grounds for Kharrufa's enthusiasm are suggested in his comment that the law helped to further the "unity of Muslims." The qadi was part of the broad 20th-century movement of Muslim reformers who sought to eliminate what they saw as the divisive effects of the legal schools in order to forge a unified Muslim identity and Islamic law for the modern era. He writes that the July 14 revolution, which had "liberated Iraqi soil from colonialism and the Iraqi dinar from the [British] sterling," had likewise "liberated the Iraqi judicial system through this [personal status] law, freeing it from the rigid boundaries [*nitaq al-jumud*] of a single school [*madhhab wahid*] into the expansiveness of the wide, developed Islamic *fiqh*," or system of jurisprudence.[44]

Scholarly assumptions that opposition to the personal status law was based on its secular undermining of Islamic clerical authority cannot account for the enthusiasm with which Sunni jurists such as Kharrufa greeted most of its provisions as well as its very promulgation as a unified code under the purview of the state. These assumptions do not take seriously the efforts by many Muslim reformers in this period to unify Muslims through the unification of Islamic family law or their frequent willingness to align themselves with the modern nation-state to achieve this aim. The assumptions have also led to the repetition in the scholarship of the historical inaccuracy that the 1959 personal status law itself was repealed by the Ba'thists after the 1963 coup.[45] But as pointed out earlier, the new regime modified only two provisions of the law, those on inheritance and polygamy. This would lead to a split between the Ba'th and the Shi'i 'ulama' who had supported, or at least not opposed, the coup in the hope that the entire law would then be repealed. But it did not damage the Ba'thists' relationship with many leading Sunni 'ulama', who had asked only for the alteration of those two provisions.

The origins of the Shi'i Islamist movement that would largely replace communism as the most important political opposition movement in southern and central Iraq by the early 1970s is usually traced to the formation of several political groups around 1960. Scholars give different dates for the founding of the Da'wa Party in Najaf by young radical scholars, ranging from 1957 to the mid-1960s. Faleh Jabar makes a reasonable case that the party most likely came together in 1959.[46] But it was not until 1960 that the older, more quietist 'ulama'—"stunned and dismayed" by the promulgation of the personal status law—lent their support to the formation of a political organization representing the entire Shi'i clerical establishment, Jama'at al-'Ulama', and to a newspaper promulgating its platform, al-Adwa' al-Islamiyya.[47] The Islamic Party, which included both Sunnis and Shi'a, was also formed in 1960.[48]

The impact of the personal status law on the Najafi public sphere is suggested by a dramatic shift in articles published in the Shi'i literary journal al-Najaf before and after the law's promulgation.[49] Prior to January 1960, al-Najaf ran numerous articles by 'ulama' and lay Shi'i intellectuals positively assessing the July revolution in particular and the concept and meaning of "revolution" in general.[50] Other articles defended the land reform law of September 1958 and the annulment of the tribal code in 1959. The latter was described by one writer as the nullification of "some of the harmful tribal customs that divide the country into two classes: a tiny class in the city who live under the rule of law and another large class whose despicable crimes of murder, appropriation, and slavery are minimized by tribal law."[51] In Iraqi public discourse at the time, accusations of tribal law legitimizing murder were usually references to "honor killings"

of women. The journal also published articles and poems criticizing polygamy for being cruel to women, though nothing was said about the law
in this regard.[52] *Al-Najaf*'s authors as well as its readers, through letters to
the editor, insisted on the importance of expanding "women's rights" and
asserted that one of the most important gains of the July revolution was
the advances made or promised in this area.[53]

After the promulgation of the personal status law, there was a radical
transformation in the tone and political positions of *al-Najaf* in relation to
women's rights, Qasim's regime, and the communist threat. Clear indica-
tions of the shift appeared almost instantly, by the February 1960 issue.[54] A
number of essays dealt directly with the personal status law. But the broader
effect of the shift is vividly illustrated in a pair of articles written by the
same author, Husayn Fahmi al-Khazraji, and published in the journal in
1959 and 1962. The September 1959 essay, titled "The Problem of the Iraqi
Woman," asserted that the question of women's work and status was "one
of the most important social issues that must be addressed by social reformers in our country today." Since "the woman's intelligence is manifested in
social service in addition to the domain of family life," it was necessary to
"open space for her" to work in the social field. By "granting the woman
her independence, freedom, and rights, she will . . . help raise her country
and her society from the depths of ignorance and . . . ancient customs to the
heights of civilization and progress, and we will then be able to say that Iraq
has caught up with the caravan of human civilization."[55] Three years later,
the author's tone had changed markedly. In an article titled "A Nation That
Entrusts Its Affairs to a Woman Will Not Prosper" (a reference to a hadith,
or saying, of the Prophet Muhammad), he writes that any society that tries
to erase the "clear differences" between the sexes "will end in turmoil and
corruption, because that is a revolution against nature, and nature has a
single order that does not vary according to the differences between nations,
epochs, or cities, nor to alterations in the environment and whether it is
advancing or decaying, nor to changes in the education or culture of the
individual."[56] While these positions were not irreconcilable, there is little
doubt that the sociopolitical context and affective registers in which they
were pronounced had shifted considerably.

The most sustained critique of the Iraqi personal status law by a
contemporary Shi'i scholar was Muhammad Bahr al-'Ulum's *Adwa' 'ala
Qanun al-Ahwal al-Shakhsiyya* (Insights into the personal status law),
published in 1963 shortly after the new Ba'th regime had revised the law.

Bahr al-ʿUlum asserts that "the most important popular demand" after the 1963 coup had been for the new regime to review the 1959 personal status law.[57] But after leaving the Iraqi people waiting in anticipation and "great hope," the government repealed only the equal-inheritance clause of the law, "with no regard for the many critiques that have opposed it as a whole" and that had established clear grounds for repeal.[58] The effect that this early disappointment of Shiʿi scholars with the new government may have had on future Shiʿi-Baʿthist relations, and the degree to which it may have violated any agreements or understandings between the party and the Najafi ʿulamaʾ prior to the coup, cannot be pursued here, though they are not well understood in the current literature.[59]

The rest of Bahr al-ʿUlum's book is a detailed critique of the 1959 law. It is directed partly at Sunni ʿulamaʾ who legitimize the practice of state rulers picking and choosing precepts from among the legal schools in order to construct a unified, fixed code, a practice not considered valid by Shiʿi ʿulamaʾ. He begins by noting the consistent opposition of Muhsin al-Hakim—the highest ranking Shiʿi *mujtahid*—to the personal status law since the day it was promulgated, which never deviated from the simple demand that the state "leave Muslims alone in their religious matters and [let them] draw their interpretations freely from their own doctrinal [*madhhabiyya*] sources, without giving preference to some of them over others."[60]

Bahr al-ʿUlum goes on to argue that the personal status law freezes legal practice in time and "closes the gates of *ijtihad*" or independent juristic reasoning. *Ijtihad* is performed by a living judge in a particular time, and it is not permissible to "pass a personal status law that must be followed by every judge in every generation." The author concedes that the Jaʿfari school of Shiʿi law permits more types of *ijtihad* than the Sunni schools, and thus the argument might seem to be less relevant to Sunnis. But he counters this possible objection by asserting that the personal status law violates even the doctrines of "our brothers from *ahl al-sunna*," which all require that the gates of at least one type of *ijtihad*, namely *ijtihad fi al-madhhab* (referring to juristic reasoning that varies by legal school) remain open. Bahr al-ʿUlum further points out that many Sunni scholars in modern times have called for opening the gates of absolute ijtihad (*al-ijtihad al-mutlaq*), especially for new events that require "new opinions."[61] The author thus questions the notion that Shiʿi opposition to the law was less modern than was Sunni or secular support for it. Indeed, the future-oriented language of progress pervades his text as it did most commentaries on the law. Compelling any sect to follow the precepts of a legal school different from its own would create problems that were both "religious" and "social," because it would "obstruct humanity's progress in building a [new] human nature for a better society, shimmering with happiness and freedom under the canopy of Islam."[62]

Bahr al-'Ulum's analyses of temporal change in relation to law can be grouped into two basic positions. On the one hand, he asserts that the 1959 law was based on the notion that legal principles can change, which contradicts the eternal nature of the shari'a.[63] On the other hand, he argues that legal practices in the Islamic tradition of jurisprudence are more dynamic and sensitive to temporal change and spatial difference than is the personal status law. Shi'i court users and judges "are not bound to a time and place," in the sense that people may travel to the court and judge of their choice, and jurists are not appointed by anyone for a fixed duration of time. In addition to closing the gates of *ijtihad*, the personal status law "closes the gates of *taqlid*."[64] *Taqlid* is the practice by which each Shi'i individual chooses one living *mujtahid* or Islamic legal scholar to emulate, and whose interpretation of the law she or he follows. It helps ensure that the interpretation of unchanging legal principles is relevant to the time and place—hence the requirement that the *mujtahid* be still alive—and also gives laypeople control over the ranking and authority of individual *mujtahid*s.

The People of the State and the People of Revolution

Bahr al-'Ulum's critique of the fixity of the modern nation-state's law, and of its incompatibility with the extraterritorial and open-ended traditions of Islamic jurisprudence, points suggestively to some of the questions about time and modernity that this book has explored. I have argued that a central paradox of modernization and development is the way in which the forms of stasis that accompany modernity often sit rather uneasily with the notion of continuous change that is likewise a central claim of modernity. I have also suggested that the modern nation-state and the modern family are somehow key to the productive maintenance of this paradox, and ultimately it is the law that binds them together. The marriage crisis discourse that was examined in previous chapters, and that also entered frequently into discussions around the personal status law, was always a national discourse. Such a crisis could only unfold within the territorial borders of a nation-state, and what this crisis demanded was a national family law, a law the territorial state could call its own.[65]

Wael Hallaq has written that the "sovereign will of the modern state" is "represented in its own legal will and therefore in the state's law. There is no modern nation-state that does not have *its own* law."[66] In an argument that resonates with Bahr al-'Ulum's critique of the 1959 Iraqi personal status law, Hallaq notes how different this sovereign legal will of the modern state is from earlier Islamic conceptions of both law and the state. The shari'a is both "pluralist" and "extraterritorial," and its temporality has never been that of the state, whether modern or premodern. Yet Islamic law was compatible with, albeit separate from, the temporality of the premodern Islamic state. Hallaq notes that the Arabic word *dawla*, which since the late nineteenth "has come to refer to *the totality of the modern state*," previously "meant nothing of the sort."

The term *dawla* essentially connoted a dynastic rule that comes to power in one part of the world, Islamic or non-Islamic, and then passes away. This idea of rotation and of successive change of dynasties is integral to the concept. Thus the [Islamic] Community remains fixed and cannot come to an end until the Day of Judgment, whereas the *dawla* that governs it is temporary and ephemeral, having no intrinsic, organic, or permanent ties to the Community and its Shari'a. It is a means to an end.[67]

The Muslim ruler of the cyclical and ephemeral *dawla* "did not possess a sovereign will that was inherently represented by his law." This understanding of *dawla* is still present in the "lexical meaning of the term," namely the "occurrence of something consecutively," or "a change from one situation to another."[68] The original lexical meaning of *dawla* is thus completely opposed to that of the term "state," which implies a condition of stasis.

In elaborating this argument, Hallaq makes the obvious reference to the 14th-century historian Ibn Khaldun, whose conception of historical time introduced, centuries before the European Enlightenment, both a social analysis and a kind of linearity into existing cyclical conceptions of civilizational time as rising and falling. But Khaldunian time also maintained the dynamic cyclicality that is still carried in the Arabic term *dawla* and that Hallaq contrasts to the fixity of the modern state. In Ibn Khaldun's narrative of historical time, a new civilization is founded by nomads invading and overthrowing a previous one, progresses over time into maturity, and begins to decline as its luxury and opulence increase, until it is overthrown by a new group of nomads, whereupon the cycle begins anew.

In 1962, the last full year of Qasim's regime and a year before the publication of Bahr al-'Ulum's work on the personal status law, the Iraqi sociologist 'Ali al-Wardi published his *Mantiq Ibn Khaldun* (Ibn Khaldun's logic), in which he explored some similar ideas about the temporal nature of the state. Al-Wardi writes that for Ibn Khaldun, "there is no state [*dawla*] that remains forever strong. . . . Every state has a life span, like the life span of a person. It begins and flourishes and then grows old and dies." Occasionally its life cycle is extended due to exceptional circumstances, but "the cycle nevertheless continues, and it is inevitable that the state will die in the end just like the individual dies."[69] The analogy of the human life cycle in this imaginary is quite different from the one commonly used in modern developmentalist narratives. The difference is that the Khaldunian narrative is not based on the denial of death, and thus the analogy does not end with the attainment of sovereign adulthood, implicitly envisioned as a permanent state in 20th-century modernization discourses that drew on the analogy.

While al-Wardi views Ibn Khaldun as the first thinker to have introduced modern conceptions of social science to historical analysis, he also links the Khaldunian narrative of the rise and fall of states to earlier Islamic conceptions of moral decline and revival. The Islamic community gradually moves away from Islamic ideals, in a process of moral deviation or degeneration, but this inevitable trajectory of decline is punctuated by periods of "renewal" or "revival"; hence the hadith that "at the beginning of every century God will send to this community one who will renew its religion." According to al-Wardi, this understanding of moral decline and revival has helped to fuel regularly repeated revolutions in Islamic history, giving Islamic civilization its "creative, dynamic" quality as well as its "fertility of intellectual production."[70]

The Islamic conceptions of moral decline and revival are interwoven in al-Wardi's analysis with the Khaldunian narrative of the historical rise and fall of states, since states by their nature "start out good and gradually worsen. They are close to the spirit of religion at first, and then their leaders submerge themselves in luxury, generation after generation. Every generation becomes more comfortable than the previous one and further from the demands of good work, until they finally end in collapse."[71] And both conceptions are linked in al-Wardi's thought to the necessary and repeated political work of revolution. Here he explicitly diverges from Ibn Khaldun, whom he notes condemned as immoral any rebellion against a ruler that did not have a good chance of success. Al-Wardi writes that Ibn Khaldun neglected the actual history of revolutions, which provides abundant proof that a revolution might end in failure but still have a positive social influence, by arousing public sentiment and opening the minds of the people. "It often happens that failed revolutions pave the way for the successful revolution that follows them."[72] We can borrow from Ibn Khaldun's "intellectual revolution," al-Wardi concludes, while "rejecting his condemnation of social revolutions."[73]

In Chapter 4, I looked at some of al-Wardi's work written before the revolution, especially his highly controversial 1954 *Wu'az al-Salatin* (The sultans' preachers). The most famous argument of that book attributed Iraq's underdevelopment in part to the proliferation of "sexual deviance" in Iraq, which in turn it attributed to a combination of women's seclusion, unhealthy family life, and ineffective moral pedagogies based on speeches and sermons. But that argument takes up only a few pages near the beginning of the book. In the rest of it, al-Wardi argues in detail that much of Islamic history in general, and Iraqi history in particular, can be understood as a repeated struggle between two camps: "the people of the state" and "the people of revolution" (*arbab al-dawla* and *arbab al-thawra*), groups he refers to elsewhere as "the sultans and the revolutionaries," "the rich and the revolutionary," and "the conservatives and the renewers [*mujaddidun*]," among other terms.[74] As soon as the revolutionaries succeed, they begin their inevitable moral decline into the corrupt people of the state, and a new group of revolutionaries must emerge to fight against the injustice that is intrinsic to every state.

Al-Wardi's narrative raises some questions about Lee Edelman's US-centered claim that "we are no more able to conceive of a politics without a fantasy of the future than we are to conceive of a future without the figure of the Child."[75] Arguing that martyrdom is an agentive force in history, al-Wardi writes that the actions of 'Ali—the Prophet's son-in-law and the first Shi'i Imam—are "not the actions of a person who wants to rule. They are the actions of a person who wants to die," and to "arouse through his death other revolutionaries. And thus does the caravan of revolutionaries wind on from generation to generation."[76] Like "the great revolutionary" Muhammad, 'Ali understood that "fighting the tyrants and the wealthy" cannot be accomplished through "speeches and resounding sermons."[77] It is precisely when al-Wardi turns his attention to death and the past (the memories of martyrs), rather than birth and the future (heteronormative time), that he makes his most radical political engagements, recalling Walter Benjamin's assertion that revolutionary sentiment is nourished "by the image of enslaved ancestors rather than that of liberated grandchildren."[78]

What links the early and later arguments in *Wuʿaz al-Salatin* (about sexual deviance and revolution, respectively) is al-Wardi's critique of what he called "Aristotelian" reason, which had led to the ineffective reliance on rational persuasion to change people's morals or impel them to action.[79] But while the discussions of deviance and of revolution are similar in their insistence on the role of irrational forces in driving human conduct, on another register the argument has been turned upside down. Al-Wardi is no longer addressing the people of the state, that is, those with the institutional power to undermine customs of women's seclusion and shape the desires and habits of the rising generation. He is now advising the people of revolution on strategies for "fighting the tyrants and the wealthy," albeit through a similar awareness of the power of sentiments operating below the level of reason. This is because "history does not move forward on the basis of rational thought," which "has no danger in it; it is cold and does not create anguish or move the heart."[80] This was advice not on how to achieve the disciplinary conduct of conduct but on how to "move the heart" toward revolution. The revolutionary martyr, according to al-Wardi, is one who has learned how to harness the powers of his unreason—since there is nothing rational about martyrdom—in order to inch the world once again toward justice, even in the face of inevitable failure.

Postcolonial Heterotemporalities

In 1959, the regime of 'Abd al-Karim Qasim commissioned the Iraqi artist Jawad Salim to build a public monument commemorating the revolution of July 14, 1958. The product of this commission, *Nusb al-Hurriyya*, or the Monument to Freedom, is a huge bronze and limestone sculpture that still stands in Baghdad's Liberation Square (Figure 1). The work was completed in 1961, shortly after Salim died of a heart attack at age forty-one while working on the installation in Baghdad—brought on, it is widely believed, by the stress of the project. Kanan Makiya asserts that *Nusb al-Hurriyya* is "probably the most important work of public art ever commissioned from a modern Arab artist."[1] It is known to inspire lofty superlatives and hyperbolic comparisons; Iraqi artist Khalid al-Rahhal has identified "two important epics in Iraq—the first is the epic of Gilgamesh and the second is the epic of freedom by Jawad Salim."[2] Today, the monument is widely recognized throughout the Arab world as a symbol of both Iraq and the revolutionary era of the 1950s—or, in the words of one commentator, as "a memory of a time and a memory of a place."[3]

As Iraqi art theorist and artist Shakir Hasan Al Sa'id notes, *Nusb al-Hurriyya* is largely about "the relationship between the body and history" (*al-'alaqa bayn al-jasad wa-l-tarikh*), and thus, I argue, about the relationship between time, selfhood, and sovereignty and about the role of sexual difference in stabilizing that relationship.[4] But the monument both performs normalizing work in many of the senses I have explored throughout this book and evokes disruptions in modern temporal experiences and imaginaries. Reading these disruptive potentialities points us beyond continuities between the colonial and postcolonial eras in the Middle East and toward the ruptures that decolonization sometimes opened up, or toward what we might, with a nod to Dipesh Chakrabarty, call postcolonial heterotemporalities.[5] One way this happens is through the work's intertwining of linear and cyclical imaginaries of time.

Lara Deeb proposes that conceptions of temporality in contemporary Lebanese Shi'i political discourses are better grasped through frameworks of "paradigmatic" and "syntagmatic" time than through those of "cyclical" and "linear" time. The martyrdom of the Prophet's grandson Husayn at the Battle of Karbala is both paradigmatic, in that it serves as a pattern or model allowing other events that fit the pattern to exist in a relationship of substitution with one another, and syntagmatic, in that it is "the point of origin for a sequential historical narrative."[6] For Deeb, one value of these frameworks is that they avoid the use of the cyclical metaphor of time. "Both of these narrative readings describe linear temporal frameworks, involving notions of time that is nonrepeating, irreversible, and sequential (no time travel allowed), although they involve different relationships between the linear flow of time and the events that take place along the time line."[7]

I follow Deeb in questioning the ways in which "the cyclical-linear binary is linked to other binary oppositions, such as modern-not modern, secular-religious, and national-mythic."[8] But my critique of this linkage takes a somewhat different tack. Metaphors of cyclical time are not always scholarly impositions on source material, and it may not always be the case that "deployment of notions of 'return' or 'cyclicality' in reference to 'religious time' masks lingering assumptions about secularity and modernity."[9] In any case, foreclosing explorations of such metaphors in advance risks participating in the recuperation of linear-progressive time as "true" time.[10] In *Nusb al-Hurriyya*, spatial metaphors

FIGURE 1. Jawad Salim, *Nusb al-Hurriyya*, 1961. Bronze on travertine, 50m × 8m, Liberation Square, Baghdad. Photo credit: Atheer Muhammad, 2018.

of cyclical time often work to give historical change more sustainable purchase than it typically achieves in linear-temporal imaginaries.[11]

The most common way of "reading" *Nusb al-Hurriyya* is as a linear-historical narrative—moving from right to left like a line of Arabic text—that starts on the right with the rearing horse, proceeds through the Iraqi nationalist movement and the July revolution it produced, and ends on the left with a sovereign and developed nation. This has been almost the only method of reading the work in both English-language scholarship and Arabic-language popular commentary. But a rich tradition of Arabic-language art criticism on the monument has long recognized its polysemic qualities, including its heterogeneous depictions of temporality. Al Sa'id, in what is probably the most theoretically sophisticated analysis of the work to date, proposes that it be read through three intersecting spatio-temporal axes, or planes: a horizontal or consecutive/diachronic plane, a vertical or simultaneous/synchronic plane, and an axial (front/back) plane. Even when we remain on the horizontal plane, the basis of the conventional right-to-left narrative reading, he insists that we find ourselves "from the first moment in front of myth, not historical reality," and that the monument's figures are moving through time in multiple directions. "We cannot locate a beginning in the work, whether horizontally, vertically, or axially. . . . The movement of the horse's neck, which proposes a beginning, diverts us in spite of ourselves to the end."[12] Engaging especially with Al Sa'id's analysis, I explore ways in which *Nusb al-Hurriyya* can be read both along and against its linear-temporal (or horizontal-diachronic) grain to shed light on some of the complex interplays between time, selfhood, and sovereignty during Iraq's revolutionary era.

Historical Time

I begin with Kanan Makiya's description:

[*Nusb al-Hurriyya*] is a visual narrative of the 1958 revolution told through symbols which the artist had been developing in the whole body of his work. Strikingly modern, yet clearly paying homage to its sources in Assyrian and Babylonian wall-relief traditions, the monument is organized as fourteen separate bronze castings averaging eight metres [26 feet] in height. These are meant to be "read" like a verse of Arabic poetry, from right to left, from the events leading up to the revolution, to the revolution itself and an ensuing harmony.[13]

In this reading, the work appears to be a remarkably literal illustration of Benedict Anderson's argument that modern nationhood depends on the capacity to imagine homogeneous linear-historical time.[14] Yet one immediate observation to make about Makiya's account is that, even following the linear narrative reading, the movement of temporal progression from right to left is not in fact uniform. Only about half of the figures are depicted in forward (i.e., leftward) motion. Neither the figures on the far right edge of the monument, representing the nation's distant past, nor those to the left of the central revolutionary scene, representing its future, are traveling from right to left. They frame the historical events but are not themselves moving in historical time.

The figures on the far right, however, are struggling precisely to set this time into motion. This scene comprises a rearing horse, its erstwhile rider, and three other men struggling to contain the ensuing chaos: a prehistorical and prepolitical past in which human and animal can hardly be distinguished (Figure 2). Al Sa'id writes that the scene

is full of beginnings but also the preservation of what came before. . . . [T]he horse is jumping to the right with its front legs, upward with its neck, and toward the left with its head. The overall movement is a spiral—from right to top to top left. The first figure appears to be moving to the right but is trying to fix his hands on the horse's saddle and turning his head to the left, while [the second figure] is gripping the horse's saddle or part of its harness with both hands and pulling it forcefully to the left with the strength and thrust of his body.[15]

That the horse has thrown its rider and is no longer under the control of its masters evokes the loss of some kind of original sovereignty, which might be read as Iraqi, Arab, or Islamic, depending on the historical event that the scene evokes in a viewer. As a depiction of the 1920 revolt against the British mandate, the scene references the event that, in Iraqi nationalist discourse, launches modern Iraq into historical time and also marks the onset of British colonial rule. As a representation of Arab knowledges—nomadism, horsemanship, the tools of the golden age of Arab-Islamic civilization strewn around the fallen rider—it suggests an Arabist narrative. In a more strictly Islamic

FIGURE 2. A Beginning. Jawad Salim, *Nusb al-Hurriyy*a, 1961. Photo credit: Atheer Muhammad, 2018.

reading, the depiction of a horse and fallen rider, especially in an Iraqi context, is almost guaranteed to evoke the Battle of Karbala, which for Shiʻi Muslims is "the axis around which all of history revolves."[16]

Regardless of the particular historical narrative evoked, the artist has condensed, in a single vivid scene, the ambivalent nationalist relation to the past, or rather the nonambivalent relation to two very different national pasts. Something that was right, in a distant and valorized past, has clearly gone wrong, in a nearer and tragic past. Salim's vision of this more recent past may not be as dark as Qasim's, who proclaimed in 1959 that it was the responsibility of Iraqi artists to "nourish the noble spirit in the rising generation and to cleanse their souls of the filth of the past, the past of darkness, the past of treachery. I don't mean the glorious past."[17] But the rupture between two pasts is clear enough in both, as it was in all national-ist discourse of the time. It was a necessary device of the drive to purge the

FIGURE 3. The Couple. Jawad Salim, *Nusb al-Hurriyya*, 1961.
Photo credit: Atheer Muhammad, 2018.

colonial and monarchical past from the nationalist and revolutionary present without compromising the historicity of the nation. And it is this national historicity, or rather historical time itself, that is born from the tragedy of the monument's first scene, the single irrepressible motion driven "leftwards by force of the horse's arching neck."[18]

The next set of figures emerges out of this struggle, carrying forward the leftward motion released by the spiraling horse (Figure 3). Evoking the nationalist mobilizations of the monarchical era, a man and a woman march forward in unison, hoisting political placards in the air. The female demonstrator, destined to become one of the monument's most iconic figures, was instantly recognized by observers as a young, modern, and revolutionary Iraqi woman claiming her equality with the man striding at her side. To the left of the couple floats the figure of a child. Historical time is thus set into motion through three very particular bodies, strongly individuated and clearly differentiated by sex and age, forming a stark contrast to the ahistorical and undifferentiated mass of (male) human and animal bodies in the first scene. The two adult figures are clearly marked as urban and modern, by their placards, which establish their literacy; their clothes, which are snug-fitting and straight-lined; their disciplined bodies, attesting to both modern schooling and political organization; and of course, their resolute march forward, abandoning the past for the future even as the man's left fist draws sustenance from the former. The depiction of a male and a female together in the public sphere marks this set of figures apart from all the other scenes of the monument as the only representation of a heterosocial community, and the child confirms that it is a heterosexual one as well. The stability and power of the conjugal family structure are what enable the progressive linear motion and futurity of the nation—that is, its history. A properly modern masculinity comes into being at the very moment that women enter the public sphere.[19]

The monument's primal nomadic scene, with its figures turned inward, onto their own drama, has no public. At best, it depicts one precociously prepolitical figure attempting to find or create a public with a clumsy attempt to raise his own placard, as some have read the vertical male figure in that scene.[20] The second scene, by contrast, is unmistakably oriented toward a public, as indicated by the placards, the demonstrators' raised fists, and the female figure's direct gaze outward, at the viewers or the monument's own public. In some ways, this triangular configuration resonates with Jürgen Habermas's account of the modern European public sphere as originating

in the private sphere of the bourgeois family, not in the sense of differentiating itself from that sphere but in the sense of being actually constituted
by private (reading) individuals with "audience-oriented subjectivities."[21]
In *Nusb al-Hurriyya*, the audience-oriented subjectivities of the conjugal
family are what bring a national public into being and, through it, a nation
moving forward in historical time.

Yet it is worth noting that the conjugal structure is not depicted here in
the binary *spatial* terms of a masculine public and a feminine private sphere.
If the couple resonates in some ways with a familiar modernization narrative,
nothing in its representation suggests a scene of private domesticity or even,
outside the mere existence of the child, of a gendered division of labor. They
are certainly not at home; they are both (all three?) engaged in dangerous
political action in the public sphere. Indeed, many contemporary observers saw in them not so much universal qualities of modernity as particular
sensibilities of Iraqi urban life in the 1950s: leftist heterosocialized activists
as representatives of the so-called generation of '58, formed in the crucible
of the mass urban protests of the postwar era.

As many observers have noticed, the child in this scene is the monument's only fully three-dimensional figure. The effect of this is intensified
by the fact that it is one of the few figures in the narrative's "historical"
sequence—that is, from the male demonstrator to the revolutionary soldier—that exhibits no sign of leftward motion or interest. It faces outward,
its arms stretching into the three-dimensional space that it alone occupies;
it even hovers slightly away from the wall to which all the other figures are
firmly fixed. It is the first hint we have of another way of locating past and
future in the monument, in which the future is located outward, where
the viewer stands. In the political imaginary of reproductive futurism, the
nation's future is of course embodied in the figure of the child. But, following Lee Edelman, this figure should not be confused with any "historical
child."[22] Likewise, the future it embodies should not be confused with any
historical future; it is not a future bound to the present. Unlike all of its
companion figures, the child figure is barely even attached to the wall behind it, which, as nearly all critics remind us, is a tribute to the wall-relief
art of ancient Mesopotamia, a historical origin of the nation. The figure
embodies the nation's distant and conflict-free future, no doubt, but at the
cost of being literally severed from any agentive connection to the political
present or the immediate, historically bound future. It is as if the child has
been released from the burden of time altogether.

FIGURE 4. The Wailing Woman. Jawad Salim, *Nusb al-Hurriyya*, 1961. Photo credit: Atheer Muhammad, 2018.

Gendered Time

The next scene depicts three primary female figures evoking somewhat different nationalist visions of femininity. The first, carrying on the vital leftward motion, is dressed in a long *'abaya*, her posture and affect evoking the female homosocial work of wailing in grief and/or urging men into battle (Figure 4).[23] The tribute to mourning as women's work is elaborated in the next scene, depicting a woman curled over the body of her martyred adult son (Figure 5). The faces of two other grieving women can be seen in the background. Both the grieving mother and the figure just beyond/below her, a woman cradling her newborn child, modify the monument's linear forward movement with their markedly circular shapes (which are enlarged mirror images of the circles carved out of the folds of the wailing woman's *'abaya*), evoking the cyclical-feminine time of mourning and reproduction without which linear-historical time would come to an end (with the death of the martyr) and the nation would not emerge.

Muhsin al-Musawi has analyzed the prevalent use of "regeneration themes" adapted from ancient Sumerian and Babylonian literature in 20th-century Iraqi nationalist art, themes that were often joined with Shi'i narratives of redemptive suffering. This "combination of ancient hymns and canticles with Shi'i rituals" marked even "the most leftist secular discourse."[24] He notes the frequent reference of artists to poems attributed to Enheduanna, the daughter of King Sargon of Akkad around 2350 BC. An especially popular poem attributed to her, "Lament for the Fall of Ur," evokes the politicized conception of mourning that often appeared in Iraqi art of this period. The poem narrates the destruction of the third dynasty of Ur, as the god Enil:

> called the storm
> the people mourned
> winds of abundance he took away from the land
> the people mourn
> good winds he took away from Sumer
> the people mourn
> deputed evil winds
> the people mourn[25]

Here, the cyclical repetition of the work of mourning can be heard as a kind of ominous drumbeat, not slowing down time but hastening it, much as in Salim's monument the figures of the monument's historical sequence—and the female homosocial scenes both lie at the heart of and traverse the largest part of this sequence—drive the ever-accelerating rhythm of linear-cyclical nationalist time, heralding the coming temporal explosion of revolution.

There is clearly a modern/traditional dichotomy established in the contrast between these female figures and the female demonstrator in the earlier scene: on the one hand, a modern woman engaged in a heteroso-cial public sphere, a heterosexual companionate marriage, and organized political activism; on the other, traditional women living in homosocial community as they carry out the now politicized work of mourning and mothering. Yet, by marking the latter figures with what in the urban na-tionalist imagination were unmistakable signs of tradition, the artist did

FIGURE 5. The Mother of the Martyr and the Mother of the Infant. Jawad Salim, *Nusb al-Hurriyya*, 1961. Photo credit: Atheer Muhammad, 2018.

not bind them to a stagnant familial space or to a past time: the irrelevance of any past/future binary is underscored by the very ordering of the figures in linear time. Both types of femininity play critical roles in bringing the sovereign nation into being; in this sense, the modern and the traditional are just different ways of being a patriotic Iraqi woman.

The two modes of living patriotic femininity do share a common denominator, however: in both, women's reproductive labor is essential to national becoming. Yasin al-Nasir has argued that "there is not a figure in the monument that lacks the symbolism of mother and child, whether explicit or implicit."[26] But if the theme of motherhood is implicit in much of the work, it is clearly quite explicit here. There is a striking paucity of active male figures in the historical sequence up to the revolution, which represents the entirety of the Iraqi nationalist movement in the colonial-monarchical era. In the whole sequence, there are four primary female figures and two secondary ones, compared to one active male figure, the urban demonstrator, in addition to one ambiguously gendered child, one adult male corpse, and one undoubtedly male infant to replace him and enact the revolution.

The scarcity of active male figures does not translate into the absence of male agency, however. Rather, it could be argued that there is only one male represented in the entire sequence, the educated urban nationalist, who is not only universal—through his achievement of full individuality and autonomy—but also eternal. However often the corrupt regime guns him down, the nation will throw him up again. In the second sequence, he emerges directly from the nation's primordial past (keeping one fist in contact with it); in the central revolutionary sequence, which he carriers out single-handedly, he emerges from a woman's body. In both cases, he becomes the universal subject of national historical time by differentiating himself from the authentic core of the nation: its women, peasants, and tribal nomads. This happens a final time in the last, futuristic sequence, where the male industrial worker stands alone at the monument's edge, set apart from the equally necessary but far less individuated peasants, women, children, and animals of the nation's future. Joan Scott writes that "since the Enlightenment, the abstract individual of political theory has been presumed to be masculine, while the feminine has been synonymous with the particular and the concrete." Scott notes Simone de Beauvoir's expression of this contrast in terms of "man's transcendence, his disembodiment, and woman's immanence, her confinement to the body."[27] The repetition of the universal (i.e., male) subject of historical time in Salim's monument is a repetition of this masculine transcendence of the body, which—despite the dangers it poses to that very body—does not contradict the autonomy of the male nationalist but is a condition of its possibility.

The irruption of death into the nationalist narrative alters the role of the child figure in these two scenes. In the previous scene, the linear trajectory of progress seems to open onto a timeless space, through the displacement of the child into a conflict-free future. As in the reproductive-futurist discourse critiqued by Lee Edelman, which is built around the denial of death, the first figure of the child enacts a "logic of *repetition* that fixes identity through identification with the future of the social order."[28] In the mourning sequence, by contrast, the child or infant (the one in his mother's arms) may grow up to enact a revolution, or he may grow up to die a martyr, since we have no way of knowing how many times the cyclical pattern repeats itself before it produces the revolution. But what we can be sure of is that he grows up, and that he does so to become a political subject: the regeneration of historical time demands it.

If much of female agency in *Nusb al-Hurriyya* is located in the reproductive realm, the *way* in which the nation's women reproduce its universal male subject clearly goes beyond banal biological observations. After all, almost the entirety of the historical sequence is devoted to representing it. In Partha Chatterjee's well-known argument, anticolonial thought constructs two domains, the outer/material/masculine and the inner/spiritual/feminine, and then "declares the domain of the spiritual its sovereign territory and refuses to allow the colonial power to intervene in that domain." Chatterjee accepts Anderson's analyses of homogeneous linear time and of "modular" forms of nationalism that are developed in the West and adopted in the colony and the postcolony—but he accepts them *only* for the outer, masculine domain of nationalism, the domain that permits the adoption of Western technology and universal conceptions of progress. He proposes that it is within the inner, protected, feminine domain where "nationalism launches its most powerful, creative, and historically significant project: to fashion a 'modern' national culture that is nevertheless not Western."[29] One of Chatterjee's most important insights is that this anticolonial binary cannot be directly aligned with the private/public spheres of Western capitalist modernity.

Yet my reading of *Nusb al-Hurriyya* suggests that the relation between sexual difference and linear-historical time in Iraqi nationalist discourse was more complex and dynamic than can be depicted by simply locating the

latter within the outer, masculine sphere. In neither the traditional homosocial sequence of the monument nor the modern heteronormative scene that
precedes it does feminine reproductive time exactly unfold within an inner
sphere assigned the role of preserving tradition, nor is it simply contrasted
with a masculine public time of material progress. There do indeed seem to
be (at least) two different temporalities at work here, constituted through
their contrast with one another: one masculine, linear, and heterosexual and
the other feminine, cyclical, and homosocial. But this interplay is not adequately captured through the binary *spatial* categories of the public/private
spheres of capitalist modernity or the outer/inner spheres of anticolonial
nationalism. Feminine time in *Nusb al-Hurriyya* does not really compensate
for the future-directed modern temporality of the larger narrative, thereby
safeguarding the nation's authentic past. Rather, it functions as that temporality's deep motive force, accelerating historical time and propelling the
nation into its future. Or, to be more precise, into its revolution, which
explodes directly out of the feminine sequence.

Revolutionary Time

The following scene depicts the liberation of a political prisoner, while
the monument's central figure, a muscular soldier, takes an exaggerated step
forward in time to smash through the bars of the larger prison, the old regime
itself (Figure 6). A disc hangs above the soldier's head, presumably representing dawn, the actual time of the revolution and the endlessly recycled metaphor
of the new age it inaugurated—perhaps even a reference to a different part
of the Sumerian poem on the destruction of Ur attributed to Enheduanna:

> dawn and the rise of the bright sun
> he locked up with good winds
> let not the bright sun rise upon the country
> like a twilight star it dawned[30]

Indeed, the scene can be read as a visual composite of the most perva-
sive rhetorical tropes (some might say clichés) for temporalizing the July
revolution, as expressed, for instance, in this unoriginal example from the
governor of Nasiriyya province: "With the break of dawn on July 14 [the
revolution] broke forth, to set right what had been corrupted over centuries
of darkness and . . . to see with open eyes Iraq's giant leap forward in every
field."[31] It may be its resonance with now deeply unfashionable language

such as this—along with retrospective knowledge of revolutionary Iraq's actual historical future, and especially the unwillingness of its military officers to consent to democratic institutions—that has made this scene the least admired of the monument, at least among recent commentators.[32]

The soldier is hailed, on the other side, by the figure of Freedom, who is gendered female and draws on certain other European conventions, such as the torch in her right hand, for representing this particular abstraction. (The torch is also one of many direct references in the monument to Picasso's *Guernica*.) In a somewhat peculiar way, Freedom seems to be rushing toward the soldier in the wrong direction, against the vital leftward movement established by the rearing horse and accelerated in each subsequent scene. When viewed together with all of the figures to her left, who are also either facing backward, toward the past, or directly outward, toward the viewer, she seems to signal the stopping of historical time altogether.

Some commentators have pointed out that the radical dislocation produced by the revolutionary scene, the abrupt shift in directional flow, opens up another way of reading *Nusb al-Hurriyya*. As al-Nasir writes, "time does not flow in [only] one direction" (*al-zaman la yasir bi-itijah wahid*) in Salim's monument.[33] Rather than proceeding in linear fashion from right to left, past to future, this method of reading begins with the revolutionary present and works outward in both directions simultaneously. When this

FIGURE 6. The Soldier of July 14. Jawad Salim, *Nusb al-Hurriyya*, 1961. Photo credit: Atheer Muhammad, 2018.

method is used, it quickly becomes apparent that many of the figures in the revolution's past mirror figures in its future, and vice versa. Revolutionary time in this reading ruptures the linearity of historical time, whether the former is understood as a centrifugal explosion that irreparably tears the past from the future and sends them flying in opposite directions, or as a more centripetal movement, a kind of temporal "setting right" that establishes harmony between the nation's past and its future.

Either way, one can picture the entire monument in this reading not as a fixed horizontal line but as the spoke of a wheel, perpetually rotating around the axis of the July revolution, itself represented by the disc fixed above the soldier's head. A close look at the disc reveals that it is crossed by straight lines that meet it in the middle, like spokes. Two of the lines, which form a vertical X, appear slightly more prominent than the others, echoing the three X shapes of the main human figures in this sequence. The repetitions of the X, combined with other suggestions of rotation—including the strange axis-like line connecting the prison bars to the soldier's thigh—produce a vertiginous effect on any viewer who begins to imagine the monument as a wheel. Is the soldier's left hand really pulling the prison bars apart, or is he just hanging on? The cyclicality of this reading evokes Ibn Khaldun's famous account of historical time, in which nomads overthrow a settled civilization and establish a new one, which progresses and then declines before meeting its inevitable demise in the form of a new nomadic invasion.

The modern experience of revolutionary time has a complex relationship to the equally modern apprehension of homogeneous historical time. In European history, the two are not disconnected in spite of their apparent contradiction.[34] Still, nationalist revolutionaries in Europe's colonies ultimately directed the urgency of absolute temporal rupture precisely against the European Enlightenment promise of gradual progress. As Chakrabarty writes, to the repeated "not yet" of the self-proclaimed modernizing colonizer, the colonized nationalist finally responds: "now."[35] If it is true that the "not yet" has never been slow to make its reappearance, it is also common for the "now" of the revolutionary event to never quite lose its force. In *Nusb al-Hurriyya*, it is the center toward which the nation's past and future are both directed; in the steady gaze of several of the figures of the future backward, toward the revolution, its memory and its possibility remain as a permanent presence.

The nonlinear "now" of revolutionary time is even more dominant in yet a third way of reading the monument's overall temporal structure, one in which time does not flow in any direction. Many observers have seen in the rightmost set of figures, the horse and struggling men, a famous scene

FIGURE 7. Woman in a Bathhouse. Jawad Salim, *Nusb al-Hurriyya*, 1961. Photo credit: Atheer Muhammad, 2018.

of July 14 itself: the destruction by Iraqi masses of two statues of men on horseback: the first of General Maude, the British conqueror of Baghdad in 1917, and the second of King Faysal, installed by the British in 1921. Apparently these were two of only three public statues in Baghdad prior to the revolution, and their spontaneous dismantling on July 14 made a "deep impression" on Jawad Salim, whose own public sculpture would soon replace them.[36] Following this method of reading, the entire monument captures no time but the revolutionary moment, with its angry and jubilant masses, its disciplined demonstrators, its loyal soldiers, its just-released prisoners, its martyrs and mourners, its mothers sheltering their infants from the turmoil, and its dreams of a better tomorrow.

Future Time

In the monument's final sequence, in Makiya's words, the "restless motion, anger, tension and pain of the revolution ceases. Peace descends. Repose enters the people's hearts. Iron bars turn into branches; and eyes close with serenity because peace is an offering which knows no fear."[37] The female figure to the left of Freedom is reclining, eyes closed, in what seems from the suggestion of wavy movements across her legs to be a pool or a bath (Figure 7). According to 'Abbas al-Sarraf, she is a "girl at the threshold of marriage, prepared to meet her waiting groom,"[38] implying that now that Iraq has attained its sovereignty, Iraqis can settle down to the business of marriage, sex, and procreation. The figure is also often seen as representing nature, with the water running over her legs, the tree branches behind her head, and the bird perched on her shoulder. Many have interpreted the bird, which looks like a dove or a pigeon, as a symbol of peace, though Al Sa'id proposes that it can also be read as a link integrating the monument in time and space with its Baghdadi environment: that it is "a secret companion" for every other bird who "comes to land on the shoulders of the monument's figures from time to time."[39] The bird further works as a visual pun in Arabic: a pigeon (al-hamam) symbolizing the bathhouse (al-hammam) in which the woman rests, and thus symbolizing Baghdad itself through reference to the city's legendary bathing institutions, a spatial embodiment of continuity from ancient to modern times.

To the left are two more female figures, depicted as women harvesting and also representing the Tigris and Euphrates rivers; the latter woman is pregnant (Figure 8). Between them is the figure of an adolescent girl with a tray on her head. It might be noted that Makiya's account of the futuristic scene no longer really applies, once the reclining woman is left aside;

while historical time does seem to have stopped, "repose" is not exactly what has replaced it. All three figures are hard at work, as are the two male peasants to the left of them and the lone male worker on the monument's far left edge (Figure 9). A sheet of metal is curled around the right side of the worker's body, signaling the industrial materials of his labor as well as the historical closure effected by this sequence. These figures inhabit not just a posthistorical utopia (or not just *any* posthistorical utopia) but, more specifically, a land made prosperous through their agricultural and industrial labor, and they are no longer directed toward the future—which would be redundant, since they *are* the future, and there is only one future

FIGURE 8. The Tigris and Euphrates, or Rural Women Harvesting. Jawad Salim, *Nusb al-Hurriyya*, 1961. Photo credit: Atheer Muhammad, 2018.

in the national developmentalist imagination—but toward the ongoing exploitation of Iraq's natural wealth for the benefit of its people. That is, they inhabit a developed country.

As Sa'id notes, in moving from forms in which the "side and forward views coincide" to forms that face us squarely, we have "broken through to stillness . . . except that this is a stillness bursting with movement," with the figures confronting us in "an axial, not a vertical or horizontal," direction. One wonders, though, about the temporal quality of this stillness that is "bursting with movement," especially given that Al Sa'id also reads into this sequence the theme of "rebellion against rebellion itself."[40] The stillness marks the imagined depoliticization of the Iraqi public sphere, which, as seen in Chapters 6 and 7, was a not entirely successful project of the post-revolutionary state. That the stillness is "bursting with movement" indicates what depoliticization aimed to ensure: a stable national space for economic development to unfold. We might, then, conceive of the future "sequence" in *Nusb al-Hurriyya* not as the end of historical time in Anderson's sense, but as the end of the eventfulness of nationalist, revolutionary time and the

FIGURE 9. Men of the Future. Jawad Salim, *Nusb al-Hurriyya*, 1961. Photo credit: Atheer Muhammad, 2018.

proper beginning of homogeneous linear time: the opening up of a fully modern temporality instituting the "fantasy of timeless, even, and limitless development" within the territory of the sovereign nation-state and through the productive agency of disciplined, self-governing citizens.[41]

Using the nonlinear method of reading that starts from the revolutionary center and moves outward in both directions simultaneously, the three primary male figures of the far left scene—the two peasants and the worker—mirror the three male figures struggling furiously with the horse in the far right scene, while the apparently placid, domesticated, and wealth-producing ox mirrors the ungovernable horse. The male figures in both scenes are strong, muscular, and determined. But the marks of their difference signal the reconstruction of Iraqi masculinity through the nationalist struggle and the July revolution— from the noble but somewhat wild, possibly violent, and unquestionably disorganized nomads of the past to the cooperative, disciplined, and produc- tive male workers and farmers of the future. Jabra Ibrahim Jabra writes: "The posture of the worker is a posture of pride. In this active posture, this belief in the future, the epic of freedom reaches its conclusion."[42] It is precisely the worker's *posture*—his modern, masculine bodily comportment—that effects the end of history in the nation's long and difficult march toward freedom, and in this "conclusion," the future he believes in can be none other than the future he already inhabits. (If he has any doubts, the thick metal-and-stone slab blocking any further leftward motion or even view should dispel them.) In this posture is the promise, or the dream, that the revolution is, or will become, far more than a political or even economic revolution; its effects will be as deep as those described by Koselleck as the aim of the Chinese Cultural Revolution: "to impel disruption into Chinese sensibility, dictating revolution into the body as it were."[43]

The reconstruction of feminine bodies is somewhat less clear. The three adult female figures in future time—the woman in the pool and the two women harvesting—mirror the three rural/traditional adult female figures in the historical sequence: the wailing woman, the mother of the martyr, and the mother of the infant. Unlike the female figures of the past, however, or the males of the future, the females of the future double as symbolic figures standing for Nature and the Tigris and Euphrates rivers. It would seem that rural women, once released from historical time (through its coming to an end), revert to the cyclical-biological time of nature and fertility.

What becomes of urban women in this imaginary? The male worker of the future does not have a female counterpart visible in the public space depicted in the monument. The metanarratives of modernization and development had difficulty imagining any role for urban women in the process of industrialization beyond that of housewife, raiser of children, and consumer of the new domestic products of national industry. Once the revolution was accomplished, that is, urban women were to return to the private sphere, or rather to enter a properly modern private sphere for the first time. This sphere would have resisted representation in Salim's epic, oriented as every sequence is to and about a national public. In other words, the first real differentiation of Iraq into properly gendered public and private spheres is imagined to occur *after* the revolution that brings the sovereign nation into being.

The heterosocial/sexual demonstrators thus constitute the only set of figures in the monument's historical sequence that do not seem to be fully mirrored by a set of figures in its future sequence. Their singular failure to find a place in the nation's future points to the imagined and attempted depoliticization of the public sphere after the revolution. But it also points to how the female counterparts of the two most likely heirs to the male demonstrator—the revolutionary soldier and the industrial worker—are unrepresentable in the national public space that the revolution has transformed. According to present-day notions of progress, this might signify a strange regression. After all, the female counterparts of the past urban nationalist, the past tribal nomads, and the future laboring peasants are all accounted for: so why not those of the two most indisputably modern male figures in the monument? But in the 1950s, modernization and development were widely understood, on a global level, to be constituted by male industrial productivity and female reproductive domesticity. As *Nusb al-Hurriyya* shows, this was not the only way that women's reproductive and political roles could be envisioned in contemporary Iraqi nationalist imaginations. It was just the most futuristic, the most developed, way.

Counter-Memory and Heterotemporalities

The monument's future sequence is now often viewed as utopian, and sometimes criticized as such. This is perhaps an obvious reading, though it might be remembered that at the time the work was created most people did not see the development of underdeveloped countries as utopian—after all, developed countries actually existed. Moreover, the sequence primarily depicts hard manual work regulated through rather familiar divisions of labor: urban/rural, male/female, adult/child, and human/animal. As utopias go, this is surely a modest one, and it is arguably only retrospective comparison with revolutionary Iraq's actual dystopian future that makes it appear otherwise. In this sense, Salim's vision is not so much a utopia as it is a future truly past and gone.

But my aim here is not really to challenge the representation of historical reality lying at the end of the linear narrative of time through which *Nusb al-Hurriyya* is most often read. Rather, it is to introduce a few complications related to that representation's connection to just this linear narrative, and to ask how strong a hold the monument's historical sequence really has on its future sequence, even within the aesthetic limits of the work itself. As Al Sa'id argues, such complications—that is, the work's marks of tension, disruption, contradiction, and breakdown—call for more attention to the "counter-memory" (*al-dhakira al-mudadda*) that shadows nationalist memory at every step of the way in Salim's epic of freedom.[44] Al Sa'id sometimes frames this counter-memory as a plane of "verticality" in the work that repeatedly cuts through its "horizontal" plane, or "the progress of human freedom in its political and humanist sense." He also links it to the "ruptures" in Salim's own life during the monument's construction—the heart attacks that preceded the one that would kill him and the "psychological breakdowns" they incited—and to the "latent counter-imagination of the artist," manifesting in the work as "everything he did not dream of before its realization" and even as "every mistake he made during its execution."[45] This is what, according to Al Sa'id, allows us to see *Nusb al-Hurriyya* anew with each viewing. Despite our knowledge of the conventional reading, which rests on the work's "superficial" plane of horizontality, "the horse breaks loose" again every time, and "we perceive in the monument something that gives us freedom of imagination."[46]

One of the most glaring vertical "cuts" may be the gaping white space between Freedom's backside and the future, by far the largest physical gap in the horizontal sequence of events. There is only one other noticeable, though shorter, visual pause in the narrative, which marks the unseen irruption of power between the defiant uprisings and the corpse of the martyr. Following the linear-historical method of reading, the void after Freedom aligns precisely with the post-revolutionary present of the monument's construction and thus might be read as a question mark regarding both how the story really ends and how the future-oriented and present-transcending time of the revolution itself is to be experienced or depicted. Koselleck notes how the Enlightenment notion of progress ended up leading not simply to a homogeneous experience of linear time but to an ever-widening gap between "the space of experience" and "the horizon of expectation." This is never more vivid than during modern revolutionary time, when the revolution "appears to unchain a yearned-for future while the nature of this future robs the present of materiality and actuality."[47] The white space in *Nusb al-Hurriyya* that corresponds to the revolutionary present in which the artist lived (and, as Al Sa'id reminds us, in which he knew that he would die) marks this otherwise unrepresentable gap.[48]

Following the reading of the monument as capturing only the revolutionary present, beginning with the destruction of the statues of General Maude and King Faysal, the white space can similarly be seen as marking the gap between the revolutionaries' actions and their dreams of the future, or even between the revolutionaries and the Iraqi masses. That the two male peasants and one of the female peasants are turned toward the revolutionary events, as if pausing only momentarily in their work to watch them unfold from afar, lends support to this reading. And then there are the closed eyes of that first figure after the void, the blissfully bathing woman, which Makiya interprets as symbolizing "peace [as] an offering which knows no fear."[49] But there was no shortage of fear in Iraq during the revolutionary years in which Salim designed and sculpted the monument, least of all among the country's peace activists. The main peace movement organization—the icon of which was a dove—was the Partisans of Peace, led by communists, who were involved in a deadly street war with the Ba'thists throughout the Qasim era. Moreover, an offering of peace is probably not the only possible interpretation of closed eyes as a visual clue. They could instead point to the dreamlike and ephemeral quality of the future sequence, perhaps even evincing something more ominous about what the historical, undreamed future might hold when the nation finally awakes to its present.

Few commentators, it seems, have attempted to account for the unsettling aspects of the figure of Freedom itself in the monument: her apparent flight toward the past; the posture with which she turns her back on both the future and the viewer; her mangled body and the hollowed-out, skull-like appearance of her face; and what could be seen as her desperate gaze backward and her scream (Figure 10). The common interpretation is that the figure "surges out into the daylight looking towards its liberator," and that "asked why freedom had no feet, Salim is reported to have said: 'Feet stick to the ground; I wanted her to soar high.'"[50] But Freedom does not

FIGURE 10. Freedom. Jawad Salim, *Nusb al-Hurriyya*, 1961. Photo credit: Atheer Muhammad, 2018.

look toward her liberator in the form of the soldier. At best, she looks up, though she can easily be seen as looking backward and upside-down with rolled eyes, toward the monument's viewer (Figure 11). Salim may or may not have said what he is reported to have said about the symbolism of her missing feet.[51] But a glance at the monument is enough to see that the artist did not let Freedom soar very high after all. Her head is lower than the heads of most other figures, and the bottom of her footless leg is one of the lowest points of the entire monument. Far from soaring, she appears to be sinking, with her front leg even lower than the back.[52] Indeed, Al Sa'id proposes that Freedom's invisible feet, along with the wavy folds of the garment around her legs, suggest that she is wading through water rather than soaring through the air.[53]

One of the earliest full-length books on *Nusb al-Hurriyya*, al-Sarraf's 1972 work, paid more attention than later analyses to the marks of dismemberment and pain on Freedom's face and body. Al-Sarraf compared the figure favorably to the serene, whole, and unrealistic "goddess of beauty"—one plump and healthy breast revealed—representing Freedom in Eugène Delacroix's famous painting "Freedom Guides the People." Jawad Salim's torn and mangled figure, in stark contrast to Delacroix's Freedom, "speaks clearly and openly of her tragedy; she appears as that wounded girl whose body is rent by bullets, knives, and whips because she is a perpetual victim of human institutions: wounded by religion, hindered by morality, imprisoned by politics." Al-Sarraf's ultimate interpretation may differ little from that of other observers, since "in spite of the torture, [Freedom] carries the torch high in order to light existence with it," but his analysis opens up a variety of other possible readings.[54] For example, when his vivid descriptions of the figure's mangled body are joined with the peculiarity of its seemingly desperate and decidedly nonlinear movements in/against time (which al-Sarraf does not address), Salim's Freedom begins to develop an uncanny resemblance to the Angel of History famously described by Walter Benjamin.

His face is turned toward the past. Where we perceive a chain of events, he sees one single catastrophe which keeps piling wreckage upon wreckage and hurls it in front of his feet. The angel would like to stay, awaken the dead, and make whole what has been smashed. But a storm is blowing in from Paradise; it has got caught in his wings with such violence that the angel can no longer close them. The storm irresistibly propels him into the future to which his back is turned, while the pile of debris before him grows skyward. This storm is what we call progress.[55]

Familiar Futures: A Final Reading

Earlier I suggested that the metal slab next to the worker's body in *Nusb al-Hurriyya* marks the end of eventful history and the opening up of even, limitless development. But the way in which the slab curves outward, toward the future located with the viewing public, can alternately convey another sense of cyclicality, this time a rotation along what Al Saʿid calls the axial plane of the work, thereby "swooshing everything back to the beginning again," toward the nomads and the horse.[56] In Chapter 7, I discussed the sociologist ʿAli al-Wardi's revision of the Khaldunian conception of history, in which he posits Islamic history as a cyclically repeating struggle between the "people of the state" and the "people of revolution." The sense of movement suggested by the curve of the slab proposes a similar reading of the "end" of *Nusb al-Hurriyya*, in which the post-revolutionary state does not inaugurate a period of even, timeless development but rather heralds the beginning of the Khaldunian era of decline, as the erstwhile revolutionaries become the civilized and eventually corrupt people of the state, and a new people of revolution emerges.

FIGURE 11. The Face of Freedom. Jawad Salim, *Nusb al-Hurriyya*, 1961. Photo credit: Atheer Muhammad, 2018.

Two figures of the future now come into sharper view: the ox and the strange human figure positioned below it (see Figure 9). The ox (*thawr*), as a visual pun in Arabic, similar to other such puns in the monument, reminds us of the revolution (*thawra*). Its stance, legs planted and head lowered, at first glance appears docile or, in Al Sa'id's word, "stagnant"—especially when compared to the rearing horse that mirrors it on the other end of the monument—thereby seeming to domesticate the pun and, with it, the revolution. But the ox's massive body can alternately appear "like a desolate mountain containing in its depths an enormous volcanic eruption [*thawra*]," and its lowered head threatening rather than submissive, glowering right at us, as the monument's viewers, and ready to charge again at any moment.[57] *Thawra* was the most common word in Iraq for the events of July 14; its sense of volcanic eruption contrasts with the other available option, *inqilab*, which is closer to the English "revolution" in its sense of rotation or turning upside-down.[58]

The human figure below the ox, positioned in a warrior-like stance with its back to the viewers, may be the most perplexing of the entire monument. Many commentators ignore it entirely. An exception is Jabra, who reads it as depicting the marsh dwellers who raise water buffalos in Iraq's southern river valleys. Jabra's clues here are the figure's invisible feet, the waviness of the garments around its legs, and its positioning near the animal, which could be a buffalo rather than an ox, and whose feet are also not visible. As al-Musawi notes, the marshlands have often functioned in Iraqi art as "a historical space" that "valorizes a politic of revolt."[59] In Jabra's reading, the two other prominent footless figures in the monument—the wailing woman and the figure of Freedom—similarly evoke the marsh dwellers, suggesting that we see them as returning figures of revolt, or perhaps the same returning figure of revolt. The three are depicted in almost identical postures, from different angles, the main difference being whether their arms are bent at the elbow or extended upward or outward. They also appear at precisely the three moments in the work in which linear time threatens to open onto a static future.

Another, and not incompatible, way to read the figure below the ox is to return to the rightmost sequence of the work. In the "mirror" reading, which starts with the revolutionary present and works outward in both directions, the three men struggling with the horse on the right are mirrored by the two male peasants and the worker on the left. This leaves a fourth figure in the first scene, the fallen rider. In the historical reading of that scene as the Battle of Karbala, this figure is of course Husayn, the Prophet's grandson and the Third Shi'i Imam, whose mirror image in the final scene, the figure below the ox, then becomes the Twelfth, or "Hidden," Imam, the *mahdi* who will return at the end of time to fill the world with justice.

In contrast to the wheel-like rotation suggested by the revolutionary sequence, the axial-cyclical motion of the final scene seems to simultaneously open toward, or explode into, a less predictable future, especially if it happens to be propelled by a charging ox. In whatever form the ox's human companion might be seen—as marsh-dwelling rebel, the returning figure of freedom, or the *mahdi*—the two figures together impel an irruption, or what Al Sa'id calls a vertical cut, into the only apparently seamless rationality of the disciplinary order of the developmental state. This cut is the return of revolution, not as *inqilab* but as *thawra,* and not once and for all but again and again.

Notes

Introduction

1. Majid Shubbar, ed., *Khutab al-Za'im 'Abd al-Karim Qasim 1958–1959* (London: Alwar-rak, 2007), 25–26. Translation adapted from Hanna Batatu, *The Old Social Classes and the Revolutionary Movements of Iraq* (Princeton: Princeton University Press, 1978), 802.

2. Reinhart Koselleck, *Futures Past: On the Semantics of Historical Time*, trans. Keith Tribe (New York: Columbia University Press, 2004).

3. "Nass al-Dustur al-Mu'aqqat li-l-Jumhuriyya al-'Iraqiyya," *Ittihad al-Sha'b*, July 18, 1959, 4.

4. "Women's Procession," *Iraq Times*, January 4, 1959, 3.

5. Sayid J. S. Hannoush, Iraqi Ministry of Development, letter to the editor of the *Illustrated London News*, republished in the *Iraq Times*, January 25, 1959.

6. "Iraqi Women on the March," *Iraqi Review* 1, no. 9 (July 30, 1959): 19. The *Iraqi Review* was the weekly English-language supplement to the ICP daily *Ittihad al-Sha'b*.

7. Denise Riley, *"Am I That Name?": Feminism and the Category of "Women" in History* (Minneapolis: University of Minnesota Press, 1988), 47.

8. For example, see "Dawr Jumhuriyyatina fi Siyanat al-Silm al-'Alami," *Ittihad al-Sha'b*, July 18, 1959, 2; and Husayn Jamil, "Masdar Quwwat al-Hizb al-Watani al-Dimuqrati," *al-Ahali*, April 29, 1960, 1. On discourses of *jumud* in 20th-century Egypt, see Omnia El Shakry, *The Great Social Laboratory: Subjects of Knowledge in Colonial and Postcolonial Egypt* (Stanford: Stanford University Press, 2007), 8.

9. See Muhammad Hadid, *Mudhakkirati: al-Sira' min Ajli al-Dimuqratiyya fi al-'Iraq* (Beirut: Dar al-Saqi, 2006), 445–50; and Yeheskel Kojaman, *Thawrat 14 Tammuz 1958 fi al-'Iraq wa-Siyasat al-Hizb al-Shuyu'i* (London: Biddles, 1985), 102–14.

10. The law, while widely trumpeted as a victory of the secular nation-state over religious sectarianism, did not apply to Iraq's Christian and Jewish minorities. See Chapter 7 for my interpretation of this apparent anomaly.

11. For a discussion of the failure theme in scholarship on the revolution, see Eric Davis, *Memories of State: Politics, History, and Collective Identity in Modern Iraq* (Berkeley: University of California Press, 2005), 111ff.

12. Lee Edelman, *No Future: Queer Theory and the Death Drive* (Durham: Duke University Press, 2004), 41.

13. Partha Chatterjee, *The Nation and Its Fragments: Colonial and Postcolonial Histories* (Princeton: Princeton University Press, 1993), 203. In the Iraq context, see Samira Haj, *The Making of Iraq, 1900–1963: Capital, Power, and Ideology* (Albany: State University of New York Press, 1997), 84–85.

14. Edelman, *No Future*, 2.

15. Muhammad Bahr al-'Ulum, *Adwa' 'ala Qanun al-Ahwal al-Shakhsiyya al-'Iraqi* (Najaf: Matba'at al-Nu'man, 1963), 27.

16. On the temporality of the Islamic discursive tradition, see Samira Haj, *Reconfiguring Islamic Tradition: Reform, Rationality, and Modernity* (Stanford: Stanford University Press, 2008); and Talal Asad, *Formations of the Secular: Christianity, Islam, Modernity* (Stanford: Stanford University Press, 2003), 222–24.

17. Koselleck, *Futures Past*, 23.

18. On the colonial spatialization of time as constitutive of modernity, see Timothy Mitchell, "The Stage of Modernity," in *Questions of Modernity*, ed. Timothy Mitchell, 1–34 (Minneapolis: University of Minnesota, 2000); and On Barak, *On Time: Technology and Temporality in Modern Egypt* (Berkeley: University of California Press, 2013), 243.

19. Kristin Ross, *Fast Cars, Clean Bodies: Decolonization and the Reordering of French Culture* (Cambridge, MA: MIT Press, 1995), 10, emphasis added.

20. Reinhart Koselleck, *The Practice of Conceptual History: Timing History, Spacing Concepts*, trans. Todd Samuel Presner (Stanford: Stanford University Press, 2002), 150. I am referring to the Andersonian notion of calendar time as a means of ordering quotidian life in the modern nation-state, not in the Benjaminian sense of calendars as "monuments of historical consciousness." For a discussion of the difference, see Kathleen Davis, *Periodization and Sovereignty: How Ideas of Feudalism and Secularization Govern the Politics of Time* (Philadelphia: University of Pennsylvania Press, 2008), 101. On the uniformity of modern clock and calendar time see also Vanessa Ogle, *The Global Transformation of Time 1870–1950* (Cambridge, MA: Harvard University Press, 2015), 7–17.

21. Benedict Anderson, *Imagined Communities: Reflections on the Origin and Spread of Nationalism* (London: Verso Books, 1983), 12.

22. Walter Benjamin, *Illuminations: Essays and Reflections*, trans. Hannah Arendt (New York: Schocken Books, 1968), 261.

23. As Kathleen Davis points out, however, Anderson does not offer a "radically alternative method of thinking events in time," as does Benjamin. See Davis, *Periodization and Sovereignty*, 101.

24. Eric Hobsbawm and Terence Ranger, eds., *The Invention of Tradition* (Cambridge: Cambridge University Press, 1983).

25. See Julia Kristeva, "Women's Time," trans. Alice Jardine and Harry Blake, *Signs* 7, no. 1 (1981): 13–35.

26. Edelman, *No Future*, 2–3.

27. Edelman, 11.

28. Edelman, 25.

29. "It is as though the 'not yet' is what keeps capital going." Dipesh Chakrabarty, *Provincializing Europe: Postcolonial Thought and Historical Difference* (Princeton: Princeton University Press, 2000), 65.

30. On internal sovereignty as the assertion of power over human bodies, see Thomas Blom Hansen and Finn Stepputat, "Introduction," in *Sovereign Bodies: Citizens, Migrants, and States in the Postcolonial World*, ed. Thomas Blom Hansen and Finn Stepputat, 1–36 (Princeton: Princeton University Press, 2005).

31. I am using Foucault's early definitions of these terms, found in Michel Foucault, *The History of Sexuality*, vol. 1, *An Introduction*, trans. Robert Hurley (New York: Vintage Books, 1990), 139.

32. Jacques Donzelot, *The Policing of Families* (Baltimore: Johns Hopkins University Press, 1977), 5.

33. Donzelot, xxvi.

34. Donzelot, 45.

35. Donzelot, 71.

36. James Ferguson, *The Anti-Politics Machine: "Development," Depoliticization, and Bureaucratic Power in Lesotho* (Minneapolis: University of Minnesota Press, 1994).

37. For overviews, see Immanuel Wallerstein, *World-Systems Analysis: An Introduction* (Durham: Duke University Press, 2004); and Samir Amin, *Unequal Development: An Essay on the Social Formations of Peripheral Capitalism*, trans. Brian Pearce (New York: Monthly Review Press, 1976).

38. For example, see Arturo Escobar, *Encountering Development: The Making and Unmaking of the Third World* (Princeton: Princeton University Press, 1995); David Ekbladh, *The Great American Mission: Modernization and the Construction of an American World Order* (Princeton: Princeton University Press, 2010); Nils Gilman, *Mandarins of the Future: Modernization Theory in Cold War America* (Baltimore: Johns Hopkins University Press, 2003); and Michael E. Latham, *Modernization as Ideology: American Social Science and "Nation Building" in the Kennedy Era* (Chapel Hill: University of North Carolina Press, 2000).

39. An exemplary exception, though focused on colonial India and not the age of development, is Manu Goswami's *Producing India: From Colonial Economy to National Space* (Chicago: University of Chicago Press, 2004).

40. See Susan Pedersen, *The Guardians: The League of Nations and the Crisis of Empire* (Oxford: Oxford University Press, 2015), 262–63.

41. Toby Dodge, *Inventing Iraq: The Failure of Nation Building and a History Denied* (New York: Columbia University Press, 2005), xxxii, xii–xiii.

42. Timothy Mitchell, *Carbon Democracy: Political Power in the Age of Oil* (London: Verso, 2011), 80.

43. Mitchell, 9.

44. See Jacob Norris, *Land of Progress: Palestine in the Age of Colonial Development, 1905–1948* (Oxford: Oxford University Press, 2013), 10; and Priya Satia, "Developing Iraq:

Britain, India and the Redemption of Empire and Technology in the First World War," *Past and Present* 197 (2007): 211–55. Sherene Seikaly identifies a narrative in mandate Palestine that looked to "neocolonial Iraq as a model" for "developing economic resources." See Seikaly, *Men of Capital: Scarcity and Economy in Mandate Palestine* (Stanford: Stanford University Press, 2016), 44–45.

45. Priya Satia, "'A Rebellion of Technology': Development, Policing, and the British Arabian Imaginary," in *Environmental Imaginaries of the Middle East and North Africa*, ed. Diana K. Davis and Edmund Burke (Athens: Ohio University Press, 2011), 25.

46. Satia, 44n5.

47. H. W. Arndt, "Economic Development: A Semantic History," *Economic Development and Cultural Change* 29, no. 3 (1981): 458.

48. Quoted in Arndt, "Economic Development," 460.

49. Arndt, "Economic Development," 458–59. For an argument that identifies a non-Marxist intransitive use of "economic development" in the 1930s, see Doug Porter, "Scenes from Childhood: The Homesickness of Development Discourses," in *Power of Development*, ed. Jonathan Crush (London: Routledge, 1995), 69. There is a similar debate over when the term started to include the welfare of the population, which happened around the same time. Evidence commonly invoked for the argument that it (barely) preceded the end of the World War II is the 1940 Colonial Development and Welfare Act, though it might be noted that "Welfare" still needed to be *added* to "Development."

50. Gilbert Rist, *The History of Development: From Western Origins to Global Faith* (London: Zed Books, 2002), 61. See also Antony Anghie, *Imperialism, Sovereignty and the Making of International Law* (Cambridge: Cambridge University Press, 2007).

51. See Rist, *History of Development*, 60.

52. Quincy Wright, "The Government of Iraq," *American Political Science Review* 20 (1926): 768–69.

53. Joseph Morgan Hodge, *Triumph of the Expert: Agrarian Doctrines of Development and the Legacies of British Colonialism* (Athens: Ohio University Press, 2007), 49–50.

54. F. D. Lugard, *The Dual Mandate in British Tropical Africa* (London: Archon Books, 1965). On the 19th-century shift, see Mantena Karuna, "The Crisis of Liberal Imperialism," *Histoire@Politique* 2, no. 11 (2010), https://www.cairn.info/revue-histoire-politique-2010-2-page-2.htm.

55. Quoted in Anghie, *Imperialism, Sovereignty*, 159. On Lugard and the mandate system, see also Rist, *History of Development*, 61–62; Mitchell, *Carbon Democracy*, 99–101; and Pedersen, *Guardians*, 108–10.

56. Hodge, *Triumph of the Expert*, 118.

57. Frederick Lugard, "Education in Tropical Africa," *Edinburgh Review* 242, no. 493 (July 1925): 3, cited in Hodge, *Triumph of the Expert*, 118.

58. See Hodge, *Triumph of the Expert*, 128–32; Mahmood Mamdani, *Citizen and Subject: Contemporary Africa and the Legacy of Late Colonialism* (Princeton: Princeton University Press, 1996); and Andrew Zimmerman, *Alabama in Africa: Booker T. Washington, the German Empire, and the Globalization of the New South* (Princeton: Princeton University Press, 2010).

59. On the history of adolescence in this period, see Nancy Lesko, *Act Your Age!: A Cultural Construction of Adolescence*, 2nd ed. (Routledge, 2012). On childhood, see, among many others, Thomas Popkewitz, *Cosmopolitanism and the Age of School Reform: Science, Education, and Making Society by Making the Child* (New York: Routledge, 2008).

60. In Lee Edelman's argument, the denial of death—or, more specifically, of the death drive—is crucial to the operation of reproductive futurism (Edelman, *No Future*).

61. On how the language of the mandate system was shaped by evolutionism, see Rist, *History of Development*, 61. On engagements with Darwin in Arabic during this time, see Marwa Elshakry, *Reading Darwin in Arabic, 1860–1950* (Chicago: University of Chicago Press, 2013).

62. On recapitulation theory in the turn-of-the-century writings of the American psychologist G. Stanley Hall, see Lesko, *Act Your Age!*, 47–48. An exception that deals with the influence of psychology, including Freud's work, on the interwar lawyers who developed the mandate system is Anghie, *Imperialism, Sovereignty*, 133. On the importance of psychological concepts to postwar development discourse, see Sara Fieldston, *Raising the World: Child Welfare in the American Century* (Cambridge, MA: Harvard University Press, 2015), esp. chap. 6. On psychoanalytic thought in Egypt, see Omnia El Shakry, *The Arabic Freud: Psychoanalysis and Islam in Modern Egypt* (Princeton: Princeton University Press, 2017).

63. Hodge writes that "it would be hard to escape the overwhelmingly agrarian vision that was being projected onto the future of colonial, soon to be 'third world,' peoples" (Hodge, *Triumph of the Expert*, 262). For related arguments, see Nathan Citino, *Envisioning the Arab Future: Modernization in U.S.–Arab Relations, 1945–1967* (Cambridge: Cambridge University Press, 2017), 98; and Daniel Immerwahr, *Thinking Small: The United States and the Lure of Community Development* (Cambridge, MA: Harvard University Press, 2015).

64. On indirect rule as the production of zones of sovereignty for native despots, see Mitchell, *Carbon Democracy*, 80, 108.

65. Achille Mbembe, "Necropolitics," *Public Culture* 15 (2003): 11–40. For an argument—different from mine—that posits French practices of violence in mandate Syria as spectacular in the Foucauldian sense, see Daniel Neep, *Occupying Syria under the French Mandate: Insurgency, Space and State Formation* (Cambridge: Cambridge University Press, 2012).

66. Mbembe, "Necropolitics," 12–13.

67. Elizabeth Freeman, *Time Binds: Queer Temporalities, Queer Histories* (Durham: Duke University Press, 2010), xi.

68. Historians routinely differentiate Arab nationalism (*qawmiyya*) from the so-called territorial nationalisms (*wataniyyat*)—a difference built into the two Arabic words for "nationalism," which are not adequately translatable into English—without exploring what it means for Arabism, especially in the interwar period, to have been a nonterritorial nationalism.

69. For example, in Egypt, the focus of much of the scholarship on feminine domesticity in the region, government-sponsored domestic education began expanding as early as the 1860s. See Lisa Pollard, *Nurturing the Nation: The Family Politics of Modernizing, Colonizing, and Liberating Egypt, 1805–1923* (Berkeley: University of California Press, 2005), 104; Mona L. Russell, *Creating the New Egyptian Woman: Consumerism, Education, and National Identity, 1863–1922* (Basingstoke: Palgrave Macmillan, 2004), 138; and Beth Baron, *The*

Women's Awakening in Egypt: Culture, Society, and the Press (New Haven: Yale University Press, 1994), 140–41.

70. Government of Iraq, "Raqm 188 li-Sanat 1959: Qanun al-Ahwal al-Shakhsiyya," *al-Waqa'i' al-'Iraqiyya*, December 30, 1959, 7–8.

71. See Shahla Haeri, *Law of Desire: Temporary Marriage in Shi'i Iran* (Syracuse: Syracuse University Press, 1989).

72. Edelman, *No Future*, 25.

73. On assembling an archive, see Omnia El Shakry, "'History without Documents': The Vexed Archives of Decolonization in the Middle East," *American Historical Review* 120, no. 3 (2015): 920–34.

74. El Shakry, *Great Social Laboratory*, 219.

75. Jacques Derrida, *Specters of Marx: The State of the Debt, The Work of Mourning & the New International*, trans. Peggy Kamuf (New York: Routledge, 1994), 14–16; 'Ali al-Wardi, *Wu'az al-Salatin* (London: Alwarrak, 2013), 134; see also 345–46.

Chapter 1

1. Quoted in Susan Pedersen, "Getting Out of Iraq—in 1932: The League of Nations and the Road to Normative Statehood," *American Historical Review* 115 (2010): 975.

2. Arnold Talbot Wilson, *Mesopotamia, 1917–1920: A Clash of Loyalties* (London: Oxford University Press, 1931), 249.

3. On Foucault's concept of government as the conduct of conduct, see Colin Gordon, "Governmental Rationality: An Introduction," in *The Foucault Effect: Studies in Governmentality*, ed. Graham Burchell et al. (Chicago: University of Chicago Press, 1991), 2. On discipline and biopolitics, see Michel Foucault, *History of Sexuality*, vol. 1, *An Introduction*, trans. Robert Hurley (New York: Vintage Books, 1990); and Michel Foucault, *Discipline & Punish: The Birth of the Prison*, trans. Alan Sheridan, 2nd ed. (New York: Vintage Books, 1995).

4. Antony Anghie, *Imperialism, Sovereignty and the Making of International Law* (Cambridge: Cambridge University Press, 2007), 135, 156. Anghie acknowledges that "the actual powers of the League to implement its vision of the sovereign nation-state were extremely limited and problematic." But his own argument seems unaffected by this brief caveat. He goes on to assert that labor regimes "provided the League with a means of entering into the very being of the native, of disciplining and civilizing him" and argues explicitly that the mandate system relied on discipline in the Foucauldian sense rather than on "force" (pp. 149, 165, 186–90).

5. David Scott, *Refashioning Futures: Criticism after Postcoloniality* (Princeton: Princeton University Press, 1999), 40.

6. On extraction as a focus of British occupying forces in Iraq during and after the war, see Kristian Coates Ulrichsen, "The British Occupation of Mesopotamia, 1914–1922," *Journal of Strategic Studies* 30, no. 2 (2007): 349–77. On the "turnaround from a conviction that Europe had a 'civilizing mission' in the colonies to a law-and-order obsession with holding the line," a shift he places around the turn of the 20th century, see Mahmood Mamdani, *Citizen and Subject: Contemporary Africa and the Legacy*

of Late Colonialism (Princeton: Princeton University Press, 1996), 50. For an argument locating a similar shift in the mid-19th century, see Mantena Karuna, "The Crisis of Liberal Imperialism," *Histoire@Politique* 2, no. 11 (2010): 2.

7. Priya Satia, " 'A Rebellion of Technology': Development, Policing, and the British Arabian Imaginary," in *Environmental Imaginaries of the Middle East and North Africa,* ed. Diana K. Davis and Edmund Burke (Athens: Ohio University Press, 2011), 38–39. See also Priya Satia, "The Defense of Inhumanity: Air Control and the British Idea of Arabia," *American Historical Review* 111, no. 1 (2006): 16; Priya Satia, *Spies in Arabia: The Great War and the Cultural Foundations of Britain's Covert Empire in the Middle East* (Oxford: Oxford University Press, 2008), 10.

8. Anghie, *Imperialism, Sovereignty,* 156; Scott, *Refashioning Futures,* 16.

9. Achille Mbembe argues that "the notion of biopower is insufficient to account for contemporary forms of subjugation of life to the power of death," and calls for more attention to how "late-modern colonial occupation differs in many ways from early-modern occupation, particularly in its combining of the disciplinary, the biopolitical, and the necropolitical." See Mbembe, "Necropolitics," *Public Culture* 15 (2003): 12, 39–40, 27.

10. Omnia El Shakry, *The Great Social Laboratory: Subjects of Knowledge in Colonial and Postcolonial Egypt* (Stanford: Stanford University Press, 2007), 2.

11. In addition to El Shakry's work, see, for example, Samera Esmeir, *Juridical Humanity: A Colonial History* (Stanford: Stanford University Press, 2012); Wilson Chacko Jacob, *Working Out Egypt: Effendi Masculinity and Subject Formation in Colonial Modernity, 1870–1940* (Durham: Duke University Press, 2011); Beth Baron, *Egypt as a Woman: Nationalism, Gender, and Politics* (Berkeley: University of California Press, 2005); Saba Mahmood, *Politics of Piety: The Islamic Revival and the Feminist Subject* (Princeton: Princeton University Press, 2005); Talal Asad, *Formations of the Secular: Christianity, Islam, Modernity* (Stanford: Stanford University Press, 2003), chap. 7; and Timothy Mitchell, *Colonising Egypt* (Berkeley: University of California Press, 1991).

12. Mitchell, *Colonising Egypt,* 98; Jacob, *Working Out Egypt,* 47.

13. Satia, *Spies in Arabia;* Satia, "Defense of Inhumanity"; Jafna Cox, "A Splendid Training Ground: The Importance to the Royal Air Force of Its Role in Iraq, 1919–32," *Journal of Imperial and Commonwealth History* 13, no. 2 (1985): 157–84; Toby Dodge, *Inventing Iraq: The Failure of Nation Building and a History Denied* (New York: Columbia University Press, 2005); David E. Omissi, *Air Power and Colonial Control: The Royal Air Force, 1919–1939* (Manchester: Manchester University Press, 1990); Mohammad Tarbush, *The Role of the Military in Politics: A Case Study of Iraq to 1941* (London: Kegan Paul, 1982).

14. British violence is discussed extensively in the Arabic-language historiography on the occupation and mandate periods, starting with Muhammad Mahdi al-Basir, *Tarikh al-Qadiyya al-'Iraqiyya* (Baghdad: Matba'at al-Fallah, 1924). See also 'Abd al-Razzaq al-Hasani, *al-'Iraq fi Dawray al-Ihtilal wa-l-Intidab* (Beirut: Dar al-Rafidayn, 2013); and 'Ali al-Wardi, *Lamahat Ijtima'iyya min Tarikh al-'Iraq al-Hadith* (Qumm: Maktabat al-Sadr, 2004), 5:2.

15. Samira Haj, *The Making of Iraq, 1900–1963: Capital, Power, and Ideology* (Albany: State University of New York Press, 1997); Noga Efrati, *Women in Iraq: Past Meets Present* (New York: Columbia University Press, 2012).

16. Dodge, *Inventing Iraq*; Peter Sluglett, *Britain in Iraq: Contriving King and Country*, 2nd ed. (New York: Columbia University Press, 2007); Orit Bashkin, *The Other Iraq: Pluralism and Culture in Hashemite Iraq* (Stanford: Stanford University Press, 2009), 231. On education, see also 'Abd al-Razzaq al-Hilali, *Tarikh al-Ta'lim fi al-'Iraq fi 'Ahd al-Ihtilal al-Biritani, 1914–1921* (Baghdad: Mutba'at al-Ma'arif, 1975). Omar Dewachi notes the difficulties caused by the minimal finances Britain devoted to health care in mandate Iraq. See Dewachi, *Ungovernable Life: Mandatory Medicine and Statecraft in Iraq* (Stanford: Stanford University Press, 2017), 15.

17. Dodge, *Inventing Iraq*, 73ff.

18. Dodge, 2. A similar kind of cultural analysis, focused on contradictions in British perceptions of Iraq during and after World War I, can be found in Satia, *Spies in Arabia*.

19. Sluglett, *Britain in Iraq*, 27.

20. See Sluglett, 69-70. On mandate polices to protect British imports rather than Iraqi industry, see Muhammad Salman Hasan, *al-Tatawwur al-Iqtisadi fi al-'Iraq, 1864–1958* (Baghdad: Maktabat al-'Asriyya), 356.

21. Nancy Lesko, *Act Your Age!: A Cultural Construction of Adolescence*, 2nd ed. (Routledge, 2012), 50.

22. Philip Willard Ireland, *Iraq: A Study in Political Development* (London: Cape, 1937), 141.

23. Erez Manela, *The Wilsonian Moment: Self-Determination and the International Origins of Anticolonial Nationalism* (Oxford: Oxford University Press, 2007), 39; Timothy Mitchell, *Carbon Democracy: Political Power in the Age of Oil* (London: Verso, 2011), 79.

24. See Leonard V. Smith, "Wilsonian Sovereignty in the Middle East: The King-Crane Commission Report of 1919," in *The State of Sovereignty: Territories, Laws, Populations*, ed. Douglas Howland and Luise White (Bloomington: Indiana University Press, 2009), 57.

25. See also Mitchell, *Carbon Democracy*; and Mark Mazower, *No Enchanted Palace: The End of Empire and the Ideological Origins of the United Nations* (Princeton: Princeton University Press, 2009). Wilsonian self-determination was also not at odds with Wilson's racist domestic policies, as is often claimed; rather, it was racial segregation on a global scale. As John Kelly and Martha Kaplan point out, the Wilsonian nation-state was "tooled and naturalized in the era of 'separate but equal.'" See Kelly and Kaplan, "Legal Fictions after Empire," in *The State of Sovereignty: Territories, Laws, Populations*, ed. Douglas Howland and Luise White, 169–195 (Bloomington: Indiana University Press, 2009), 171.

26. For a critique, see Sara Pursley, "'Lines Drawn on an Empty Map': Iraq's Borders and the Legend of the Artificial State," *Jadaliyya*, June 2, 2015.

27. Thomas Blom Hansen and Finn Stepputat, "Introduction," in *Sovereign Bodies: Citizens, Migrants, and States in the Postcolonial World*, ed. Thomas Blom Hansen and Finn Stepputat (Princeton: Princeton University Press, 2005), 11.

28. Henry Dobbs, "Iraq State from the Autumn of 1920," Report prepared by the High Commissioner, Baghdad, for the Colonial Secretary, 6 August 1925, CO730/77, *Records of Iraq 1914–1966*, vol. 3, *1921–1924*, 4–5. On the global anticolonial uprisings of 1919–20, see also Manela, *Wilsonian Moment*.

29. 'Abd al-Razzaq al-Hasani, *Tarikh al-Wizarat al-'Iraqiyya* (Sidon: Matba'at al-'Irfan, 1965), 1:170.

30. Satia, *Spies in Arabia*, 18.

31. Wilson, *Mesopotamia*, 290. See also al-Wardi, *Lamahat*, 5.1:55–58.

32. al-Wardi, *Lamahat*, 5.2:134.

33. Wilson, *Mesopotamia*, 300.

34. Wilson, 302.

35. See, for example, al-Basir, *al-Qadiyya al-'Iraqiyya*, 186ff; al-Wardi, *Lamahat*, 5.2:42–43, 156, 222; and 'Abd Allah al-Fayyad, *al-Thawra al-'Iraqiyya al-Kubra Sanat 1920* (Baghdad: Matba'at al-Irshad, 1963).

36. For similar discourses in French mandate Syria, see Daniel Neep, *Occupying Syria under the French Mandate: Insurgency, Space and State Formation* (Cambridge: Cambridge University Press, 2012), 57.

37. Quoted in Satia, *Spies in Arabia*, 248.

38. "Proclamation to the Tribes and Communities of the 'Iraq," in *Iraq Administration Reports 1914–1932*, ed. Robert L. Jarman, 7:78–83. For the Arabic version see al-Hilali, *Tarikh al-Ta'lim*, 236–37; and al-Fayyad, *al-Thawra al-'Iraqiyya*, 320.

39. See Pursley, " 'Lines Drawn on an Empty Map.' "

40. The most noteworthy aspect of the uprising, as it played out in the tribal regions of the Middle Euphrates, was precisely that it was not tribal, in that it involved the joining of many different tribes, some sworn enemies of one another, in order to make nontribal demands on a nontribal enemy in alliance with nontribal actors in Baghdad and other cities. Since it is impossible to define the revolt by the social or spatial origins of its participants, given the variety of these, we might as well define it by its stated demands: it was an anticolonial uprising.

41. For example, see Dodge, *Inventing Iraq*, 22.

42. Wilson, *Mesopotamia*, 248.

43. al-Wardi, *Lamahat*, 5.2:291.

44. Wilson, 74–76. For the details in this paragraph, see also al-Wardi, *Lamahat*, 5.2:253–335; and al-Fayyad, *al-Thawra al-'Iraqiyya*, 181–84. These accounts are similar, except that the tax complaints and the whipping of the boy are not mentioned by Wilson.

45. Quoted in Mamdani, *Citizen and Subject*, 77.

46. The very sectarian discourses that emerged out of the conflict shaped its later narration. Ignoring the initial Shi'i clerical support for Faysal, and the timing of the withdrawal of that support, has enabled the analysis of Iraq's formation through the categories of sect and tribe. This analysis, prevalent in the British primary sources and some of the English-language secondary scholarship on Iraq, has unfortunately shaped work by some of the "new" British imperial historians.

47. Omissi, *Air Power and Colonial Control*, 211.

48. Tarbush, *Role of the Military in Politics*, 17.

49. Satia, "Defense of Inhumanity," 27, 31.

50. Satia, 33.

51. Satia, 29.

52. Foucault, *Discipline & Punish*.

53. Satia, "Defense of Inhumanity," 39.

54. Daniel R. Headrick, *Power over Peoples: Technology, Environments, and Western Imperialism, 1400 to the Present* (Princeton: Princeton University Press, 2010), 319.

55. Omissi, *Air Power and Colonial Control*, 174.

56. Gertrude Bell, letter of July 2, 1924, in *The Letters of Gertrude Bell: Selected and Edited by Lady Bell*, vol. 2 (New York: Boni and Liveright, 1927), 701.

57. Cox, "A Splendid Training Ground," 172.

58. Satia, *Spies in Arabia*, 249.

59. Satia, 250.

60. *Records of Iraq 1914–1966*, 3:472. See also Sluglett, *Britain in Iraq*, 187–91.

61. "Administration Report of the Gharraf Area, for the Year 1921," in *Iraq Administration Reports 1914–1932*, ed. Robert L. Jarman, 7:158.

62. "Administration Report of Suq Al Shuyukh District, 1922," in *Iraq Administration Reports 1914–1932*, ed. Robert L. Jarman, 7:169.

63. Dina Rizk Khoury, "Reflections on Imperial, Colonial, and Post-Colonial Citizenship in Iraq," paper presented at *Dissections* workshop, CUNY Graduate Center, May 1, 2015. See also Satia, *Spies in Arabia*, 10–11.

64. Quoted in Sluglett, *Britain in Iraq*, 168.

65. Quoted in Wilson, *Mesopotamia*, 173.

66. See Sluglett, *Britain in Iraq*, 169–72.

67. Dobbs, *Iraq State from the Autumn of 1920*, 82.

68. Hanna Batatu, *The Old Social Classes and the Revolutionary Movements of Iraq* (Princeton: Princeton University Press, 1978), 95.

69. Quoted in Haj, *Making of Iraq*, 30.

70. Haj, 30.

71. "Tribal Criminal and Civil Disputes Regulation," in *Iraq Administration Reports 1914–1932*, ed. Robert L. Jarman, 8:144.

72. Khayri al-'Umari, *Hikayat Siyasiyya min Tarikh al-'Iraq al-Hadith* (Cairo: Dar al-Hilal, 1969), 178; Sluglett, *Britain in Iraq*, 172.

73. Dobbs, *Iraq State from the Autumn of 1920*, 83.

74. Wilson, *Mesopotamia*, 172; Dobbs, *Iraq State from the Autumn of 1920*, 83–84.

75. al-Wardi, *Lamahat*, 5.2: 22–23.

76. "Report by His Majesty's Government in the United Kingdom to the Council of the League of Nations on the Administration of Iraq for the Year 1926," in *Iraq Administration Reports 1914–1932*, ed. Robert L. Jarman, 8:220–21.

77. Wilson, *Mesopotamia*, 97.

78. Timothy Mitchell, *Rule of Experts: Egypt, Techno-Politics, Modernity* (Berkeley: University of California Press, 2002), 79. For an argument about the relation of civil, tribal, and personal status law in the construction of Jordan as a nation-state, see Joseph Massad, *Colonial Effects: The Making of National Identity in Jordan* (New York: Columbia University Press, 2011), esp. chap. 2.

79. Mitchell, 77–78.

80. "Report by His Majesty's Government in the United Kingdom of Great Britain and Northern Ireland to the Council of the League of Nations on the Administration of Iraq for the Year 1929," in *Iraq Administration Reports 1914–1932*, ed. Robert L. Jarman, 9:316.

81. Lionel Smith, "Note on the Present State of Education in Iraq," reprinted in E. C. Hodgkin, "Lionel Smith on Education in Iraq," *Middle Eastern Studies* (April 1983): 258.

82. Smith, 258.

83. Smith, 258–59.

84. Jerome Farrell, "The Education Department and Its Relation to the Mandate and the League of Nations," Baghdad, 6 November 1921, Great Britain, Colonial Office 730/14/17117, cited in Sluglett, *Britain in Iraq*, 201.

85. Reeva S. Simon, *Iraq between the Two World Wars: The Militarist Origins of Tyranny*, rev. ed. (New York: Columbia University Press, 2004), 76.

86. Leela Gandhi, *Affective Communities: Anticolonial Thought, Fin-de-Siècle Radicalism, and the Politics of Friendship* (Durham: Duke University Press, 2006), 47, 52.

87. Quoted in Gandhi, 52.

88. Iwan Bloch, *The Sexual Life of Our Time, in Its Relations to Modern Civilisation* (1908), 534, cited in Gandhi, *Affective Communities*, 49.

89. Bashkin, *Other Iraq*, 231; Satiʿ al-Husri, *Mudhakkirati fi al-ʿIraq, 1921–1941* (Beirut: Dar al-Taliʿa, 1967), 2:302.

90. The report even expressed ambivalence about the expansion of primary schooling: "It is not hoped, or even wished, that all children shall complete the Primary Course." See "Report by His Brittanic Majesty's Government on the Administration of Iraq for the period April 1923–December 1924," in *Iraq Administration Reports 1914–1932*, ed. Robert L. Jarman, 7:718.

91. F. B. Riley, "Education in a Backward Country," *Phi Delta Kappan* 7, no. 4 (1925), 3.

92. "Report by His Brittanic Majesty's Government to the Council of the League of Nations on the Administration of Iraq for the Year 1927," in *Iraq Administration Reports 1914–1932*, ed. Robert L. Jarman, 8:503.

93. al-Husri, *Mudhakkirati*, 2:13.

94. al-Husri, 2:15.

95. al-Hasani, *Tarikh al-Wizarat*, 2:8–10.

96. Dobbs, *Iraq State from the Autumn of 1920*, 71.

97. Dobbs, 89.

98. Fadil Barrak, *Dawr al-Jaysh al-ʿIraqi fi Hukumat al-Difaʿ al-Watani wa-l-Harb maʿa Biritaniya Sanat 1941* (Baghdad: Dar al-ʿArabiyya, 1979), 214–15.

99. Husayn Jamil, *al-ʿIraq: Shahada Siyasiyya, 1908–1930* (London: Dar al-Laam, 1987), 248.

100. al-Hasani, *Tarikh al-Wizarat*, 1:169.

101. Note prepared by Middle East Department, Colonial Office, by the Instructions of the Committee, to Implement the Skeleton Statement Circulated as I.R.Q.2., 11 December 1922, FO 371/7772, in *Records of Iraq 1914–1966*, 3:108. Some scholars continue, somewhat inexplicably, to question the British government's interest in oil as a major factor in its Iraq policy, based largely on its own public denials of such interest at the time and its claims that little was known about the quantities of oil in Mosul. But these assertions were disproven long ago; see, for example, Sluglett, *Britain in Iraq*, 75.

102. Note on the Turkish Petroleum Company, 13 December 1923, CO 730/44, in *Records of Iraq 1914–1966*, vol. 3, *1921–1924*, 413.

103. Sluglett, *Britain in Iraq*, 71.

104. For the British explanation of its actions, see Foreign Office to Secretary-General, League of Nations, August 24, 1925 [FO 371/10825], in *Records of Iraq, 1914–1966*, 4:676–78. On the arrests, see also Sarah Shields, "Mosul, the Ottoman Legacy and the League of Nations," *International Journal of Contemporary Iraqi Studies* 3, no. 2 (2009): 217–30.

105. al-Hasani, *Tarikh al-Wizarat*, 2:29.

106. Note prepared by Middle East Department, Colonial Office . . . to Implement the Skeleton Statement, 3:108.

107. "Report by His Brittanic Majesty's Government on the Administration of Iraq for the period April 1923–December 1924," 7:728.

108. Mitchell, *Carbon Democracy*, 47–48.

109. al-Wardi, *Lamahat*, 5.2:223–26, 230–31; Haj, *Making of Iraq*, esp. chap. 1.

110. Wilson, *Mesopotamia*, 93.

111. Report by His Majesty's Government in the United Kingdom to the Council of the League of Nations on the Administration of Iraq for the Year 1926," 8:234. See also Mamdani, *Citizen and Subject*, 156–57.

112. "Report by His Majesty's Government in the United Kingdom to the Council of the League of Nations on the Administration of Iraq for the Year 1927," 8:381.

113. The relevant Iraqi legislation includes the Forcible Assistance Law of 1923 and Articles 100 and 119 of the Baghdad Penal Code of 1919. See "Report by His Majesty's Government in the United Kingdom to the Council of the League of Nations on the Administration of Iraq for the Year 1926," 8:220–21. On forced labor regulations of the League of Nations, see Pedersen, *Guardians*, 233, 242, 259; and Anghie, *Imperialism, Sovereignty*, 167.

114. On forced labor to build the railroad, and the shaykhs' opposition to it, see al-Fayyad, *al-Thawra al-'Iraqiyya*, 135. On corvée labor projects as "development projects," see Abbas Kadhim, *Reclaiming Iraq: The 1920 Revolution and the Founding of the Modern State* (Austin: University of Texas Press, 2012), 67–68.

115. Pedersen, *Guardians*, 259. Pedersen notes how "'development' could intensify compulsion" in the Belgian interwar mandate territories of Rwanda and Burundi (p. 239). In scholarship on the mandate system, uses of compulsory labor in the British mandate territories have received less attention than those in the mandates of other European powers.

116. Wilson, *Mesopotamia*, 312. On how "enhanced resource extraction" by British occupying forces during and after the war fueled the grievances that led to the revolt, see Ulrichsen, "British Occupation of Mesopotamia," 349.

117. Quoted in Kadhim, *Reclaiming Iraq*, 67.

Chapter 2

Parts of this chapter are derived from Sara Pursley, "The Stage of Adolescence: Anticolonial Time, Youth Insurgency, and the Marriage Crisis in Hashimite Iraq," published in *History of the Present* 3, no. 2 (Fall 2013): 160–97, by the University of Illinois Press.

1. Al-Husri asserted that Faysal's plan was for Iraqis to take power gradually from the British, starting with the education system. Sati' al-Husri, *Mudhakkirati fi al-'Iraq, 1921–1941* (Beirut: Dar al-Tali'a, 1967), 1:13–14.

2. al-Husri, 1:57.

3. al-Husri, 1:571.

4. Quoted in 'Abd Allah al-Fayyad, *al-Thawra al-'Iraqiyya al-Kubra Sanat 1920* (Baghdad: Matba'at al-Irshad, 1963), 136.

5. See 'Abd al-Razzaq al-Hilali, *Tarikh al-Ta'lim fi al-'Iraq fi 'Ahd al-Ihtilal al-Biritani, 1914–1921* (Baghdad: Mutba'at al-Ma'arif, 1975). On similar British policies in Egypt, see Gregory Starrett, *Putting Islam to Work: Education, Politics, and Religious Transformation in Egypt* (Berkeley: University of California Press, 1998), 32–33, 46–47.

6. But see Orit Bashkin, *The Other Iraq: Pluralism and Culture in Hashemite Iraq* (Stanford: Stanford University Press, 2009), 249–54; and Sara Pursley, "The Stage of Adolescence: Anticolonial Time, Youth Insurgency, and the Marriage Crisis in Hashimite Iraq," *History of the Present* 3, no. 2 (November 2013): 160–97.

7. Probably the most well-developed argument for the centrality of this struggle in Iraq's history is made by Eric Davis, *Memories of State: Politics, History, and Collective Identity in Modern Iraq* (Berkeley: University of California Press, 2005).

8. But see Peter Wien, *Iraqi Arab Nationalism: Authoritarian, Totalitarian and Pro-Fascist Inclinations, 1932–1941* (London: Routledge, 2006).

9. al-Husri, *Mudhakkirati*, 2:271–72.

10. al-Husri, 2:527–28.

11. al-Husri, 1:221–24, 2:302.

12. Sati' al-Husri, *Ahadith fi al-Tarbiya wa-l-Ijtima'* (Beirut: Dar al-'Ilm li-l-Malayyin, 1962), 115, 336; on psychology, see also 120–33.

13. On similar projects by anticolonial elites elsewhere to "appropriate an ego," see Warwick Anderson et al., "Introduction: Globalizing the Unconscious," in *Unconscious Dominions: Psychoanalysis, Colonial Trauma, and Global Sovereignties*, ed. W. Anderson et al. (Durham: Duke University Press, 2011), 9. For a discussion of how "pedagogy and psychology developed hand in hand" in early 20th-century Iran, see Cyrus Schayegh, *Who Is Knowledgeable Is Strong: Science, Class, and the Formation of Modern Iranian Society, 1900–1950* (Berkeley: University of California Press, 2009), 166ff.

14. Elizabeth Freeman, *Time Binds: Queer Temporalities, Queer Histories* (Durham: Duke University Press, 2010), 3.

15. According to Eric Weitz, the Treaty of Lausanne was a "tectonic shift" on the global historical scale, "even if it is barely known today except to specialists on the region." Weitz labels the outcome of this shift "the Paris system," which he argues replaced "the Vienna system" established among European states in 1815. Vienna "centered on dynastic legitimacy and state sovereignty within clearly defined borders," while Paris "focused on populations and an ideal of state sovereignty rooted in national homogeneity." Weitz's analysis is useful in pointing to the global significance of the Treaty of Lausanne. But I would qualify his argument in two ways. First, while the treaty's reasoning may well have been informed by an "ideal of state sovereignty rooted in national homogeneity," the treaty itself makes no assumption of national homogeneity. Rather, what it assumes is that every state will have a "majority race" and, by extension, "minority races." This is precisely because the treaty was focused, contra Weitz, on the production of state sovereignty within territorial borders, my second qualification to his argument. Thus, while the treaty assigned default nationalities to former Ottoman subjects based on their "habitual residence," it also allowed any adult

male former Ottoman subject who was "differing in race" from the majority of people in the territory in which he resided to opt for the nationality of a former Ottoman state in which he was a member of the "majority race." In this latter case, he was required to move to that state's territory within twelve months. State sovereignty itself was still defined in terms of territory, not population. Weitz, "From the Vienna to the Paris System: International Politics and the Entangled Histories of Human Rights, Forced Deportations, and Civilizing Missions," *American Historical Review* 113, no. 5 (2008): 1314, 1338.

16. Talal Asad has noted that in modernization discourses, from the Enlightenment to the postwar age of development, "one assumption has been constant: to make history, the agent must create the future, remake herself, and help others to do so, where the criteria of successful remaking are seen to be universal. Old universes must be subverted and a new universe created. . . . Actions seeking to maintain the 'local' status quo, or to follow local models of social life, do not qualify as history making. From the Cargo Cults of Melanesia to the Islamic Revolution in Iran, they merely attempt (hopelessly) 'to resist the future' or 'to turn back the clock of history.'" Asad, *Genealogies of Religion: Discipline and Reasons of Power in Christianity and Islam* (Baltimore: Johns Hopkins University Press, 1993), 19.

17. On temporal distancing, see Johannes Fabian, *Time and the Other: How Anthropology Makes Its Object*, rev. ed. (New York: Columbia University Press, 2002).

18. Thomas Blom Hansen and Finn Stepputat, eds., "Introduction," in *Sovereign Bodies: Citizens, Migrants, and States in the Postcolonial World* (Princeton: Princeton University Press, 2005), 1.

19. 'Abd al-Razzaq al-Hasani, *Tarikh al-Wizarat al-'Iraqiyya* (Sidon: Matba'at al-'Irfan, 1965), 1:118.

20. Since the 1920 revolt, Iraq's "original borders" had been regularly defined in nationalist discourse as stretching "from the northern border of Mosul province to the Persian Gulf." See Sara Pursley, "'Lines Drawn on an Empty Map': Iraq's Borders and the Legend of the Artificial State," *Jadaliyya*, June 2, 2015.

21. al-Hilali, *Tarikh al-Ta'lim*, 39, 62–63.

22. On early Shi'i clerical and southern tribal support for Faysal, or another son of Sharif Husayn, see Muhammad Mahdi al-Basir, *Tarikh al-Qadiyya al-'Iraqiyya* (Baghdad: Matba'at al-Fallah, 1924), 72, 116; al-Fayyad, *al-Thawra al-'Iraqiyya*, 211ff; Khayri al-'Umari, *Hikayat Siyasiyya min Tarikh al-'Iraq al-Hadith* (Cairo: Dar al-Hilal, 1969), 70; and 'Ali al-Wardi, *Lamahat Ijtima'iyya min Tarikh al-'Iraq al-Hadith* (Qumm: Maktabat al-Sadr, 2004), 5.1:79–80, 5.1:214ff, 5.2:236, 6.2:209. British officials spread the assertion that "the Shi'a" were opposed to a "Sunni" government, a claim that continues to be repeated by British imperial historians. For an example of this narrative in the British primary sources, see Arnold Talbot Wilson, *Mesopotamia, 1917–1920: A Clash of Loyalties* (London: Oxford University Press, 1931), 2:113, 314. For critiques of the narrative, see al-Wardi, *Lamahat*, 6.1:109, 176; and al-Fayyad, *al-Thawra al-'Iraqiyya*, 245–47. Al-Fayyad notes that he was not able to find a single "fatwa or opinion from any important person among the Shi'a saying that a Shi'i ruler should be appointed" to govern Iraq (p. 247). I have not seen one either.

23. al-Wardi, *Lamahat*, 6.1:165–66, 202–204; Husayn Jamil, *al-'Iraq: Shahada Siyasiyya, 1908–1930* (London: Dar al-Laam, 1987), 73–82; al-'Umari, *Hikayat Siyasiyya*, 85, 89; al-Hasani, *Tarikh al-Wizarat*, 1:85.

24. Both British and Iraqi officials occasionally claimed that there was no mandate in Iraq, only a treaty between equals, but the treaty's failure to nullify the mandate contradicted that claim, and the League of Nations officially accepted the treaty as giving effect to the mandate. Susan Pedersen, *The Guardians: The League of Nations and the Crisis of Empire* (Oxford: Oxford University Press, 2015), 483n11.

25. al-Hasani, *Tarikh al-Wizarat*, 83–84; al-Wardi, *Lamahat*, 6.1:175–76, 194.

26. al-Hasani, *Tarikh al-Wizarat*, 1:84–85.

27. Jamil, *al-'Iraq*, 79; al-Wardi, *Lamahat*, 6.1:179, 194.

28. al-Wardi, *Lamahat*, 6.1:201.

29. al-Hasani, *Tarikh al-Wizarat*, 1:85.

30. al-Wardi, *Lamahat*, 6.1:202, 204.

31. al-Wardi, 6.1:203–204.

32. al-Wardi, 6.1:203–4.

33. Muhammad Mahdi Jawahiri, *Mudhakkirati* (Beirut: Dar al-Muntazar, 1999), 1:116–17; Jamil, *al-'Iraq*, 113–14; al-Wardi, *Lamahat*, 6.1:208–9.

34. al-Wardi, *Lamahat*, 6.1:217–18.

35. al-Wardi, 6.1:223.

36. al-Wardi, 6.1:218.

37. al-Wardi, 6.1: 218, 223–24.

38. Bashkin, *Other Iraq*, 170–71.

39. al-Hasani, *Tarikh al-Wizarat*, 1:128.

40. al-Hasani, 1:132–33.

41. al-Wardi, *Lamahat*, 6.1: 235. These claims echoed earlier British assertions that the Shi'i 'ulama' opposing the British occupation were "spiritual tyrants whose principle ambition was to stem the rising tide of emancipation" (Wilson, *Mesopotamia*, x).

42. Sati'al-Husri, *Abhath Mukhtara fi al-Qawmiyya al-'Arabiyya* (Cairo: Dar al-Ma'arif, n.d.), 39ff.

43. al-Husri, *Mudhakkirati*, 2:480. See also al-Husri, *Abhath Mukhtara*, 42–43.

44. Sati' al-Husri, *Ara' wa-Ahadith fi al-Wataniyya wa-l-Qawmiyya* (Beirut: Markaz Dirasat al-Wahda al-'Arabiyya, 1984), 61; al-Husri, *Mudhakkirati*, 1:215.

45. al-Husri, *Abhath Mukhtara*, 43–44.

46. William L. Cleveland, *The Making of an Arab Nationalist: Ottomanism and Arabism in the Life and Thought of Sati' Al-Husri* (Princeton: Princeton University Press, 1971), 36–37.

47. Cleveland, 38. See also Reeva S. Simon, *Iraq between the Two World Wars: The Militarist Origins of Tyranny*, rev. ed. (New York: Columbia University Press, 2004), 69–73.

48. Cleveland, *Making of an Arab Nationalist*, 37, 112.

49. It was also later exaggerated by al-Husri, in an addendum to his reprint of the 1922 curriculum in his memoirs (al-Husri, *Mudhakkirati*, 1:216).

50. Cleveland, *Making of an Arab Nationalist*, 63.

51. The curriculum is reprinted in al-Husri, *Mudhakkirati*, 1:215.

52. al-Husri, 1:215.

53. al-Husri, 2:123.

54. al-Husri, 1:215.

55. Benedict Anderson, *Imagined Communities: Reflections on the Origin and Spread of Nationalism* (London: Verso Books, 1983).

56. al-Husri, *Mudhakkirati*, 1:215.

57. al-Husri, 1:215.

58. al-Husri, 2:483.

59. al-Husri, 2:479.

60. al-Husri, 1:228.

61. al-Husri, 1:105ff.

62. al-Husri, *Ahadith fi al-Tarbiya wa-l-Ijtima'*, 115–16. On al-Husri's critique of "learning without education," see also Bashkin, *Other Iraq*, 253.

63. al-Husri, *Mudhakkirati*, 1:213.

64. al-Husri, 1:214. The British curriculum is reprinted on pp. 106–7; the new curriculum on p. 212.

65. al-Husri, *Ara' wa-Ahadith fi al-Wataniyya wa-l-Qawmiyya*, 34; al-Husri, *Mudhakkirati*, 2:480–81.

66. For example, al-Husri, *Ahadith fi al-Tarbiya wa-l-Ijtima'*, 330–33.

67. al-Husri, *Abhath Mukhtara*, 44.

68. al-Husri, *Ara' wa-Ahadith fi al-Wataniyya wa-l-Qawmiyya*, 150.

69. al-Husri, *Mudhakkirati*, 1:215–16.

70. al-Husri, 1:214.

71. al-Husri, 1:218.

72. al-Husri, 1:217.

73. al-Husri, *Ahadith fi al-Tarbiya wa-l-Ijtima'*, 58.

74. I translate *al-tarbiya al-akhlaqiyya* as "moral education" when al-Husri seems to be describing the project to produce a good, rather than bad, essential character in the future citizen, and as "ethical pedagogy" when he is discussing techniques and spatio-temporal regimes that work on students' quotidian emotions and habits, their bodily tempos and routines. Since the classical age of Islam, *tahdhib al-akhlaq*, or the cultivation of ethics or morals, has referred to the repetition of ethical practices to discipline the body and soul. In the modern period, *akhlaq* came to be used more frequently in reference to a person's essential moral character. *Tarbiya*, which can be translated as "education," "cultivation," "training," or "pedagogy," is distinct from *ta'lim*, "education," or the transmission or acquisition of knowledge. On Islamic technologies of the self, see Samira Haj, *Reconfiguring Islamic Tradition: Reform, Rationality, and Modernity* (Stanford: Stanford University Press, 2008); Saba Mahmood, *Politics of Piety: The Islamic Revival and the Feminist Subject* (Princeton: Princeton University Press, 2005); and Asad, *Genealogies of Religion*.

75. al-Husri, *Ahadith fi al-Tarbiya wa-l-Ijtima'*, 36–38.

76. al-Husri, *Mudhakkirati*, 1:325–33.

77. al-Husri, 1:322–24.

78. al-Husri, *Ahadith fi al-Tarbiya wa-l-Ijtima'*, 76.

79. See Cleveland, *Making of an Arab Nationalist*, 32–33.

80. al-Husri, *Mudhakkirati*, 1:214–15.

81. According to Timothy Mitchell, Le Bon was "probably the strongest individual European influence in turn-of-the-century Cairo on the political thought of Egypt's emergent bourgeoisie." Mitchell, *Colonising Egypt* (Berkeley: University of California Press, 1991), 123.

82. al-Husri, *Ahadith fi al-Tarbiya wa-l-Ijtima'*, 330–33.

83. al-Husri, 336.

84. al-Husri, 323–24. See also Cleveland, *Making of an Arab Nationalist*, 106n61.

85. Sati' al-Husri, *Ara' wa-Ahadith fi al-'Ilm wa-l-Akhlaq wa-l-Thaqafa* (Beirut: Markaz Dirasat al-Wahda al-'Arabiyya, n.d.), 172.

86. al-Husri, 169–70.

87. al-Husri, *Ahadith fi al-Tarbiya wa-l-Ijtima'*, 34–36, 50; al-Husri, *Mudhakkirati*, 2:280.

88. al-Husri, *Mudhakkirati*, 2:280.

89. See, for example, Johan Franzén, *Red Star over Iraq: Iraqi Communism before Saddam* (Columbia University Press, 2011), 18; and "Thawra fi Mafhum al-Watan," *al-'Irfan* 49, no. 2 (October 1961): 122–24.

90. D.G. Horn, "This Norm Which Is Not One: Reading the Female Body in Lombroso's Anthropology," in *Deviant Bodies: Critical Perspectives on Difference in Science and Popular Culture*, ed. J. Terry and J. Urla (Bloomington, IN: Indiana University Press, 1995), 122, cited in Lesko, *Act Your Age!*, 58. See also Lynn Fendler, "What Is It Impossible to Think? A Genealogy of the Educated Subject," in *Foucault's Challenge: Discourse, Knowledge, and Power in Education*, ed. Thomas Popkewitz, 39–63 (New York: Teachers College Press, 1998).

91. Marwa Elshakry, *Reading Darwin in Arabic, 1860–1950* (Chicago: University of Chicago Press, 2013), 226.

92. al-Husri, *Ahadith fi al-Tarbiya wa-l-Ijtima'*, 401.

93. al-Husri, *Mudhakkirati*, 2:308–309.

94. al-Husri, 2:309.

95. al-Husri, 2:311.

96. al-Husri, 2:308.

97. al-Husri, *Ahadith fi al-Tarbiya wa-l-Ijtima'*, 50.

98. al-Husri, *Mudhakkirati*, 2:307.

99. al-Husri, 2:306.

100. al-Husri, 2:307.

101. Freeman, *Time Binds*, xi.

102. The Iraqi, rather than Arab, framework of the army was a concern of some Arab nationalists at the time; see Fadil Barrak, *Dawr al-Jaysh al-'Iraqi fi Hukumat al-Difa' al-Watani wa-l-Harb ma'a Biritaniya Sanat 1941* (Baghdad: Dar al-'Arabiyya., 1979), 175–76.

103. Iraqi sources give various dates for the founding of al-Futuwwa; it seems it was introduced in fits and starts from 1932 to 1939, with several setbacks due to various kinds of opposition (see Wien, *Iraqi Arab Nationalism*, esp. 89–90).

104. Wilson Chacko Jacob, *Working Out Egypt: Effendi Masculinity and Subject Formation in Colonial Modernity, 1870–1940* (Durham: Duke University Press, 2011), 234. This may need more research, but the interwar Iraqi version of *al-futuwwa* seems to bear little resemblance to the interwar Egyptian figure of *al-futuwwa* theorized by Jacob as an "internal Other,"

standing for a tradition whose "immanent concept" of sovereignty "made it problematic within the time-space of the nation-state," and whose "constitutive exclusion" was "essential to the historical process of working out modern Egypt" (pp. 25, 229).

105. al-Husri, *Mudhakkirati*, 2:380.

106. Reeva Simon, in *Iraq between the Two World Wars*, links al-Futuwwa and other interwar military education projects to the Hitler Youth and to the rise of Ba'thist dictatorship in the 1970s (see esp. chap. 4). (On the front cover of the paperback edition of her book, this causal relation is stated flatly: "How the German-based military education of an Iraqi elite led to the regime of Saddam Hussein.") This argument is challenged by Peter Wien, who argues that al-Futuwwa should be seen as primarily an anticolonial project (Wien, *Iraqi Arab Nationalism*, esp. 93).

107. Bashkin, *Other Iraq*, 60, 233–35; Orit Bashkin, "'When Mu'awiya Entered the Curriculum': Some Comments on the Iraqi Educational System in the Interwar Period," *Comparative Education Review* 50, no. 3 (2006): 356.

108. Cited in Sami Shawkat, *Hadhihi Ahdafuna* (Baghdad: Wizarat al-Ma'arif, 1939), 8.

109. Shawkat, 8–9.

110. Shawkat, 7.

111. Shawkat, 84–85.

112. al-Husri, *Mudhakkirati*, 2:132–33.

113. On masculinity in contemporary Iraqi Arab nationalist thought, including that of Shawkat and al-Husri, see Wien, *Iraqi Arab Nationalism*, esp. 90–105; and Peter Wien, "'Watan' and 'Rujula': The Emergence of a New Model of Youth in Interwar Iraq," in *Youth and Youth Culture in the Contemporary Middle East*, ed. Jørgen Bæk Simonsen, 10–20 (Aarhus: Aarhus University Press, 2005).

114. al-Husri, *Mudhakkirati*, 2:309.

115. al-Husri, 1:217.

116. Quoted in Matta Akrawi, "Curriculum Construction in the Public Primary Schools of Iraq in the Light of a Study of the Political, Economic, Social, Hygienic and Educational Conditions and Problems of the Country, with Some Reference to the Education of Teachers" (PhD diss., Teachers College, Columbia University, 1942), 192.

117. See Akrawi, 156–58.

Chapter 3

Parts of this chapter are derived from Sara Pursley, "Building the Nation through the Production of Difference: The Gendering of Education in Iraq, 1928–58," published in *Writing the Modern History of Iraq: Historiographical and Political Challenges*, ed. Jordi Tejel et al., 119–41 (London: Imperial College Press, 2012); and Sara Pursley, "'Education for Real Life': Pragmatist Pedagogies and American Interwar Expansion in Iraq," published in *The Routledge Handbook of the History of the Middle East Mandates*, ed. Cyrus Schayegh and Andrew Arsan, 88–105 (New York: Routledge, 2015).

1. Paul Monroe, ed., *Report of the Educational Inquiry Commission* (Baghdad: Government Press, 1932), 148.

2. Monroe, 55, 73.

3. Monroe, 112. This proposal relates to the elementary schools; on similar recommendations for the girls' secondary schools, see pp. 132, 162.

4. Monroe, 133.

5. Uday Singh Mehta, *Liberalism and Empire: A Study in Nineteenth-Century British Liberal Thought* (Chicago: University of Chicago Press, 1999), 192.

6. Monroe, *Report*, 120.

7. For an example of British discourses in mandate Palestine that called for the curriculum in rural girls' schools to focus on "hygiene" rather than "bookwork," see Ellen Fleischmann, *The Nation and Its "New" Women: The Palestinian Women's Movement 1920–1948* (Berkeley: University of California Press, 2003), 37. For British critiques of "bookish" education in early 20th-century Egypt, see Gregory Starrett, *Putting Islam to Work: Education, Politics, and Religious Transformation in Egypt* (Berkeley: University of California Press, 1998), 51.

8. See Megan J. Elias, *Stir It Up: Home Economics in American Culture* (Philadelphia: University of Pennsylvania Press, 2010); and Sarah Stage and Virginia B. Vincenti, eds., *Rethinking Home Economics: Women and the History of a Profession* (Ithaca: Cornell University Press, 1997).

9. See Reeva S. Simon, *Iraq between the Two World Wars: The Militarist Origins of Tyranny*, rev. ed. (New York: Columbia University Press, 2004), chap. 4; and Peter Sluglett, *Britain in Iraq: Contriving King and Country*, 2nd ed. (New York: Columbia University Press, 2007), chap. 8.

10. Orit Bashkin, *The Other Iraq: Pluralism and Culture in Hashemite Iraq* (Stanford: Stanford University Press, 2009), 240.

11. On patriotic motherhood, see Elizabeth Thompson, *Colonial Citizens: Republican Rights, Paternal Privilege, and Gender in French Syria and Lebanon* (New York: Columbia University Press, 2000).

12. Beth Baron, *The Women's Awakening in Egypt: Culture, Society, and the Press* (New Haven: Yale University Press, 1994), 159–61. See also Kenneth Cuno, *Modernizing Marriage: Family, Ideology, and Law in Nineteenth- and Early Twentieth-Century Egypt* (Syracuse: Syracuse University Press, 2015); Beth Baron, *Egypt as a Woman: Nationalism, Gender, and Politics* (Berkeley: University of California Press, 2005); Lisa Pollard, *Nurturing the Nation: The Family Politics of Modernizing, Colonizing, and Liberating Egypt, 1805–1923* (Berkeley: University of California Press, 2005); Afsaneh Najmabadi, *Women with Mustaches and Men without Beards: Gender and Sexual Anxieties of Iranian Modernity* (Berkeley: University of California Press, 2005); Mona L. Russell, *Creating the New Egyptian Woman: Consumerism, Education, and National Identity, 1863–1922* (Basingstoke: Palgrave Macmillan, 2004); Fleischmann, *The Nation and Its "New" Women: The Palestinian Women's Movement 1920–1948*; and Akram Fouad Khater, *Inventing Home: Emigration, Gender, and the Middle Class in Lebanon, 1870–1920* (Berkeley: University of California Press, 2001). For studies in Iraqi women's history, see Noga Efrati, "Competing Narratives: Histories of the Women's Movement in Iraq, 1910–1958," *International Journal of Middle East Studies* 40 (2008): 445–66; Noga Efrati, "Negotiating Rights in Iraq: Women and the Personal Status Law," *Middle East Journal* 59, no. 4 (August 2005): 577–96; Noga Efrati, "The Other 'Awakening' in Iraq: The Women's Movement in the First Half of the Twentieth Century," *British Journal of Middle Eastern Studies* 31 (2004): 153–73;

Peter Wien, "Mothers of Warriors: Girls in a Youth Debate of Interwar Iraq," in *Girlhood: A Global History*, ed. Jennifer Helgren and Colleen A. Vasconcellos, 289–303 (New Brunswick: Rutgers University Press, 2010); Orit Bashkin, "Representations of Women in the Writings of the Intelligentsia in Hashemite Iraq, 1921–1958," *Journal of Middle East Women's Studies* (Winter 2008): 53–82; Nadje Sadig al-Ali, *Iraqi Women: Untold Stories from 1948 to the Present* (London: Zed Books, 2007); and Jacqueline Ismael and Shereen Ismael, "Gender and State in Iraq," in *Gender and Citizenship in the Middle East*, ed. Suad Joseph, 185–211 (Syracuse: Syracuse University Press, 2000).

13. Omnia El Shakry, "Schooled Mothers and Structured Play: Child Rearing in Turn-of-the-Century Egypt," in *Remaking Women: Feminism and Modernity in the Middle East*, ed. Lila Abu-Lughod (Princeton: Princeton University Press, 1998), 126.

14. Afsaneh Najmabadi, "Crafting an Educated Housewife in Iran," in *Remaking Women: Feminism and Modernity in the Middle East*, ed. Lila Abu-Lughod (Princeton: Princeton University Press, 1998), 94.

15. For exceptions that pay serious attention to the imbrications of class and gender in the production of modern domesticity, see Sherene Seikaly, *Men of Capital: Scarcity and Economy in Mandate Palestine* (Stanford: Stanford University Press, 2016); and Omnia El Shakry, *The Great Social Laboratory: Subjects of Knowledge in Colonial and Postcolonial Egypt* (Stanford: Stanford University Press, 2007).

16. Numerous studies have focused on the symbolic or metaphorical aspects of these discourses, sometimes arguing that the rise of "the woman question" was "not really about women at all" (Pollard, *Nurturing the Nation*, 13). See also Hanan Kholoussy, *For Better, for Worse: The Marriage Crisis That Made Modern Egypt* (Stanford: Stanford University Press, 2010).

17. Baron, *Egypt as a Woman*, 6.

18. See Ann Laura Stoler, *Along the Archival Grain: Epistemic Anxieties and Colonial Common Sense* (Princeton: Princeton University Press, 2010).

19. There was some initial disagreement over the Monroe Report's assertion that home economics "receive little or no attention" in the girls' curriculum. Al-Husri responded by claiming that domestic education for girls was implemented "many years ago"; but later, after the debate had escalated, the only example he came up with was a directive issued to girls' primary schools for the addition of a home economics requirement in 1928. Matta Akrawi conceded that al-Husri issued this directive, though he claimed it was not actually implemented by girls' schools. Key leaders of the opposing sides thus seem to have settled on 1928 as the date of the first official home economics requirement for girls in the public school system. In his dissertation (written in the mid-1930s but not deposited until 1942), Akrawi provided additional evidence for this by reprinting the ministry's official "Course of Study" for Iraq's primary schools from 1922 to 1928, which, as he noted, "contained no provision for differentiation according to the needs of urban and rural schools, or of boys' and girls' schools." I am not claiming that domestic education did not exist within present-day Iraq's borders prior to the 1930s. It would surely have been taught in Protestant missionary schools, which spread domestic education around the world starting in the mid-19th century. It was also taught in Ottoman schools for girls established between 1899 and 1914 and probably by local initiative

in individual government schools during the 1920s. Research into the curricula used in all these institutions would flesh out the story of modern domestic education in Iraq. But for my purposes, it remains significant that there was no such centrally mandated education for girls in public schools during Iraq's first post-Ottoman decade, and that expansion of this type of education generated much public debate in subsequent decades. See Monroe, *Report*, 112; Matta Akrawi, "Curriculum Construction in the Public Primary Schools of Iraq in the Light of a Study of the Political, Economic, Social, Hygienic and Educational Conditions and Problems of the Country, with Some Reference to the Education of Teachers" (PhD Diss., Teachers College, Columbia University, 1942), 195–97; and Sati' al-Husri, *Mudhakkirati fi al-'Iraq, 1921–1941* (Beirut: Dar al-Tali'a, 1967), 2:167, 186.

20. See, respectively, Simon, *Iraq between the Two World Wars*, 83; and Muhsin al-Musawi, *Reading Iraq: Culture and Power in Conflict* (London: I. B. Tauris, 2006), 42.

21. Robert Vitalis, *America's Kingdom: Mythmaking on the Saudi Oil Frontier* (London: Verso, 2009), xxx.

22. Quoted in David M. Ment, "Education, Nation-Building and Modernization after World War I: American Ideas for the Peace Conference," *Paedagogica Historica* 41:1 (2005): 161.

23. Ment, 176.

24. Ment, 177.

25. David M. Ment, "The American Role in Education in the Middle East: Ideology and Experiment, 1920–1940," *Paedagogica Historica* 47, no. 1–2 (2011): 173–89.

26. Paul Monroe, "Influence of the Growing Perception of Human Interrelationship on Education," *American Journal of Sociology* 18, no. 5 (1913): 629.

27. Monroe, 623.

28. Monroe, 622–23.

29. Monroe, 636.

30. Monroe, 638.

31. Paul Monroe, "Education and Nationalism," in *Essays in Comparative Education: Republished Papers* (New York: Teachers College Press, 1927), 3.

32. Monroe, 4.

33. Ment, "American Role," 176; Monroe, "Mission Education," in Monroe, *Essays*, 181.

34. Monroe, "Problems of Mission Education," in Monroe, *Essays*, 222.

35. Gita Steiner-Khamsi and Hubert O. Quist, "The Politics of Educational Borrowing: Reopening the Case of Achimota in British Ghana," *Comparative Education Review* 44, no. 3 (2000): 274.

36. Quoted in Steiner-Khamsi and Quist, 286.

37. Monroe, "Mission Education," 182.

38. Liping Bu, "International Activism and Comparative Education: Pioneering Efforts of the International Institute of Teachers College, Columbia University," *Comparative Education Review* 41, no. 4 (1997): 420; Inderjeet Parmar, *Foundations of the American Century: The Ford, Carnegie, and Rockefeller Foundations in the Rise of American Power* (New York: Columbia University Press, 2015), 61–62; and Louis Harlan, *Booker T. Washington: The Wizard of Tuskegee, 1901–1915* (Oxford: Oxford University Press, 1983), 130.

39. See Edgar Wallace Knight, *The Influence of Reconstruction on Education in the South* (New York: Arno Press, 1969); and Clinton B. Allison, "The Appalling World of Edgar Wallace Knight," *Journal of Thought* 18, no. 3 (1983): 7–14. In a process Andrew Zimmerman calls "the globalization of the New South," German and British colonial administrations in West Africa also drew on the model, importing specialists from Hampton and Tuskegee, thus "combining the European colonial civilizing mission with American industrial education." See Andrew Zimmerman, *Alabama in Africa: Booker T. Washington, the German Empire, and the Globalization of the New South* (Princeton: Princeton University Press, 2010), 168. On British colonial borrowings from Tuskegee, see also Steiner-Khamsi and Quist, "The Politics of Educational Borrowing"; and Michael Omolewa, "Educating the 'Native': A Study of the Education Adaptation Strategy in British Colonial Africa, 1910–1936," *Journal of African American History* 91, no. 3 (2006): 267–87.

40. Thomas Popkewitz, Preface to *Inventing the Modern Self and John Dewey: Modernities and the Traveling of Pragmatism in Education*, ed. Thomas Popkewitz (New York: Palgrave Macmillan, 2005), ix.

41. Popkewitz, x, viii.

42. Thomas Popkewitz, *Cosmopolitanism and the Age of School Reform: Science, Education, and Making Society by Making the Child* (New York: Routledge, 2008), 63, 55–56, 66–68.

43. See Simon, *Iraq between the Two World Wars*, chap. 4.

44. El Shakry, *Great Social Laboratory*, 116.

45. See Samira Haj, *The Making of Iraq, 100–1963: Capital, Power, and Ideology* (Albany: State University of New York Press, 1997), esp. chap. 1.

46. Muhammad Fadhil al-Jamali, *The New Iraq: Its Problem of Bedouin Education* (New York: Bureau of Publications, Columbia Teachers College, 1934), 7.

47. al-Jamali, 100–101.

48. Monroe, *Report*, 161.

49. Monroe, 153.

50. Monroe, 55.

51. Akrawi, "Curriculum Construction," 209.

52. See, for example, Akrawi, 135.

53. Akrawi, 215.

54. Akrawi, 215.

55. Monroe, *Report*, 117, 120.

56. Sati' al-Husri, *Naqd Taqrir Lajnat Munru: Rasa'il Muwajjaha ila al-Ustadh Bul Munru* (Baghdad: Matba'at al-Najah, 1932), 126. See also al-Husri, *Mudhakkirati*, 2:167.

57. al-Husri, *Naqd Taqrir*, 130–33.

58. Akrawi, "Curriculum Construction," 177.

59. al-Jamali, *New Iraq*, 9–10.

60. al-Jamali, 12.

61. Akrawi, "Curriculum Construction," 216.

62. Akrawi, 237.

63. Roderic D. Matthews and Matta Akrawi, *Education in Arab Countries of the Near*

East: Egypt, Iraq, Palestine, Transjordan, Syria, Lebanon (Washington, DC: American Council on Education, 1949), 166.

64. See, for example, Muhammad Husayn Al Yasin, "Hajat Madarisina al-Thanawiyya ila al-Tawjih," *al-Mu'allim al-Jadid* 12, no. 1 (September 1948): 25; Amat Sa'id, "al-Ta'lim al-Niswi," *al-Mu'allim al-Jadid* 12, no. 5–6 (July 1949): 87; and the editorial "al-Ta'lim al-Niswi fi al-'Iraq bayn al-Ams wa-l-Yawm," *al-Mu'allim al-Jadid* 17, no. 1–2 (September 1953): 3.

65. Akrawi, "Curriculum Construction," 198.

66. Popkewitz, *Cosmopolitanism and the Age of School Reform*, 68.

67. Akrawi, "Curriculum Construction," 203.

68. Akrawi, 204.

69. Akrawi, 204.

70. Badi' Sharif, "Mashakil al-Tawjih al-Thaqafi fi I'dad Jil al-Mustaqbal," *al-Mu'allim al-Jadid* 12, no. 5 (July 1949): 12.

71. Akrawi, "Curriculum Construction," 74. On arguments in interwar Iran that "good parenting also required psychological knowledge," see Cyrus Schayegh, *Who Is Knowledgeable Is Strong: Science, Class, and the Formation of Modern Iranian Society, 1900–1950* (Berkeley: University of California Press, 2009), 172.

72. Sluglett, *Britain in Iraq*, 193–96.

73. Monroe, *Report*, 38.

74. Reprinted in al-Husri, *Mudhakkirati*, 2:237.

75. al-Husri, 2:238.

76. al-Husri, 2:239.

77. Paul Monroe, "Philippine Education, 1913," in *Essays*, 11, 47, 46.

78. Monroe, "Education in Latin America," in *Essays*, 174.

79. Monroe, "Education in China, 1922," in *Essays*, 51; Monroe, "Students and Politics in China, 1926," in *Essays*, 88–96.

80. Muhammad Fadil al-Jamali, "al-Tifl wa-l-Umma," *al-Mu'allim al-Jadid* 3, no. 3 (June 1938): 166.

81. al-Jamali, 168.

82. Akrawi, "Curriculum Construction," 200.

83. al-Jamali, *New Iraq*, 10.

84. Monroe, *Report*, 29.

85. The association of pragmatist pedagogies with democratization has been the cause of considerable confusion in the historiography. For example, Reeva Simon depicts the battle between al-Jamali and al-Husri as "the struggle of youth against the established status quo," even while noting that, in the particular conflict she is discussing, al-Jamali was supported by Prime Minister Nuri Sa'id and the Iraqi monarch, two rather question-able representatives of the struggle against the status quo (Simon, *Iraq between the Two World Wars*, 87).

86. Matthews and Akrawi, *Education in Arab Countries of the Near East*, 155.

87. Victor Clark, *Compulsory Education in Iraq* (Paris: United Nations Educational, Cultural and Scientific Organization, 1951), 26.

88. Clark, 15.

89. al-Husri, *Mudhakkirati*, 2:265. Here al-Husri contrasted "practical pedagogy" with "intellectual pedagogy" (*al-tarbiya al-fikriyya*), clearly preferring the latter.

90. Clark, *Compulsory Education in Iraq*, 21.

91. Monroe, *Report*, 70.

92. International Bank for Reconstruction and Development, *The Economic Development of Iraq* (Baltimore: Johns Hopkins University Press, 1952), 402.

93. Monroe, *Report*, 110.

94. Popkewitz, *Cosmopolitanism and the Age of School Reform*, 78. Emphasis added.

95. Popkewitz, 54.

96. Popkewitz, 29, 92.

97. Popkewitz, 57, 60. The "homeless mind" that according to Popkewitz became the object and end of pragmatist pedagogy has striking similarities to the "mobile personality" posited by US modernization theorist Daniel Lerner in 1958 as the "psychological prerequisite" of the "modernizing take-off" in the Middle East. See Daniel Lerner, *The Passing of Traditional Society: Modernizing the Middle East*, 2nd ed. (New York: Free Press, 1964), 48–49.

98. Rima Apple, "Liberal Arts or Vocational Training? Home Economics Education for Girls," in *Rethinking Home Economics: Women and the History of a Profession*, ed. Sarah Stage and Virginia B. Vincenti (Ithaca: Cornell University Press, 1997), 80.

99. al-Husri, *Mudhakkirati*, 2:114.

100. al-Husri, 2:132.

101. Ruz Gharib, "Harakat Tadbir al-Manzil," *al-Mu'allim al-Jadid* 3, no. 3 (June 1938): 207.

102. Monroe, *Report*, 133.

103. Clark, *Compulsory Education in Iraq*, 38.

104. Monroe, *Report*, 132.

105. There was, however, some interesting debate on just this point. A 1942 article in *al-Mu'allim al-Jadid* argued that a girl's education, especially in the sciences, should not focus on domesticity precisely because the acceleration of time in the modern era meant that her future work could not be predicted. See Ihssan 'Abid, "Hal Yakhtalif Manhaj al-'Ulum li-l-Banat 'an li-l-Wilad?," *al-Mu'allim al-Jadid* 7, no. 6 (June 1942): 513–20.

106. Akrawi, "Curriculum Construction," 181.

107. Iraqi Ministry of Education, "Summary of the Present Primary Course of Study," reprinted in Akrawi, "Curriculum Construction," 193–95.

108. Akrawi, "Curriculum Construction," 181.

109. Matthews and Akrawi, *Education in Arab Countries of the Near East*, 152.

110. Matthews and Akrawi, 149.

111. 'Abd al-Majid Hasan, "Dawr I'dad al-Mu'allimat fi al-'Iraq," *al-Mu'allim al-Jadid* 20, no. 3 (June 1957): 2.

112. "Manahij al-Fanun al-Baytiyya," *al-Mu'allim al-Jadid* 15, no. 5 (August 1952): 60; Matthews and Akrawi, *Education in Arab Countries of the Near East*, 177; Hind Kadry, *Women's Education in Iraq* (Washington, DC: Embassy of Iraq, 1958), 6.

113. Hasan, "Dawr I'dad al-Mu'allimat."

114. Hanna Batatu, *The Old Social Classes and the Revolutionary Movements of Iraq* (Princeton: Princeton University Press, 1978), 477.

115. Hasan, "Dawr I'dad al-Mu'allimat," 2.

116. Matthews and Akrawi, *Education in Arab Countries of the Near East*, 168.

117. Matthews and Akrawi, 166–67; Mahir al-Kasey, *Youth Education in Iraq and Egypt 1920–1980: A Contribution to Comparative Education within the Arab Region* (Leuven: Helicon, 1983), 50.

118. Kadry, *Women's Education in Iraq*, 12; Muhammad Husayn Al Yasin, "Letter to UNESCO: Report on Iraqi Education," 1953, Correspondence file 37 A 57 (567): Educational Mission – Iraq – General, UNESCO Archives.

119. Kadry, *Women's Education in Iraq*, 14–16.

120. In the 1957–58 school year, there were 391 women enrolled at Queen 'Aliya College; 352 at the higher teacher training college; 263 at the college of arts and sciences; and a total of 171 at other academic colleges. There were also a few hundred women studying in professional schools, including 99 at the medical school and 120 at the women's school of nursing and midwifery in the 1955–56 school year. See Kadry, 22–23.

121. For example, a history of public education in the country, produced by the Iraqi government, noted that the gradual expansion of vocational education since the early 1930s, including home economics, was "a result of various recommendations" of the Monroe Report, the World Bank, UNESCO, and US missions. Iraq, *Education in Iraq* (Washington, DC: Office of the Cultural Attaché, Embassy of Iraq, 1957), 49.

Chapter 4

This chapter is derived in part from Sara Pursley, "The Stage of Adolescence: Anticolonial Time, Youth Insurgency, and the Marriage Crisis in Hashimite Iraq," published in *History of the Present*, 3, no. 2 (Fall 2013): 160–97, by the University of Illinois Press.

1. Muhammad Husayn Al Yasin, "Hajat Madarisina al-Thanawiyya ila al-Tawjih," *al-Mu'allim al-Jadid* 12, no. 1 (September 1948): 22.

2. 'Abd al-Hadi al-Mukhtar, "Hal min al-Daruri Tadris al-Thawra al-Faransiyya fi Madarisna?," *al-Mu'allim al-Jadid* 10, no. 4–5 (September 1946): 23. On the removal of the study of revolutions from the school curriculum, see Gha'ib Tu'ma Farman, *al-Hukm al-Aswad fi al-'Iraq* (Cairo: Dar al-Fikr, 1957), 51.

3. Mahmud al-Jumard, "Tilmidhat wa-Talamidh al-Madaris al-Thanawiyya wa-Awqat al-Faragh," *al-Mu'allim al-Jadid* 18, no. 1 (December 1954): 69, 75.

4. Sati' al-Husri, *Ahadith fi al-Tarbiya wa-l-Ijtima'* (Beirut: Dar al-'Ilm li-l-Malayyin, 1962), 48–49.

5. Omnia El Shakry, "Youth as Peril and Promise: The Emergence of Adolescent Psychology in Postwar Egypt," *International Journal of Middle East Studies* 43 (2011): 592, 595.

6. El Shakry, 592.

7. El Shakry, 592, 595.

8. El Shakry, 595.

9. See, for example, 'Abd al-Rahman al-Bazzaz, "Tathqif al-Mar'a," *al-Mu'allim al-Jadid* 17, no. 2 (September 1953): 41.

10. See Farman, *al-Hukm al-Aswad*, 29–34; and Orit Bashkin, *The Other Iraq: Pluralism and Culture in Hashemite Iraq* (Stanford: Stanford University Press, 2009), 114–16, 241.

11. As Hanna Batatu writes, "the principal vehicles of hostility to the existing social order

were the teachers and students, and the center of gravity of the Communist movement lay not in the factories or other workers' establishments but in the colleges and schools." See Batatu, *The Old Social Classes and the Revolutionary Movements of Iraq* (Princeton: Princeton University Press, 1978), 645.

12. Batatu, 645–47.

13. Bashkin, *Other Iraq*, 242.

14. Lisa Rofel, *Other Modernities: Gendered Yearnings in China after Socialism* (Berkeley: University of California Press, 1999), 7.

15. While he does not make an argument specifically about generations, Michael Eppel's use of the term *effendiyya* is often explicitly in contrast to "traditional" and equivalent to "Westernized," "modernized," or even just "modern." For example, he writes that after the 1950s, "it no longer made sense to use the term *effendiyya*," because "[c]ompulsory education, across-the-board modernization, spreading patterns of modern discourse—all made the characteristics of the *effendiyya* nearly universal. Thus, the term lost its utility in characterizing social groups." See Eppel, "Note about the Term *Effendiyya* in the History of the Middle East," *International Journal of Middle East Studies* 41 (2009): 538. Peter Wien uses the term "Young Effendiyya" in a refreshingly specific way, to refer to a particular (interwar) generation, though the term loses some cohesion when he maintains it to describe members of the same generation when they are no longer young. See Wien, *Iraqi Arab Nationalism: Authoritarian, Totalitarian and Pro-Fascist Inclinations, 1932–1941* (London: Routledge, 2006).

16. See, for example, Rofel, *Other Modernities*, 7; and Michael Eppel, "Note about the Term *Effendiyya* in the History of the Middle East," 235.

17. Batatu, *Old Social Classes*, 403; Muhsin al-Musawi, *Reading Iraq: Culture and Power in Conflict* (London: I. B. Tauris, 2006), 67.

18. Jacques Donzelot, *The Policing of Families* (Baltimore: Johns Hopkins University Press, 1977), 78–79. For similar motivations driving the expansion of universal education in Britain, see Steve Humphries, *Hooligans or Rebels?: An Oral History of Working Class Childhood and Youth, 1889–1939* (Oxford: Blackwell, 1981).

19. Donzelot, *Policing of Families*, 81.

20. Donzelot, 69.

21. Bushra Perto, interview, January 14, 2008, London.

22. Perto, interview.

23. Mubejel Baban, interview, November 27, 2007, London.

24. As al-Musawi writes of Iraqi nationalist claims to a cultural disposition inclined since ancient times toward the pursuit of knowledge, "reference to a specific character and temper may not be consistently tenable . . . but narrative as such gains currency through repetition and circulation" (al-Musawi, *Reading Iraq*, 26). See also Bashkin, *Other Iraq*, 90–91.

25. Batatu, *Old Social Classes*, 647.

26. Perto, interview.

27. Baban, interview.

28. See Bashkin, *Other Iraq*, 116.

29. Perto, interview, November 23, 2007, London. After her expulsion, Perto's father,

a civil servant, packed her off to Geneva, where she continued her chemistry studies and hooked up with the international communist movement.

30. Farman, *al-Hukm al-Aswad*, 37, 50.

31. US Embassy Baghdad to Department of State, Foreign Despatch no. 980, June 29, 1953, RG84/787, NARA. See also Farman, *al-Hukm al-Aswad*, 78–79.

32. Amana al-Salman, "Ara' fi Islah wa-Tahsin al-Ta'lim al-Niswi," *al-Mu'allim al-Jadid* 17, no. 1–2 (September 1953): 94.

33. Safa' Khulusi, "Tawhid aw Ikhtilaf Manhaj al-Ta'lim bayn al-Banin wa-l-Banat," *al-Mu'allim al-Jadid* 17, no. 1–2 (September 1953): 61, 63.

34. al-Jumard, "Tilmidhat wa-Talamidh al-Madaris al-Thanawiyya," 69.

35. al-Jumard, 69, 75.

36. al-Jumard, 74. See also Al Yasin, "Hajat Madarisina al-Thanawiyya."

37. al-Jumard, "Tilmidhat wa-Talamidh al-Madaris al-Thanawiyya," 69–70.

38. al-Bazzaz, "Tathqif al-Mar'a," 41.

39. al-Bazzaz, 43.

40. al-Bazzaz, 43.

41. al-Bazzaz, 45–46.

42. al-Salman, "Ara' fi Islah wa-Tahsin al-Ta'lim al-Niswi," 94; Mahmud al-Jumard, "al-Ta'lim al-Mukhtalit," *al-Mu'allim al-Jadid* 17, no. 1–2 (September 1953): 83. See also Kamil Khalaf, "Ahamiyyat al-Tarbiya al-Jinsiyya," *al-Mu'allim al-Jadid* 19, no. 1 (February 1956): 58–59.

43. "Manahij al-Fanun al-Baytiyya," *al-Mu'allim al-Jadid* 15, no. 5 (August 1952): 60.

44. al-Jumard, "al-Ta'lim al-Mukhtalit," 86.

45. 'Abd al-Hamid Kazim, "Dawr al-Mu'allim fi al-Islah al-Ijtima'i," *al-Mu'allim al-Jadid* 20, no. 5–6 (December 1957): 2–3.

46. al-Bazzaz, "Tathqif al-Mar'a," 41.

47. al-Salman, "Ara' fi Islah wa-Tahsin al-Ta'lim al-Niswi," 94.

48. "al-Ta'lim al-Niswi fi al-'Iraq bayn al-Ams wa-l-Yawm," editorial, *al-Mu'allim al-Jadid* 17, no. 1–2 (September 1953): 3.

49. "al-Ta'lim al-Niswi fi al-'Iraq bayn al-Ams wa-l-Yawm," 4.

50. 'Abd al-Majid Hasan Wali, "Markaz al-Mar'a fi al-Kiyan al-'A'ili," *al-Mu'allim al-Jadid* 17, no. 1–2 (September 1953): 78–81. On a similar discourse in the 1930s, see Sami Shawkat, *Hadhihi Ahdafuna* (Baghdad: Wizarat al-Ma'arif, 1939), 80.

51. See Noga Efrati, *Women in Iraq: Past Meets Present* (New York: Columbia University Press, 2012), chap. 2.

52. Joel Francis Harrington, *Reordering Marriage and Society in Reformation Germany* (Cambridge: Cambridge University Press, 1995), 25; Barbara Alpern Engel, *Breaking the Ties That Bound: The Politics of Marital Strife in Late Imperial Russia* (Ithaca: Cornell University Press, 2011); Lisa Duggan and Nan D. Hunter, *Sex Wars: Sexual Dissent and Political Culture* (New York: Routledge, 2006), 223.

53. For the tip of the iceberg on 20th-century marriage crises, see Ellen Fleischmann, *The Nation and Its "New" Women: The Palestinian Women's Movement 1920–1948* (Berkeley: University of California Press, 2003), 78–85; Elizabeth Thompson, *Colonial Citizens: Repub-*

lican Rights, Paternal Privilege, and Gender in French Syria and Lebanon (New York: Columbia University Press, 2000), 220; Parvin Paidar, *Women and the Political Process in Twentieth-Century Iran* (Cambridge: Cambridge University Press, 1995), 285; Dagmar Herzog, *Sex after Fascism: Memory and Morality in Twentieth-Century Germany* (Princeton: Princeton University Press, 2005), 86; Malgorzata Fidelis, *Women, Communism, and Industrialization in Postwar Poland* (Cambridge: Cambridge University Press, 2010); Brett Lindsay Shadle, *"Girl Cases": Marriage and Colonialism in Gusiiland, Kenya, 1890–1970* (Portsmouth: Heinemann, 2006); and Christina Simmons, *Making Marriage Modern: Women's Sexuality from the Progressive Era to World War II* (New York: Oxford University Press, 2009).

54. Hanan Kholoussy, *For Better, for Worse: The Marriage Crisis That Made Modern Egypt* (Stanford: Stanford University Press, 2010), 1–2.

55. For celebrations of singlehood in the writings of a male leftist novelist in the 1930s and a female Shi'i intellectual in the 1960s (both were themselves never married), see, respectively, Orit Bashkin, "'When Mu'awiya Entered the Curriculum': Some Comments on the Iraqi Educational System in the Interwar Period," *Comparative Education Review* 50, no. 3 (2006): 346–66; and Sara Pursley, "Daughters of the Right Path: Family Law, Homosocial Publics, and the Ethics of Intimacy in the Works of Shi'i Revivalist Bint Al-Huda," *Journal of Middle East Women's Studies* 8, no. 2 (Spring 2012): 51–77.

56. Jabbir 'Umar, "Min Mushkilat Ta'limina al-Niswi," *al-Mu'allim al-Jadid* 17, no. 1–2 (September 1953): 50.

57. 'Umar, 55.

58. Ava Milam, "Report to the Government of Iraq on Education in Home Economics," FAO Report No. 48 (Rome: Food and Agriculture Organization, October 1952), 1, FAO Archives.

59. Jessie B. Brodie, "Report to the Government of Iraq on Home Economics in Queen Aliya College," FAO Report No. 320 (Rome: Food and Agriculture Organization, October 1954), 1, FAO Archives.

60. Milam, "Report to the Government of Iraq on Education in Home Economics," 3. This could also reflect a shift in the social classes that were now targeted with home economics education, since embroidery was often taught to middle- and upper-class girls. See Mona L. Russell, *Creating the New Egyptian Woman: Consumerism, Education, and National Identity, 1863–1922* (Basingstoke: Palgrave Macmillan, 2004), 105.

61. Brodie, "Report to the Government of Iraq on Home Economics in Queen Aliya College," 2.

62. Milam, "Report to the Government of Iraq on Education in Home Economics."

63. For an argument against such requirements, in an article published in *al-Mu'allim al-Jadid* in 1942, one year before the ministry implemented the first mandatory home economics courses in the girls' academic secondary schools, see Ihssan 'Abid, "Hal Yakhtalif Manhaj al-'Ulum li-l-Banat 'an li-l-Wilad?," *al-Mu'allim al-Jadid* 7, no. 6 (June 1942): 513–20.

64. Ava Milam Clark, *Adventures of a Home Economist* (Corvallis: Oregon State University Press, 1969), 333–34.

65. Home economics education for Iraqi girls certainly did not come to an end in 1958, but FAO involvement declined.

66. 'Ali al-Wardi, *Wu'az al-Salatin* (London: Alwarrak, 2013), 10. On the controversy in Iraq over this book, see also Joseph Massad, *Desiring Arabs* (Chicago: University of Chicago Press, 2007), 141–44.

67. Afsaneh Najmabadi, *Women with Mustaches and Men without Beards: Gender and Sexual Anxieties of Iranian Modernity* (Berkeley: University of California Press, 2005), 3.

68. Afsaneh Najmabadi, "Genus of Sex or the Sexing of Jins," *International Journal of Middle East Studies*, Special issue: Queer Affects, 45 (2013): 212–13. However, in a 1956 work, al-Wardi distinguished between those who acquire their sexual deviance from their environment and the "natural deviant," who exists in all societies and who is a "person with a right to live and to seek the pleasures he desires, to the extent that no harm is done to others." See 'Ali al-Wardi, *Mahzalat al-'Aql al-Bashari* (London: Dar al-Warraq li-l-Nashr, 2016), 12.

69. al-Wardi, *Wu'az al-Salatin*, 166.

70. al-Wardi, 10.

71. al-Wardi, 25, 111, 113.

72. al-Wardi, 45.

73. For analyses of secular reformist discourses on Islam that make these arguments, see, respectively, Wilson Chacko Jacob, *Working Out Egypt: Effendi Masculinity and Subject Formation in Colonial Modernity, 1870–1940* (Durham: Duke University Press, 2011), 87; Gregory Starrett, "The Hexis of Interpretation: Islam and the Body in the Egyptian Popular School," *American Ethnologist* 22 (1995): 953–69; and Talal Asad, *Formations of the Secular: Christianity, Islam, Modernity* (Stanford: Stanford University Press, 2003).

74. Despite his criticism of applications of pragmatism in Iraq, al-Husri drew explicitly on some pragmatist theories, and agreed that the fundamental duty of the modern school was to "prepare children for real life" (al-Husri, *Ahadith fi al-Tarbiya wa-l-Ijtima'*, 60).

75. al-Wardi, *Wu'az al-Salatin*, 12.

76. al-Wardi, 8-9.

77. al-Wardi, 62.

78. al-Wardi, 76.

79. al-Wardi, 11.

80. al-Wardi, 132.

81. Lee Edelman, *No Future: Queer Theory and the Death Drive* (Durham: Duke University Press, 2004), 139, 9.

82. Edelman, 2.

83. al-Wardi, *Wu'az al-Salatin*, 353–54.

84. Sara Pursley, "The Stage of Adolescence: Anticolonial Time, Youth Insurgency, and the Marriage Crisis in Hashimite Iraq," *History of the Present* 3, no. 2 (Fall 2013): 160–97.

85. al-Wardi, *Wu'az al-Salatin*, 341.

Chapter 5

1. On uses of US agrarian reform theory in the 1950s Arab world, including at Dujayla, see Nathan Citino, *Envisioning the Arab Future: Modernization in U.S.-Arab Relations, 1945–1967* (Cambridge: Cambridge University Press, 2017), chap. 4.

2. Andrew Zimmerman, "A German Alabama in Africa: The Tuskegee Expedition to German Togo and the Transnational Origins of West African Cotton Growers," *American Historical Review* 110, no. 5 (2005): 1368. On family-farming projects in German colonial Africa with some similarities to those I explore in this chapter, see also Andrew Zimmerman, *Alabama in Africa: Booker T. Washington, the German Empire, and the Globalization of the New South* (Princeton: Princeton University Press, 2010).

3. Quoted in Norman Burns, "Development Projects in Iraq," pt. 1, "The Dujaylah Land Settlement," *Middle East Journal* 5, no. 3 (1951): 362.

4. "Raqm 23 li-Sanat 1945: Qanun I'mar wa-Istithmar Aradi al-Dujayla," *al-Waqa'i' al-'Iraqiyya* (December 28, 1945): 3–4.

5. Kamil Mahdi, *State and Agriculture in Iraq: Modern Development, Stagnation and the Impact of Oil* (Reading: Ithaca Press, 2000), 167.

6. Mahdi, 167.

7. Burns, "Dujaylah Land Settlement," 363. According to Samira Haj, only 232,960 of the 2 million dunums of land reclaimed between 1952 and 1954 were distributed to small farmers, while the rest went to large landholders. See Samira Haj, *The Making of Iraq, 1900–1963: Capital, Power, and Ideology* (Albany: State University of New York Press, 1997), 34.

8. Charles Tripp, *A History of Iraq*, 2nd ed. (Cambridge: Cambridge University Press, 2000), 78; Orit Bashkin, *The Other Iraq: Pluralism and Culture in Hashemite Iraq* (Stanford: Stanford University Press, 2009), chap. 6.

9. Ja'far Khayyat, *al-Qarya al-'Iraqiyya: Dirasa fi Ahwaliha wa-Islahiha* (Beirut: Dar al-Kashshaf, 1950), 3.

10. Khayyat, 54.

11. Matta 'Aqrawi [Akrawi], "al-Ta'lim al-'Am wa-Atharuhu fi al-Nahda al-Qawmiyya," *al-Mu'allim al-Jadid* 4, no. 2 (June 1938): 105.

12. Haj, *Making of Iraq*, 11, 38.

13. Hassan Mohammad Ali, *Land Reclamation and Settlement in Iraq* (Baghdad: Baghdad Printing Press, 1955), l, m.

14. Quoted in Eric Davis, *Memories of State: Politics, History, and Collective Identity in Modern Iraq* (Berkeley: University of California Press, 2005), 213.

15. Burns, "Dujaylah Land Settlement," 363.

16. See Priya Satia, "Developing Iraq: Britain, India and the Redemption of Empire and Technology in the First World War," *Past and Present*, no. 197 (2007): 211–55; and Daniel Smail, "In the Grip of Sacred History," *American Historical Review* 110, no. 5 (2005): 1337–61.

17. Satia, "Developing Iraq," 232.

18. Quoted in Daniel Klingensmith, *"One Valley and a Thousand": Dams, Nationalism, and Development* (New Delhi: Oxford University Press, 2007), 67.

19. Odd Arne Westad, *The Global Cold War: Third World Interventions and the Making of Our Times* (Cambridge: Cambridge University Press, 2005), 12.

20. See Doreen Warriner, *Land Reform and Development in the Middle East: A Study of Egypt, Syria and Iraq* (London: Royal Institute of International Affairs, 1957), 2–5.

21. Nathan J. Citino, "The Ottoman Legacy in Cold War Modernization," *International Journal of Middle East Studies* 40 (2008): 581.

22. "US Department of State, Point 4 to Assist Iraq in its Land Development Program," Press Release No. 187, April 10, 1953, Washington, DC. Cited in Warren Edward Adams, "The Land Development Program in Iraq with Special Reference to the Dujaila Settlement, 1945 to 1954." (PhD diss., University of California, Berkeley, 1955), 259.

23. Citino, "Ottoman Legacy," 583.

24. Burns, "Dujaylah Land Settlement," 362–63.

25. Haj, *Making of Iraq*, 56.

26. Haj, 73.

27. Doris Adams, "Current Population Trends in Iraq," *Middle East Journal* 10, no. 2 (1956): 162–63.

28. Darwish Al Haidari, "The Development of Iraq" (paper presented to the Food and Agriculture Organization of the United Nations, Country Project No. 1, Iraq, October 1955), 1, FAO Archives.

29. Afif I. Tannous, "Land Reform: Key to the Development and Stability of the Arab World," *Middle East Journal* 5 (Winter 1951): 17.

30. FAO Mediterranean Development Project, *Iraq: Country Report* (Rome: Food and Agriculture Organization of the United Nations, 1959), 10.

31. Tannous, "Land Reform," 8.

32. Burns, "Dujaylah Land Settlement," 363.

33. Burns, 363; Adams, "Land Development Program in Iraq," 302; "Raqm 23 li-Sanat 1945: Qanun I'mar wa-Istithmar Aradi al-Dujayla," 4. See also Sara Pursley, "Gender as a Category of Analysis in Development and Environmental History," presentation to the "Gendering the Middle East" roundtable, *International Journal of Middle East Studies* 48, no. 3 (2016): 555–60.

34. "Raqm 23 li-Sanat 1945: Qanun I'mar wa-Istithmar Aradi al-Dujayla," 4.

35. "Raqm 23 li-Sanat 1945: Qanun I'mar wa-Istithmar Aradi al-Dujayla," 3.

36. Adams, "Land Development Program in Iraq," 311.

37. Warriner, *Land Reform and Development in the Middle East*, 166. Adams, however, suggests that the abandonment of cotton growing at Dujayla was due to an infestation in the cotton crops (Adams, "Land Development Program in Iraq," 111). It may have also related to the fact that cotton growing was often resisted by peasant cultivators, especially indebted ones, because it was a high-risk, labor-intensive cash crop that could not feed them (Haj, *Making of Iraq*, 46).

38. Adams, "Land Development Program in Iraq," 107.

39. Adams, 188. See also Muhammad Husayn Al Yasin, "al-Tarbiya al-Asasiyya fi Majalay al-Fikr wa-l-Tatbiq," *al-Mu'allim al-Jadid* 18, no. 3 (May 1955): 5.

40. Burns, "Dujaylah Land Settlement," 364. See also Adams, "Land Development Program in Iraq," 96.

41. H. J. Rousseau, "Fundamental Education in Primary Teachers Colleges in Iraq: Suggested Programme," n.d., 9, File: Rousseau H.J., Box: Iraq CPx/REP.3/258, UNESCO Archives; Brad Fisk, "Iraq's Pilot Project for Land Settlement," *Economic Geography* 28, no. 4 (1952): 348.

42. Sattareh Farman, "Letter No. 7 to Dr. Taghi Nasr, Technical Assistance Administration, United Nations," December 15, 1954, 2, File: Dujailah/Trowbridge A.B., Box: Iraq CPx/REP.3/259, UNESCO Archives.

43. Brad Fisk, "Dujaylah Land Settlement," *Middle East Journal* 5, no. 4 (1951): 527.

44. Fisk, 527.

45. All foreign and Iraqi technical specialists at Dujayla had piped water in their own residences.

46. See, for example, A. B. Trowbridge, "Bi-Monthly Report for March and April, 1953," May 1, 1953, 5, File: Dujailah/Trowbridge A.B., Box: Iraq CPx/REP.3/259, UNESCO Archives.

47. Some scholars argue that in most historical contexts, and contrary to popular belief, family farms have not been conducive to the development of capitalist agriculture. For an introduction to the debates, see T. H. Aston and C.H.E. Philpin, eds., *The Brenner Debate: Agrarian Class Structure and Economic Development in Pre-Industrial Europe* (Cambridge: Cambridge University Press, 1987). Partha Chatterjee argues that the preferred model for promoting capitalist agriculture—large consolidated landholdings employing wage labor—was not available to 20th-century postcolonial regimes, which could not have maintained their nationalist legitimacy while dispossessing the majority of the national population of land. See Partha Chatterjee, *The Nation and Its Fragments: Colonial and Postcolonial Histories* (Princeton: Princeton University Press, 1993), 212–13.

48. Michael P. Cowen and Robert W. Shenton, *Doctrines of Development* (London: Routledge, 1996), 341.

49. Al Yasin, "al-Tarbiya al-Asasiyya," 5.

50. A. B. Trowbridge, "An Outline of the UNESCO Fundamental Education Program for Dujaila, 1952–52" (unpublished paper, Baghdad, 1953), p. 1. Cited in Adams, "Land Development Program in Iraq," 146.

51. "Progress Report on UNESCO's Participation in the UN Expanded Programme of Technical Assistance," File 36A 653 (567) 224: GCP Beneficiaries – Iraq – Project 224 – Dujaila FE Centre, UNESCO Archives.

52. Ahmad Haqqi al-Hilli, "Tajriba fi al-Tarbiya al-Asasiyya," *al-Mu'allim al-Jadid* 18, no. 3 (May 1955): 9.

53. A. Fielding-Clarke, "Fundamental Education with Special Reference to Dujaila, Iraq," 1952, 11, File: Dujailah project/Fielding-Clarke, A., Box: Iraq CPx/REP.3/259, UNESCO Archives.

54. "al-Tarbiya al-Asasiyya: Ghayatuha wa-Ahdafuha," editorial, *al-Mu'allim al-Jadid* 18, no. 3 (May 1955): 3.

55. James Ferguson, *The Anti-Politics Machine: "Development," Depoliticization, and Bureaucratic Power in Lesotho* (Minneapolis: University of Minnesota Press, 1994), 87.

56. Arturo Escobar, *Encountering Development: The Making and Unmaking of the Third World* (Princeton: Princeton University Press, 1995), 36.

57. These statistics were compiled by the Iraq Technical Assistance Resource Agencies (ITARA) group, which helped coordinate the work of all UN, US, and UK technical assistance agencies in the country through regular meetings of their representatives in Baghdad. See attachment to H. J. Rousseau, "Fundamental Education Mission, Dujaila, Iraq, 4th Two-Monthly Report: July–August 1952," August 31, 1952, File: Rousseau H. J., Box: Iraq CPx/REP.3/258, UNESCO Archives.

58. A US Point Four proposal for Iraq explained: "The initial program of rural improve-

ment should be directed to reducing the present ignorance of most rural people in the fundamental principles and concepts of welfare. The major activities of the program should be concerned with the four major needs of improved farming practices, of home and village sanitation, of house building, of home and child care." Three of the four main TCA activities on Iraqi settlements were thus centered on the reform of rural homes, and two of those (sanitation and home and child care) focused primarily on women. See Gordan Macgregor and Yusuf Khaddury, "Village Development Program for Iraq" (Technical Cooperation Administration, American Embassy, Baghdad, 1952), 6, enclosed in file: Rousseau H.J./ Literacy, box: Iraq CPx/REP.3/258, UNESCO Archives.

59. Citino, *Envisioning the Arab Future*, 77.

60. Daniel Lerner, *The Passing of Traditional Society: Modernizing the Middle East*, 2nd ed. (New York: Free Press, 1964), 411–12. Emphasis in original.

61. Citino, "Ottoman Legacy," 582.

62. Quoted in Adams, "Land Development Program in Iraq," 272.

63. Quoted in Adams, 147.

64. Al Yasin, "al-Tarbiya al-Asasiyya," 4.

65. "al-Tarbiya al-Asasiyya: Ghayatuha wa-Ahdafuha," 1–2.

66. H. J. Rousseau, "Report on School Feeding in Kilo 29, Dujaila, 1953–54," June 22, 1954, 3, File: Rousseau H.J., Box: Iraq CPx/REP.3/258, UNESCO Archives.

67. "UNESCO and Iraq: A Picture Story of UN Assistance Work," *AMGRAD* (1954):8, enclosed in File: Dujailah/Trowbridge A.B., Box: Iraq CPx/REP.3/259, UNESCO Archives.

68. A. B. Trowbridge, "Objectives of the UNESCO Fundamental Education Project at Dujaila, Iraq 1953," February 8, 1953, 4, File: Dujailah/Trowbridge A.B., Box: Iraq CPx/ REP.3/259, UNESCO Archives.

69. Rousseau, "Report on School Feeding in Kilo 29, Dujaila," 1.

70. A. B. Trowbridge, "Report for Sept, Oct, and November, 1952," December 1, 1952, 5–6, File: Dujailah/Trowbridge A.B., Box: Iraq CPx/REP.3/259, UNESCO Archives.

71. A. Hurbli, "Comments on Report on Dujaila by A. B. Trowbridge," April 5, 1954, EDSP.54.326, File: Dujailah/Trowbridge A.B., Box: Iraq CPx/REP.3/259, UNESCO Archives.

72. Jane Parpart, "Lessons from the Field: Rethinking Empowerment, Gender and Development from a Post-(Post-?)Development Perspective," in *Feminist Post-Development Thought: Rethinking Modernity, Post-Colonialism and Representation*, ed. Kriemild Saunders (London: Zed Books, 2003), 43; Jane Parpart and Marchand Marianne, "Exploding the Canon: An Introduction/Conclusion," in *Feminism, Postmodernism, Development*, ed. Marianne Marchand and Jane Parpart (London: Routledge, 1995), 13.

73. Escobar, *Encountering Development*, 172–73. A very similar argument is made in Suzanne Bergeron, *Fragments of Development: Nation, Gender, and the Space of Modernity* (Ann Arbor: University of Michigan Press, 2006), 19–22.

74. See Denise Riley, *"Am I That Name?" Feminism and the Category of "Women" in History* (Minneapolis: University of Minnesota Press, 1988). See also Joan Wallach Scott's discussion of Riley's argument, in *The Fantasy of Feminist History* (Durham: Duke University Press, 2011), 10–11.

75. A. B. Trowbridge, "Annual Report: Feb. 28, 1952 to Feb. 28, 1953," February 28, 1953, 1, File: Dujailah/Trowbridge A.B., Box: Iraq CPx/REP.3/259, UNESCO Archives.

76. Margaret Hockin, "Report Covering Period Nov. 9–Dec. 9, 1951, Fundamental Education Demonstration Project Dujaila, Iraq," n.d., 4, File: Dujailah project/Hockin M.L./Women's Education, Box: Iraq CPx/REP.3/259, UNESCO Archives. Parenthesis in original.

77. Enriqueta Lopez, "Ma Ya'mal al-Nisa' fi al-Dujayla," *al-Mu'allim al-Jadid* 18, no. 3 (May 1955): 62; A. B. Trowbridge, "Bi-Monthly Report, Period of August 15 to October 15, 1954," October 15, 1954, 3, File: Dujailah/Trowbridge A.B., Box: Iraq CPx/REP.3/259, UNESCO Archives.

78. Fielding-Clarke, "Fundamental Education with Special Reference to Dujaila," 10.

79. Trowbridge, "Report for Sept, Oct, and November, 1952"; A. B. Trowbridge, "Bi-Monthly Report May and June 1953," June 30, 1953, File: Dujailah/Trowbridge A.B., Box: Iraq CPx/REP.3/259, UNESCO Archives.

80. Al Yasin, "al-Tarbiya al-Asasiyya," 5.

81. Lopez, "Ma Ya'mal al-Nisa' fi al-Dujayla," 63.

82. A. K. Kinany, "Evaluation of the Annual Report of the Fundamental Education Mission in Dujaila, Iraq," April 30, 1954, 2, File: Trowbridge A.B., Box: Iraq CPx/REP.3/258, UNESCO Archives.

83. Trowbridge, "Annual Report: Feb. 28, 1952 to Feb. 28, 1953," 6; Rousseau, "Fundamental Education in Primary Teachers Colleges in Iraq: Suggested Programme," 3.

84. A. B. Trowbridge, "Bi-Monthly Report for Period of Nov. 1 to Dec. 31 1953," January 8, 1954, File: Dujailah/Trowbridge A.B., Box: Iraq CPx/REP.3/259, UNESCO Archives.

85. Trowbridge, "Annual Report: Feb. 28, 1952 to Feb. 28, 1953," 5.

86. Lopez, "Ma Ya'mal al-Nisa' fi al-Dujayla," 62.

87. "Iraq Builds Its Future," *Iraq Times*, July 17, 1953, 8.

88. Adams, "Land Development Program in Iraq," 150.

89. Hockin, "Report Covering Period Nov. 9–Dec. 9, 1951," app., p. 2.

90. Malcolm N. Quint, "The Idea of Progress in an Iraqi Village," *Middle East Journal* 12, no. 4 (1958): 383.

91. Trowbridge, "Report for Sept, Oct, and November, 1952," 6.

92. Trowbridge, 2–3, 6; Trowbridge, "Annual Report: Feb. 28, 1952 to Feb. 28, 1953," 4.

93. Trowbridge, "Report for Sept, Oct, and November, 1952," 6.

94. A. B. Trowbridge, "Bi-Monthly Report for Period April 15 to June 15, 1954," n.d., 8, File: Dujailah/Trowbridge A.B., Box: Iraq CPx/REP.3/259, UNESCO Archives. See also Fielding-Clarke, "Fundamental Education with Special Reference to Dujaila," 19.

95. Trowbridge, "Report for Sept, Oct, and November, 1952," 6.

96. Adams, "Land Development Program in Iraq," 95.

97. Adams, 161.

98. A. B. Trowbridge, "The Aim of the Unesco Fundamental Education Mission in Iraq," October 20, 1954, 1, File: Dujailah/Trowbridge A.B., Box: Iraq CPx/REP.3/259, UNESCO Archives.

99. Trowbridge, 1.

100. UNESCO correspondent in Dujailah, "UNESCO Team at Work," *Times Educational Supplement*, May 1, 1953. Emphasis added.

101. Samera Esmeir, *Juridical Humanity: A Colonial History* (Stanford: Stanford University Press, 2012), 3–4.

102. See Ian Hacking, "The Looping Effects of Human Kinds," in *Casual Cognition*, ed. Dan Sperber et al., chap. 12. Oxford Scholarship Online, 1996.

103. Joan Smith and Immanuel Wallerstein, "Households as an Institution of the World-Economy," in *Creating and Transforming Households: The Constraints of the World-Economy*, coordinated by Joan Smith and Immanuel Wallerstein (Cambridge: Cambridge University Press, 1992), 4.

104. Mahdi, *State and Agriculture in Iraq*, 168.

105. Fisk, "Dujaylah Land Settlement," 527.

106. Mahdi, *State and Agriculture in Iraq*, 168. See also Trowbridge, "Bi-Monthly Report, Period of August 15 to October 15, 1954," 5.

107. Henry Stippler and Mohammad Darwish, *Land Tenure and Land Utilization in Shakla 8, Dujaila Project, 1965–66* (Baghdad: Ministry of Agrarian Reform, 1966), 5–6.

108. Mahdi, *State and Agriculture in Iraq*, 168.

109. Trowbridge, "Annual Report: Feb. 28, 1952 to Feb. 28, 1953," 4.

110. Cowen and Shenton, *Doctrines of Development*, 341, xii.

111. Peter Miller and Nikolas Rose, *Governing the Present: Administering Economic, Social and Personal Life* (Cambridge: Polity, 2008), 17, 29.

Chapter 6

1. Mubejel Baban, interview, November 27, 2007, London.

2. "Watha'iq Tarikhiyya," *Ittihad al-Sha'b*, July 18, 1959, 6. See also Hanna Batatu, *The Old Social Classes and the Revolutionary Movements of Iraq* (Princeton: Princeton University Press, 1978), 803–04.

3. Baban, interview.

4. Batatu, *Old Social Classes*, 804–05.

5. Uriel Dann, *Iraq under Qassem: A Political History, 1958–1963* (Jerusalem: Israel Universities Press, 1969), 32. On the detainment, torture, and killing of political prisoners, see 'Aziz al-Haj, *Dhakirat al-Nakhil: Sahafat min Ta'rikh al-Haraka al-Shuyu'iyya fi al-'Iraq* (Beirut: al-Mu'assasa al-'Arabiyya li-l-Dirasat wa-l-Nashr, 1993); Batatu, *Old Social Classes*, 690–93; and Orit Bashkin, *The Other Iraq: Pluralism and Culture in Hashemite Iraq* (Stanford: Stanford University Press, 2009), 107–11.

6. Batatu, *Old Social Classes*, 805.

7. Charles Tripp, *A History of Iraq*, 2nd ed. (Cambridge: Cambridge University Press, 2000), 149.

8. See Wm. Roger Louis and Roger Owen, eds., *A Revolutionary Year: The Middle East in 1958* (London: I. B. Tauris, 2002). On how the events of 1958 in the Arab Mashriq led to "state-formation surges," fueled by economic-development plans, see Cyrus Schayegh, "1958 Reconsidered: State Formation and the Cold War in the Early Postcolonial Arab Middle East," *International Journal of Middle East Studies* 45 (2013): 421–43.

9. "Women's Procession," *Iraq Times*, January 4, 1959, 3.

10. "Women's Procession," 3.

11. David Frizlan to Secretary of State, January 5, 1959, RG 84/787, NARA.

12. Sayid J. S. Hannoush, Iraqi Ministry of Development, letter to the editor of the *Illustrated London News*, republished in the *Iraq Times*, January 25, 1959.

13. "Iraqi Women on the March," *Iraqi Review* 1, no. 9 (July 30, 1959): 19.

14. Government of Iraq, *Thawrat 14 Tammuz fi 'Amiha al-Thani* (Baghdad: al-Lajna al-'Ulya li-Ihtifalat 14 Tammuz, 1960), 81.

15. On discourses of *jumud* in early 20th-century Egypt, see Omnia El Shakry, *Great Social Laboratory: Subjects of Knowledge in Colonial and Postcolonial Egypt* (Stanford: Stanford University Press, 2007), for example, p. 8.

16. Jacques Donzelot, *The Policing of Families* (Baltimore: Johns Hopkins University Press, 1977), 36.

17. For these terms, see Donzelot, *Policing of Families*, 69–71.

18. Caractacus, *Revolution in Iraq: An Essay in Comparative Public Opinion* (London: Gollancz, 1959), 8.

19. Reinhart Koselleck, *Futures Past: On the Semantics of Historical Time*, trans. Keith Tribe (New York: Columbia University Press, 2004).

20. See 'Amir 'Abd Allah, "al-Tariq al-Tarikhi li-Wahdat al-Umma al-'Arabiyya," *Ittihad al-Sha'b*, February 16, 18, 22, and 25, 1959. For discussions of these arguments, see Batatu, *Old Social Classes*, 830; Johan Franzén, *Red Star over Iraq: Iraqi Communism before Saddam* (Columbia University Press, 2011), 97; and Samira Haj, *The Making of Iraq, 1900–1963: Capital, Power, and Ideology* (Albany: State University of New York Press, 1997), 116.

21. For a discussion of the ICP's inclusive Iraqist orientation, see Eric Davis, *Memories of State: Politics, History, and Collective Identity in Modern Iraq* (Berkeley: University of California Press, 2005).

22. See Batatu, *Old Social Classes*, 843ff.

23. "Nass al-Dustur al-Mu'aqqat li-l-Jumhuriyya al-'Iraqiyya," *Ittihad al-Sha'b*, July 18, 1959, 4.

24. Dann, *Iraq under Qassem*, 156.

25. "al-'Iraq wa-Siyasat al-Tadamun al-'Arabi," *Ittihad al-Sha'b*, July 18, 1959, 2.

26. Haj, *Making of Iraq*, 116. For the debates within the ICP over the party's relation to Qasim, and its several shifts on that front, see also Tareq Ismael, *The Rise and Fall of the Communist Party of Iraq* (New York: Cambridge University Press, 2008), chap. 2.

27. Zaki Khayri and Su'ad Khayri, *Dirasat fi Tarikh al-Hizb al-Shuyu'i al-'Iraqi* (London: al-Jadid, 1984), 289.

28. Muhammad Hadid, *Mudhakkirati: al-Sira' min Ajli al-Dimuqratiyya fi al-'Iraq* (Beirut: Dar al-Saqi, 2006), 316.

29. Franzén, *Red Star over Iraq*, 92–96.

30. Yeheskel Kojaman, *Thawrat 14 Tammuz 1958 fi al-'Iraq wa-Siyasat al-Hizb al-Shuyu'i* (London: Biddles, 1985), 90, 102–103.

31. See, for example, Fawzi Karim, *Tahafut al-Sittiniyyin* (Damascus: al-Mada, 2006). From a different perspective, see also Fadil al-'Azzawi, *al-Ruh al-Hayya: Jil al-Sittinat fi al-'Iraq* (Damascus: Dar al-Mada, 1997), 47. I thank one of the anonymous peer reviewers for pointing me to these arguments.

32. "'Am min al-Thawra," *al-Muthaqqaf* 2, no. 10 (July 1959): 3–4.

33. Tripp, *A History of Iraq*, 154.

34. "Iraqi Women on the March."

35. "Khitab al-Duktura Naziha al-Dulaymi," *Ittihad al-Sha'b*, March 10, 1960, 8. These impressive numbers are difficult to substantiate conclusively, since most of al-Rabita's archives were lost in the aftermath of the 1963 Ba'th coup, when its leaders fled into exile along with many other ICP members who survived the coup.

36. "Iraqi Women on the March." See also Dann, *Iraq under Qassem*, 117.

37. Second Secretary of Embassy Lee Dinsmore to Secretary of State, January 6, 1959, RG84/787, NARA.

38. Second Secretary of Embassy Lee Dinsmore to Secretary of State, December 29, 1958, RG84/787, NARA.

39. Jernegan to Secretary of State, July 7, 1959, RG84/787, NARA.

40. U.S. Embassy Baghdad to Secretary of State, July 10, 1959, RG84/787, NARA.

41. "Muhadarat al-Duktura Ruz Khaduri hawl Mashakil al-Mar'a al-'Iraqiyya," *Ittihad al-Sha'b*, July 24, 1960, 4.

42. "Dawr Jumhuriyyatina fi Siyanat al-Silm al-'Alami," *Ittihad al-Sha'b*, July 18, 1959, 2.

43. "Siyadat al-Za'im 'Abd al-Karim Qasim Yalqi Khitaban," *Ittihad al-Sha'b*, July 18, 1959, 14.

44. Articles on this theme can be found in almost any issue of the Iraqi newspapers *al-Ahali* and *al-Hurriyya* in 1959 and 1960; see, for example, *al-Ahali*, March 3, 1960; and *al-Hurriyya*, April 15, 1960.

45. Haj, *Making of Iraq*, 120–26.

46. Haj, 127; Dann, *Iraq under Qassem*, 238–46, 265–90; Ismael, *Rise and Fall of the Communist Party of Iraq*, 99–102.

47. See Hadid, *Mudhakkirati*, 445–50.

48. See Kojaman, *Thawrat 14 Tammuz 1958 fi al-'Iraq wa-Siyasat al-Hizb al-Shuyu'i*, 147–48.

49. "Editorial," *Iraqi Review* 1, no. 21 (December 30, 1959): 11.

50. Batatu, *Old Social Classes*, 935.

51. Ismael, *Rise and Fall of the Communist Party of Iraq*, 102; "Ila Ikhwanina 'Ummal al-Asmant, Ila Ikhwanina 'Ummal fi Kul Makan," *al-Hurriyya*, April 15, 1960.

52. Batatu, *Old Social Classes*, 957.

53. Batatu, 946–48.

54. "Editorial," *Iraqi Review*.

55. Husayn Jamil, "Masdar Quwwat al-Hizb al-Watani al-Dimuqrati," *al-Ahali*, April 29, 1960, 1.

56. "Sina'atuna al-Wataniyya wa-Qudratuha 'ala Sadd Hajat al-Bilad al-Istihlakiyya bi-Ta'awun bayn Ashab al-Sina'a wa-l-'Ummal," *al-Ahali*, February 22, 1960, 1.

57. "Ila Ikhwanina 'Ummal al-Asmant."

58. Nur al-Din al-Wa'iz, "Ba'th al-Quwwa wa-Tahyi'at Asbabiha," *al-Hurriyya*, April 27, 1960, 2, 8.

59. Nur al-Din al-Wa'iz, "al-Ta'kid. … 'Ala al-Islah al-Dhati," *al-Hurriyya*, April 21, 1960, 2.

60. See, for example, letters published in *al-Najaf* in response to questions posed by the journal's editors to the Najafi public regarding the "most significant gains of the revolution"

in its first year, including letters written by the Shiʻi *ʻalim* Muhammad Taqi al-Hakim and by the qadi of the shariʻa court in Najaf, Hadi al-ʻAzimi. See *al-Najaf* 3, no. 5 (September 1, 1959): 13–15. As I discuss in Chapter 7, the orientation of this journal toward Qasim's regime would change dramatically after the promulgation of the 1959 personal status law.

61. Najiya Hamdi, "al-Jil al-Saʻid," *al-Muʻallim al-Jadid* 26, no. 1–2 (January 1963): 161.

62. Muhyi al-Din ʻAbd al-Hamid, "Mustaqbal al-Thaqafa fi al-ʻIraq," *al-Muʻallim al-Jadid* 23, no. 1–2 (February 1960): 6.

63. "Children's Day Celebrated," *Iraqi Review* 1, no. 2 (June 4, 1959). For similar prizes awarded in ʻAbd al-Nasir's Egypt in the 1950s, see Beth Baron, "The Origins of Family Planning: Aziza Hussein, American Experts, and the Egyptian State," *Journal of Middle East Women's Studies* 4, no. 3 (2008): 33.

64. "Mashruʻ Riʻayat al-Tufula," *Ittihad al-Shaʻb*, June 5, 1959, 6. I was not able to find this law in the official government gazette, though the government had announced it as a law and allowed the text to be published in the daily newspapers. It may have been a regulation or program of the Ministry of Health rather than an official law.

65. "Mashruʻ Riʻayat al-Tufula," 6.

66. "Raqm 42 li-Sanat 1958: Qanun al-Muʼassasat al-Ijtimaʻiyya," *al-Waqaʼiʻ al-ʻIraqiyya*, October 18, 1958, 1–2. See also Government of Iraq, *Thawrat 14 Tammuz fi ʻAmiha al-Awwal* (Baghdad: al-Lajna al-ʻUlya li-Ihtifalat 14 Tammuz, 1959), 330–31.

67. "Iʻlan Qanun al-Islah al-Ziraʻi (8/30/1958)," in *Khutab al-Zaʻim ʻAbd al-Karim Qasim*, ed. Majid Shubbar (London: Alwarrak, 2007).

68. See "al-Ummahat Masʼulat 30 bi-l-Miʼa ʻan al-Taʼakhkhur al-Dirasi li-Atfalihunna," *al-ʻAhd al-Jadid*, April 3, 1962, 4; "Thawrat al-ʻIraq al-Rifiyya," *al-Bayan*, April 15, 1962, 2.

69. ʻAbd al-Jabar ʻAwad, "al-Islah al-Ziraʻi," *al-Muthaqqaf* 2, no. 10 (July 1959): 28.

70. Hadid, *Mudhakkirati*, 339.

71. "Hamlat Usbuʻ al-Sihha wa-l-Nazafa fi Yawmiha al-Thalith," *Ittihad al-Shaʻb*, October 27, 1959, 1.

72. See Hadid, *Mudhakkirati*, 341.

73. "Second Congress of Iraqi Women," *Iraqi Review* 1, no. 27 (March 23, 1960): 6. See also Suʻad Khayri, *al-Marʼa al-ʻIraqiyya: Kifah wa-ʻAtaʼ* (Stockholm: A.R.M. All-Tryck, 1998), 17–19; Government of Iraq, *Thawrat 14 Tammuz fi ʻAmiha al-Thani*, 275.

74. "Directive to Women Teachers," *Iraq Times*, February 25, 1959, 1.

75. On temporal distancing, see Johannes Fabian, *Time and the Other: How Anthropology Makes Its Object*, rev. ed. (New York: Columbia University Press, 2002).

76. "Women Censured," *Iraq Times*, March 13, 1959, 7.

77. "Editorial Report of Recorded Broadcast of Proceedings of the 114th Session of the Supreme Military Court in Baghdad on 30 May [1959]," in *Records of Iraq 1914–1966*, 13:86.

78. "Editorial Report of Recorded Broadcast of Proceedings of the 114th Session of the Supreme Military Court in Baghdad on 30 May [1959]."

79. Husayn Fahmi al-Khazraji, "Mushkilat al-Marʼa al-ʻIraqiyya," *al-Najaf* 3, no. 6 (September 15, 1959): 13–14.

80. al-Khazraji, "Mushkilat al-Marʼa," 14.

81. "Rabitat al-Marʼa al-ʻIraqiyya Tusahim bi-Sharaf fi Mashruʻ Mukafahat al-Ummiyya al-Nabil," *Ittihad al-Shaʻb*, June 15, 1960, 5.

82. "Rabitat al-Mar'a al-'Iraqiyya Tusahim bi-Sharaf fi Mashru' Mukafahat al-Ummiyya al-Nabil," 5.

83. "Muhadarat al-Duktura Ruz Khaduri hawl Mashakil al-Mar'a al-'Iraqiyya," 4. See also "Iraqi Women on the March," 18.

84. "Second Congress of Iraqi Women," 6.

85. "*Ittihad al-Sha'b* wa-'Jarimat' Mukafahat al-Ummiyya," *Ittihad al-Sha'b*, June 9, 1960, 4. See also "al-Muthaqqaf al-Haddam," *Ittihad al-Sha'b*, June 9, 1960, 4; and "Hawla Ghalq Maqarr Rabitat al-Difa' 'an Huquq al-Mar'a fi al-'Amara," *Ittihad al-Sha'b*, October 26, 1959, 7.

86. "Rabitat al-Difa' 'an Huquq al-Mar'a Tutalib bi-I'adat Fath Marakiz Mukafahat al-Ummiyya," *Ittihad al-Sha'b*, August 30, 1959, 2.

87. James Ferguson, *The Anti-Politics Machine: "Development," Depoliticization, and Bureaucratic Power in Lesotho* (Minneapolis: University of Minnesota Press, 1994).

88. "*Ittihad al-Sha'b* wa-'Jarimat' Mukafahat al-Ummiyya," 4. "Rabitat al-Mar'a al-'Iraqiyya Tusahim bi-Sharaf fi Mashru' Mukafahat al-Ummiyya al-Nabil," 8.

89. "Wad' al-Hawajiz amam Tadawul Ittihad al-Sha'b," *Ittihad al-Sha'b*, June 9, 1960, 1, 8.

90. "Mu'tamar Ru'asa' Sihhat al-Alwiya," *Ittihad al-Sha'b*, December 9, 1959, 4; "Iqtirah Wizarat al-Sihha," *Ittihad al-Sha'b*, December 10, 1959, 4.

91. See, for example, "Nisa' al-'Iraq Yastankirna Hamlat al-Dass al-La'im 'ala Munaz-zamatihunna al-Mujahida" and "Min Rabitat al-Mar'a," *Ittihad al-Sha'b*, June 19, 1960, 5.

92. "Talibat Madrasat al-Fanun al-Baytiyya fi al-A'zamiyya Yata'arradna ila I'tida'at," *Ittihad al-Sha'b*, December 10, 1959, 5.

93. "Ilayki Ayyatuha al-'Udwiyya al-Karima," *al-Hurriyya*, September 9, 1960.

94. "Mawqifuna min al-Nazariyya al-Shuyu'iyya," *al-Hurriyya*, April 28, 1960, 3.

95. "Hafnat Turab 'ala ghayr al-Intihaziyya," *al-Hurriyya*, April 14, 1960, 10.

96. "al-Zawaj min Wijhat Nazar al-Shuyu'iyya," *Ittihad al-Sha'b*, August 29, 1959.

97. "Nida' ila al-Damir al-'Alami wa-ila al-Shu'ub al-'Arabiyya," *Ittihad al-Sha'b*, December 13, 1959, 7.

98. "Nutalib bi-l-Hurriyya li-l-Mu'taqalat fi Sujun Hukkam al-'Arabiyya al-Mutahida," *Ittihad al-Sha'b*, December 13, 1959, 7.

99. "Iraqi Women's Pledge," *Iraq Times*, March 10, 1960, 9.

100. "Siyadat al-Za'im 'Abd al-Karim Qasim Yalqi Khitaban," 14. On Qasim's references to Iraq as eternal, see also Dann, *Iraq under Qassem*, 172.

101. "al-'Iraq wa-Siyasat al-Tadamun al-'Arabi," 2.

102. For example, the minister of the interior refused to consider applications for politi-cal parties to operate if they used the term *al-sha'b* to refer to anything but the Iraqi people, "Arabs and Kurds together" (Dann, *Iraq under Qassem*, 278).

103. Andrew Sartori, *Bengal in Global Concept History: Culturalism in the Age of Capital* (Chicago: University of Chicago Press, 2008), 13.

104. Ismael, *Rise and Fall of the Communist Party of Iraq*, 106.

105. On the "grassroots" campaign of Qasim's government to dismantle the communist popular front organizations, while leaving the ICP governing structure in place, see Dann, *Iraq under Qassem*, 238.

106. Karim, *Tahafut al-Sittiniyyin*, 80–81. On uses of modernization theory to legitimize

the 1963 Ba'th coup, see Weldon Matthews, "The Kennedy Administration, Counterinsurgency, and Iraq's First Ba'thist Regime," *International Journal of Middle East Studies* 43 (2011): 635–53.

107. Women were mobilized for similar purposes. On the involvement of the Ba'thist General Federation of Iraqi Women in the "surveillance of families and reporting on dissent" in the 1980s, see Dina Rizk Khoury, *Iraq in Wartime: Soldiering, Martyrdom, and Remembrance* (Cambridge: Cambridge University Press, 2013), 79.

Chapter 7

1. See, for example, Yitzhak Nakash, *Reaching for Power: The Shi'a in the Modern Arab World* (Princeton: Princeton University Press, 2006), 96; Eric Davis, *Memories of State: Politics, History, and Collective Identity in Modern Iraq* (Berkeley: University of California Press, 2005), 146; and Uriel Dann, *Iraq under Qassem: A Political History, 1958–1963* (Jerusalem: Israel Universities Press, 1969), 246–47, 328.

2. Faleh A. Jabar, *The Shi'ite Movement in Iraq* (London: Saqi Books, 2003), 75–76, 110; Pierre-Jean Luizard, "The Nature of the Confrontation between the State and *Marja'ism*: Grand Ayatollah Muhsin Al-Hakim and the Ba'th," in *Ayatollahs, Sufis and Ideologues: State, Religion and Social Movements in Iraq*, ed. Faleh A. Jabar (London: Saqi Books, 2002), 92.

3. Noga Efrati, "Negotiating Rights in Iraq: Women and the Personal Status Law," *Middle East Journal* 59, no. 4 (August 2005): 577–96; Noga Efrati, *Women in Iraq: Past Meets Present* (New York: Columbia University Press, 2012). For early work in legal history, see J.N.D. Anderson, "A Law of Personal Status for Iraq," *International and Comparative Law Quarterly* 9, no. 4 (October 1960): 542–63; and J.N.D. Anderson, "Changes in the Law of Personal Status in Iraq," *International and Comparative Law Quarterly* 12, no. 3 (1963): 1026–31. One general historical work that devoted more than passing attention to the reforms was Uriel Dann's 1969 *Iraq under Qassem*. Dann concluded that the law reflected Qasim's "Western-style 'progressiveness'" more than his "political acumen," given that the communists dismissed it as "bourgeois reform" and the Arab nationalists were simply uninterested (247). In contrast, this chapter will show not only that the communists firmly supported the law but also that its promulgation was of considerable interest to political actors across the spectrum. A common thread running through the discourses of supporters and opponents alike was their agreement on the importance of laws regulating family structures and relations to the construction of a sovereign national future.

4. Government of Iraq, "Raqm 188 li-Sanat 1959: Qanun al-Ahwal al-Shakhsiyya," *al-Waqa'i' al-'Iraqiyya*, December 30, 1959, 7–8.

5. Government of Iraq, "Raqm 188," 7.

6. See Brinkley Messick, *The Calligraphic State: Textual Domination and History in a Muslim Society* (Berkeley: University of California Press, 1996). See also the works of Max Weber, for example, *Economy and Society* (Totowa: Bedminster, 1968).

7. Government of Iraq, "Raqm 188," 8. As Laura Bier writes of family law reform in 20th-century Egypt, the "codification of family law established the gendered roles of mother and wife and of husband and father as a legal basis of personhood and citizenship upon which rights and duties were accorded." See Bier, *Revolutionary Womanhood: Feminisms, Modernity, and the State in Nasser's Egypt* (Stanford: Stanford University Press, 2011), 105.

8. The term "post-revolutionary self," though I use it differently, comes from Jan Goldstein, *The Post-Revolutionary Self: Politics and Psyche in France, 1750–1850* (Cambridge, MA: Harvard University Press, 2005).

9. Government of Iraq, "Raqm 188," 8.

10. On Islamic discursive traditions, see Samira Haj, *Reconfiguring Islamic Tradition: Reform, Rationality, and Modernity* (Stanford: Stanford University Press, 2008); Ebrahim Moosa, *Ghazālī and the Poetics of Imagination* (Chapel Hill: University of North Carolina Press, 2005); and Talal Asad, *Formations of the Secular: Christianity, Islam, Modernity* (Stanford: Stanford University Press, 2003).

11. Asad, *Formations of the Secular*, 227–28. See also Saba Mahmood, *Religious Difference in a Secular Age: A Minority Report* (Princeton: Princeton University Press, 2016); and Hussein Ali Agrama, *Questioning Secularism: Islam, Sovereignty, and the Rule of Law in Modern Egypt* (Chicago: University of Chicago Press, 2012). Kenneth Cuno notes that family law also did not appear as a legal category in Europe before the 19th century. See Cuno, *Modernizing Marriage: Family, Ideology, and Law in Nineteenth- and Early Twentieth-Century Egypt* (Syracuse: Syracuse University Press, 2015), 78. Moreover, in constructing premodern family law as the unchanging heart of the shari'a, the secularization narrative also fails to consider ways in which state authority *has* extended into the regulation of marriage and other family affairs throughout Islamic history. On how Ottoman regulations from the 16th through the 19th centuries intervened in marriage law, such as to ban marriage between Sunnis and Shi'a (and/or between Ottoman and Iranian citizens) in southern Iraq, see Karen M. Kern, *Imperial Citizen: Marriage and Citizenship in the Ottoman Frontier Provinces of Iraq* (Syracuse: Syracuse University Press, 2011).

12. Government of Iraq, "Raqm 188," 1.

13. Anderson, "Law of Personal Status for Iraq," 542. Egyptian law is similarly divided: "Despite declaring that Christians have their own family law, the Egyptian government regards Islamic family law as the 'general law' of the country" (Mahmood, *Religious Difference in a Secular Age*, 136).

14. Anderson, "Law of Personal Status for Iraq," 547.

15. Anderson, 547.

16. For an extended analysis of similar forms of legal reasoning in Egypt, see Mahmood, *Religious Difference in a Secular Age*. Mahmood argues that "modern secular governance has contributed to the exacerbation of religious tensions in postcolonial Egypt, hardening interfaith boundaries and polarizing religious differences" (p. 1). A key way this has happened is through family law, which "is predicated upon the public-private divide—foundational to the modern secular political order—that relegates religion, family, and sexuality to the private sphere, thereby entwining their legal and moral fates" (p. 115).

17. Max Weiss, *In the Shadow of Sectarianism: Law, Shi'ism, and the Making of Modern Lebanon* (Cambridge, MA: Harvard University Press, 2010), 123. See also Muhammad Bahr al-'Ulum, *Adwa' 'ala Qanun al-Ahwal al-Shakhsiyya al-'Iraqi* (Najaf: Matba'at al-Nu'man, 1963), 21.

18. Bahr al-'Ulum, 21.

19. Messick, *Calligraphic State*.

20. Government of Iraq, "Raqm 188," 1.

21. Discussions of conjugal life in the revolutionary-era press were extensive and deserve a separate study. See, for example, "Mashru' al-Zawaj," *al-Mustaqbal*, April 8, 1962, 8; "Hal al-Rajul huwa al-Mas'ul 'an al-Burud al-Jinsi 'ind al-Mar'a?," *Sawt al-Ahrar*, April 3, 1962, 7.

22. See Shahla Haeri, *Law of Desire: Temporary Marriage in Shi'i Iran* (Syracuse: Syracuse University Press, 1989).

23. This appears to be changing in the 21st century. For example, some Shi'i jurists now permit *mut'a* contracts between a man and an egg-donor woman who have never met, for the purpose of legitimizing *in vitro* fertilization of the man's "permanent" wife. See Morgan Clarke and Marcia C. Inhorn, "Mutuality and Immediacy between *Marja'* and *Muqallid*: Evidence from Male in Vitro Fertilization Patients in Shi'i Lebanon," *International Journal of Middle East Studies* 43, no. 3 (August 2011): 409–27.

24. Quoted in and translated by Haeri, *Law of Desire*, 34–35.

25. I am working on a separate article that provides this analysis.

26. Bahr al-'Ulum, *Adwa' 'ala Qanun al-Ahwal al-Shakhsiyya*, 26–27, 70–76.

27. Anderson, "Law of Personal Status for Iraq," 546.

28. In her study of Ottoman court records, Judith Tucker found that when "legal disputes about *talaq* found their way into court" due to disagreement "about whether a divorce had actually taken place," it was "usually with the wife pressing for the court's validation of the divorce." See Tucker, *Women, Family, and Gender in Islamic Law* (Cambridge: Cambridge University Press, 2008), 105. For a case in contemporary Egypt of a man who succeeded in getting his pronouncement of *talaq* invalidated in court by claiming that he had been drunk when making it, although his wife, who wanted the divorce validated, as well as eyewitnesses testified that he was sober, see Agrama, *Questioning Secularism*, 116–17.

29. Government of Iraq, "Raqm 188," 5.

30. Bahr al-'Ulum, *Adwa' 'ala Qanun al-Ahwal al-Shakhsiyya*, 142–45.

31. Beth Baron, *The Women's Awakening in Egypt: Culture, Society, and the Press* (New Haven: Yale University Press, 1994), 160–61.

32. Jacques Donzelot, *The Policing of Families* (Baltimore: Johns Hopkins University Press, 1977), 44.

33. Government of Iraq, "Raqm 188," 8.

34. For a critique of this and other aspects of the law from an Iraqi feminist perspective, see Su'ad Khayri, *al-Mar'a al-'Iraqiyya: Kifah wa-'Ata'* (Stockholm: A.R.M. All-Tryck, 1998), 20. For a fascinating account of how European law shaped the modern enforcement in Islamic countries of a husband's right to prevent his wife from leaving the marital home, see Cuno, *Modernizing Marriage*, chap. 6.

35. Government of Iraq, "Raqm 188," 6.

36. On Qasim's attempt to use this argument, and the response of the 'ulama, see 'Ala' al-Din Kharrufa, "al-Mirath bi-Qanun al-Ahwal al-Shakhsiyya," *al-Hurriyya*, May 29, 1960, 3.

37. "al-Zawaj wa-l-Haya al-'A'iliyya fi al-Ittihad al-Sufiyati," *Ittihad al-Sha'b*, November 6, 1959, 6–8.

38. "al-Zawaj wa-l-Haya al-'A'iliyya fi al-Ittihad al-Sufiyati."

39. For example, in Naziha al-Dulaimi, "al-Mar'a al-'Iraqiyya" (unpublished manuscript, 1952). I thank Mubejel Baban for providing me with this manuscript.

40. See Ahmad Jamal al-Din, "al-Ahwal al-Shakhsiyya wa-Huquq al-Mar'a," *Ittihad al-Sha'b*, August 8, 1960, 5.

41. Jamal al-Din, "al-Ahwal al-Shakhsiyya," 5.

42. Hanna Batatu, *The Old Social Classes and the Revolutionary Movements of Iraq* (Princeton: Princeton University Press, 1978), 1018.

43. 'Ala' al-Din Kharrufa, "al-Mirath bi-Qanun al-Ahwal al-Shakhsiyya," *al-Hurriyya*, May 29, 1960, 3. For a more extended explication of the 1959 law by Kharrufa, see 'Ala' al-Din Kharrufa, *Sharh Qanun al-Ahwal al-Shakhsiyya: Raqm 188, Sanat 1959* (Baghdad: Matba'at al-'Ani, 1962).

44. Kharrufa, "al-Mirath bi-Qanun al-Ahwal al-Shakhsiyya," 3.

45. Dann, *Iraq under Qassem*, 247.

46. Jabar, *Shi'ite Movement in Iraq*, 95–100.

47. Jabar, 110–13.

48. Dann, *Iraq under Qassem*, 300.

49. The journal's editor was the *'alim* Hadi Fayad, later the dean of the Kuliyat al-Fiqh (College of Jurisprudence). Fayad launched *al-Najaf* in 1957, and its publication continued for five years. See http://www.almoajam.org/poet_details.php?id=7750 (accessed February 20, 2012).

50. See, for example, "Thawratan," *al-Najaf* 3, no. 2 (July 14, 1959); and Muhammad Taqi al-Hakim, "al-Thawra=Hadm wa-Bina'," *al-Najaf* 3, no. 2 (July 14, 1959): 30–31.

51. Ahmad Husayn al-Rahim, "'Uruq al-Nar fi Thawrat 14 Tammuz," *al-Najaf* 3, no. 2 (July 14, 1959): 7.

52. See Muhammad al-Hijri, "Fi 'Urs," *al-Najaf* 3, no. 3 (August 1, 1959): 13.

53. See, for example, 'Abd al-Muhsin al-Hakim, "Jawab al-Ustadh al-Sayyid 'Abd al-Muhsin al-Hakim," *al-Najaf* 3, no. 6 (September 15, 1959): 17.

54. The shift also coincided with some sort of split within the journal's editorial staff. Reporting the resignation of the assistant editor in its January 15, 1960, issue, the journal duly noted that he had "asked that the readers be told that he has no relationship to anything printed in the journal in the future." The journal's editor remained the same through the dramatic about-face in its assessment of Qasim's regime and women's rights.

55. Husayn Fahmi al-Khazraji, "Mushkilat al-Mar'a al-'Iraqiyya," *al-Najaf* 3, no. 6 (September 15, 1959): 13–14.

56. Husayn Fahmi al-Khazraji, "Lan Yaflah Qawm Asnadu Amrahum ila Imra'a," *al-Najaf* 4, no. 19–20 (April 24, 1962): 14–15.

57. Bahr al-'Ulum, *Adwa' 'ala Qanun al-Ahwal al-Shakhsiyya*, 7.

58. Bahr al-'Ulum, 7–8.

59. For example, Yitzhak Nakash notes a Ba'th-Shi'i alliance against the personal status law, but incorrectly suggests that the *mujtahid*s were satisfied by the Ba'thist government's annulment of the inheritance clause (Nakash, *Reaching for Power*, 96).

60. Bahr al-'Ulum, *Adwa' 'ala Qanun al-Ahwal al-Shakhsiyya*, 9.

61. Bahr al-'Ulum, 26–27.

62. Bahr al-'Ulum, 247.

63. Bahr al-'Ulum, 32.

64. Bahr al-'Ulum, 26–28.

65. For a draft personal status law in the 1940s, which was never promulgated but was shaped by the marriage crisis discourse of that era, see Efrati, *Women in Iraq*, chap. 2.

66. Wael Hallaq, *The Impossible State: Islam, Politics, and Modernity's Moral Predicament* (New York: Columbia University Press, 2013), 59, 66.

67. Hallaq, 62–63.

68. Hallaq, 66, 190n144.

69. 'Ali al-Wardi, *Mantiq Ibn Khaldun* (London: Alwarrak, 2009), 96. See also Ibrahim al-Haidari, *'Ali al-Wardi: Shakhsiyyatuhu wa-Manhajuhu wa-Afkarahu al-Ijtima'iyya* (Köln: Al-Kamel Verlag, 2006), 89–94.

70. al-Wardi, 262. On the Islamic concept of revival, see also Haj, *Reconfiguring Islamic Tradition*.

71. al-Wardi, 97.

72. al-Wardi, 259.

73. al-Wardi, 317.

74. 'Ali al-Wardi, *Wu''az al-Salatin* (London: Alwarrak, 2013), 348, 351, 352; 'Ali al-Wardi, *Mahzalat al-'Aql al-Bashari* (London: Dar al-Warraq li-l-Nashr, 2016), 240.

75. Lee Edelman, *No Future: Queer Theory and the Death Drive* (Durham: Duke University Press, 2004), 11.

76. al-Wardi, *Wu''az al-Salatin*, 293, 300.

77. al-Wardi, *Mahzalat al-'Aql al-Bashari*, 235.

78. Elizabeth Freeman, *Time Binds: Queer Temporalities, Queer Histories* (Durham: Duke University Press, 2010), 19. According to Freeman, Benjamin thus "anticipate[s] Lee Edelman's *No Future* by many decades," but it seems to me that this is not quite right. Edelman's analysis honors the death drive; Benjamin's, like al-Wardi's, honors the dead.

79. See Sara Pursley, "'Ali al-Wardi and the Miracles of the Unconscious," *Psychoanalysis and History* (forthcoming).

80. al-Wardi, *Wu''az al-Salatin*, 352, 335. In his book *al-Ahlam bayn al-'Ilm wa-l-'Aqida* (London: Alwarrak, 2009), originally published the year after the revolution, al-Wardi asserted that he had engaged in "evasions" in his work published during the Hashimite era, since the other option was to "express my opinion clearly and go to prison" (p. 386). This may help to explain the radical shift that seems to occur in some of his books, including *Wu''az al-Salatin* (The sultans' preachers), following the introduction.

Epilogue

Parts of this chapter are derived from Sara Pursley, "Futures Past: Nation, Gender, Time in Jawad Salim's *Monument to Freedom*," *Kufa Review* 5, no. 3 (May 2014), www.uokufa.edu.iq/journals/index.php/Kufa_Review/article/view/2623.

1. Kanan Makiya, *The Monument: Art, Vulgarity and Responsibility in Iraq* (Berkeley: University of California Press, 1991), 81.

2. "Jawad Salim wa-Nusb al-Hurriyya: Dhakirat Zaman, Dhakirat Makan," Annabaa, April 2, 2007, http://www.annabaa.org/nbanews/62/197.htm (accessed July 27, 2010).

3. "Jawad Salim wa-Nusb al-Hurriyya."

4. In making this point, Shakir Hasan Al Sa'id quotes Michel Foucault in Arabic translation: *inna al-jasad huwa al-sath alladhi tartasim 'alayhi al-ahdath* (the body is the surface on which events are inscribed). See Al Sa'id, *Jawad Salim: al-Fannan wa-l-Akharun* (Baghdad: Wizarat al-Thaqafa wa-l-I'lam, 1991), 202.

5. Dipesh Chakrabarty, *Provincializing Europe: Postcolonial Thought and Historical Difference* (Princeton: Princeton University Press, 2000), 95, 239.

6. Lara Deeb, "Emulating and/or Embodying the Ideal: The Gendering of Temporal Frameworks and Islamic Role Models in Shi'i Lebanon," *American Ethnologist* 36, no. 2 (2009): 248.

7. Deeb, 246.

8. Deeb, 244.

9. Deeb, 243.

10. On uses of the cyclical metaphor by Egyptian intellectuals engaged with Islamic discourses, including those of Ibn Khaldun, see Omnia El Shakry, *The Great Social Laboratory: Subjects of Knowledge in Colonial and Postcolonial Egypt* (Stanford: Stanford University Press, 2007), esp. 221–22.

11. As Stephen Jay Gould has shown, even the modern science of geology is dependent on both linear and cyclical metaphors of time. Narrating the earth's cyclical regeneration through volcanos and other recurring phenomena is no less pertinent to understanding geological change than is studying the "contingent pathways of evolutionary change." See Gould, *Time's Arrow, Time's Cycle: Myth and Metaphor in the Discovery of Geological Time* (Cambridge, MA: Harvard University Press, 1987), 197.

12. Al Sa'id, *Jawad Salim*, 159.

13. Makiya, *Monument*, 83.

14. Benedict Anderson, *Imagined Communities: Reflections on the Origin and Spread of Nationalism* (London: Verso Books, 1983).

15. Al Sa'id, *Jawad Salim*, 193.

16. Kamran Scot Aghaie, "Introduction: Gendered Aspects of the Emergence and Historical Development of Shi'i Symbols and Rituals," in *The Women of Karbala*, ed. Kamran Scot Aghaie (Austin: University of Texas Press, 2005), 9.

17. "al-Za'im Yaftatih Mahrajan al-Risafi," *al-Mu'allim al-Jadid* 22, no. 5 (May 1959): 2–3.

18. Makiya, *Monument*, 83.

19. Afsaneh Najmabadi has examined similar constructions in modern Iran, in which the heterosocialization of public space was connected to the "heteronormalization of eros and sex [as] a condition of 'achieving modernity.'" See Najmabadi, *Women with Mustaches and Men without Beards: Gender and Sexual Anxieties of Iranian Modernity* (Berkeley: University of California Press, 2005), 146.

20. The more common reading is that the figure is raising a saddle in the air. But see Jabra Ibrahim Jabra, *Jawad Salim wa-Nusb al-Hurriyya: Dirasa fi Atharihi wa-Ara'ihi* (Baghdad: Wizarat al-'Alam, 1974), 136.

21. Craig Calhoun, "Introduction," in *Habermas and the Public Sphere*, ed. Craig Calhoun (Cambridge, MA: MIT Press, 1992), 10-11. See also Michael Warner, *Publics and Counterpublics* (New York: Zone Books, 2005).

22. Lee Edelman, *No Future: Queer Theory and the Death Drive* (Durham: Duke University Press, 2004), 11.

23. On mourning as women's work, see Lila Abu-Lughod, "Islam and the Gendered Discourses of Death," *International Journal of Middle East Studies* 25 (1993): 187–205. For examples of Iraqi nationalist narratives of women urging men into battle, see "Iraqi Women on the March," *Iraqi Review*, 1, no. 9 (July 30, 1959), 18.

24. Muhsin al-Musawi, *Reading Iraq: Culture and Power in Conflict* (London: I. B. Tauris, 2006), 29.

25. al-Musawi, 28.

26. Yasin al-Nasir, "Qira'a fi Nusb al-Hurriyya. ... Sirr al-Fann fi Nusb al-Hurriyya ... al-Ta'ayush ma'a Jami' al-'Uhud al-Siyasiyya," *al-Zaman*, 20 January 2003.

27. Joan Wallach Scott, *The Fantasy of Feminist History* (Durham: Duke University Press, 2011), 18.

28. Edelman, *No Future*, 25.

29. While his framework is derived from a historical analysis of India, Partha Chatterjee explicitly proposes that these two domains are a "fundamental feature of anticolonial nationalisms in Asia and Africa." See Partha Chatterjee, *The Nation and Its Fragments: Colonial and Postcolonial Histories* (Princeton: Princeton University Press, 1993), 6.

30. al-Musawi, *Reading Iraq*, 28.

31. Government of Iraq, *Manhaj Ihtifalat wa-Mahrajanat al-Dhikra al-Rabi'a li-Thawrat 14 Tammuz al-Majida li-Liwa' al-Nasiriyya* (Baghdad: Matba'at al-Irshad, 1962).

32. See, for example, Makiya, *Monument*, 87, 120.

33. Al-Nasir, "Qira'a fi Nusb al-Hurriyya."

34. See Reinhart Koselleck, *Futures Past: On the Semantics of Historical Time*, trans. Keith Tribe (New York: Columbia University Press, 2004), 48.

35. Chakrabarty, *Provincializing Europe*, 9.

36. Makiya, *Monument*, 81–82; Jabra, *Jawad Salim wa-Nusb al-Hurriyya*, 136.

37. Makiya, *Monument*, 84.

38. 'Abbas al-Sarraf, *Jawad Salim* (Baghdad: Wizarat al-I'lam, 1972), 146.

39. Al Sa'id, *Jawad Salim*, 203.

40. Al Sa'id, 199–200.

41. On the global postwar fantasy of "timeless, even, and limitless" development and the end of "eventful" time, see Kristin Ross, *Fast Cars, Clean Bodies: Decolonization and the Reordering of French Culture* (Cambridge, MA: MIT Press, 1995), 10.

42. Jabra, *Jawad Salim wa-Nusb al-Hurriyya*, 158.

43. Koselleck, *Futures Past*, 43.

44. Al Sa'id, *Jawad Salim*, chap. 7.

45. Al Sa'id, 206–7.

46. Al Sa'id, 203.

47. Koselleck, *Futures Past*, 23.

48. Nada Shabout notes that in Al Sa'id's theoretical work on modern Arab art, "the 'temporal now' is . . . expressed through spatial means. For example, an opening in the picto-

rial surface is a temporal void." See Shabout, *Modern Arab Art: Formation of Arab Aesthetics* (Gainesville: University Press of Florida, 2007), 112.

49. Makiya, *Monument*, 84.

50. Makiya, 84.

51. Makiya's source here is Jabra, who does not cite his own source, though his use of the passive voice ("When Jawad was asked why he didn't give her feet . . . ") might suggest that it was not Jabra who asked (Jabra, *Jawad Salim wa-Nusb al-Hurriyya*, 152). In any event, Freedom is only one of several prominent figures in the monument who are conspicuously lacking feet, a fact routinely ignored by decades of commentators who have repeated Jabra's uplifting interpretation of Freedom's own missing appendages. For an example of a female figure with amputated feet in Salim's earlier art that clearly cannot be read through a "soaring high" interpretation, see his painting *Kayd al-Nisa'*.

52. I am not suggesting that Freedom's form need be read as a literal representation of a body laid out within a realistic depiction of space. Salim was strongly influenced by Cubism, after all, and there are many tributes to Picasso's *Guernica* in the monument, including in the figure of Freedom (though it might be noted that Cubism is not the dominant style in most of the other figures of the monument). I am simply questioning the tradition of reading Freedom's form as symbolic triumph by interpreting its apparent bodily distortions (e.g., its "missing" feet) as simplistic spatial metaphors (e.g., "soaring high") that themselves rely on certain assumptions of spatial realism.

53. Al Sa'id, *Jawad Salim*, 200.

54. al-Sarraf, *Jawad Salim*, 146.

55. Walter Benjamin, *Illuminations: Essays and Reflections*, trans. Hannah Arendt (New York: Schocken Books, 1968), 257–58.

56. I thank Kate Liska for proposing this reading.

57. Al Sa'id, *Jawad Salim*, 203.

58. *Inqilab* is now used most often to mean "coup," but in interwar and early postwar Iraq it could also mean "revolution." No doubt the Iraqi choice in 1958 was influenced, if not determined, by the already established use of *thawra* for the events of 1952 in Egypt. Still, the fact that Persian speakers continue to use *inqilab* for "revolution," including the events of 1979 in Iran, suggests that the shift to *thawra* in the Arabic-speaking world was not a foregone conclusion. I thank Ervand Abrahamian for this point.

59. al-Musawi, *Reading Iraq*, 30.

Bibliography

Primary Sources

Archival Collections and Official Records

Confidential U.S. State Department Central Files: Iraq, 1950–1954, Internal Affairs, RG84/787. US National Archives and Records Administration (NARA).

Confidential U.S. State Department Central Files: Iraq, 1955–1959, Internal Affairs, RG84/787. US National Archives and Records Administration (NARA).

Iraq Administration Reports, 1914–1932. 10 vols. Cambridge: Cambridge Archive Editions, 1992.

United Nations Educational, Cultural and Scientific Organization (UNESCO) Archives. Paris.

United Nations Food and Agricultural Organization (FAO) Archives. Online.

Records of Iraq 1914–1966. 15 vols. Cambridge: Cambridge Archive Editions, 2001.

al-Waqa'i' al-'Iraqiyya (Iraqi Government Gazette), 1921–1963.

Journals and Newspapers

al-Ahali
al-'Ahd al-Jadid
al-Bayan
al-Hurriyya
Iraqi Review
Iraq Times
al-'Irfan
Ittihad al-Sha'b

al-Mu'allim al-Jadid
al-Mustaqbal
al-Muthaqqaf
al-Najaf
Sawt al-Ahrar
al-Thawra
al-Zaman

Additional Sources

'Abd al-Hamid, Muhyi al-Din. "Mustaqbal al-Thaqafa fi al-'Iraq." al-*Mu'allim al-Jadid* 23, no. 1–2 (February 1960): 3–9.

'Abid, Ihssan. "Hal Yakhtalif Manhaj al-'Ulum li-l-Banat 'an li-l-Wilad?" *al-Mu'allim al-Jadid* 7, no. 6 (June 1942): 513–20.

Abu-Lughod, Lila. "Islam and the Gendered Discourses of Death." *International Journal of Middle East Studies* 25, no. 2 (May 1993): 187–205.

Adams, Doris. "Current Population Trends in Iraq." *Middle East Journal* 10, no. 2 (1956): 151–165.

Adams, Warren Edward. "The Land Development Program in Iraq with Special Reference to the Dujaila Settlement, 1945 to 1954." PhD diss., University of California, Berkeley, 1955.

Aghaie, Kamran Scot. "Introduction: Gendered Aspects of the Emergence and Historical Development of Shi'i Symbols and Rituals." In *The Women of Karbala*, edited by Kamran Scot Aghaie, 1–21. Austin: University of Texas Press, 2005.

Agrama, Hussein Ali. *Questioning Secularism: Islam, Sovereignty, and the Rule of Law in Modern Egypt*. Chicago: University of Chicago Press, 2012.

Akrawi, Matta. "Curriculum Construction in the Public Primary Schools of Iraq in the Light of a Study of the Political, Economic, Social, Hygienic and Educational Conditions and Problems of the Country, with Some Reference to the Education of Teachers." PhD diss., Teachers College, Columbia University, 1942.

Ali, Hassan Mohammad. *Land Reclamation and Settlement in Iraq*. Baghdad: Baghdad Printing Press, 1955.

Ali, Nadje Sadig al-. *Iraqi Women: Untold Stories from 1948 to the Present*. London: Zed Books, 2007.

Allison, Clinton B. "The Appalling World of Edgar Wallace Knight." *Journal of Thought* 18, no. 3 (1983): 7–14.

"'Am min al-Thawra." *al-Muthaqqaf* 2, no. 10 (July 1959): 1–5.

Amin, Samir. *Unequal Development: An Essay on the Social Formations of Peripheral Capitalism*. Translated by Brian Pearce. New York: Monthly Review Press, 1976.

Anderson, Benedict. *Imagined Communities: Reflections on the Origin and Spread of Nationalism*. London: Verso Books, 1983.

Anderson, J.N.D. "Changes in the Law of Personal Status in Iraq." *International and Comparative Law Quarterly* 12, no. 3 (1963): 1026–31.

———. "A Law of Personal Status for Iraq." *International and Comparative Law Quarterly* 9, no. 4 (October 1960): 542–63.

Anderson, Warwick, Deborah Jenson, and Richard C. Keller. "Introduction: Globalizing the Unconscious." In *Unconscious Dominions: Psychoanalysis, Colonial Trauma, and Global Sovereignties*, edited by W. Anderson, Deborah Jenson, and Richard C. Keller, 1–20. Durham: Duke University Press, 2011.

Anghie, Antony. *Imperialism, Sovereignty and the Making of International Law*. Cambridge: Cambridge University Press, 2007.

Apple, Rima. "Liberal Arts or Vocational Training? Home Economics Education for Girls." In *Rethinking Home Economics: Women and the History of a Profession*, edited by Sarah Stage and Virginia B. Vincenti, 79–95. Ithaca: Cornell University Press, 1997.

Aqrawi, Matta. "al-Ta'lim al-'Am wa-Atharuhu fi al-Nahda al-Qawmiyya." *al-Mu'allim al-Jadid* 4, no. 2 (June 1938): 97–105.

Arndt, H. W. "Economic Development: A Semantic History." *Economic Development and Cultural Change* 29, no. 3 (1981): 457–66.

Asad, Talal. *Formations of the Secular: Christianity, Islam, Modernity.* Stanford: Stanford University Press, 2003.

———. *Genealogies of Religion: Discipline and Reasons of Power in Christianity and Islam.* Baltimore: Johns Hopkins University Press, 1993.

Aston, T. H., and C.H.E. Philpin, eds. *The Brenner Debate: Agrarian Class Structure and Economic Development in Pre-Industrial Europe.* Cambridge: Cambridge University Press, 1987.

'Awad, 'Abd al-Jabar. "al-Islah al-Zira'i." *al-Muthaqqaf* 2, no. 10 (July 1959): 26–29.

'Azzawi, Fadil al-. *al-Ruh al-Hayya: Jil al-Sittinat fi al-'Iraq.* Damascus: Dar al-Mada, 1997.

Bahr al-'Ulum, Muhammad. *Adwa' 'ala Qanun al-Ahwal al-Shakhsiyya al-'Iraqi.* Najaf: Matba'at al-Nu'man, 1963.

Barak, On. *On Time: Technology and Temporality in Modern Egypt.* Berkeley: University of California Press, 2013.

Baron, Beth. *Egypt as a Woman: Nationalism, Gender, and Politics.* Berkeley: University of California Press, 2005.

———. "The Origins of Family Planning: Aziza Hussein, American Experts, and the Egyptian State." *Journal of Middle East Women's Studies* 4, no. 3 (2008): 31–57.

———. *The Women's Awakening in Egypt: Culture, Society, and the Press.* New Haven: Yale University Press, 1994.

Barrak, Fadil. *Dawr al-Jaysh al-'Iraqi fi Hukumat al-Difa' al-Watani wa-l-Harb ma'a Biritaniya Sanat 1941.* Baghdad: Dar al-'Arabiyya, 1979.

Bashkin, Orit. *The Other Iraq: Pluralism and Culture in Hashemite Iraq.* Stanford: Stanford University Press, 2009.

———. "Representations of Women in the Writings of the Intelligentsia in Hashemite Iraq, 1921–1958." *Journal of Middle East Women's Studies* (Winter 2008): 53–82.

———. "'When Mu'awiya Entered the Curriculum': Some Comments on the Iraqi Educational System in the Interwar Period." *Comparative Education Review* 50, no. 3 (2006): 346–66.

Basir, Muhammad Mahdi al-. *Tarikh al-Qadiyya al-'Iraqiyya.* Baghdad: Matba'at al-Fallah, 1924.

Batatu, Hanna. *The Old Social Classes and the Revolutionary Movements of Iraq.* Princeton: Princeton University Press, 1978.

Bazzaz, 'Abd al-Rahman al-. "Tathqif al-Mar'a." *al-Mu'allim al-Jadid* 17, no. 2 (September 1953): 40–49.

Bell, Gertrude. *The Letters of Gertrude Bell: Selected and Edited by Lady Bell.* New York: Boni and Liveright, 1927.

Benjamin, Walter. *Illuminations: Essays and Reflections.* Translated by Hannah Arendt. New York: Schocken Books, 1968.

Bergeron, Suzanne. *Fragments of Development: Nation, Gender, and the Space of Modernity.* Ann Arbor: University of Michigan Press, 2006.

Bier, Laura. *Revolutionary Womanhood: Feminisms, Modernity, and the State in Nasser's Egypt.* Stanford: Stanford University Press, 2011.

Bu, Liping. "International Activism and Comparative Education: Pioneering Efforts of the International Institute of Teachers College, Columbia University." *Comparative Education Review* 41, no. 4 (1997): 413–34.

Burns, Norman. "Development Projects in Iraq." Pt. 1, "The Dujaylah Land Settlement." *Middle East Journal* 5, no. 3 (1951): 362–66.

Calhoun, Craig. "Introduction." In *Habermas and the Public Sphere*, edited by Craig Calhoun. Cambridge, MA: MIT Press, 1992.

Caractacus. *Revolution in Iraq: An Essay in Comparative Public Opinion.* London: Gollancz, 1959.

Chakrabarty, Dipesh. *Provincializing Europe: Postcolonial Thought and Historical Difference.* Princeton: Princeton University Press, 2000.

Chatterjee, Partha. *The Nation and Its Fragments: Colonial and Postcolonial Histories.* Princeton: Princeton University Press, 1993.

Citino, Nathan J. *Envisioning the Arab Future: Modernization in U.S.–Arab Relations, 1945–1967.* Cambridge: Cambridge University Press, 2017.

———. "The Ottoman Legacy in Cold War Modernization." *International Journal of Middle East Studies* 40 (2008): 579–97.

Clark, Victor. *Compulsory Education in Iraq.* Paris: United Nations Educational, Cultural and Scientific Organization, 1951.

Clarke, Morgan, and Marcia C. Inhorn. "Mutuality and Immediacy Between *Marjaʿ* and *Muqallid*: Evidence from Male in Vitro Fertilization Patients in Shiʿi Lebanon," *International Journal of Middle East Studies* 43, no. 3 (August 2011): 409–27.

Cleveland, William L. *The Making of an Arab Nationalist: Ottomanism and Arabism in the Life and Thought of Satiʿ Al-Husri.* Princeton: Princeton University Press, 1971.

Cooper, Frederick. "Alternatives to Empire: France and Africa after World War II." In *The State of Sovereignty: Territories, Laws, Populations*, edited by Douglas Howland and Luise White, 94–123. Bloomington: Indiana University Press, 2009.

Cowen, Michael P., and Robert W. Shenton. *Doctrines of Development.* London: Routledge, 1996.

Cox, Jafna. "A Splendid Training Ground: The Importance to the Royal Air Force of Its Role in Iraq, 1919–32." *Journal of Imperial and Commonwealth History* 13, no. 2 (1985): 157–84.

Cuno, Kenneth. *Modernizing Marriage: Family, Ideology, and Law in Nineteenth- and Early Twentieth-Century Egypt.* Syracuse: Syracuse University Press, 2015.

Dann, Uriel. *Iraq under Qassem: A Political History, 1958–1963.* Jerusalem: Israel Universities Press, 1969.

Davis, Eric. *Memories of State: Politics, History, and Collective Identity in Modern Iraq.* Berkeley: University of California Press, 2005.

Davis, Kathleen. *Periodization and Sovereignty: How Ideas of Feudalism and Secularization Govern the Politics of Time.* Philadelphia: University of Pennsylvania Press, 2008.

Deeb, Lara. "Emulating and/or Embodying the Ideal: The Gendering of Temporal Frameworks and Islamic Role Models in Shiʿi Lebanon." *American Ethnologist* 36, no. 2 (2009): 242–57.

Derrida, Jacques. *Specters of Marx: The State of the Debt, The Work of Mourning & the New International*. Translated by Peggy Kamuf. New York: Routledge, 1994.

Dewachi, Omar. *Ungovernable Life: Mandatory Medicine and Statecraft in Iraq*. Stanford: Stanford University Press, 2017.

Dodge, Toby. *Inventing Iraq: The Failure of Nation Building and a History Denied*. New York: Columbia University Press, 2005.

Donzelot, Jacques. *The Policing of Families*. Baltimore: Johns Hopkins University Press, 1977.

Duggan, Lisa, and Nan D. Hunter. *Sex Wars: Sexual Dissent and Political Culture*. New York: Routledge, 2006.

Dulaimi, Naziha al-. "al-Mar'a al-'Iraqiyya." Unpublished manuscript, 1952.

Edelman, Lee. *No Future: Queer Theory and the Death Drive*. Durham: Duke University Press, 2004.

Efrati, Noga. "Competing Narratives: Histories of the Women's Movement in Iraq, 1910–1958." *International Journal of Middle East Studies* 40 (2008): 445–66.

———. "Negotiating Rights in Iraq: Women and the Personal Status Law." *Middle East Journal* 59, no. 4 (August 2005): 577–96.

———. "The Other 'Awakening' in Iraq: The Women's Movement in the First Half of the Twentieth Century." *British Journal of Middle Eastern Studies* 31 (2004): 153–73.

———. *Women in Iraq: Past Meets Present*. New York: Columbia University Press, 2012.

Ekbladh, David. *The Great American Mission: Modernization and the Construction of an American World Order*. Princeton: Princeton University Press, 2010.

El Shakry, Omnia. *The Arabic Freud: Psychoanalysis and Islam in Modern Egypt*. Princeton: Princeton University Press, 2017.

———. *The Great Social Laboratory: Subjects of Knowledge in Colonial and Postcolonial Egypt*. Stanford: Stanford University Press, 2007.

———. "'History without Documents': The Vexed Archives of Decolonization in the Middle East." *American Historical Review* 120, no. 3 (2015): 920–34.

———. "Schooled Mothers and Structured Play: Child Rearing in Turn-of-the-Century Egypt." In *Remaking Women: Feminism and Modernity in the Middle East*, edited by Lila Abu-Lughod, 126–170. Princeton: Princeton University Press, 1998.

———. "Youth as Peril and Promise: The Emergence of Adolescent Psychology in Postwar Egypt." *International Journal of Middle East Studies* 43 (2011): 591–610.

Elias, Megan J. *Stir It Up: Home Economics in American Culture*. Philadelphia: University of Pennsylvania Press, 2010.

Elshakry, Marwa. *Reading Darwin in Arabic, 1860–1950*. Chicago: University of Chicago Press, 2013.

Engel, Barbara Alpern. *Breaking the Ties That Bound: The Politics of Marital Strife in Late Imperial Russia*. Ithaca: Cornell University Press, 2011.

Eppel, Michael. "Note about the Term *Effendiyya* in the History of the Middle East." *International Journal of Middle East Studies* 41 (2009): 535–39.

Escobar, Arturo. *Encountering Development: The Making and Unmaking of the Third World*. Princeton: Princeton University Press, 1995.

Esmeir, Samera. *Juridical Humanity: A Colonial History*. Stanford: Stanford University Press, 2012.

Fabian, Johannes. *Time and the Other: How Anthropology Makes Its Object*. Rev. ed. New York: Columbia University Press, 2002.

FAO Mediterranean Development Project. *Iraq: Country Report*. Rome: Food and Agriculture Organization of the United Nations, 1959.

Farman, Gha'ib Tu'ma. *al-Hukm al-Aswad fi al-'Iraq*. Cairo: Dar al-Fikr, 1957.

Fayyad, 'Abd Allah al-. *al-Thawra al-'Iraqiyya al-Kubra Sanat 1920*. Baghdad: Matba'at al-Irshad, 1963.

Fendler, Lynn. "What Is It Impossible to Think? A Genealogy of the Educated Subject." In *Foucault's Challenge: Discourse, Knowledge, and Power in Education*, edited by Thomas Popkewitz and Marie Brennan, 39–63. New York: Teachers College Press, 1998.

Ferguson, James. *The Anti-Politics Machine: "Development," Depoliticization, and Bureaucratic Power in Lesotho*. Minneapolis: University of Minnesota Press, 1994.

Fidelis, Malgorzata. *Women, Communism, and Industrialization in Postwar Poland*. Cambridge: Cambridge University Press, 2010.

Fieldston, Sara. *Raising the World: Child Welfare in the American Century*. Cambridge, MA: Harvard University Press, 2015.

Fisk, Brad. "Dujaylah Land Settlement." *Middle East Journal* 5, no. 4 (1951): 526–27.

———. "Dujaila: Iraq's Pilot Project for Land Settlement." *Economic Geography* 28, no. 4 (1952): 343–54.

Fleischmann, Ellen. *The Nation and Its "New" Women: The Palestinian Women's Movement 1920–1948*. Berkeley: University of California Press, 2003.

Foucault, Michel. *Discipline & Punish: The Birth of the Prison*. Translated by Alan Sheridan. 2nd ed. New York: Vintage Books, 1995.

———. *The History of Sexuality*. Vol. 1, *An Introduction*. Translated by Robert Hurley. New York: Vintage Books, 1990.

Franzén, Johan. *Red Star over Iraq: Iraqi Communism before Saddam*. New York: Columbia University Press, 2011.

Freeman, Elizabeth. *Time Binds: Queer Temporalities, Queer Histories*. Durham: Duke University Press, 2010.

Gandhi, Leela. *Affective Communities: Anticolonial Thought, Fin-de-Siècle Radicalism, and the Politics of Friendship*. Durham: Duke University Press, 2006.

Gharib, Ruz. "Harakat Tadbir al-Manzil." *al-Mu'allim al-Jadid* 3, no. 3 (June 1938): 206–13.

Gilman, Nils. *Mandarins of the Future: Modernization Theory in Cold War America*. Baltimore: Johns Hopkins University Press, 2003.

Goldstein, Jan. *The Post-Revolutionary Self: Politics and Psyche in France, 1750–1850*. Cambridge, MA: Harvard University Press, 2005.

Gordon, Colin. "Governmental Rationality: An Introduction." In *The Foucault Effect: Studies in Governmentality*, edited by Graham Burchell, Colin Gordon, and Peter Miller. Chicago: University of Chicago Press, 1991.

Goswami, Manu. *Producing India: From Colonial Economy to National Space*. Chicago: University of Chicago Press, 2004.

Gould, Stephen Jay. *Time's Arrow, Time's Cycle: Myth and Metaphor in the Discovery of Geological Time*. Cambridge, MA: Harvard University Press, 1987.

Government of Iraq, *Manhaj Ihtifalat wa-Mahrajanat al-Dhikra al-Rabi'a li-Thawrat 14 Tammuz al-Majida li-Liwa' al-Nasiriyya* (Baghdad: Matba'at al-Irshad, 1962).

Government of Iraq, *Thawrat 14 Tammuz fi 'Amiha al-Awwal.* Baghdad: al-Lajna al-'Ulya li-Ihtifalat 14 Tammuz, 1959.

Government of Iraq, *Thawrat 14 Tammuz fi 'Amiha al-Thani.* Baghdad: al-Lajna al-'Ulya li-Ihtifalat 14 Tammuz, 1960.

Hacking, Ian. "The Looping Effects of Human Kinds." In *Casual Cognition,* edited by Dan Sperber, David Premack, and Ann James Premack. Oxford Scholarship Online, 1996. Retrieved from http://www.oxfordscholarship.com/view/10.1093/acprof :oso/9780198524021.001.0001/acprof-9780198524021-chapter-12.

Hadid, Muhammad. *Mudhakkirati: al-Sira' min Ajli al-Dimuqratiyya fi al-'Iraq.* Beirut: Dar al-Saqi, 2006.

Haeri, Shahla. *Law of Desire: Temporary Marriage in Shi'i Iran.* Syracuse: Syracuse University Press, 1989.

Haidari, Ibrahim al-. *'Ali al-Wardi: Shakhsiyyatuhu wa-Manhajuhu wa-Afkarahu al-Ijtima'iyya.* Köln: Al-Kamel Verlag, 2006.

Haj, 'Aziz al-. *Dhakirat al-Nakhil: Safahat min Ta'rikh al-Haraka al-Shuyu'iyya fi al'Iraq.* Beirut: al-Mu'assasa al-'Arabiyya li-l-Dirasat wa-l-Nashr, 1993.

Haj, Samira. *The Making of Iraq, 1900–1963: Capital, Power, and Ideology.* Albany: State University of New York Press, 1997.

———. *Reconfiguring Islamic Tradition: Reform, Rationality, and Modernity.* Stanford: Stanford University Press, 2008.

Hakim, 'Abd al-Muhsin al-. "Jawab al-Ustadh al-Sayyid 'Abd al-Muhsin al-Hakim." *al-Najaf* 3, no. 6 (September 15, 1959): 17.

Hakim, Muhammad Taqi al-. "al-Thawra=Hadm wa-Bina'." *al-Najaf* 3, no. 2 (July 14, 1959): 4, 27–28.

Hallaq, Wael. *The Impossible State: Islam, Politics, and Modernity's Moral Predicament.* New York: Columbia University Press, 2013.

Hamdi, Najiya. "al-Jil al-Sa'id." *al-Mu'allim al-Jadid* 26, no. 1–2 (January 1963): 158–62.

Hansen, Thomas Blom, and Finn Stepputat. "Introduction." In *Sovereign Bodies: Citizens, Migrants, and States in the Postcolonial World,* edited by Thomas Blom Hansen and Finn Stepputat, 1–36. Princeton: Princeton University Press, 2005.

Harlan, Louis. *Booker T. Washington: The Wizard of Tuskegee, 1901–1915.* Oxford: Oxford University Press, 1983.

Harrington, Joel Francis. *Reordering Marriage and Society in Reformation Germany.* Cambridge: Cambridge University Press, 1995.

Hasan, 'Abd al-Majid. "Dawr I'dad al-Mu'allimat fi al-'Iraq." *al-Mu'allim al-Jadid* 20, no. 3 (June 1957): 1–6.

Hasan, Muhammad Salman. *al-Tatawwur al-Iqtisadi fi al-'Iraq, 1864–1958.* Baghdad: Maktabat al-'Asriyya, 1965.

Hasani, 'Abd al-Razzaq al-. *al-'Iraq fi Dawray al-Ihtilal wa-l-Intidab.* Beirut: Dar al-Rafidayn, 2013.

———. *Tarikh al-Wizarat al-'Iraqiyya.* Sidon: Matba'at al-'Irfan, 1965.

Headrick, Daniel R. *Power over Peoples: Technology, Environments, and Western Imperialism, 1400 to the Present*. Princeton: Princeton University Press, 2010.

Herzog, Dagmar. *Sex after Fascism: Memory and Morality in Twentieth-Century Germany*. Princeton: Princeton University Press, 2005.

Hijri, Muhammad al-. "Fi 'Urs." *al-Najaf* 3, no. 3 (August 1, 1959): 13–16.

Hilali, 'Abd al-Razzaq al-. *Tarikh al-Ta'lim fi al-'Iraq fi 'Ahd al-Ihtilal al-Biritani, 1914–1921*. Baghdad: Mutba'at al-Ma'arif, 1975.

Hilli, Ahmad Haqqi al-. "Tajriba fi al-Tarbiya al-Asasiyya." *al-Mu'allim al-Jadid* 18, no. 3 (May 1955): 9–14.

Hobsbawm, Eric, and Terence Ranger, eds. *The Invention of Tradition*. Cambridge: Cambridge University Press, 1983.

Hodge, Joseph Morgan. *Triumph of the Expert: Agrarian Doctrines of Development and the Legacies of British Colonialism*. Athens: Ohio University Press, 2007.

Humphries, Steve. *Hooligans or Rebels?: An Oral History of Working Class Childhood and Youth, 1889–1939*. Oxford: Blackwell, 1981.

Husri, Sati' al-. *Abhath Mukhtara fi al-Qawmiyya al-'Arabiyya*. Cairo: Dar al-Ma'arif, n.d.

———. *Ahadith fi al-Tarbiya wa-l-Ijtima'*. Beirut: Dar al-'Ilm li-l-Malayyin, 1962.

———. *Ara' wa-Ahadith fi al-'Ilm wa-l-Akhlaq wa-l-Thaqafa*. Beirut: Markaz Dirasat al-Wahda al-'Arabiyya, n.d.

———. *Ara' wa-Ahadith fi al-Wataniyya wa-l-Qawmiyya*. Beirut: Markaz Dirasat al-Wahda al-'Arabiyya, 1984.

———. *Mudhakkirati fi al-'Iraq, 1921–1941*. 3 vols. Beirut: Dar al-Tali'a, 1967.

———. *Naqd Taqrir Lajnat Munru: Rasa'il Muwajjaha ila al-Ustadh Bul Munru*. Baghdad: Matba'at al-Najah, 1932.

Immerwahr, Daniel. *Thinking Small: The United States and the Lure of Community Development*. Cambridge, MA: Harvard University Press, 2015.

International Bank for Reconstruction and Development. *The Economic Development of Iraq*. Baltimore: Johns Hopkins University Press, 1952.

Iraq. *Education in Iraq*. Washington, DC: Office of the Cultural Attaché, Embassy of Iraq, 1957.

Ireland, Philip Willard. *Iraq: A Study in Political Development*. London: Cape, 1937.

Ismael, Jacqueline, and Shereen Ismael. "Gender and State in Iraq." In *Gender and Citizenship in the Middle East*, edited by Suad Joseph, 185–211. Syracuse: Syracuse University Press, 2000.

Ismael, Tareq. *The Rise and Fall of the Communist Party of Iraq*. New York: Cambridge University Press, 2008.

Jabar, Faleh A. *The Shi'ite Movement in Iraq*. London: Saqi Books, 2003.

Jabra, Jabra Ibrahim. *Jawad Salim wa-Nusb al-Hurriyya: Dirasa fi Atharihi wa-Ara'ihi*. Baghdad: Wizarat al-I'lam, 1974.

Jacob, Wilson Chacko. *Working Out Egypt: Effendi Masculinity and Subject Formation in Colonial Modernity, 1870–1940*. Durham: Duke University Press, 2011.

Jamali, Muhammad Fadhil al-. *The New Iraq: Its Problem of Bedouin Education*. New York: Bureau of Publications, Columbia Teachers College, 1934.

———. "al-Tifl wa-l-Umma." *al-Mu'allim al-Jadid* 3, no. 3 (June 1938): 166–69.

Jamil, Husayn. *al-'Iraq: Shahada Siyasiyya, 1908–1930*. London: Dar al-Laam, 1987.

Jawahiri, Muhammad Mahdi. *Mudhakkirati*. Beirut: Dar al-Muntazar, 1999.

Jumard, Mahmud al-. "al-Ta'lim al-Mukhtalit." *al-Mu'allim al-Jadid* 17, no. 1–2 (September 1953): 82–88.

———. "Tilmidhat wa-Talamidh al-Madaris al-Thanawiyya wa-Awqat al-Faragh." *al-Mu'allim al-Jadid* 18, no. 1 (December 1954): 69–75.

Kadhim, Abbas. *Reclaiming Iraq: The 1920 Revolution and the Founding of the Modern State*. Austin: University of Texas Press, 2012.

Kadry, Hind. *Women's Education in Iraq*. Washington, DC: Embassy of Iraq, 1958.

Karim, Fawzi. *Tahafut al-Sittiniyyin*. Damascus: al-Mada, 2006.

Karuna, Mantena. "The Crisis of Liberal Imperialism." *Histoire@Politique* 2, no. 11 (2010). Retrieved from https://www.cairn.info/revue-histoire-politique-2010-2-page-2.htm.

Kasey, Mahir al-. *Youth Education in Iraq and Egypt 1920–1980: A Contribution to Comparative Education within the Arab Region*. Leuven: Helicon, 1983.

Kazim, 'Abd al-Hamid. "Dawr al-Mu'allim fi al-Islah al-Ijtima'i." *al-Mu'allim al-Jadid* 20, no. 5–6 (December 1957): 1–5.

Kelly, John, and Martha Kaplan. "Legal Fictions after Empire." In *The State of Sovereignty: Territories, Laws, Populations*, edited by Douglas Howland and Luise White, 169–195. Bloomington: Indiana University Press, 2009.

Kern, Karen M. *Imperial Citizen: Marriage and Citizenship in the Ottoman Frontier Provinces of Iraq*. Syracuse: Syracuse University Press, 2011.

Khalaf, Kamil. "Ahamiyyat al-Tarbiya al-Jinsiyya." *al-Mu'allim al-Jadid* 19, no. 1 (February 1956): 58–59.

Kharrufa, 'Ala al-Din. *Sharh Qanun al-Ahwal al-Shakhsiyya: Raqm 188, Sanat 1959*. Baghdad: Matba'at al-'Ani, 1962.

Khater, Akram Fouad. *Inventing Home: Emigration, Gender, and the Middle Class in Lebanon, 1870–1920*. Berkeley: University of California Press, 2001.

Khayri, Su'ad. *al-Mar'a al-'Iraqiyya: Kifah wa-'Ata'*. Stockholm: A.R.M. All-Tryck, 1998.

Khayri, Zaki, and Su'ad Khayri. *Dirasat fi Tarikh al-Hizb al-Shuyu'i al-'Iraqi*. London: al-Jadid, 1984.

Khayyat, Ja'far. *al-Qarya al-'Iraqiyya: Dirasa fi Ahwaliha wa-Islahiha*. Beirut: Dar al-Kashshaf, 1950.

Khazraji, Husayn Fahmi al-. "Lan Yaflah Qawm Asnadu Amrahum ila Imra'a." *al-Najaf* 4, no. 19–20 (April 24, 1962): 14–15.

———. "Mushkilat al-Mar'a al-'Iraqiyya." *al-Najaf* 3, no. 6 (September 15, 1959): 13–14.

Kholoussy, Hanan. *For Better, for Worse: The Marriage Crisis That Made Modern Egypt*. Stanford: Stanford University Press, 2010.

Khoury, Dina Rizk. *Iraq in Wartime: Soldiering, Martyrdom, and Remembrance*. Cambridge: Cambridge University Press, 2013.

———. "Reflections on Imperial, Colonial, and Post-Colonial Citizenship in Iraq." Paper presented at Dissections workshop, CUNY Graduate Center, May 1, 2015.

Khulusi, Safa'. "Tawhid aw Ikhtilaf Manhaj al-Ta'lim bayn al-Banin wa-l-Banat." *al-Mu'allim al-Jadid* 17, no. 1–2 (September 1953): 61–64.

Klingensmith, Daniel. *"One Valley and a Thousand": Dams, Nationalism, and Development*. New Delhi: Oxford University Press, 2007.

Knight, Edgar Wallace. *The Influence of Reconstruction on Education in the South*. New York: Arno Press, 1969.

Kojaman, Yeheskel. *Thawrat 14 Tammuz 1958 fi al-'Iraq wa-Siyasat al-Hizb al-Shuyu'i*. London: Biddles, 1985.

Koselleck, Reinhart. *Futures Past: On the Semantics of Historical Time*. Translated by Keith Tribe. New York: Columbia University Press, 2004.

———. *The Practice of Conceptual History: Timing History, Spacing Concepts*. Translated by Todd Samuel Presner. Stanford: Stanford University Press, 2002.

Kristeva, Julia. "Women's Time." Translated by Alice Jardine and Harry Blake. *Signs* 7, no. 1 (1981): 13–35.

Latham, Michael E. *Modernization as Ideology: American Social Science and "Nation Building" in the Kennedy Era*. Chapel Hill: University of North Carolina Press, 2000.

Lerner, Daniel. *The Passing of Traditional Society: Modernizing the Middle East*. 2nd ed. New York: Free Press, 1964.

Lesko, Nancy. *Act Your Age!: A Cultural Construction of Adolescence*. 2nd ed. London: Routledge, 2012.

Lopez, Enriqueta. "Ma Ya'mal al-Nisa' fi al-Dujayla." *al-Mu'allim al-Jadid* 18, no. 3 (May 1955): 62–64.

Louis, Wm. Roger, and Roger Owen, eds. *A Revolutionary Year: The Middle East in 1958*. London: I. B. Tauris, 2002.

Lugard, F. D. *The Dual Mandate in British Tropical Africa*. London: Archon Books, 1965.

Luizard, Pierre-Jean. "The Nature of the Confrontation between the State and *Marja'ism*: Grand Ayatollah Muhsin Al-Hakim and the Ba'th." In *Ayatollahs, Sufis and Ideologues: State, Religion and Social Movements in Iraq*, edited by Faleh A. Jabar, 90–100. London: Saqi Books, 2002.

Mahdi, Kamil. *State and Agriculture in Iraq: Modern Development, Stagnation and the Impact of Oil*. Reading: Ithaca Press, 2000.

Mahmood, Saba. *Politics of Piety: The Islamic Revival and the Feminist Subject*. Princeton: Princeton University Press, 2005.

———. *Religious Difference in a Secular Age: A Minority Report*. Princeton: Princeton University Press, 2016.

Makiya, Kanan. *The Monument: Art, Vulgarity and Responsibility in Iraq*. Berkeley: University of California Press, 1991.

Mamdani, Mahmood. *Citizen and Subject: Contemporary Africa and the Legacy of Late Colonialism*. Princeton: Princeton University Press, 1996.

"Manahij al-Fanun al-Baytiyya." *al-Mu'allim al-Jadid* 15, no. 5 (1952): 60.

Manela, Erez. *The Wilsonian Moment: Self-Determination and the International Origins of Anticolonial Nationalism*. Oxford: Oxford University Press, 2007.

Massad, Joseph. *Colonial Effects: The Making of National Identity in Jordan*. New York: Columbia University Press, 2011.

———. *Desiring Arabs*. Chicago: University of Chicago Press, 2007.

Matthews, Roderic D., and Matta Akrawi. *Education in Arab Countries of the Near East: Egypt, Iraq, Palestine, Transjordan, Syria, Lebanon*. Washington, DC: American Council on Education, 1949.

Matthews, Weldon. "The Kennedy Administration, Counterinsurgency, and Iraq's First Ba'thist Regime." *International Journal of Middle East Studies* 43 (2011): 635–53.

Mazower, Mark. *No Enchanted Palace: The End of Empire and the Ideological Origins of the United Nations.* Princeton: Princeton University Press, 2009.

Mbembe, Achille. "Necropolitics." *Public Culture* 15 (2003): 11–40.

Mehta, Uday Singh. *Liberalism and Empire: A Study in Nineteenth-Century British Liberal Thought.* Chicago: University of Chicago Press, 1999.

Ment, David M. "The American Role in Education in the Middle East: Ideology and Experiment, 1920–1940." *Paedagogica Historica* 47, no. 1–2 (2011): 173–89.

———. "Education, Nation-Building and Modernization after World War I: American Ideas for the Peace Conference." *Paedagogica Historica* 41, no. 1 (2005): 159–78.

Messick, Brinkley. *The Calligraphic State: Textual Domination and History in a Muslim Society.* Berkeley: University of California Press, 1996.

Milam Clark, Ava. *Adventures of a Home Economist.* Corvallis: Oregon State University Press, 1969.

Miller, Peter, and Nikolas Rose. *Governing the Present: Administering Economic, Social and Personal Life.* Cambridge: Polity, 2008.

Mitchell, Timothy. *Carbon Democracy: Political Power in the Age of Oil.* London: Verso, 2011.

———. *Colonising Egypt.* Berkeley: University of California Press, 1991.

———. *Rule of Experts: Egypt, Techno-Politics, Modernity.* Berkeley: University of California Press, 2002.

———. "The Stage of Modernity." In *Questions of Modernity,* edited by Timothy Mitchell, 1–34. Minneapolis: University of Minnesota, 2000.

Monroe, Paul. *Essays in Comparative Education: Republished Papers.* New York: Teachers College Press, 1927.

———. "Influence of the Growing Perception of Human Interrelationship on Education." *American Journal of Sociology* 18, no. 5 (1913): 622–40.

———, ed. *Report of the Educational Inquiry Commission.* Baghdad: Government Press, 1932.

Moosa, Ebrahim. *Ghazālī and the Poetics of Imagination.* Chapel Hill: University of North Carolina Press, 2005.

Mukhtar, 'Abd al-Hadi al-. "Hal min al-Daruri Tadris al-Thawra al-Faransiyya fi Madarisna?" *al-Mu'allim al-Jadid* 10, no. 4–5 (September 1946): 23–24.

Musawi, Muhsin al-. *Reading Iraq: Culture and Power in Conflict.* London: I. B. Tauris, 2006.

Najmabadi, Afsaneh. "Crafting an Educated Housewife in Iran." In *Remaking Women: Feminism and Modernity in the Middle East,* edited by Lila Abu-Lughod, 91–125. Princeton: Princeton University Press, 1998.

———. "Genus of Sex or the Sexing of Jins." *International Journal of Middle East Studies,* Special issue, "Queer Affects," 45 (2013): 211–31.

———. *Women with Mustaches and Men without Beards: Gender and Sexual Anxieties of Iranian Modernity.* Berkeley: University of California Press, 2005.

Nakash, Yitzhak. *Reaching for Power: The Shi'a in the Modern Arab World.* Princeton: Princeton University Press, 2006.

Neep, Daniel. *Occupying Syria under the French Mandate: Insurgency, Space and State Formation.* Cambridge: Cambridge University Press, 2012.

Norris, Jacob. *Land of Progress: Palestine in the Age of Colonial Development, 1905–1948.* Oxford: Oxford University Press, 2013.

Ogle, Vanessa. *The Global Transformation of Time 1870–1950.* Cambridge, MA: Harvard University Press, 2015.

Omissi, David E. *Air Power and Colonial Control: The Royal Air Force, 1919–1939.* Manchester: Manchester University Press, 1990.

Omolewa, Michael. "Educating the 'Native': A Study of the Education Adaptation Strategy in British Colonial Africa, 1910–1936." *Journal of African American History* 91, no. 3 (2006): 267–87.

Paidar, Parvin. *Women and the Political Process in Twentieth-Century Iran.* Cambridge: Cambridge University Press, 1995.

Parmar, Inderjeet. *Foundations of the American Century: The Ford, Carnegie, and Rockefeller Foundations in the Rise of American Power.* New York: Columbia University Press, 2015.

Parpart, Jane. "Lessons from the Field: Rethinking Empowerment, Gender and Development from a Post-(Post-?)Development Perspective." In *Feminist Post-Development Thought: Rethinking Modernity, Post-Colonialism and Representation,* edited by Kriemild Saunders, 41–56. London: Zed Books, 2003.

Parpart, Jane, and Marchand Marianne. "Exploding the Canon: An Introduction/Conclusion." In *Feminism, Postmodernism, Development,* edited by Marianne Marchand and Jane Parpart, 1–22. London: Routledge, 1995.

Pedersen, Susan. "Getting Out of Iraq—in 1932: The League of Nations and the Road to Normative Statehood." *American Historical Review* 115 (2010): 975–1000.

———. *The Guardians: The League of Nations and the Crisis of Empire.* Oxford: Oxford University Press, 2015.

Pollard, Lisa. *Nurturing the Nation: The Family Politics of Modernizing, Colonizing, and Liberating Egypt, 1805–1923.* Berkeley: University of California Press, 2005.

Popkewitz, Thomas. *Cosmopolitanism and the Age of School Reform: Science, Education, and Making Society by Making the Child.* New York: Routledge, 2008.

———. Preface to *Inventing the Modern Self and John Dewey: Modernities and the Traveling of Pragmatism in Education.* Edited by Thomas Popkewitz, vii–xi. New York: Palgrave Macmillan, 2005.

Porter, Doug. "Scenes from Childhood: The Homesickness of Development Discourses." In *Power of Development,* edited by Jonathan Crush, 63–87. London: Routledge, 1995.

Pursley, Sara. "'Ali al-Wardi and the Miracles of the Unconscious." *Psychoanalysis and History* (forthcoming).

———. "Building the Nation through the Production of Difference: The Gendering of Education in Iraq, 1928–58." In *Writing the Modern History of Iraq: Historiographical and Political Challenges,* edited by Jordi Tejel, Peter Sluglett, Riccardo Bocco, and Hamit Bozarslan, 119–41. London: Imperial College Press, 2012.

———. "Daughters of the Right Path: Family Law, Homosocial Publics, and the Ethics of Intimacy in the Works of Shi'i Revivalist Bint Al-Huda." *Journal of Middle East Women's Studies* 8, no. 2 (Spring 2012): 51–77.

———. "'Education for Real Life': Pragmatist Pedagogies and American Interwar Expansion in Iraq." In *The Routledge Handbook of the History of the Middle East Mandates*, edited by Cyrus Schayegh and Andrew Arsan, 88–105. New York: Routledge, 2015.

———. "Futures Past: Nation, Gender, Time in Jawad Salim's *Monument to Freedom*." *Kufa Review* 5, no. 3 (May 2014).

———. "Gender as a Category of Analysis in Development and Environmental History." Presentation to the "Gendering the Middle East" roundtable. *International Journal of Middle East Studies* 48, no. 3 (2016): 555–60.

———. "'Lines Drawn on an Empty Map': Iraq's Borders and the Legend of the Artificial State." *Jadaliyya*, June 2, 2015. Retrieved from http://www.jadaliyya.com/Details/32140/Lines -Drawn-on-an-Empty-Map-Iraq's-Borders-and-the-Legend-of-the-Artificial-State-Part-1.

———. "The Stage of Adolescence: Anticolonial Time, Youth Insurgency, and the Marriage Crisis in Hashimite Iraq." *History of the Present* 3, no. 2 (November 2013): 160–97.

Quint, Malcolm N. "The Idea of Progress in an Iraqi Village." *Middle East Journal* 12, no. 4 (1958): 369–84.

Rahim, Ahmad Husayn al-. "'Uruq al-Nar fi Thawrat 14 Tammuz." *al-Najaf* 3, no. 2 (July 14, 1959): 7, 26–27.

Riley, Denise. *"Am I That Name?" Feminism and the Category of "Women" in History*. Minneapolis: University of Minnesota Press, 1988.

Riley, F. B. "Education in a Backward Country." *Phi Delta Kappan* 7, no. 4 (1925): 1–5.

Rist, Gilbert. *The History of Development: From Western Origins to Global Faith*. London: Zed Books, 2002.

Rofel, Lisa. *Other Modernities: Gendered Yearnings in China after Socialism*. Berkeley: University of California Press, 1999.

Ross, Kristin. *Fast Cars, Clean Bodies: Decolonization and the Reordering of French Culture*. Cambridge, MA: MIT Press, 1995.

Russell, Mona L. *Creating the New Egyptian Woman: Consumerism, Education, and National Identity, 1863–1922*. Basingstoke: Palgrave Macmillan, 2004.

Sa'id, Amat. "al-Ta'lim al-Niswi." *al-Mu'allim al-Jadid* 12, no. 5–6 (July 1949): 85–88.

Sa'id, Shakir Hasan Al. *Jawad Salim: al-Fannan wa-l-Akharun*. Baghdad: Wizarat al-Thaqafa wa-l-I'lam.

Salman, Amana al-. "Ara' fi Islah wa-Tahsin al-Ta'lim al-Niswi." *al-Mu'allim al-Jadid* 17, no. 1–2 (September 1953): 89–94.

Sarraf, 'Abbas al-. *Jawad Salim*. Baghdad: Wizarat al-I'lam, 1972.

Sartori, Andrew. *Bengal in Global Concept History: Culturalism in the Age of Capital*. Chicago: University of Chicago Press, 2008.

Satia, Priya. "The Defense of Inhumanity: Air Control and the British Idea of Arabia." *American Historical Review* 111, no. 1 (2006): 16–51.

———. "Developing Iraq: Britain, India and the Redemption of Empire and Technology in the First World War." *Past and Present* 197 (2007): 211–55.

———. "'A Rebellion of Technology': Development, Policing, and the British Arabian Imaginary." In *Environmental Imaginaries of the Middle East and North Africa*, edited by Diana K. Davis and Edmund Burke, 23–59. Athens: Ohio University Press, 2011.

———. *Spies in Arabia: The Great War and the Cultural Foundations of Britain's Covert Empire in the Middle East*. Oxford: Oxford University Press, 2008.

Schayegh, Cyrus. "1958 Reconsidered: State Formation and the Cold War in the Early Postcolonial Arab Middle East." *International Journal of Middle East Studies* 45 (2013): 421–43.

———. *Who Is Knowledgeable Is Strong: Science, Class, and the Formation of Modern Iranian Society, 1900–1950*. Berkeley: University of California Press, 2009.

Scott, David. *Refashioning Futures: Criticism after Postcoloniality*. Princeton: Princeton University Press, 1999.

Scott, Joan Wallach. *The Fantasy of Feminist History*. Durham: Duke University Press, 2011.

Seikaly, Sherene. *Men of Capital: Scarcity and Economy in Mandate Palestine*. Stanford: Stanford University Press, 2016.

Shabout, Nada M. *Modern Arab Art: Formation of Arab Aesthetics*. Gainesville: University Press of Florida, 2007.

Shadle, Brett Lindsay. *"Girl Cases": Marriage and Colonialism in Gusiiland, Kenya, 1890–1970* (Portsmouth: Heinemann, 2006).

Sharif, Badi'. "Mashakil al-Tawjih al-Thaqafi fi I'dad Jil al-Mustaqbal." *al-Mu'allim al-Jadid* 12, no. 5 (July 1949): 8–13.

Shawkat, Sami. *Hadhihi Ahdafuna*. Baghdad: Wizarat al-Ma'arif, 1939.

Shields, Sarah. "Mosul, the Ottoman Legacy and the League of Nations, *International Journal of Contemporary Iraqi Studies* 3, no. 2 (2009): 217–230.

Shubbar, Majid, ed. *Khutab al-Za'im 'Abd al-Karim Qasim 1958–1959*. London: Alwarrak, 2007.

Simmons, Christina. *Making Marriage Modern: Women's Sexuality from the Progressive Era to World War II*. New York: Oxford University Press, 2009.

Simon, Reeva S. *Iraq between the Two World Wars: The Militarist Origins of Tyranny*. Rev. ed. New York: Columbia University Press, 2004.

Sluglett, Peter. *Britain in Iraq: Contriving King and Country*. 2nd ed. New York: Columbia University Press, 2007.

Smail, Daniel. "In the Grip of Sacred History." *American Historical Review* 110, no. 5 (2005): 1337–61.

Smith, Joan, and Immanuel Wallerstein. "Households as an Institution of the World-Economy." In *Creating and Transforming Households: The Constraints of the World-Economy*, coordinated by Joan Smith and Immanuel Wallerstein, 3–26. Cambridge: Cambridge University Press, 1992.

Smith, Leonard V. "Wilsonian Sovereignty in the Middle East: The King-Crane Commission Report of 1919." In *The State of Sovereignty: Territories, Laws, Populations*, edited by Douglas Howland and Luise White, 56–74. Bloomington: Indiana University Press, 2009.

Smith, Lionel. "Note on the Present State of Education in Iraq." Reprinted in E. C. Hodgkin, "Lionel Smith on Education in Iraq," *Middle Eastern Studies* (April 1983): 253–60.

Stage, Sarah, and Virginia B. Vincenti, eds. *Rethinking Home Economics: Women and the History of a Profession*. Ithaca: Cornell University Press, 1997.

Starrett, Gregory. "The Hexis of Interpretation: Islam and the Body in the Egyptian Popular School." *American Ethnologist* 22 (1995): 953–69.

———. *Putting Islam to Work: Education, Politics, and Religious Transformation in Egypt.* Berkeley: University of California Press, 1998.

Steiner-Khamsi, Gita, and Hubert O. Quist. "The Politics of Educational Borrowing: Reopening the Case of Achimota in British Ghana." *Comparative Education Review* 44, no. 3 (2000): 272–99.

Stippler, Henry, and Mohammad Darwish. *Land Tenure and Land Utilization in Shakla 8, Dujaila Project, 1965–66.* Baghdad: Ministry of Agrarian Reform, 1966.

Stoler, Ann Laura. *Along the Archival Grain: Epistemic Anxieties and Colonial Common Sense.* Princeton: Princeton University Press, 2010.

"al-Ta'lim al-Niswi fi al-'Iraq bayn al-Ams wa-l-Yawm." Editorial. *al-Mu'allim al-Jadid* 17, no. 1–2 (September 1953): 3–7.

Tannous, Afif I. "Land Reform: Key to the Development and Stability of the Arab World." *Middle East Journal* 5 (Winter 1951): 1–20.

"al-Tarbiya al-Asasiyya: Ghayatuha wa-Ahdafuha." Editorial. *al-Mu'allim al-Jadid* 18, no. 3 (May 1955): 1–3.

Tarbush, Mohammad. *The Role of the Military in Politics: A Case Study of Iraq to 1941.* London: Kegan Paul, 1982.

"Thawratan," *al-Najaf* 3, no. 2 (July 14, 1959): 30–31.

Thompson, Elizabeth. *Colonial Citizens: Republican Rights, Paternal Privilege, and Gender in French Syria and Lebanon.* New York: Columbia University Press, 2000.

Tripp, Charles. *A History of Iraq.* 2nd ed. Cambridge: Cambridge University Press, 2000.

Tucker, Judith. *Women, Family, and Gender in Islamic Law.* Cambridge: Cambridge University Press, 2008.

Ulrichsen, Kristian Coates. "The British Occupation of Mesopotamia, 1914–1922." *Journal of Strategic Studies* 30, no. 2 (2007): 349–77.

'Umar, Jabbir. "Min Mushkilat Ta'limina al-Niswi," *al-Mu'allim al-Jadid* 17, no. 1–2 (September 1953): 50–60.

'Umari, Khayri al-. *Hikayat Siyasiyya min Tarikh al-'Iraq al-Hadith.* Cairo: Dar al-Hilal, 1969.

Vitalis, Robert. *America's Kingdom: Mythmaking on the Saudi Oil Frontier.* London: Verso, 2009.

Wali, 'Abd al-Majid Hasan. "Markaz al-Mar'a fi al-Kiyan al-'A'ili." *al-Mu'allim al-Jadid* 17, no. 1–2 (September 1953): 78–81.

Wallerstein, Immanuel. *World-Systems Analysis: An Introduction.* Durham: Duke University Press, 2004.

Wardi, 'Ali al-. *al-Ahlam bayn al-'Ilm wa-l-'Aqida.* London: Alwarrak, 2009.

———. *Lamahat Ijtima'iyya min Tarikh al-'Iraq al-Hadith.* Qumm: Maktabat al-Sadr, 2004.

———. *Mahzalat al-'Aql al-Bashari.* London: Dar al-Warraq li-l-Nashr, 2016.

———. *Mantiq Ibn Khaldun.* London: Alwarrak, 2009.

———. *Wu'az al-Salatin.* London: Alwarrak, 2013.

Warner, Michael. *Publics and Counterpublics.* New York: Zone Books, 2005.

Warriner, Doreen. *Land Reform and Development in the Middle East: A Study of Egypt, Syria and Iraq.* London: Royal Institute of International Affairs, 1957.

Weber, Max. *Economy and Society.* Totawa: Bedminister, 1968.

Weiss, Max. *In the Shadow of Sectarianism: Law, Shi'ism, and the Making of Modern Lebanon.* Cambridge, MA: Harvard University Press, 2010.

Weitz, Eric. "From the Vienna to the Paris System: International Politics and the Entangled Histories of Human Rights, Forced Deportations, and Civilizing Missions." *American Historical Review* 113, no. 5 (2008): 1313–43.

Westad, Odd Arne. *The Global Cold War: Third World Interventions and the Making of Our Times*. Cambridge: Cambridge University Press, 2005.

Wien, Peter. *Iraqi Arab Nationalism: Authoritarian, Totalitarian and Pro-Fascist Inclinations, 1932–1941*. London: Routledge, 2006.

———. "Mothers of Warriors: Girls in a Youth Debate of Interwar Iraq." In *Girlhood: A Global History*, edited by Jennifer Helgren and Colleen A. Vasconcellos, 289–303. New Brunswick: Rutgers University Press, 2010.

———. " 'Watan' and 'Rujula': The Emergence of a New Model of Youth in Interwar Iraq." In *Youth and Youth Culture in the Contemporary Middle East*, edited by Jørgen Bæk Simonsen, 10–20. Aarhus: Aarhus University Press, 2005.

Wilson, Arnold Talbot. *Mesopotamia, 1917–1920: A Clash of Loyalties*. London: Oxford University Press, 1931.

Wright, Quincy. "The Government of Iraq." *American Political Science Review* 20 (1926): 743–69.

Yasin, Muhammad Husayn Al. "Hajat Madarisina al-Thanawiyya ila al-Tawjih." *al-Mu'allim al-Jadid* 12, no. 1 (September 1948): 22–27.

———. "al-Tarbiya al-Asasiyya fi Majalay al-Fikr wa-l-Tatbiq." *al-Mu'allim al-Jadid* 18, no. 3 (May 1955): 4–8.

"al-Za'im Yaftatih Mahrajan al-Risafi." *al-Mu'allim al-Jadid* 22, no. 5 (May 1959): 1–3.

Zimmerman, Andrew. *Alabama in Africa: Booker T. Washington, the German Empire, and the Globalization of the New South*. Princeton: Princeton University Press, 2010.

———. "A German Alabama in Africa: The Tuskegee Expedition to German Togo and the Transnational Origins of West African Cotton Growers." *American Historical Review* 110, no. 5 (2005): 1362–98.

Index

Stanford Studies in Middle Eastern and Islamic Societies and Cultures

Joel Beinin and Laleh Khalili, editors

Editorial Board
Asef Bayat, Marilyn Booth, Laurie Brand, Timothy Mitchell, Jillian Schwedler, Rebecca L. Stein, Max Weiss

———————

Michael Farquhar, *Circuits of Faith: Migration, Education, and the Wahhabi Mission*
2016

Gilbert Achcar, *Morbid Symptoms: Relapse in the Arab Uprising*
2016

Jacob Mundy, *Imaginative Geographies of Algerian Violence: Conflict Science, Conflict Management, Antipolitics*
2015

Ilana Feldman, *Police Encounters: Security and Surveillance in Gaza under Egyptian Rule*
2015

Tamir Sorek, *Palestinian Commemoration in Israel: Calendars, Monuments, and Martyrs*
2015

Adi Kuntsman and Rebecca L. Stein, *Digital Militarism: Israel's Occupation in the Social Media Age*
2015

Laurie A. Brand, *Official Stories: Politics and National Narratives in Egypt and Algeria*
2014

Kabir Tambar, *The Reckonings of Pluralism: Citizenship and the Demands of History in Turkey*
2014

Diana Allan, *Refugees of the Revolution: Experiences of Palestinian Exile*
2013

Shira Robinson, *Citizen Strangers: Palestinians and the Birth of Israel's Liberal Settler State*
2013

Joel Beinin and Frédéric Vairel, editors, *Social Movements, Mobilization, and Contestation in the Middle East and North Africa*
2013 (Second Edition), 2011